Women and Reproductive Health

Women and Reproductive Health

An Educational Insight in the New Millennium

S.C. Jhansi

SHIPRA

Rs. 1600

ISBN: 978-81-7541-540-9

First Published in India in 2010

Women and Reproductive Health- An Educational Insight in the New Millennium

Published by:
SHIPRA PUBLICATIONS
LG 18-19, Pankaj Central Market,
I.P. Ext., Patparganj, Delhi 110092, India
Ph.: +91 11 22235152/6152
info@shiprapublication.com
www.shiprapublication.com

Foreword

Since the 1994 International Conference on Population and Development (ICPD) in Cairo and the 1995 Fourth World Conference on Women (FWCW) in Beijing, reproductive health (RH) has become a global, regional and national priority in almost, if not all, the countries in the world today. According to paragraph 7.2 of the ICPD Programme of Action (ICPD POA):

> Reproductive health is a state of complete physical, mental and social well being and not merely the absence of disease or infirmity, in all matters relating to the reproductive system and to its functions and processes. Reproductive Health therefore, implies that people are able to have a satisfying and safe sex life and that they have the capability to reproduce and the freedom to decide if, when and how often to do so.

Time and time again governments and leaders have pledged their commitments to reproductive health and to the enhancements of human development and well being of their people. These commitments were made in national, regional and international forums. Declarations, Platforms for Action/Programmes of Action were adopted by consensus. The most significant ones include the ICPD POA and the Beijing Platform for Action. In the Pacific, the Post Vila Declaration on Population and Development, the Yanuca Island Declaration on Healthy Island, the Suva Declaration on sustainable human development and the Pacific response to the ICPD POA are examples of these commitments.

The Research studies done in the developing countries have shown that educating girls and women's empowerment is a powerful ally in the eradication of poverty. Educated women are also better able to care for their own health and that of their children and families. Education and employment enable women to demand and exercise their fundamental rights, including the right to health and reproductive choice. Educated women tend to delay marriage, later delay their first delivery and have fewer children overall than those who are illiterate.

The present book is useful for population scientists, students of demography, public health personnel and as well as to Non-Governmental Organizations working in the field of health, education and social development. It will also be the need of:

- the university libraries,
- colleges,
- research institutes, and
- community level organizations world over.

The book touches upon relevant RH issues as well as some of the programmes undertaken by United Nations and other agencies. I strongly recommend this volume for teaching at under-graduate and postgraduate levels and for researcher in interdisciplinary fields. Furthermore, the population data used in this book will serve as a base line for initiating larger work for the development of the society.

I congratulate Dr. Jhansi for bringing out this publication on reproductive health which has gained enhanced significant importance in recent time.

Dr. C.P. Prakasam
Retired Professor,
Department of Public Health and Mortality Studies,
International Institute for Population Sciences
Govandi Station Road, Deonar,
Mumbai, 400088.

Contents

1

Female Reproductive System

All living things reproduce. Reproduction—the process by which organisms make more organisms like themselves—is one of the things that sets living things apart from nonliving matter. But even though the reproductive system is essential to keeping a species alive, unlike other body systems, it's not essential to keeping an individual alive.

In the human reproductive process, two kinds of sex cells, or gametes, are involved. The male gamete, or sperm, and the female gamete, the egg or ovum, meet in the female's reproductive system to create a new individual. Both the male and female reproductive systems are essential for reproduction. The female needs a male to fertilize her egg, even though it is she who carries offspring through pregnancy and childbirth.

Humans, like other organisms, pass certain characteristics of themselves to the next generation through their genes, the special carriers of human traits. The genes that parents pass along to their children are what make children similar to others in their family, but they are also what make each child unique. These genes come from the male's sperm and the female's egg, which are produced by the male and female reproductive systems.

About the Female Reproductive System

Most species have two sexes: male and female. Each sex has its own unique reproductive system. They are different in shape and structure, but both are specifically designed to produce, nourish, and transport either the egg or sperm.

Unlike the male, the human female has a reproductive system located entirely in the pelvis. The external part of the female reproductive organs is called the vulva, which means covering. Located between the legs, the vulva covers the opening to the vagina and other reproductive organs located inside the body.

The fleshy area located just above the top of the vaginal opening is called the mons pubis. Two pairs of skin flaps called the labia (which mean lips) surround the vaginal opening. The clitoris, a small sensory organ, is located toward the front of the vulva where the folds of the labia join. Between the labia are openings to the urethra (the canal that carries urine from the bladder to the outside of the body) and vagina. Once girls become sexually mature, the outer labia and the mons pubis are covered by pubic hair. A female's internal reproductive organs are the vagina, uterus, fallopian tubes, and ovaries.

The vagina is a muscular, hollow tube that extends from the vaginal opening to the uterus. The vagina is about 3 to 5 inches (8 to 12 centimeters) long in a grown woman. Because it has muscular walls, it can expand and contract. This ability to become wider or narrower allows the vagina to accommodate something as slim as a tampon and as wide as a baby. The vagina's muscular walls are lined with mucous membranes, which keep it protected and moist.

The vagina serves three purposes:

a) It is where the penis is inserted during sexual intercourse.
b) It is the pathway that a baby takes out of a woman's body during childbirth, called the birth canal.
c) It provides the route for the menstrual blood (the period) to leave the body from the uterus.

A thin sheet of tissue with one or more holes in it called the hymen that partially covers the opening of the vagina. Hymens are often different from female to female. Most women find their hymens have stretched or torn after their first sexual experience, and the hymen may bleed a little (this usually causes little, if any, pain). Some women who have had sex don't have much of a change in their hymens, though.

The vagina connects with the uterus, or womb, at the cervix (which means neck). The cervix has strong, thick walls. The opening of the cervix is very small (no wider than a straw), which is why a tampon can never get lost inside a girl's body. During childbirth, the cervix can expand to allow a baby to pass.

The uterus is shaped like an upside-down pear, with a thick lining and muscular walls—in fact, the uterus contains some of the strongest muscles in the female body. These muscles are able to expand and contract to accommodate a growing fetus and then help push the baby out during labor. When a woman isn't pregnant, the uterus is only about 3 inches (7.5 centimeters) long and 2 inches (5 centimeters) wide.

At the upper corners of the uterus, the fallopian tubes connect the uterus to the ovaries. The ovaries are two oval-shaped organs that lie to the upper right and left of the uterus. They produce, store, and release eggs into the fallopian tubes in the process called ovulation. Each ovary measures about 1½ to 2 inches (4 to 5 centimeters) in a grown woman.

There are two fallopian tubes, each attached to a side of the uterus. The fallopian tubes are about 4 inches (10 centimeters) long and about as wide as a piece of spaghetti. Within each tube is a tiny passageway no wider than a sewing needle. At the other end of each fallopian tube is a fringed area that looks like a funnel. This fringed area wraps around the ovary but doesn't completely attach to it. When an egg pops out of an ovary, it enters the fallopian tube. Once the egg is in the fallopian tube, tiny hairs in the tube's lining help push it down the narrow passageway toward the uterus.

The ovaries are also part of the endocrine system because they produce female sex hormones such as:

a) estrogen, and
b) progesterone.

Reproductive Anatomy and Physiology

Effective public health programmes, research, and policy relating to human sexuality, pregnancy, contraception, and the transmission of sexually transmitted infections (including HIV) depends upon knowledge of the structure *(anatomy)* and function *(physiology)* of the male and female reproductive systems.

Sexual and Reproductive Development

Human beings are sexual throughout life. Sexuality encompasses more than sexual behaviour—it is not only the physical, but the mental and spiritual as well. Sexuality is a core component of personality and a fundamental part of human life. While the problems usually associated with sexual behaviour are real and need to be addressed, human sexuality also has significant meaning and value in each individual's life.

Reproductive Biology

Reproductive physical maturity and the capacity for human reproduction begin during *puberty*, a period of rapid growth and change experienced by both males and females. Puberty is not an isolated event, but a process which takes place over several years.

During puberty, the *hypothalamus* (a gland located at the base of the brain which regulates temperature, sleep, emotions, sexual function and behaviour) produces *hormones* (chemicals that originate in a gland or organ and travel through the blood to another organ, stimulating it by chemical action to increase functional activity and secretions).

These hormones stimulate the *gonads*, the reproductive glands (the testes in males and the ovaries in females) to produce *testosterone* (males) and *estrogen* and *progesterone* (females).

Male puberty generally occurs between the ages of 13-15 and is characterized by the secretion of the male hormone *testosterone*, which stimulates *spermatogenesis* (sperm production), and the development of *secondary sexual characteristics* (increased height and weight, broadening shoulders, growth of the testes and penis, pubic and facial hair growth, voice deepening, and muscle development).

Female puberty generally occurs between the ages of 9-13, and results in *ovulation* and *menstruation*, which involve cyclic hormonal changes in estrogen and progesterone. Secondary sexual characteristics (growth of pubic and underarm hair, breast enlargement, vaginal and uterine growth, widening hips, increased height, weight and fat distribution) also occur as part of the female pubertal process.

Functions of Female Reproductive System

The female reproductive system enables a woman to:

a) produce eggs (ova)
b) have sexual intercourse
c) protect and nourish the fertilized egg until it is fully developed
d) give birth

Sexual reproduction couldn't happen without the sexual organs called the gonads. Although most people think of the gonads as the male testicles, both sexes actually have gonads: In females the gonads are the ovaries. The female gonads produce female gametes (eggs); the male gonads produce male gametes (sperm). After an egg is fertilized by the sperm, the fertilized egg is called the zygote.

When a baby girl is born, her ovaries contain hundreds of thousands of eggs, which remain inactive until puberty begins. At puberty, the pituitary gland, located in the central part of the brain, starts making hormones that stimulate the ovaries to produce female sex hormones, including estrogen. The secretion of these hormones causes a girl to develop into a sexually mature woman.

Toward the end of puberty, girls begin to release eggs as part of a monthly period called the menstrual cycle. Approximately once a month, during ovulation, an ovary sends a tiny egg into one of the fallopian tubes.

Unless the egg is fertilized by a sperm while in the fallopian tube, the egg dries up and leaves the body about 2 weeks later through the uterus—this is menstruation. Blood and tissues from the inner lining of the uterus combine to form the menstrual flow, which in most girls lasts from 3 to 5 days. A girl's first period is called menarche.

It is common for women and girls to experience some discomfort in the days leading to their periods. Premenstrual syndrome (PMS) includes both physical and emotional symptoms that many girls and women get right before their periods, such as acne, bloating, fatigue, backaches, sore breasts, headaches, constipation, diarrhea, food cravings, depression, irritability, or difficulty concentrating or handling stress. PMS is usually at its worst during the 7 days before a girl's period starts and disappears once it begins.

Many girls also experience abdominal cramps during the first few days of their periods caused by prostaglandins, chemicals in the body that make the smooth muscle in the uterus contract. These involuntary contractions can be either dull or sharp and intense.

It can take up to 2 years from menarche for a girl's body to develop a regular menstrual cycle. During that time, her body is adjusting to the hormones puberty brings. On average, the monthly cycle for an adult woman is 28 days, but the range is from 23 to 35 days.

If a female and male have sex within several days of the female's ovulation, fertilization can occur. When the male ejaculates (when semen leaves a male's penis), between 0.05 and 0.2 fluid ounces (1.5 to 6.0 milliliters) of semen is deposited into the vagina. Between 75 and 900 million sperm are in this small amount of semen, and they "swim" up from the vagina through the cervix and uterus to meet the egg in the fallopian tube. It takes only one sperm to fertilize the egg.

About a week after the sperm fertilizes the egg, the fertilized egg (zygote) has become a multicelled blastocyst. A blastocyst is about the size of a pinhead, and it's a hollow ball of cells with fluid inside. The blastocyst burrows itself into the lining of the uterus, called the endometrium. The hormone estrogen causes the endometrium to become thick and rich with blood. Progesterone, another hormone released by the ovaries, keeps the endometrium thick with blood so that the blastocyst can attach to the uterus and absorb nutrients from it. This process is called implantation.

As cells from the blastocyst take in nourishment, another stage of development, the embryonic stage, begins. The inner cells form a flattened circular shape called the embryonic disk, which will develop into a baby. The outer cells become thin membranes that form around the baby. The cells multiply thousands of times and move to new positions to eventually become the embryo.

After approximately 8 weeks, the embryos is about the size of an adult's thumb, but almost all of its parts—the brain and nerves, the heart and blood, the stomach and intestines, and the muscles and skin—have formed.

During the fetal stage, which lasts from 9 weeks after fertilization to birth, development continues as cells multiply, move, and change. The fetus floats in amniotic fluid inside the amniotic sac. The fetus receives oxygen and nourishment from the mother's blood via the placenta, a disk-like structure that sticks to the inner lining of the uterus and connects to the fetus via the umbilical cord. The amniotic fluid and membrane cushion the fetus against bumps and jolts to the mother's body.

Pregnancy lasts an average of 280 days—about 9 months. When the baby is ready for birth, its head presses on the cervix, which begins to relax and widen to get ready for the baby to pass into and through the vagina. The mucus that has formed a plug in the cervix loosens, and with amniotic fluid, comes out through the vagina when the mother's water breaks.

When the contractions of labor begin, the walls of uterus contract, as they are stimulated by the pituitary hormone oxytocin. The contractions cause the cervix to widen and begin to open. After several hours of this widening, the cervix is dilated (opened) enough for the baby to come through. The baby is pushed out of the uterus, through the cervix, and along the birth canal. The baby's head usually comes first; the umbilical cord comes out with the baby and is cut after the baby is delivered.

The last stage of the birth process involves the delivery of the placenta, which is now called the afterbirth. After it has separated from the inner lining of the uterus, contractions of the uterus push it out, along with its membranes and fluids.

Box 1: Assisted Reproductive Technology

Infertility is often defined as not being able to get pregnant after trying for one year. Of the approximately 62 million women of reproductive age in 2002, about 1.2 million, or 2 per cent, had an infertility-related medical appointment within the previous year, and 8 per cent had an infertility-related medical visit at some point in the past. (Infertility services include medical tests to diagnose infertility, medical advice and treatments to help a woman become pregnant, and services other than routine prenatal care to prevent miscarriage.) Additionally, 7 per cent of married couples in which the woman was of reproductive age (2.1 million couples) reported that they had not used contraception for 12 months and the woman had not become pregnant (2002 National Survey of Family Growth).

Thus, for many people who want to start a family, the dream of having a child is not easily realized. Assisted Reproductive Technology (ART) has been used in the United States since 1981 to help women become pregnant, most commonly through the transfer of fertilized human eggs into a woman's uterus (*in vitro fertilization*). However, deciding whether to undergo this expensive and time-consuming treatment can be difficult.

What is Assisted Reproductive Technology (ART)?: Although various definitions have been used for ART, the definition used by CDC is based on the 1992 Fertility Clinic Success Rate and Certification Act that requires CDC to publish the annual ART success rates report. According to this definition, ART includes all fertility treatments in which both eggs and sperm are handled. In general, ART procedures involve surgically removing eggs from a woman's ovaries, combining them with sperm in the laboratory, and returning them to the woman's body or donating them to another woman.

Problems of the Female Reproductive System

Female may sometimes experience reproductive system problems. Below are some examples of disorders that affect the female reproductive system.

- *Problems of the Vulva and Vagina*
    - *Vulvovaginitis*: Vulvovaginitis is an inflammation of the vulva and vagina. It may be caused by irritating substances (such as

laundry soaps or bubble baths). Poor personal hygiene (such as wiping from back to front after a bowel movement) may also cause this problem. Symptoms include redness and itching in the vaginal and vulvar areas and sometimes vaginal discharge. Vulvovaginitis can also be caused by an overgrowth of *Candida*, a fungus normally present in the vagina.

- *Non-menstrual Vaginal Bleeding*: Non-menstrual vaginal bleeding is most commonly due to the presence of a vaginal foreign body, often wadded-up toilet paper. It may also be due to urethral prolapse, a condition in which the mucous membranes of the urethra protrude into the vagina and form a tiny, doughnut-shaped mass of tissue that bleeds easily. It can also be due to a straddle injury (such as when falling onto a beam or bicycle frame) or vaginal trauma from sexual abuse.
- *Labial Adhesions*: *Labial Adhesions*, the sticking together or adherence of the labia in the midline, usually appear in infants and young girls. Although there are usually no symptoms associated with this condition, labial adhesions can lead to an increased risk of urinary tract infection. Sometimes topical estrogen cream is used to help separate the labia.

- *Problems of the Ovaries and Fallopian Tubes*:
  - *Ectopic Pregnancy*: *Ectopic pregnancy* occurs when a fertilized egg, or zygote, doesn't travel into the uterus, but instead grows rapidly in the fallopian tube. A woman with this condition can develop severe abdominal pain and should see a doctor because surgery may be necessary.
  - *Endometriosis*: *Endometriosis* occurs when tissue normally found only in the uterus starts to grow outside the uterus—in the ovaries, fallopian tubes, or other parts of the pelvic cavity. It can cause abnormal bleeding, painful periods, and general pelvic pain.
  - *Ovarian Tumors*: *Ovarian tumors*, although they're rare, can occur. Girls with ovarian tumors may have abdominal pain and masses that can be felt in the abdomen. Surgery may be needed to remove the tumor.
  - *Ovarian Cysts*: *Ovarian cysts* are non-cancerous sacs filled with fluid or semisolid material. Although they are common and generally harmless, they can become a problem if they grow very large. Large cysts may push on surrounding organs, causing abdominal pain. In most of the cases, cysts disappear and treatment is unnecessary. If the cysts are painful, a doctor may prescribe birth control pills to alter their growth, or they may be removed by a surgeon.
  - *Polycystic Ovary Syndrome*: Polycystic ovary syndrome is a

hormone disorder in which too many male hormones (androgens) are produced by the ovaries. This condition causes the ovaries to become enlarged and develop many fluid-filled sacs, or cysts. It often first appears during the teen years. Depending on the type and severity of the condition, it may be treated with drugs to regulate hormone balance and menstruation.

- *Ovarian Torsion*, or the twisting of the ovary, can occur when an ovary becomes twisted because of a disease or a developmental abnormality. The torsion blocks blood from flowing through the blood vessels that supply and nourish the ovaries. The most common symptom is lower abdominal pain. Surgery is usually necessary to correct it.

- *Menstrual Problems*: A variety of menstrual problems can affect girls, including:
  - *Dysmenorrhea* is when a girl has painful periods.
  - *Menorrhagia* is when a girl has a very heavy periods with excess bleeding.
  - *Oligomenorrhea* is when a girl misses or has infrequent periods, even though she's been menstruating for a while and isn't pregnant.
  - *Amenorrhea* is when a girl has not started her period by the time she is 16 years old or 3 years after starting puberty, has not developed signs of puberty by age 14, or has had normal periods but has stopped menstruating for some reason other than pregnancy.
  - *Infections of the Female Reproductive System*:
  - *Sexually Transmitted Diseases (STDs)*: These include infections and diseases such as pelvic inflammatory disease (PID), human immunodeficiency virus/acquired immunodeficiency syndrome (HIV/AIDS), human papillomavirus (HPV, or genital warts), syphilis, chlamydia, gonorrhea, and genital herpes. Most are spread from one person to another by sexual contact.
  - *Toxic Shock Syndrome*: This uncommon illness is caused by toxins released into the body during a type of bacterial infection that is more likely to develop if a tampon is left in too long. It can produce high fever, diarrhea, vomiting, and shock.

Menstrual Problems

Everyone knows the teen years can be difficult—for both teens and parents. All those physical changes during puberty can make adolescents feel awkward and unsure of themselves.

This is particularly true for girls when it comes to menstruation. For a girl, getting her first period is a physical milestone and a sign of becoming a woman.

But it can also be confusing and scary, particularly if she encounters certain problems like irregular periods or premenstrual syndrome (PMS).

Common Menstrual Problems

Most issues teens confront when they start menstruating are completely normal. In fact, many girls and women have had to deal with one or more of them at one time or another:

- **Premenstrual Syndrome (PMS):** PMS includes both physical and emotional symptoms that many females get right before their periods, such as:
    - acne
    - bloating
    - fatigue
    - backaches
    - sore breasts
    - headaches
    - constipation
    - diarrhea
    - food cravings
    - depression or feeling blue
    - irritability
    - difficulty concentrating
    - difficulty handling stress

Different girls may have some or all of these symptoms in varying combinations. PMS is usually at its worst during the 7 days before the period starts and disappears soon after it begins. But girls usually don't develop symptoms associated with PMS until several years after menstruation starts—if ever.

Although the exact cause of PMS is unknown, it seems to occur because of changing hormone levels, and their effect on chemicals in the brain. During the second half of the menstrual cycle, the amount of progesterone in the body increases. Then, about 7 days before the period starts, levels of both progesterone and estrogen drop.

Some girls' bodies seem to be more sensitive to these hormone changes than others. Talk to your daughter's doctor if her symptoms are severe or interfere with her normal activities.

- *Cramps*: Many girls experience abdominal cramps during the first few days of their periods. They're caused by prostaglandin, a chemical in the body that makes the smooth muscle in the uterus contract. These involuntary contractions can be either dull or sharp and intense. The good news is that cramps usually only last a few days. But call your

daughter's doctor if she has severe cramps that keep her home from school or from doing stuff with her friends.
- *Irregular Periods*: It can take 2 to 3 years from a girl's first period for her body to develop a regular cycle. During that time, the body is essentially adjusting to the influx of hormones unleashed by puberty. And what's "regular" varies from person to person. The typical cycle of an adult female is 28 days, although some are as short as 21 days and others are as long as 45.
- Changing hormone levels might make a girl's period last a short time during one month (just a few days) and a long time the next (up to a week). She may skip months, get two periods almost right after each other, or alternate between heavy and light bleeding from one month to another.
- But any girl who's sexually active and skips a period should see a doctor to make sure she's not pregnant. And if your daughter's period still hasn't settled into a relatively predictable pattern after 3 years, or if she has four or five regular periods and then skips her period or becomes irregular, make an appointment with her doctor to check for possible problems. Also let your daughter's doctor know if her cycle is less than 21 days or more than 45 days, or if she doesn't get a period for 3 months at any time after first beginning to menstruate.
- *Delayed Menarche*: Girls go through puberty at different rates. Some reach menarche (the medical term for the first period or the beginning of menstruation) as early as 9 or 10 years old and others don't have their first periods until they're well into their teen years. So, if your daughter is a "late bloomer," it doesn't necessarily mean there's something wrong with her.
- When girls get their periods actually depends a lot on genetics. Girls often start menstruating at approximately the same age their mothers or grandmothers did. Also, certain ethnic groups, on average, go through puberty earlier than others. For instance, African-American girls, on average, start puberty and get their periods before Caucasian girls do.

Problems that May be Cause for Concern

Although most period problems are harmless, a few conditions can be more serious and require medical attention:

Amenorrhea (the Absence of Periods): Girls who haven't started their periods by the time they're 16 years old or 3 years after they've shown the first signs of puberty have primary amenorrhea, which is usually caused by a genetic abnormality, a hormone imbalance, or a structural problem. Hormones are also often responsible for secondary amenorrhea, which is when a girl who had normal periods suddenly stops menstruating for more than 6 months or three of her usual cycles.

Since pregnancy is the most common cause of secondary amenorrhea, it should always be ruled out when a girl skips periods. In addition to hormone imbalances, other things that can cause both primary and secondary amenorrhea include:

- stress
- significant weight loss or gain
- anorexia (amenorrhea can be a sign that a girl is losing too much weight and may have anorexia)
- stopping birth control pills
- thyroid conditions
- ovarian cysts
- other conditions that can affect hormone levels

Something that can also cause primary and secondary amenorrhea is excessive exercising (often distance running, ballet, figure skating or gymnastics) combined with a poor diet, which usually results in inappropriate weight loss or failure to gain weight during growth. But this doesn't include the usual gym class or school sports team, even those that practice often. To exercise so much that she delays her period, a girl would have to train vigorously for several hours a day, most days of the week, and not get enough calories, vitamins, and minerals.

Menorrhagia (Extremely Heavy, Prolonged Periods): It's normal for a girl's period to be heavier on some days than others. But signs of menorrhagia (excessively heavy or long periods) can include soaking through at least one sanitary napkin (pad) an hour for several hours in a row or periods that last longer than 7 days. Girls with menorrhagia sometimes stay home from school or social functions because they're worried they won't be able to control the bleeding in public.

The most frequent cause of menorrhagia is an imbalance between the levels of estrogen and progesterone in the body, which allows the endometrium (the lining of the uterus) to keep building up. When the endometrium is finally shed during menstruation, the resulting bleeding is particularly heavy.

Because many adolescents have slight hormone imbalances during puberty, menorrhagia isn't uncommon in teens. But in some cases, heavy menstrual bleeding can be caused by problems such as:

a) fibroids (benign growths) or polyps in the uterus
b) thyroid conditions
c) clotting disorders
d) inflammation or infection in the vagina or cervix

Dysmenorrhea (Painful Periods): There are two types of dysmenorrhea, which is severely painful menstruation that can interfere with a girl's ability to attend school, study, or sleep:

- *Primary Dysmenorrhea* is very common in teens and is not caused by a disease or other condition. Instead, the culprit is prostaglandin, the same chemical behind cramps. Large amounts of prostaglandin can lead to nausea, vomiting, headaches, backaches, diarrhea, and severe cramps. Fortunately, these symptoms usually last for only a day or two.
- *Secondary Dysmenorrhea* is pain caused by some physical condition like polyps or fibroids in the uterus, endometriosis, pelvic inflammatory disease (PID), or adenomyosis (uterine tissue growing into the muscular wall of the uterus).

  Having cramps for a day or two each month is common, but if your daughter has symptoms severe enough to keep her from her normal activities, discuss it with her doctor.

Endometriosis: In this condition, tissue normally found only in the uterus starts to grow outside the uterus—in the ovaries, fallopian tubes, or other parts of the pelvic cavity. It can cause abnormal bleeding, dysmenorrhea, and general pelvic pain.

Treating Menstrual Problems

To determine whether a problem requires treatment, the doctor will ask several questions and do a thorough physical exam. The doctor may do a pelvic exam, a Pap smear, blood tests (to check hormone levels), or urine tests. If there might be a structural problem or some sort of growth, an ultrasound or CAT scan may be performed. Together, these tests can help the doctor determine how a condition should be handled.

Growths such as polyps or fibroids can often be removed and endometriosis can often be treated with medications or surgery. If a hormone imbalance is to blame, the doctor will likely suggest hormone therapy with birth control pills or other hormone-containing medications.

And for menstrual pain with no underlying medical cause, anti-inflammatory medicines are the most effective treatment. Conditions like clotting disorders or thyroid problems may require treatment with medications as well.

Reproductive Healthcare

- The cervix, the lower portion of the uterus, can be visualized during a gynecological examination by inserting a speculum into the vagina. The Pap smear, developed in the 1940's by Dr. George Papaniclaou, is a simple and cost-effective screening test that involves the collection of a sample of cells from the cervix, which are examined microscopically. The Pap smear screens for infections and/or cell changes which, can detect indications of cervical cancer. In the developed world, Pap smear screening has been instrumental in reducing morbidity and mortality associated with cervical cancer. Cervical screening technologies have expanded to include liquid cytology, although the traditional Pap smear is still used.

- Despite the availability of Pap smear screening in the developed world, studies of its use reveal racial, economic and ethnic disparities. In the developing world, programmes for screening and treating cervical cancer are rare.

The *ovaries,* two small almond-shaped structures located on each side of the uterus, are the female *gonads* (reproductive glands). Female babies are born with over 400,000 *ova* (the gametes, also referred to as *egg cells* or *oocytes*), which are stored in the ovaries. The female body does not produce any additional ova. The ovaries produce *estrogen* and *progesterone.* The ovaries are close to, but not actually connected to the *fallopian tubes,* thin tube-like structures that are the site of *fertilization*, the fusion of the *male* and *female gametes*.

Box 2: Menopause

Menopause, the end of menstruation, occurs between the ages of 45 and 55 (with the average age of 51.3). An entirely normal developmental and physiological process, it can be accompanied by symptoms including hot flashes, fatigue, moodiness, insomnia, decreased libido and sexual response, changes in memory, weight gain, and vaginal dryness. Until cessation of ovarian function is confirmed through a blood test, and/or one year of no menses, women may continue to ovulate and therefore require contraception to prevent unintended pregnancy.

The Menstrual/Hormonal Cycle

The *hormonal cycle* facilitates maturation and rupture of the ovarian follicle resulting in the release of an ovum (the female reproductive or germ cell). Each month a series of changes take place which prepares the uterus for pregnancy. This cycle (*menstrual cycle*) is described below:

The first day of menstruation (referred to as Day 1) occurs when levels of estrogen and progesterone are low. In response to these low levels, the hypothalamus secretes *gonadotrophin releasing hormone (GnRH)* which triggers the *anterior pituitary gland* to release two hormones: *follicle stimulating hormone (FSH)*, and *luteinizing hormone (LH)*.

FSH stimulates the development of many follicles within the ovary. One dominant follicle takes over. As it continues to grow, it produces increasing amounts of estrogen, which stimulates the release of LH, and inhibits FSH, which suppresses further follicular development.

When LH levels are highest (*LH surge*), the ovarian follicle "ruptures" and releases one ovum, which is "swept" into the fallopian tube by hair-like projections called cilia that line the *fimbriae* (the fringe-like end of the fallopian tube that is closest to the ovary). This process is called ovulation. Increasing estrogen levels causes the *cervical mucous* (vaginal secretions) to become clear and profuse and the os to dilate. These two actions may facilitate the transport of semen (containing sperm) from the vagina, through the uterus, and into the fallopian tube.

Following ovulation, the ruptured follicle is transformed into the *corpus luteum,* a glandular mass that continues to produce estrogen and high levels of *progesterone*. The progesterone causes the endometrium to thicken, preparing it for implantation of a fertilized egg. If fertilization takes place during ovulation, hormonal levels remain high, essential for the maintenance of the pregnancy.

If fertilization does not occur, the corpus luteum shrinks and levels of both estrogen and progesterone decrease. The withdrawal of estrogen and progesterone cause the blood vessels of the endometrial (uterine) lining to "break" resulting in vaginal bleeding (*menstruation*). The average menstrual cycle is 28-35 days, and menstrual flow usually continues for three to seven days, although there are variations among women.

Following menstruation, estrogen and progesterone levels are low, triggering the hypothalamus to once again release GnRH, starting the entire cycle again. If fertilization does take place, menstruation will not reoccur for the duration of the pregnancy

Mechanism of Action for Contraception/Pregnancy

- Most hormonal methods of birth control, including emergency contraception, work by preventing or postponing ovulation, and by thickening the cervical mucous.
- The absence of a menstrual period in a sexually active woman may indicate that pregnancy has occurred. It is a presumptive, although not definitive, sign of pregnancy.

Male Reproductive System

To understand the male reproductive system, one must know the external and internal structures, and the process of *spermatogenesis* (sperm production) including the physiologic pathway of the sperm cell.

Structures

The male external structures are the *penis* and the *scrotum* (a pouch which protects the testes). The penis consists of the *glans* (the head), and the *shaft* (the body). The *glans* is covered by a fold of skin called the *foreskin* (circumcision removes the foreskin). The scrotum surrounds and protects the two *testes*, internal structures also referred to as testicles.

The testes are the male gonads and contain hundreds of tiny *seminiferous tubules* where sperm cells are produced. The *epididymis* is a small oblong body which rests on the surface of the testes where sperm mature and are stored. The *epididymis* leads into the *vas deferens* (narrow tubes which carry sperm away from the testes). The vas deferens extends to join with the ducts of the two *seminal vesicles* (located on side of the prostate gland) to form the ejaculatory ducts which extend through the body of the *prostate gland* and empty into the urethra. The prostate gland surrounds the neck of the *bladder* (the structure that stores urine) and the *urethra,* (a thin tube which extends through the penis and carries *semen* and urine outside of the body, although not simultaneously). The *Cowper's glands* (also called the *bulbourethral glands*) are found on each side of the urethra, just below the prostate gland.

Process of Spermatogenesis

Spermatogenesis begins in the *seminiferous tubules* of the testes. Sperm pass into the *epididymis* where they mature and become *motile* so they are able to move through the *vas deferens* and into the *seminal vesicles* where they mix with seminal fluids, rich in fructose and other nutrients. The prostate gland and the Cowper's glands secrete fluids which also help to nourish and transport the sperm. This mixture of fluids and sperm is called *semen*, the fluid which is expelled from a man's penis during *ejaculation.* Sexual arousal can cause fluid from the Cowper's glands to be released prior to ejaculation. This fluid is called *pre-ejaculatory fluid and does not contain sperm unless it is leftover from a previous ejaculation.* Contrary to popular belief, there is little evidence to support that pre-ejaculatory fluid contains enough sperm to cause pregnancy.

Although men continue to produce sperm throughout their lives, testosterone production decreases at about 45-65 years of age.

During *coitus* (sexual intercourse) between a male and a female, semen is released into the vagina and transported through the uterus into the fallopian tube. Although many factors contribute to whether or not a single act of intercourse will result in pregnancy, most important is whether or not a sperm cell will "meet" an ovum in the fallopian tube (*fertilization*). Fertilization can only occur if intercourse takes place before the time of *ovulation* that usually occurs "mid-cycle", or about 14 days before the woman's next menstrual period. At the time of ovulation, the ovum is released from the ovary and transported in the fallopian tube where it remains for about 24-48 hours. Pregnancy is most likely to occur if fresh semen is present when ovulation occurs.

Sperm cells remain viable within the female reproductive tract for about 72 hours. Only a single sperm cell is needed to fertilize the ovum, even though the average ejaculation contains approximately 300 million sperm.

During fertilization, the sperm enters the cell membrane of the ovum so the nuclei of the sperm and egg cells combine to form a *zygote.* The zygote will remain in the fallopian tube for approximately three days before it travels to the uterus where it will remain for approximately four to five days before *implantation* into the uterine lining.

Ectopic Pregnancy

An ectopic pregnancy is when a fertilized egg becomes implanted outside the uterus, most often in the fallopian tubes. Ectopic pregnancies are often the result of fallopian tube scarring caused by untreated sexually transmitted infections, which impedes the transport of the zygote from the fallopian tubes to the uterus. If left undiagnosed or untreated, the zygote grows in the fallopian tube, and may result in fallopian rupture. Without medical or surgical intervention, ectopic pregnancy usually results in infertility, severe infection, or death. Ectopic pregnancy can be difficult to diagnose, as it shares many symptoms with uterine pregnancy. However, Some symptoms of ectopic pregnancy include pain in the vagina, abdomen, or lower back, vaginal bleeding or spotting, dizziness, fainting, and low blood pressure.

Sex Determination

Prior to fertilization, the sperm and egg cells have only half the number of *chromosomes* (the genetic determinants of heredity) of other body cells because they go through a process of cell division called *meiosis*, which reduces the number of chromosomes from 46 to 23. The 23 chromosomes from the sperm cell combine with the 23 chromosomes from the ovum to form a single cell (zygote) consisting of 46 chromosomes.

Sex of the offspring is determined by whether the sperm contains an X or a Y sex chromosome. Female ova always carry an X chromosome. If the sperm cell contains a Y chromosome, the offspring will be a male (XY pair). If it contains an X chromosome, the offspring will be a female (XX pair). Thus, the sperm biologically determines sex.

2

Women, Reproductive Health and International Human Rights

The modern era of rights that can be applied to women's health may be said to have started with the adoption of the United Nations Charter in 1946. The Charter requires the United Nations to encourage "*respect for the principle of equal rights*" by promoting "*universal respect for, and observance of, human rights and fundamental freedoms for all without distinction as to ... sex*".

In 1948, the Universal Declaration of Human Rights was adopted by the United Nations General Assembly. This Declaration condemned discrimination on the grounds of sex and set out a network of rights relevant to the promotion and protection of health. The Declaration was developed into international human rights law by two general covenants adopted by the General Assembly in 1966, namely the International Covenant on Civil and Political Rights, and the International Covenant on Economic, Social and Cultural Rights.

A number of regional human rights conventions were also derived from the Universal Declaration, including the European Convention for the Protection of Human Rights and Fundamental Freedoms, the American Convention on Human Rights, and the African Charter on Human and Peoples' Rights. These regional conventions all prohibit discrimination on grounds of sex and require respect for various rights related to the promotion and protection of health. Other specialized conventions relevant to women's health also exist, such as the conventions on the Rights of the Child (which includes protection of the rights of girl children), on Torture and Other Cruel, Inhuman or Degrading Treatment or Punishment (which prohibits the infliction of physical or mental suffering on women), and on the Status of Refugees (which provides protection for refugee women).

The leading modern instrument on women's equal rights, however, is the Convention on the Elimination of All Forms of Discrimination against Women (the Women's Convention), which was adopted in 1979. Derived from the

Universal Declaration of Human Rights, the Women's Convention is the first international treaty in which member countries, known as States Parties, assume the legal duty to eliminate all forms of discrimination against women in civil, political, economic, social and cultural areas, including health care and family planning.

The Women's Convention, which has been widely accepted, obliges States Parties in general "to pursue by all appropriate means and without delay a policy of eliminating discrimination against women" and, in particular, "to eliminate discrimination against women in the field of health care in order to ensure ... access to health care services, including those related to family planning". When women experience disadvantage in contrast to other members of their families, communities or societies, they will be considered to suffer discrimination because they are women.

The Constitution of WHO, which was drawn up in 1946 and came into force in 1948, describes health as follows: "Health is a state of complete physical, mental and social well-being and not merely the absence of disease or infirmity." It is clear that much more than the provision of medical and nursing services is required to achieve this. Society must therefore pay attention to the full range of human rights, and not just those directly relating to health care, if health as defined by WHO is to be achieved and maintained.

Health, Sex and Gender

The concept of health as "physical, mental and social well-being" emphasizes the significance of social welfare. Medical science has a central role in health, but health is the outcome of a combination of factors—biological, genetic, environmental and socioeconomic. In the case of women, social, economic and cultural influences can be seen to play an important role in health status. In some parts of the world women are considered to be relatively insignificant. They may be conditioned to suffer low self-esteem, to accept inferior status as normal, and see the birth of a daughter as a reason for apology and distress. Legal, religious and cultural traditions may reinforce the devaluation of daughters. For instance, if women must leave the family on marriage, there is little point in investing money in their education. The cumulative impact of women's disadvantages results in many women being denied health as defined by WHO.

Neglect of women's health is linked both to their sex and to their gender. Sex is determined by genes and biology, whereas gender is a social construct that relates to feelings, values, behaviours and activities. Women suffer discrimination in health and other matters because of their sex, as for instance in cases of taboos related to menstruation. However, they suffer additional discrimination as roles associated with female gender are often not valued in social and economic terms.

Women's Health Disadvantages

The disadvantages women suffer in health may be classed as injustices in the light of human rights law. For instance, maternal mortality can be explained as being due to:

a) the immediate cause of lack of maternity care,
b) the underlying causes of exhaustion and anaemia associated with short intervals between births, and
c) structural causes such as poverty.

In the case of (a), the right to health care would require obstetric services to be available. In the case of (b), the right to education, among other rights, would enable people to become literate and thereby learn of the health benefits of child spacing and having fewer children. And in the case of (c), states may be legally responsible if they allocate national wealth disproportionately to expenditures that deny populations their basic needs.

Epidemiological and other data show how lack of basic obstetric services, antenatal care and related reproductive health services result in unnecessarily high rates of maternal mortality and morbidity. Evidence also confirms the danger to health presented by pregnancies that come too early, too late, too often and at intervals that are too closely spaced. Unsafe abortion procedures can endanger life, health and future fertility. Unwanted infertility, often a consequence of infection resulting from poor health care, leads to unmarriageability, divorce or abandonment and the health disadvantages associated with them. All these conditions can be seen as infringements of human rights, as understood within the terms of widely accepted international human rights treaties.

At the same time, fear of sexual relationships that lead to unwanted pregnancy, often linked to the physical dangers of pregnancy, impairs women's enjoyment of health as defined by WHO. Women may also be disadvantaged in protecting themselves against sexually transmitted infections, including the human immunodeficiency virus (HIV), through lack of information, through lack of power to refuse to have intercourse with their partners, or because they cannot insist that their partners use condoms. Thus, rights may be contravened even by the attitudes and customs of the communities where women live.

In order to address the health disadvantages of women, action is needed in a number of areas—many of them relating to empowerment. For instance:

- women must have greater freedom to determine their own health and life choices within families and communities;
- women must have opportunities to learn about their rights and their health;
- women must have access to accurate information about their health as

well as to high-quality women-centred care;
- women must have greater access to education and economic opportunities;
- adolescent girls must have the opportunity to develop the life skills so that they can act to protect their own health;
- men must be made aware of their role in expanding women's choices in households and communities, and in ensuring responsible sexual and family life;
- women must be supported by policies and laws that promote and ensure reproductive health and gender equality; and
- training of health care providers must stress the importance of preserving women's rights.

Rights and Reproductive Health

Preventing reproductive ill-health in women is an issue of social justice and human rights. Redefining women's reproductive ill-health as a "social injustice" rather than as a "health disadvantage" provides the legal and political basis for governments to ensure reproductive health care for all women. The challenge is to characterize women's health disadvantages as injustices that governments are obliged to remedy through political, health and legal systems.

Efforts to advance women's reproductive health through human rights must build on the existing framework of human rights, as recognized in most national constitutions and international human rights treaties. These rights include:

- the rights to life, liberty and the security of the person (these rights require governments to ensure access to appropriate health care, and to guarantee that citizens can choose when and how often to bear children);
- the rights that relate to the foundation of families and of family life (these rights require governments to provide access to health care and other services women need to establish families and enjoy life within their families);
- the rights to health care and the benefits of scientific progress, including health information and education (these rights require governments to provide reproductive and sexual health services and information to women); and
- the rights to equality and nondiscrimination (these rights require governments to ensure that all women and girls have access to services such as education and health care—regardless of age, marital status, ethnicity or socioeconomic status).

What do these rights mean in practice? It could be argued, for example, that a woman's right to life entitles her access to appropriate health services and that laws that obstruct this violate her human rights. It can be said that her right to liberty is infringed if she is not given full information about an intervention that affects her reproductive health—such as the failure rate or side-effects of a method of fertility regulation. And the right to security of the person is not respected if a girl or young woman is subjected to female genital mutilation.

The right to find a family means much more than the right to conceive and bear a child. The Convention on the Elimination of All Forms of Discrimination against Women, for instance, goes beyond this. The Convention requires states that are signatory to it to ensure that women enjoy "*rights to decide freely and responsibly on the number and spacing of their children and to have access to the information, education and means to enable them to exercise these rights*".

The right to health care is infringed if there are legal barriers to a woman's access to health services. But the right may also be said to be infringed if a government fails to provide necessary health services to women who cannot obtain them through their own means. It could further be argued that the right is violated when a woman is deterred from using health services because she will not be treated with dignity and respect, or because she fears the lack of confidentiality and privacy. The right to the benefits of scientific progress requires that women should have access to treatments and technologies based on the results of scientific research. Failure to provide such treatments and technologies for no good reason could be interpreted as a violation of this right.

The rights to equality and nondiscrimination mean that a woman should not be disadvantaged in any way, legally or otherwise, simply because of the fact of being a woman. These rights are infringed, for instance, if a woman is required to obtain another person's authorization before she can access health services.

States have a legal obligation to account for their practices regarding human rights by reporting to human rights treaty bodies. Where states do not take all appropriate means to bring laws, policies and practices into compliance with the human rights of women, they have been held, and can continue to be held, accountable by constitutional courts and treaty monitoring bodies for denying women their human rights.

The Right to Reproductive and Sexual Health

The importance of good health and education to a woman's well-being—and that of her family and society—cannot be overstated. Without reproductive health and freedom, women cannot fully exercise their fundamental human rights, such as those relating to education and employment. Yet around the world, the right to health, and especially reproductive and sexual health, is far from a reality for many women. According to the World Bank, a full one-third of the illness among women ages 15-44 in developing countries is related to pregnancy, childbirth, abortion, reproductive tract infections, and human immunodeficiency virus and acquired immune deficiency syndrome (HIV/AIDS).

> **Box 1: Quote**
>
> "*The fact is that women have been trapped. Reproduction is used, consciously or not, as a means to control women, to limit their options and to make them subordinate to men. In many societies a serious approach to reproductive health has to have this perspective in mind. We must seek to liberate women.*"—Dr. Nafis Sadik, Executive Director, UN Population Fund.

Women's disproportionate poverty, low social status, and reproductive role expose them to high health risks, resulting in needless and largely preventable suffering and deaths. Many of the women and girls who die each year during pregnancy and childbirth could have been saved by relatively low-cost improvements in reproductive healthcare; yet high levels of maternal mortality persist. The benefits of eliminating the harmful and painful practice of female genital mutilation are easily demonstrated, yet it persists for cultural and traditional reasons. And a large proportion of abortions, some resulting in death and injury, would be avoided if women and men had access to safe, affordable and effective means of contraception.

Women's health status is affected by complex biological, social and cultural factors which are interrelated and can only be addressed in a comprehensive manner. Reproductive health is determined not only by the quality and availability of health care, but also by socio-economic development levels, lifestyles and women's position in society. In fact, the International Federation of Gynecology and Obstetrics asserts that improvements in women's health require state action to correct injustices to women. In its 1994 World Report on Women's Health, the Federation states that women's health is often compromised not by lack of medical knowledge, but by infringements on women's human rights.

The Evolution of the Right to Reproductive and Sexual Health

Over the years, a human rights-based approach to reproductive health has evolved which emphasizes the rights to health, to have children by choice, and to have a safe and satisfying sex life. It is now recognized that women have the right to the fullest enjoyment of health throughout their life cycle.

Since the right to family planning was enshrined in 1968 at the Teheran Human Rights Conference, the value of family planning and of individuals and couples being able to make their own childbearing decisions has been widely accepted. Today, 60 per cent of all couples are planning when to have children by using contraception, and family size is falling in most areas of the world.

The 1994 International Conference on Population and Development in Cairo and the 1995 Fourth World Conference on Women held in Beijing expanded the right to family planning to include the right to better sexual and reproductive health. Building on the World Health Organization's definition of health, the Cairo Programme defines reproductive health as:

> "a state of complete physical, mental and social well-being and...not merely the absence of disease or infirmity, in all matters relating to the reproductive system and to its functions and processes. Reproductive health therefore implies that people are able to have a satisfying and safe sex life and that they have the capability to reproduce and the freedom to decide if, when and how often to do so. Implicit in this last condition are the right of men and women to be informed and to have access to safe, effective, affordable and acceptable methods of family planning of their choice, as well as other methods of their choice for regulation of fertility which are not against the law, and the right of access to appropriate health-care services that will enable women to go safely through pregnancy and childbirth and provide couples with the best chance of having a healthy infant" (Para 72).
>
> *Furthermore*, the Cairo Programme of Action clearly spells out the concept of reproductive rights in Chapter 7 which states in part that such rights "rest on the recognition of the basic right of all couples and individuals to decide freely and responsibly the number, spacing and timing of their children and to have the information and means to do so, and the right to attain the highest standard of reproductive and sexual health. It also includes the right of all to make decisions concerning reproduction free of discrimination, coercion, and violence as expressed in human rights documents".

The Platform for Action, which was adopted by 189 delegations at the Beijing Women's Conference, reaffirms the Cairo Programme's definition of reproductive health and advances women's wider interests. Paragraph 96 states:

> "The human rights of women include their right to have control over and decide freely and responsibly on matters related to their sexuality, including sexual and reproductive health, free of coercion, discrimination and violence. Equal relationships between women and men in matters of sexual relations and reproduction, including full respect for the integrity of the person, require mutual respect, consent and shared responsibility for sexual behaviour and its consequences."

Violence and Reproductive Health

Gender-based violence is a profound human rights abuse and health problem for women around the world. Recent World Bank estimates of the global burden of the disease indicate that in established market-based economies gender-based victimization is responsible for one out of every five healthy days of life lost to women of reproductive age.

Gender violence can occur throughout a woman's lifecycle. Types include sex-selective abortion, battering during pregnancy, coerced pregnancy, rape, female infanticide, differential food and medical care for girls, child marriage, genital mutilation, child prostitution, dating and courtship violence, psychological abuse, marital rape, sexual harassment, trafficking in women, dowry abuse and murder, and abuse of elderly women.

Box 2: Quote

"*Much of the violence against women occurs in the context of sexuality and reproduction. The health consequences of violence often occur in the context of reproductive health and seriously contribute to the burden of disease in women and young people*".—Dr. Hiroshi Nakajima, Director General of the World Health Organization.

Increasingly, reproductive health services are dealing with the issue of violence. Morning-after pills to prevent pregnancies resulting from rape are being dispensed, and health clinics are offering counselling and support services for victims of abuse and violence. The Beijing Platform for Action contains an entire chapter on violence against women, which outlines concrete policies to combat this global threat to women and girls.

Adolescents and Reproductive Health

More than half the world's population is under the age of 25, and a significant number of adolescents are sexually active. From birth through childhood and adulthood, girls and women need effective services and information to enable them to lead healthy productive lives. Boys and men also need information and services that contribute to responsible behaviour and equal treatment of women and girls.

It is estimated that about 15 million teenage women give birth each year, accounting for up to one-fifth of all births worldwide. And every year, 1 out of 20 teenagers contracts a sexually transmitted disease. To reduce the rising instances of teenage pregnancy and sexually transmitted diseases among young people, the Cairo and Beijing texts call for the removal of regulatory and social barriers to reproductive health information and care for adolescents.

The Legal Impact

The increasing emphasis on the right to reproductive and sexual health is changing the way family planning services are devised and provided. Some non-governmental groups that provide family planning services, like Profamilia in Colombia, are now staffing their clinics with legal advisers. Women who come for reproductive health services have access to advocates who can educate them about their rights and counsel them if these have been violated.

At the national level, Guyana has enacted components of a reproductive health law. State policies that protect and promote reproductive health within a wider programme of women's health have been enacted in Colombia and Brazil. South Africa has included provisions on reproductive rights in its new Constitution which was signed by President Nelson Mandela on 10 December 1996. Unlike most constitutions, which include reproductive rights in the form of general rights—to equality, freedom and security of the person, dignity, privacy, freedom of conscience and the right to life—the South African Constitution specifically refers to reproductive rights.

One clause of the South African Constitution outlaws discrimination on the grounds of pregnancy. Another clause states that everyone has the right "to be free from all forms of violence from both public and private sources". This clause guarantees bodily and psychological integrity which specifically includes the right "to make decisions concerning reproduction" and "to security and control over bodies". Decisions concerning reproduction can include decisions related to family planning, pre-natal care, safe delivery and post-natal care, as well as prevention and treatment of reproductive tract infections, sexually transmitted diseases and abortion.

Ethical Guidelines

The Cairo and Beijing documents recommend that the health professions develop, disseminate and implement ethics codes to ensure practitioners' conformity with human rights and ethical and professional standards. In March 1994, before the Population Conference in Cairo, experts developed a Declaration of Ethical Propositions at a meeting sponsored by the Development Law and Policy Programme of Columbia University's Center for Population and Family Health, and the United Nations Population Fund (UNFPA). The principles stress human dignity and respect, the right to reproductive and sexual health care and information, an equitable allocation of health services, and freedom from coercion. The Declaration concludes that "reproductive rights and reproductive health are part of a broader human good that every society should aim to achieve for all its members...To address these issues ethically, governments cannot compartmentalize their efforts but must devise strategies that are broadly integrated with social and economic development, improved education and political and legal reform."

Ethical guidelines have also been developed by medical associations such as the International Federation of Gynecology and Obstetrics and the Commonwealth Medical Association. Another promising sign is the elaboration of a Charter on Sexual and Reproductive Rights by the International Planned Parenthood Federation (IPPF), which was approved by the organization's governing body and 127 member associations in 1995. The Charter, which provides an ethical framework for IPPF's work, defines 12 rights. These include the rights to life, liberty and security of the person, equality and to be free from all forms of discrimination, privacy, freedom of thought, to information and education, to choose whether or not to marry and to found and plan a family, to decide whether and when to have children, to health care and health protection, to the benefits of scientific progress, to freedom of assembly and political participation, and to be free from torture and ill treatment.

Holding Governments Accountable

Human rights activists have long argued that governments must be held accountable for all forms of discrimination against women, and they are increasingly urging that governments be specifically held accountable for violations of reproductive rights. Although these rights were clearly elaborated at the Cairo Population Conference in 1994 and the Beijing Women's Conference in 1995, it is clear that they will mean little to the well-being of women and men, if national, regional and international human rights instruments are not used to ensure governments' compliance with their Cairo and Beijing commitments.

Widespread recognition of the legal foundations for such claims form a first step in ensuring that reproductive rights become reality. In addition to the Cairo and Beijing documents, women's reproductive rights under international human rights law are a composite of a number of separate human rights treaties including the Universal Declaration of Human Rights; the International Covenant on Economic, Social and Cultural Rights; the Convention on the Elimination of All Forms of Discrimination against Women; and the International Covenant on Civil and Political Rights. The rights of girls and mothers are protected under the Convention on the Rights of the Child.

International efforts are under way to increase cooperation between United Nations agencies, non-governmental organizations and human rights treaty bodies to better promote, implement and monitor health-related rights, especially reproductive and sexual rights.

Women's right to health and reproductive health in particular, is essential to gender equality and female empowerment. The benefits of better reproductive health for both women and men can easily be demonstrated, from the point of view of society as well as the individual. In addition to saving lives and preventing infection and suffering, better reproductive health will lead to smaller families and slower population growth.

An emphasis on human rights obligations is a tool in the battle to secure reproductive and sexual health. It reinforces the fundamental point that reproductive health programmes are essential to protect the dignity of men and women—something governments are obligated to do.

Human Rights and Women's Reproductive Health

What is the Human Right to Reproductive Health?

The issues raised in Beijing and Cairo regarding women's reproductive health and sexuality are human rights issues. Reinforcing them are universal human rights standards defined in the Universal Declaration of Human Rights, CEDAW, the International Covenant on Economic, Social and Cultural Rights, and other widely adhered to international human rights treaties and Declarations—powerful tools that must be put to use to enhance efforts for the advancement of women's reproductive and sexual health.

The Human Rights at Issue

The reproductive and sexual human rights of all women include:

- The human right to the highest attainable standard of physical and mental health, including reproductive and sexual health.
- The human right to equality in marriage, including the equal right of women and men to decide on the number and spacing of children.
- The human right to access to education and information, in particular relating to family planning to enable couples and individuals to exercise their right to decide freely and responsibly all matters of reproduction and sexuality.
- The human right to access to adequate social services, including access to safe, effective, affordable and acceptable methods of family planning of their choice, as well as other methods of their choice for regulation of fertility, and the right of access to appropriate health-care services that will enable women to go safely through pregnancy and childbirth.

The Human Right to Privacy

- The human right to freedom from discrimination and discriminatory social practices, including female genital mutilation, prenatal gender selection, and female infanticide.
- The human right to freedom from coercion and violence, sexual exploitation, forced prostitution.
- These human rights are inextricably linked to other fundamental human rights guaranteed to all women, rights that are universal, indivisible, interconnected and interdependent, including:
- The human right to equality between men and women and to full and equal partnership in the family and society.
- The human right to full respect for the inherent dignity of the person.
- The human right to full and equal participation in all aspects of public life and decision-making.
- The human right to an adequate standard of living.

Governments' Obligations to Ensuring the Human Right to Reproductive Health

What provisions of human rights law guarantee all women the Human Right to Reproductive Health? Following description includes excerpts from:

- the Convention on the Elimination of All Forms of Discrimination Against Women,
- the Universal Declaration of Human Rights,
- the International Covenant on Economic, Social and Cultural Rights,
- the International Covenant on Civil and Political Rights, and inferiority or ... superiority of the Convention on the Rights of the Child.
    - "States Parties shall take all appropriate measures ... to modify the social and cultural patterns of conduct of men and women, ... to achieve... the elimination of prejudices and customary ... practices which are based on the idea of ... inferiority or ... superiority of either of the sexes or on stereotyped roles for men and women; to ensure that family education includes a proper understanding of maternity as a social function and the recognition of the common responsibility of men and women in the upbringing and development of their children.... States Parties shall ... suppress all forms of traffic in women and exploitation of prostitution of women...."—*Convention on the Elimination of All Forms of Discrimination Against Women, Articles 5 and 6*
    - "States Parties shall ... ensure to [women] ... access to specific educational information to help to ensure the health and well-being of families, including information and advice on family planning.... States Parties shall take appropriate measures ... to introduce maternity leave with pay or ... comparable social benefits without loss of former employment, seniority or social allowances.... States Parties shall ... eliminate discrimination against women in the field of health care in order to ensure ... access to health care services, including those related to family planning....; ensure ... appropriate services in connection with pregnancy ... granting free services where necessary, as well as adequate nutrition during pregnancy and lactation.... States Parties shall ... ensure ... that [women in rural areas] ... have access to adequate health care facilities, including information counselling and services in family planning...."—*Convention on the Elimination of All Forms of Discrimination Against Women, Articles 10, 11, 12, and 14*
    - "Men and women ... are entitled to equal rights as to marriage, during marriage and at its dissolution.... Everyone has the right

to a standard of living adequate for health and well-being.... Motherhood and childhood are entitled to special care and assistance....”—*Universal Declaration of Human Rights, Articles 16 and 25*

- “The States Parties ... recognize that ... the widest possible protection and assistance should be accorded to the family.... Marriage must be entered into with the free consent of the intending spouses. Special protection should be accorded to mothers during a reasonable period before and after childbirth. During such period working mothers should be accorded paid leave or leave with adequate social security benefits.... The States Parties ... recognize the right of everyone ... to the highest attainable standard of physical and mental health”.—*International Covenant on Economic, Social and Cultural Rights, Articles 10 and 12*
- “... States Parties ... undertake to ensure the equal right of men and women to the enjoyment of all civil and political rights.... No one shall be subjected to torture or to cruel, inhuman or degrading treatment or punishment.... No one shall be held in slavery.... No one shall be subjected to ... interference with his privacy.... The family ... is entitled to protection by society and the State.... No marriage shall be entered into without the free and full consent of the intending spouses. States Parties ... shall ... ensure equality of rights and responsibilities of spouses as to marriage, during marriage and at its dissolution....”—*International Covenant on Civil and Political Rights, Articles 3, 7, 8, 17, and 23*
- “States Parties shall take measures to combat the illicit transfer and non-return of children abroad.... States Parties shall take all appropriate ... measures to protect the child from all forms of physical or mental violence, injury or abuse, maltreatment or exploitation including sexual abuse.... States Parties recognize the right of the child to the enjoyment of the highest attainable standard of health.... shall take ... measures ... to ensure appropriate pre-and post-natal health care for expectant mothers.... States Parties shall take all ... measures with a view to abolishing traditional practices prejudicial to the health of children.... States Parties undertake to protect the child from all forms of sexual exploitation and sexual abuse.... shall take all appropriate ... measures to prevent the abduction, the sale of or traffic in children....”—*Convention on the Rights of the Child, Articles 11, 19, 24, 34, and 35*

Governments' Commitments to Ensuring the Human Right to Reproductive Health

What commitments have governments made to ensure the realization of the Human Right to Reproductive Health?

Following description includes commitments made at the International Conference on Population and Development in Cairo, and the World Conference on Human Rights in Vienna.

- "The explicit recognition ... of the right of all women to control all aspects of their health, in particular their own fertility, is basic to their empowerment.... We are determined to ... ensure equal access to and equal treatment of women and men in ... health care and enhance women's sexual and reproductive health as well as education."—*Beijing Declaration, paras. 17 and 30*
- "Reproductive health is a state of complete physical, mental and social well-being and not merely the absence of disease or infirmity, in all matters relating to the reproductive system and to its functions and processes. Reproductive health ... implies that people are able to have a satisfying and safe sex life and that they have the capability to reproduce and the freedom to decide if, when and how often to do so. Implicit in this last condition are the right of men and women to be informed and to have access to safe, effective, affordable and acceptable methods of family planning of their choice, as well as other methods of their choice for regulation of fertility ... and the right of access to appropriate health-care services...."—*Beijing Platform for Action, para. 94*
- "The human rights of women and of the girl-child are an inalienable, integral and indivisible part of universal human rights.... Gender-based violence and all forms of sexual harassment and exploitation, including those resulting from cultural prejudice ... are incompatible with the dignity and worth of the human person, and must be eliminated".—*Vienna Declaration, Part I, para. 18*
- "Everyone has the right to the enjoyment of the highest attainable standard of physical and mental health. States should ... ensure, on a basis of equality of men and women, universal access to health-care services, including those related to reproductive health care, which includes family planning and sexual health. Reproductive health-care programmes should provide the widest range of services without any form of coercion. All couples and individuals have the basic right to decide freely and responsibly the number and spacing of their children and to have the information, education and means to do so."—*Cairo Programme of Action, Principle 8*

3

Reproductive Health

A Global and Regional Priority

Since the 1994 International Conference on Population and Development (ICPD) in Cairo and the 1995 Fourth World Conference on Women (FWCW) in Beijing, reproductive health has become a global, regional and national priority in almost, if not all, the countries in the world today. The definition of reproductive health was the focus of considerable negotiation at the ICPD, but in the end consensus was reached on it, as reflected in paragraph 7.2 of the ICPD Programme of Action (ICPD POA):

- Reproductive health is a state of complete physical, mental and social well being and not merely the absence of disease or infirmity, in all matters relating to the reproductive system and to its functions and processes. RH therefore implies that people are able to have a satisfying and safe sex life and that they have the capability to reproduce and the freedom to decide if, when and how often to do so. Implicit in this last condition are the right of men and women to be informed and to have access to safe, effective, affordable and acceptable methods of family planning of their choice, as well as other methods for the regulation of fertility which are not against the law, and the right of access to appropriate health care services that will enable women to go safely through pregnancy and childbirth and provide the couple with the best chance of having a healthy infant.
- In line with the above definition of RH, reproductive health care is defined as the constellation of methods, techniques and services that contribute to RH and well-being by preventing and solving RH problems. It also includes sexual health, the purpose of which is the enhancement of life and personal relations, and not merely counseling and care related to reproduction and sexually transmitted diseases.

The 1994 ICPD placed reproductive health within an ethical framework. 180 nations reached a consensus for the first time that:

- people's reproductive health needs is a matter of human rights and social justice;
- people have a right to make free and informed decisions about their reproductive lives;
- people have a right to information and care that will enable them to protect their health and that of their loved ones;
- smaller families and slower population growth are created by choice and opportunity, not control or coercion; and
- women's reproductive health and empowerment are critical to a nation's sustainability and growth.

In Cairo, the world also acknowledged that if there is in-action or complacency, or when people's sexual and reproductive rights are denied, the following scenario will be experienced:

- each year, at least 120 million women who do not want to become pregnant do not have the means to prevent it;
- each year, 15 million young women between age 15 and 19 give birth;
- each year, close to 600,000 women die of childbirth or pregnancy related causes;
- each year, about 20 million women put their health and lives at risk because they seek unsafe abortions (70, 000 women eventually die from it each year);
- each year, more than 330 million people contract STD (one in twenty adolescents involved and women are infected five times more than men);
- each year, more than 5 million people contract HIV (50 per cent of whom are young people aged 15 to 24);
- each year, 2 million girls aged 5 to 15 are put on the commercial sex market; and
- each year, there are 450,000 new cases of cancer of the cervix (neck of the womb).

The world leaders agreed that this is not an acceptable situation and something must be done about this. Ironically most of these human suffering and wastage could be prevented or avoided or at least minimised through the commitment of key stakeholders.

A Programme of Action (ICDP-POA), with specific goals was endorsed. The aims of the ICPD POA include, inter-alia, universal access to reproductive health services including family planning, reduction of infant and maternal deaths, increased access to education (particularly for girls), and gender equity and equality. Three specific long-term goals were also set to be met over the next two decades (2015), as well as intermediate goals to be achieved within a decade (2005).

The reproductive health status and trends in the Pacific, based on various sources including country reports and assessments (for the period 1994 to 1996) were quite a concern:

- an estimated 1,100 mothers die each year of complications of pregnancy and childbirth;
- over 12, 000 Pacific infants will not live to celebrate their first birthdays each year;
- an estimated 160,000 women will get pregnant each year (a significant proportion of whom are teenagers and women over 35 years with high parity—high risk pregnancies);
- an estimated 140,000 people will contract an sexually transmitted infection (STI) each year;
- the number of adolescents and young people contracting STI including HIV/AIDS, abuse drugs including alcohol, engage in commercial sex work and take to the streets or live in isolation from their families are reported to be increasing;
- complications of abortion account for a significant proportion of gynaecological admissions in hospitals; and
- violence against women including rape and sexual abuse is of concern (the extend of which remains largely undetermined).

In addition to the above issues, there are hundreds and even thousands of Pacific women who suffer from complications and consequences of pregnancy, childbirth, STI, abortions, sexual abuse and rape. Yet they remain at home and suffer in silence due to the lack of information on what to do or where to go for help, or because of injustice and negligence.

Global estimates showed that between 5-15 per cent of the burden of disease is associated with failures to address reproductive health needs. This burden hits people, particularly women, in the prime of life (when their potential, responsibilities and productivity are at their highest). The three main conditions of STI including HIV/AIDS, maternal ill health and deaths and reproductive tract cancers result in a 20 per cent loss in total years of healthy life among women of child bearing age. A further 10 per cent of healthy years of life are lost due to conditions affecting the newborn.

In 1993, the World Bank estimated the health burden of selected conditions for women aged 15 to 44. Every year, lost due to premature death is counted as a "disability-adjusted life year" (DALY), and every year spent sick or incapacitated is counted as a fraction of a DALY with the value determined by the severity of the disability. The assessment showed that the health burden of maternal conditions was ten times that of war or malaria. The health burden of domestic violence and rape was comparable to that of HIV/AIDS, TB, cancers and cardiovascular diseases.

What has not been measured, however, is the extent of social and psychological sufferings caused by violence, loss of loved ones, ignorance and total disregard and lack of respect for individuals' sexual and reproductive rights. These rights include:

- the right to survival/right to life—abrogated by maternal deaths;
- the right to the highest attainable standard of health including sexual and reproductive health;
- the right to non-discrimination on the basis of age—abrogated when young people are denied information and confidentiality about reproductive health services;
- the right to reproductive decision-making, including choice in marriage, family formation, and the number, timing and spacing of one's children; and the right to the information and the means to exercise those choices;
- the right to equality and equity for women and men to make free and informed choices in all spheres of life, free from gender discrimination; and
- the right to sexual and reproductive security, including freedom from sexual violence and coercion, and the right to privacy.

Time and time again governments and leaders have pledged their commitments to reproductive health and to the enhancements of human development and well being of their people. These commitments were made in national, regional and international forums. Declarations, Platforms for Action/Programmes of Action were adopted by consensus. The most significant ones include the ICPD POA and the Beijing Platform for Action. Principle 8 and chapters IV, VII and VIII of the ICPD POA are designed to protect and promote the health and welfare of women, men, adolescents and families with specific emphasis on reproductive health including family planning and sexual health. The Beijing Declaration numbers 17, 29 and 30 are directly related to the health of women.

In the Pacific, the Post Vila Declaration on Population and Development, the Yanuca Island Declaration on Healthy Island, the Suva Declaration on sustainable human development and the Pacific response to the ICPD POA are examples of these commitments.

A global review of the implementation of the ICPD POA and the progress in achieving its goals (referred to as the ICPD+5 review) looked at five substantive themes: creating an enabling environment for the further implementation of the ICPD POA; reproductive health including family health and sexual health, and reproductive rights; gender equality, equity and the empowerment of women; strengthening partnerships; and resource flows and financing for the implementation of the ICPD POA. The review took place at national, regional and international levels. At the Hague Forum in February 1999, all the stakeholders (NGOs, Youths, Parliamentarians, donors and government representatives) dialogued once again on how to further the implementation of the ICPD based on lessons learned and make recommendations to the United Nations General Assembly Special Session (UNGASS) on how to further the ICPD POA's implementation.

Generally, positive progress has been made in the area of policy changes, programme development and in the reduction of maternal, infant and child ill health and deaths. Access to reproductive health services and care had improved and many countries had instituted legal measures to deal with sexual violence, coercion and harmful practices such as female genital mutilation. In the Pacific, similar progress has been made—improvements in life expectancy, health and education status. Using the ICPD POA goal indicator and threshold levels as benchmarks, most of the PICs had already met the quantitative goal of access to reproductive health, mortality reduction and universal primary education.

However, these achievements are not good enough as the levels of morbidity and mortality are still considered high. The levels of infants and maternal deaths in the Melanesian and Micronesian countries are relatively high and the contraceptive prevalence rate (CPR) low. Fertility remains high in some countries and so are the unmet needs for family planning (limiting or spacing births).

The incidence of RTI and STI, among adolescents and youths in particular, are said to be increasing. In terms of services, there is inadequate/lack of services to meet the needs of adolescents/youth and men reproductive health and sexual health needs.

A review of the implementation of the Beijing Platform for Action has concluded that progress to more gender equity in the PICs has taken place. Many governments have made changes to their national legislations or policies in order to improve the status of women. These include family laws and procedures to punish gender violence, the sensitization of decision-makers about gender issues, efforts to raise girls' and women's access to education and training, and the need for gender disaggregated data and the integration of gender aspect into planning and development processes. Again, despite thee notable achievements much remain to be done, particularly in respect to fulfilling women's sexual and reproductive rights and choices and protection from violence and abuse.

A major setback for the successful implementation of the ICPD POA was the lack of translating international commitments into realities. The total cost of the POA was estimated to be $17 billion per year by the turn of the century, climbing to $22 billion by 2015.

Two-thirds of the budget would come from developing countries and one-third from the more developed. So far, the developing countries had provided well over 60 per cent of their share whilst the developed countries (donors) have provided only 30 per cent of their share. The worst thing is that donor support seems to be declining rather than increasing in the past years.

In the Pacific, the 1997/98 government expenditures (as percentage of government spending) on health services ranged from 3.0 per cent (Tokelau) to 17.9 per cent (Kiribati. A significant proportion being allocated to curative/ clinical services, staffing and drug supplies. In reality, the budgetary provision for sexual health and reproductive health services is very minimal.

The situation is further compounded by the global economic recession and the structural reforms taking place in most of the Pacific countries. Although health sector reform strategies may include "essential services package" or "basic package" that incorporates many aspects of reproductive health care, the drive for cost-reductions and organisational efficiencies may impact negatively on reproductive health services and care.

The RH/FP-SH programmes supported by the UNFPA have experienced a 40 per cent cut in funding this year attributed to the decline in donor contributions. The serious shortfalls in resources will definitely lead to the following consequences (1995-2000 period):

a) an increase of 97 to 170 million individuals and couples with unmet needs for family planning;
b) an increase of 130 to 230 million unintended pregnancies;
c) an increase of 50 to 90 million abortions;
d) an increase of 300,000 to 540,000 maternal deaths; and
e) increases in infant and child deaths.

Commitments

Sustaining Commitment through Advocacy

- Advocate tirelessly for political commitment to reproductive health and help to forge partnerships between stakeholders (government, NGOs and the private sector).
- Advocate for necessary legal and policy framework for the successful implementation of reproductive health programmes including services.
- Consider Parliamentary initiatives and support groups for mobilisation of resources.

Attacking Poverty and Promoting Education

The linkages between health, poverty and education are well established and known. Poverty is now the single greatest cause of ill health in the world today and action to improve health should be coordinated with initiatives to reduce poverty.

About 70 per cent of the world's poor are female, according to international aid experts. In a situation of poverty, women often have the least access to food, health, education and employment, which in turn violates the right of control over their reproductive function. Important links between poverty and reproductive health is the growing recourse to abortion and an increase in STI due to prostitution.

Research has shown that educating girls and women is a powerful ally in the eradication of poverty. Educated women are also better able to care for their own health and that of their children and families. Education and employment enable women to demand and exercise their fundamental rights, including the right to health and reproductive choice. Educated women tend to marry later, have their first children later and have fewer children overall than those who are illiterate.

Utilize Useful Lessons Learned

Institute appropriate reproductive health services and approaches based on useful lessons learned. These include:

a) the life-cycle approach;
b) integrated health programmes
c) prenatal care, attended birth;
d) quality of care; and
e) lifting the barriers to access information and services.

Promoting Reproductive Rights

Enhancing:

a) sexual and reproductive self-determination as regards adolescent sexuality,
b) adolescents' right to reproductive health services,
c) planned pregnancies,
d) non-coercion and violence against women, and
e) gender equity and equality.

Partnership and Collaboration

The need for partnerships and collaboration cannot be overemphasized. The implications of any inaction or complacency are serious, as outlined in this paper. NGOs and Civil Society Organisations; strengths and comparative advantages should be utilized more effectively. Likewise, the involvement of donors and other development agencies is critical for the mobilization of much needed funding and support.

Pacific island governments have pledged their commitment to population and reproductive health through various international declarations and Programme of Action (POA) particularly the ICPD POA and the Beijing Platform for Action on women. The ICPD+5 and the Beijing+5 reviews showed that encouraging progress has been made so far in the enhancement of Pacific peoples reproductive health status—but much more need to be done.

The current levels of infant and maternal deaths (equivalent to 33 jumbo jets, each with 400 passengers on board, crashing and killing everyone per year in the Pacific) are unacceptably high. The reproductive needs and rights (particularly of men, women and young people) are yet to be adequately met or fulfilled.

The magnitude of disease burden and human suffering caused by in-action cannot be overemphasized. The benefits of investing in reproductive health particularly in the fulfillment of adolescents and women's reproductive needs and rights are enormous. This global consensus should be made into reality in the Pacific.

4

Meeting the Reproductive Health Needs of Women with HIV

Meeting the Reproductive Health Needs of Women with HIV

Introduction

During the past decade, HIV counselling and testing services have expanded in both urban and rural areas of sub-Saharan Africa, even becoming routine in some medical settings. With this expansion, more women who are infected with HIV are becoming aware of their status. Recent population-based studies and health surveys from 12 African countries suggest that between 10 per cent and 25 per cent of women with HIV now know that they are infected.

As more HIV-infected women learn of their status, they will be able to make informed choices about their reproductive health—including whether to have children and how to prevent further transmission of the virus. A knowledgeable healthcare provider can help with these difficult decisions.

Fertility Desires

A recent review of how HIV status affects people's reproductive intentions and behaviours found that the fertility desires of HIV-infected women are not that different from those of uninfected women. According to a summary of 19 studies that were conducted in developing countries, most women with HIV still want to have children. Others do not want children, and so need effective contraception to prevent unintended pregnancies. Like the fertility desires of uninfected women, these desires are not static and may change over time.

Research also shows that HIV-infected women who do *not* want more children have a high risk of unintended pregnancy. Studies and surveys from Zimbabwe and Uganda even suggest that HIV-infected women who do not want more children may be more likely than their uninfected counterparts to report that they are not using contraception. This could be due to a fear of social stigma or discrimination, which could inhibit women with HIV from seeking family planning and other reproductive health services.

At least one study, from Malawi, suggests that HIV-infected women are more likely to put off childbearing and to use contraception after they receive HIV counselling and testing and find out their status. This suggests that counselling HIV-infected women about their reproductive health options may influence their health decisions. Professionals who offer family planning or HIV services can talk with their HIV-infected patients to determine their fertility desires and reproductive health needs. Regardless of their own personal views about whether HIV-infected women should be sexually active or have children, healthcare professionals should also provide accurate, unbiased information about the medical risks and benefits of both contraception and pregnancy.

Contraception

Nearly all modern methods of contraception, including the intrauterine device (IUD) and hormonal methods are safe for most women with HIV.

The only methods that are not recommended for women with HIV are spermicides and diaphragms. If used frequently, spermicides containing the surfactant nonoxynol-9 can actually increase the risk of acquiring HIV. Thus, theoretically, women who are already infected with HIV may have a higher risk of being re-infected with a different strain of HIV when they use spermicides often. Diaphragms are not recommended because they need to be used with spermicides.

In 2004, the World Health Organization (WHO) changed its international guidelines for use of the IUD by women with HIV, making the method more available to infected women. This change was implemented after research from Kenya showed that women with HIV are no more likely than women without HIV to experience complications from IUD use. Also, the use of an IUD does not increase the chance that a woman with HIV will transmit the virus to her sexual partners. As long as she has regular access to medical services, an HIV-infected woman can safely begin using an IUD in most circumstances. However, IUD insertion is not generally recommended for a woman who has AIDS unless she is taking antiretroviral (ARV) drugs and responding well to them. This is because AIDS can suppress a woman's immune system, which may put her at risk of infection during an IUD insertion. On the other hand, if an IUD user develops AIDS after her IUD is already in place, she can generally continue using the method.

WHO places no restrictions on the use of hormonal methods—including combined oral contraceptive pills, progestin-only pills, injectables, or contraceptive implants—for women who have HIV. Women who have AIDS but are not receiving ARV drugs can also use hormonal methods without restrictions.

New guidelines from WHO specifically address the use of hormonal methods by women taking ARV drugs. According to the new guidelines, a woman on any ARV drugs can use the injectable depot medroxyprogesterone acetate (DMPA) without any restrictions. Research has shown, however, that some ARV drugs decrease the level of active steroids that some of the methods rely on for their contraceptive effectiveness. Because most of the studies did not actually measure contraceptive effectiveness, it is not clear whether the decreases in active steroids are clinically relevant. No data are available on the interactions between contraceptive steroids and some ARV drugs, such as stavudine, which is a component of first-line therapy for HIV in some parts of Africa.

Based on research concerning these possible interactions, a woman who is taking ARV drugs other than the protease inhibitor ritonavir can still generally use oral contraceptives, contraceptive implants, and the injectable norethisterone enanthate (NET-EN), but WHO suggests that she also use condoms—to compensate for any potential decreases in contraceptive effectiveness and to prevent HIV transmission. According to the new guidelines, a woman should not use oral contraceptives or combined injectable contraceptives if her ARV regimen contains ritonavir, because this particular drug has been shown to reduce the blood concentration of contraceptive hormones more than the other drugs studied.

Pregnancy

Although HIV can affect fertility, making it harder for an infected woman to conceive a child, most HIV-infected women who become pregnant can have a healthy baby if proper medical care is available. But before deciding to become pregnant, HIV-infected women should understand the risks that pregnancy can pose, especially if they have advanced HIV or AIDS.

Pregnancy does not facilitate the progression of HIV to AIDS, but it is not without other risks. When compared with uninfected women, women with HIV are about three to six times more likely to miscarry. They are also more likely to go into labour early, to deliver prematurely, and to have a baby that is too small or weighs too little. Other complications of pregnancy that are more common among HIV-infected women include postpartum fever (but no other signs of infection) and anaemia.

Children of HIV-infected women are also at risk of increased morbidity and mortality, most likely due to increased chances that their mothers will be sick or die. For the same reasons, the children of infected women are at risk of orphanhood, inadequate nutrition, and missed educational opportunities.

In order to improve their own health—and thus the odds of having a healthy baby—some pregnant women who have high viral loads can take ARV drugs after their first trimester of pregnancy. However, not all ARV drugs are safe during pregnancy. The drug efavirenz, for example, can be toxic to a developing fetus. Health professionals who are caring for women with advanced HIV or AIDS should discuss this issue with their patients. A woman with advanced disease may need to rethink her decision to become pregnant until her health improves or until she has access to the ARV drugs she needs.

Perhaps the biggest risk to the infants of HIV-infected mothers—but one that is largely preventable with access to appropriate medical care—is the risk of mother-to-child transmission. In Africa, the rate of mother-to-child transmission is estimated to be between 25 per cent and 40 per cent if no efforts are made to prevent infection. The severity of the mother's HIV infection is the most significant factor in predicting mother-to-child transmission, and the highest rates of transmission happen when the mother's viral load exceeds 100 000 copies per milliliter of blood. Most of the infections occur during pregnancy or delivery, but the virus can also be transmitted to the baby during the postpartum period, through breastfeeding.

Several strategies have been shown to reduce the risk of mother-to-child transmission. One of the most effective strategies is ART for both a mother and her newborn baby. For instance, studies have shown that different regimens of zidovudine or nevirapine can reduce rates of transmission by 47 per cent or more. Avoidance of breastfeeding is another effective way to reduce mother-to-child transmission, if infant formula is available and affordable. If formula is not an option, exclusive breastfeeding is advised since it appears to be associated with a lower risk of mother-to-child transmission than a mix of formula and breastfeeding. Finally, a planned caesarean section is more protective against mother-to-child transmission than a vaginal delivery, although caesarean sections can be associated with increased health risks to the mother.

Unfortunately, access to ART, infant formula, and safe caesarean sections remains a challenge in many parts of Africa. But, if all three precautions can be taken, rates of mother-to-child transmission drop significantly. In developing countries, where access is relatively good, fewer than 2 per cent of babies acquire HIV from their HIV-infected mothers.

Condom Use

Whether or not a woman decides to have children, she must also be aware of the best ways to prevent further HIV acquisition and transmission. Consistent condom use can protect an HIV-infected woman against re-infection with another strain of HIV or from acquiring a sexually transmitted infection such as 'gonorrhea' and 'chlamydia'. It can also reduce the risk that she will transmit the virus to an uninfected partner.

If a woman is trying to conceive, unprotected intercourse should be limited to the day of ovulation and a few days before ovulation is expected. Male or female condoms should be used during every act of sexual intercourse in which an infected woman is not trying to conceive. If her infection is controlled by ARV drugs, she may be unlikely to infect others. However, because ARV treatment may not completely eliminate her risk of infecting others, she should still be encouraged to use condoms.

Meeting the Sexual and Reproductive Health Needs of People Living with HIV

What it means to be a man, woman or young person living with HIV can be very different now than 25 years ago when AIDS was first identified, in large part because of the availability of antiretroviral treatment. For those with access to treatment services, a diagnosis of HIV infection is no longer an imminent death sentence; although still incurable, HIV now can be managed as a chronic disease. Today, the push for universal access to life-saving drugs is a major focus of attention at national and global levels. And although realization of that ambitious goal may be a long way off, especially in the developing world, significant progress in the campaign for treatment access is being made even there. The number of people in low-and middle-income countries receiving treatment more than tripled between 2003 and 2005, from 400,000 to 1.3 million.

As the prognosis for people living with HIV has improved worldwide, AIDS activists and the global public health community has increased their focus on quality-of-life issues as well as length-of-life issues. Regardless of HIV status, the ability to express oneself sexually and the desire to experience parenthood are, for many, central to what it means to be human. Therefore, acknowledging these needs and aspirations is essential to vindicating the basic human rights of HIV-positive people. At the same time, because the large majority of HIV infections worldwide occur as a result of sexual intercourse, global HIV prevention efforts must address the sexual and reproductive health needs of people living with HIV to succeed. For both of these reasons, meeting the sexual and reproductive health goals and service needs of people with HIV must be considered a global priority.

Aspirations and Needs

The Desire to have Children

The intersection between HIV status and childbearing desires is complicated. On the one hand, HIV-positive men and women report strong pressure from family members, people in their community and health care providers to give up the idea of having children, either because of the risk of perinatal HIV transmission or out of concern for the welfare of children raised by parents who may die prematurely of AIDS. On the other hand, childbearing in most societies plays a central role in the social identity of both men and women, and couples are expected to have children. In that sense, it is not surprising that the preponderance of research from both developed and developing countries suggests that HIV status does not depress fertility desires.

The bottom line is that a significant proportion of HIV-positive men and women report that they want to have a child or another child in the future. And when they are asked why, they talk about the pleasure and happiness that comes with being a parent—answers that, not surprisingly, are similar to those given by HIV-negative people. Moreover, pregnancy may be a time of high self-esteem for women, and parenting may help combat the dehumanizing effects of living with HIV for women and men. At the same time, those living with HIV who are considering parenthood raise concerns about the effect a pregnancy may have on a woman's health, the risk of transmitting the virus to their newborn, and whether they will be able to have a long, healthy life in which to love and support the child.

In fact, evidence (mostly from developed countries) indicates that pregnancy does not have an adverse effect on HIV disease progression; however, for a variety of reasons that are not entirely clear, HIV infection appears to place women who are pregnant at increased risk of complications and is regarded as an indirect cause of maternal death. A meta-analysis combining the results of 31 studies conducted in a range of countries suggests that HIV infection may be associated with increased risk of miscarriage, preterm delivery and low birth weight, although these associations are not strong.

Fortunately, the risk of perinatal transmission of HIV is below 2 per cent with antiretroviral treatments, safe delivery and safe infant-feeding; absent these critical interventions, the risk ranges from 20-45 per cent. But because low-income countries often lack the infrastructure to deliver even relatively modest interventions, progress in expanding access has been slow. At the end of 2005, fewer than 10 per cent of HIV-positive pregnant women were estimated to be receiving services to prevent mother-to-child transmission of HIV, resulting in 1,800 infants born with HIV every day.

Men and women living with HIV who are considering becoming a parent—biologically or by adoption—clearly need special counseling and support; however, there are other issues as well. Studies suggest that HIV may have an adverse effect on both male and female fertility. In addition, there is the issue of how HIV-discordant couples—in which one partner is infected and the other is not—can safely pursue pregnancy. Artificial insemination can reduce the risk of infection when the woman is HIV-positive. Pregnancy is more problematic, however, when the man is HIV-positive. In this case, couples can reduce the risk of transmission by limiting unprotected sex to the short time during a woman's menstrual cycle when she is fertile and her partner's viral load is undetectable; because experience with this technique in resource-limited settings is lacking, the World Health Organization (WHO) considers it to be "inadequate for making recommendations." Another option is "sperm washing," a process in which sperm are separated from HIV-causing agents in seminal fluid before being used for insemination; however, this technique is currently too costly for many people with HIV, especially those in low-resource settings.

The Need to Prevent Unplanned Pregnancy and Childbearing

Many people living with HIV will want to prevent pregnancy, either to time and space their childbearing or to avoid it entirely. Because condoms are the only method that protects against HIV and other sexually transmitted infections (STIs), WHO recommends that providers encourage men and women with HIV who are seeking to avoid pregnancy to use condoms, with or without another contraceptive method. According to WHO's Medical Eligibility Criteria for Contraceptive Use, hormonal methods (such as oral contraceptives, injectables, implants, emergency contraception and the vaginal ring) are appropriate for women with HIV, including those who take antiretroviral drugs. For women receiving treatment, however, potential drug interactions should be considered in light of the fact that the limited data available suggest that some antiretroviral drugs may alter hormonal blood levels in women using oral contraceptives and possibly other hormonal methods. The IUD can be used by women with HIV, but insertion is not recommended for those who have developed AIDS and are not on antiretroviral therapy. Female sterilization and vasectomy are additional options, except for women and men with an acute HIV-related illness; in such cases, the procedure should be delayed until the condition is resolved. Spermicides—as well as diaphragms and cervical caps, which are used in conjunction with spermicides—are not recommended for women living with HIV, on the basis of findings that question the safety of nonoxynol-9.

However, even among those who use contraceptives, many women with HIV inevitably will have and may seek to end an unplanned pregnancy. Both early surgical abortion and medication abortion are considered safe for women with HIV; if provided by a qualified professional using standard technique in sanitary conditions, injuries and deaths are rare. Unsafe abortions, which are risky for all women, are particularly dangerous for women with HIV, because of these women's somewhat increased risk of infection and hemorrhage.

To preserve their health and rights, people living with HIV must be able to make informed decisions about their sexual and reproductive health and have access to appropriate services. Concerted actions on several fronts may be needed: to ensure that men and women with HIV are not coerced or pressured into terminating a pregnancy or into using certain contraceptive methods, such as sterilization; to expand contraceptive services; to offer psychosocial support for men and women contemplating childbearing; and to provide nondirective, nonjudgmental and confidential counseling to HIV-positive women, including those faced with unplanned pregnancies. And where unsafe abortion exists, governments must try to create a consensus in favour of addressing its harmful social and health consequences.

The Ability to Protect Sexual Health

Because people living with HIV may have compromised immune systems, they are biologically more vulnerable than others to certain STIs. In addition, it is theorized, but not proven, that they may be at risk of reinfection with another strain of HIV. "Safer sex" practices can reduce an individual's risk of HIV and other STIs. Currently, this is best accomplished by using male or female condoms, although some sexual behaviours (such as non-penetrative sex) can also reduce risk.

[Even as the AIDS vaccine field progresses, research is currently underway on a range of new prevention technologies. Perhaps most notably, scientists in several countries are working to determine whether tenofovir, an antiretroviral drug used to treat HIV disease, is safe and effective for use as an oral pre-exposure prophylaxis, while other researchers are investigating microbicides, gels or creams that prevent the transmission of HIV and other STIs when applied topically.]

Individuals tend to increase their condom use after learning their HIV status. Correct and consistent condom use over long periods, however, is difficult for most people, and even the most well-intentioned may experience prevention "fatigue." Some people living with HIV report not using condoms because their partners also have HIV or because they or their partners refuse to use the method. Some may be reluctant to disclose their HIV status or negotiate condom use with their partners for fear that it would raise suspicions about infidelity, cause conflict or violence, or lead to the end of the relationship. Discordant couples may forgo condoms when they think the HIV-positive partner's viral load is too low to permit transmission. This may not in fact be the case, however, and it also leaves them at risk of STIs if the couple is not monogamous and of unintended pregnancy if no other contraceptive method is used. Finally, even highly motivated condom users may be stymied by the cost or simple lack of availability of male or female condoms.

HIV prevention programmes aimed at people living with HIV are a critical component of HIV prevention efforts. People living with HIV, however, need support from all levels of society to practice prevention. At a minimum, they need access to health services and to providers of both HIV services and sexual and reproductive health services who are capable and sufficiently trained to meet their needs. Providers must be comfortable talking about sexual intimacy, risky behaviours and other sensitive issues with their clients—some of whom may be youth, men who have sex with men, sex workers or injecting drug users. In particular, young people and men traditionally have not been the targets of sexual and reproductive health programmes, and their needs have been largely ignored in the body of research on sexual and reproductive health for people living with HIV. It is crucial that providers offer youth-friendly services and recognize men's needs in their own right.

Overarching Challenges

Clearly, there is a compelling need for specific services that address the sexual and reproductive health of people living with HIV. Of course, such services are not delivered in a vacuum. They are set against a backdrop of large-scale challenges that impede service delivery and people's ability to access health care. At the same time, meeting the sexual and reproductive health needs of people living with HIV could make an important contribution to resolving these overarching challenges.

Weak Health Systems

First, the health services of many countries have been badly undermined by inadequate investment over decades and by the burden of AIDS itself. Virtually everywhere, there is a shortage of available health care personnel. And where personnel are available, some have received no training or even basic information about HIV and sexual and reproductive health. Moreover, health care providers in low-resource settings often lack basic supplies, such as needles, gloves and alcohol swabs, that allow them to take universal precautions, making them all the more reluctant to provide sexual and reproductive health services to people living with HIV.

These problems are exacerbated by the fact that sexual and reproductive health services and HIV services have generally evolved as separate and parallel programmes, often resulting in sharp divisions between these two areas among donors, within country governments and in frontline service provision.

Breaking down these barriers and finding ways to provide more integrated services for people living with HIV could play an important role in strengthening fragile health care systems and in bridging the divide between sexual and reproductive health and HIV. Other key actions, such as intensified training and ensuring safety in the workplace, would go a long way toward improving the quality of care for people living with HIV.

Social and Cultural Issues

The second overarching challenge to effectively meeting the sexual and reproductive health needs of people living with HIV is a set of interlocking social issues that degrade people and impede their access to services: sexual taboos, gender inequality, and stigma and discrimination around HIV itself. HIV programming is hampered by these persistent, deep-seated social and cultural factors; at the same time, dealing with these issues through HIV programming would make for a more just world.

In many societies, even talking about sex is taboo. Because many policymakers may not want to be perceived as promoting sexual activity, they may be reluctant to expand the capacity of health care providers to effectively provide sexual health services to people—especially youth—living with HIV. This is a serious mistake. Failure to acknowledge the central role that sexuality plays in the lives of virtually all people, including people living with HIV, is self-defeating. What is also self-defeating is failure to realistically confront HIV as an STI. Not only is this an obstacle to innovation where integration is concerned, it may also exacerbate the spread of HIV. This problem is made worse by persistent gender inequalities. In particular, women's inability to have control over their sexuality and sexual experiences not only increases their chances of acquiring HIV, but also undermines their ability to cope with the social, economic and physical impacts of HIV.

Finally, HIV-related stigma and discrimination are pervasive at the national and local levels. Judgmental attitudes toward people living with HIV persist, making it difficult for people with HIV to disclose their status for fear of hostility or discrimination and of negatively affecting the quality of care they receive. Far too often, health care professionals have refused to care for HIV patients, disclosed clients' HIV status without consent, provided highly directive counseling on contraceptive methods and pressured women to undergo abortion or sterilization. All of this is compounded by the fact that many men and women with HIV are among society's most vulnerable individuals and are already struggling against adverse conditions such as poverty, oppression and discrimination.

Social attitudes and biases are reflected in policies that target people living with HIV, despite the fact that 189 countries at the United Nations (UN) General Assembly Special Session on HIV/AIDS in 2001 committed themselves to ensuring that people living with HIV and AIDS experience "the full enjoyment of all human rights and fundamental freedoms." (This statement was reaffirmed at the 2006 UN General Assembly High Level Meeting on AIDS.) Governments have an obligation to devise laws and policies that create a safe and secure environment and to protect the rights of HIV-positive individuals to make free and responsible choices for their sexual and reproductive health.

Moving Forward

In designing policies and programmes to address the sexual and reproductive health needs of men and women living with HIV, policymakers, public health experts and national-level programme planners must, of course, consider the best available scientific data. To be successful, they must also take advantage of the perspectives, expertise and accumulated experiences of people living with HIV. Associations and networks of HIV-positive people and community-based organizations run by and for people with HIV have a key role to play at all stages in the process—from programme and policy design to the delivery and evaluation of sexual and reproductive health services. This includes involving HIV-positive men, women and youth in decisions about how and which services should be made available—for example, whether services are offered through a referral system or by adapting existing health services, such as family planning programmes, programmes for the prevention of mother-to-child transmission of HIV or drug rehabilitation programmes. Moreover, governments and donors must invest in the capacity of organizations run by and for people with HIV to participate fully in policy and programme design of sexual and reproductive health services.

Three decades into the global AIDS pandemic, it is abundantly clear that enormous challenges remain, both in containing and reducing HIV infection rates and in helping people with HIV live longer, healthier lives. At the same time, the picture for people living with HIV is getting brighter. For a growing number of people with access to life-saving antiretroviral drugs, HIV is now a chronic disease rather than an imminent death sentence. Because sex and childbearing are central to the lives of almost everyone, including those living with HIV, effective programmes must fully accept the human right of HIV-positive men and women to decide whether and when to have children and to pursue a safe and satisfying sex life. At the same time, HIV prevention programmes must actively involve people living with HIV, working with them to decrease the risk of transmitting the virus to others while also making sure that HIV-negative people share in that responsibility. In support of their efforts, governments and policy-making bodies at all levels also need to take into account—and begin to meaningfully address—the sexual and reproductive health needs, aspirations and rights of people living with HIV. Not only do the lives of people with HIV stand to benefit, but global HIV prevention efforts and the health and well-being of the entire global community will benefit as well.

5

Rights to Sexual and Reproductive Health

The ICPD and the Convention on the Elimination of All Forms of Discrimination against Women

The International Conference on Population and Development (ICPD) held in Cairo in 1994 marked the acceptance of a new paradigm in addressing human reproduction and health. For the first time, there was a clear focus on the needs of individuals and on the empowerment of women, and the emergence of an evolving discourse about the connection between human rights and health, linking new conceptions of health to the struggle for social justice and respect for human dignity.

The new attention to human rights in the ICPD marked a departure from the previous approach that treated women instrumentally, as tools through which to implement population programmes and policies. The reproductive health and rights approach adopted at ICPD is premised on a view that values women intrinsically and is genuinely concerned about their health and well-being. Women's reproductive capacity was transformed from an object of population control to a matter of women's empowerment to exercise personal autonomy in relation to their sexual and reproductive health within their social, economic and political contexts. Women's health, in general, and their sexual and reproductive health, in particular, is determined not only by their access to health services but by their status in society and pervasive gender discrimination. The ICPD thus posits the human rights of women—their right to personal reproductive autonomy and to collective gender equality—as a primary principle in the development of reproductive health and population programmes.

The ICPD Programme of Action

The Programme of Action adopted at the ICPD is a consensus document, the end product of a process of negotiation and compromise involving over 180

States. A separate chapter addresses gender equality and empowerment of women, placing the eradication of sex discrimination as a priority objective of the international community in relation to policies and programmes of population and development. Chapter VII, entitled "*Reproductive Rights and Reproductive Health*", articulates the principle of autonomy and is also central.

Reproductive health is defined in paragraph 7.2 of the Programme of Action as "a state of complete physical, mental and social well-being ... in all matters related to the reproductive system", which "implies that people are able to have a satisfying and safe sex life and that they have the capability to reproduce and the freedom to decide if, when and how often to do so."

The ICPD referred to the term "reproductive rights" as embracing "certain human rights that are already recognized in ... international human rights documents and other consensus documents". The most mentionable "consensus documents" are the Universal Declaration of Human Rights, and the Declaration and Programme of Action of the World Conference on Human Rights, Vienna, June 1993.

The human rights already recognized in "international human rights documents" include "the right of everyone to the enjoyment of the highest attainable standard of physical and mental health" as guaranteed by Article 12 of the International Covenant on Economic, Social and Cultural Rights (1964) (ICESCR). Other health-related human rights fall within the scope of certain fundamental freedoms protected under the International Covenant on Civil and Political Rights (1964) (ICCPR). These include the right to life, the right to liberty and security of the person, and the right to privacy, to mention just a few. In addition, the Convention on the Elimination of All Forms of Discrimination Against Women (1978) (known as CEDAW and hereinafter referred to as the Women's Convention) is particularly pertinent to the enjoyment of sexual and reproductive rights.

Reproductive rights, according to the ICPD, "rest on the recognition of the basic right of all couples and individuals to decide freely and responsibly the number, spacing and timing of their children and to have the information and means to do so, and the right to attain the highest standard of sexual and reproductive health." The language is taken from Article 16(1)(e) of the Women's Convention, which states that States Parties shall ensure on a basis of equality of men and women:

> "the same rights to decide freely and responsibly on the number and spacing of their children, and to have access to the information, education and means to enable them to exercise these rights".

Reproductive rights, according to the ICPD, also include the right "to make decisions concerning reproduction free of discrimination, coercion and violence, as expressed in human rights documents." This aspect of reproductive rights can also be derived from the Women's Convention.

Before proceeding to examine the Convention more closely, it is worth noting that a subsequent consensus document of the international community, that is, the Platform for Action of the Fourth World Conference on Women (FWCW), held in Beijing in 1995, reiterated the paradigm shift of the ICPD. One of the critical areas of concern identified at the Beijing Conference referred to inequalities and inadequacies in access to health care and related services, adopting a life cycle approach to women's health from infancy to old age. The Beijing Declaration stated that "the explicit recognition and reaffirmation of the right of all women to control all aspects of their health, in particular their own fertility, is basic to their empowerment". The Platform for Action adopted at Beijing included one notable addition to the ICPD in further explicating women's human rights in respect of their sexuality.

The Women's Convention

Both the ICPD and the FWCW acknowledged the intrinsic relation of gender equality to women's health, including sexual and reproductive health. Both of these are consensus documents, expressing *political will*. As opposed to this, international human rights documents—treaties or conventions—are sources of international *law*, and as such are considered to be legally binding. The Women's Convention is the core human rights treaty to address discrimination against women, and is sometimes referred to as the international bill of women's rights. In general, States Parties to the Convention undertake to pursue a policy of eliminating discrimination in all its forms, and to guarantee women the exercise and enjoyment of human rights and fundamental freedoms on a basis of equality with men. Its covers all areas of women's lives in both the public and private spheres, including discrimination in relation to the right to health and health services.

The Committee on the Elimination of Discrimination Against Women (the CEDAW Committee) is established under article 17. It is composed of 23 expert members elected by States Parties from among their nationals and serving in their personal capacity. The Committee's main function is to monitor implementation of the Convention by considering periodic reports submitted by States Parties on the measures they have adopted to give effect to the provisions of the Convention and on the progress made in this respect. The Committee may also make general recommendations based on the examination of reports and information received from the States Parties. Some of these general recommendations address formal matters, such as the reporting obligations of States Parties, while others are explications of substantive matters and constitute authoritative interpretations of the rights guaranteed under the Convention.

Health—Related Rights under the Women's Convention

Article 16(1)(e) of the Convention guarantees the right to decide on the number and spacing of children, but that is only one of the articles that address women's rights in relation to health. Article 12 is central. It formulates (in paragraph 1) States Parties' obligation "to take all appropriate measures to eliminate discrimination against women in the field of health care in order to ensure, on a basis of equality of men and women, access to health care services, including those related to family planning." It further stipulates (in paragraph 2) their undertaking to "ensure to women appropriate services in connection with pregnancy, confinement and the post-natal period, granting free services where necessary, as well as adequate nutrition during pregnancy and lactation."

It should be noted that the Women's Convention is the only one of the six human rights treaties in the United Nations system to mention family planning. In addition to the aforementioned articles, the right of access to specific educational information and advice on family planning is guaranteed under article 10(h). And article 14(b) specifies, in particular, the right of women in rural areas to have access to adequate health care facilities, including information, counselling and services in family planning. The Convention also refers to women's right to protection of health and to safety in working conditions, including "the safeguarding of the function of reproduction", in article 11(1) (f).

Many other provisions of the Convention have an implicit or indirect bearing on women's rights in relation to health, some of which have been explicated in the General Recommendations of the CEDAW Committee in relation to female genital mutilation; sexual violence; HIV/AIDS; and reproduction.

Here there are two key concepts: autonomy and discrimination:

- *Autonomy*: Autonomy means the right of a woman to make decisions concerning her fertility and sexuality free of coercion and violence. Much turns on our understanding of coercion and violence. Key to this is the notion of choice. In health care contexts, the rights to informed consent and confidentiality are instrumental to ensuring free decision making by the client. These rights impose certain correlative duties upon health care providers and deliverers of services. They are bound to disclose information of proposed treatments and their alternatives so as to obtain the informed consent of the client, and they must respect her right to refuse treatment. Likewise, they are bound to maintain secrecy so as to allow her to make private decisions without the interference of others whom she has not chosen to consult, and who might not have her best interests at heart. "Autonomy" also means that a woman seeking health care in relation to her fertility and sexuality is entitled to be treated as an individual in her own right—the sole client of the health care provider, and fully competent to make decisions concerning her own health. This is a matter, among other things, of the woman's right to equality before the law as to her legal capacity.

As mentioned earlier, the human right of women to control their fertility and sexuality free of coercion is guaranteed implicitly by the Women's Convention. The right to autonomy in making health decisions in general, and sexual and reproductive decisions in particular, derives from the fundamental human right to liberty. The word "autonomy" itself is not mentioned expressly in the Convention, but the value of autonomy is certainly implicit in the fundamental freedoms it guarantees to women, on a basis of equality with men. Autonomy is intimately and intrinsically connected with many fundamental human rights, such as liberty, dignity, privacy, security of the person, and bodily integrity. These form the basis for asserting rights to informed consent and confidentiality in relation to health services and health care. Moreover, article 15 guarantees women's right to equality before the law and to full legal capacity. This includes women's right to make free and informed decisions about health care, medical treatment and research. Women have the right to be fully informed of their options in health care, including likely benefits and potential adverse effects of proposed methods of treatment and available alternatives, including the option of refusing treatment.

One of the most eloquent explications of the meaning of "autonomy" is that of Isaiah Berlin in his essay, *Two Concepts of Liberty*. For Berlin "liberty" in the ordinary sense is a "negative" right to freedom, in that one is entitled to be free in certain areas from the interference of others. "I am normally said to be free to the degree to which no man or body of men interferes with my activity." But "liberty" also has a "positive" sense. It is not merely freedom "from" but freedom "to". This positive right to freedom is "autonomy", in the sense that one is entitled to recognition of one's capacity, as a human being, to exercise choice in the shaping of one's life.

"This 'positive' sense of the word 'liberty' derives from the wish on the part of the individual to be his own master. I wish my life and decisions to depend on myself, not on external forces of whatever kind. I wish to be the instrument of my own, not of other men's, acts of will. I wish to be a subject, not an object; to be moved by reasons, by conscious purposes, which are my own, not causes which affect me, as it were, from outside. I wish to be somebody, not nobody; a doer—deciding, not being decided for, self-directed and not acted upon by external nature or by other men as if I were a thing, or an animal, or a slave incapable of playing a human role, that is, of conceiving goals and policies of my own and realizing them. This is at least part of what I mean when I say that I am rational, and that it is my reason that distinguishes me as a human being from the rest of the world. I wish, above all, to be conscious of myself as a thinking, willing, active being, bearing responsibility for my choices and able to explain them by references to my own ideas and purposes. I feel free to the degree that I believe this to be true, and enslaved to the degree that I am made to realize that it is not."

- *Equality, Discrimination and Difference*: The second concept that deserves some explication is that of discrimination. Equality implies non-discrimination, and discrimination is violation of the right to equality. Article 1 of the Convention defines the term 'discrimination against women' as any distinction, exclusion or restriction made on the basis of sex which has the *effect* or purpose of impairing or nullifying the recognition, enjoyment or exercise by women irrespective of their marital status, on a basis of equality of men and women, of human rights and fundamental freedoms in the political, economic, social, cultural, civil or any other field"

(emphasis added—CS).

Two comments are in place:

- *First,* the Convention adopts an "effect" approach, whereby discrimination is condemned even if it is not purposeful. This is of particular significance in the area of health, where much of the discrimination is evident in differences in the health status of women and men, but is the result of certain patterns of behaviour, sometimes described as "natural". These patterns persist by the mere inertia of habit if no intervention is undertaken for the removal of discriminatory barriers, or if we fail to pay attention to the factors that comprise the "real" differences—some biological or physiological, and some social—between women and men in relation to their health. It should be mentioned in this context that the Committee has noted that discrimination under the Convention is not restricted to action by or on behalf of governments. This means that states may also be responsible for acts of discrimination perpetrated in the private sphere by non-governmental actors, including health care providers.
- *The second* comment is that the definition of discrimination under the Convention applies to all women, irrespective of their marital status. This is of significance in two respects. First, it expresses the underlying recognition of the institution of marriage as constructing women's social status, which is relevant in the health area, where women are sometimes denied care and services because they are not married. Second, it also gives expression to an underlying theme of feminist theory on gender equality—that equality is not a matter of a woman's personal relations with men, but rather a matter of women's discrimination, as a group, in a society that is structured collectively by gendered patterns of power (one of which is the traditional marital relation).

The area of health is particularly interesting in terms of equality theory because of what has already been noted: "real" differences between women and men—some biological (or physiological), and some social. Women's health needs are different from men's due to both biological differences and societal factors. This is particularly true as regards women's reproductive and sexual health, not only because biological differences are of the essence, but also because discrimination against women is closely associated with prejudices and stereotypes based on patriarchal notions of women's sexual and reproductive roles and functions.

Social Construction of Difference

While the Convention acknowledges the maternal function of women, social and cultural patterns of conduct often glorify motherhood in a manner that circumscribes women's right to autonomy in exercising life choices. Cultural and religious attitudes may value women according to their ability to produce children. Their health may consequently be jeopardized by repeated pregnancies spaced too closely together, often as the result of efforts to produce male children. Women who have not borne children may be cast out of marriages on the assumption that they, rather than their male partners, are infertile. Women may be denied access to health care that is unrelated to their reproductive functions, and their health needs may be considered secondary to those of their children or, in the case of pregnant women—to the health of their fetuses.

Stereotypes of women's sexuality underlie codes of chastity that circumscribe women's freedom of movement and their participation in public life. Certain practices harmful to women's health are related to discriminatory attitudes about women's sexuality that deny them the right to a satisfying sex life. These entail unnecessary interventions, such as female genital mutilation, forced virginity examinations and hymen repair. Women's sexuality is frequently subordinated to the satisfaction of male needs, exposing them to risks of sexual abuse and violence. As a consequence of unequal power relations based on gender, women and girls are often unable to refuse sex or negotiate safe sex; they therefore face risks of contracting sexually transmitted diseases, including HIV/AIDS.

Biological Difference

While such social phenomena are clearly mediated by gender discrimination, health-related discrimination might be attributed in part to biological differences between women and men. Contemporary feminist legal theory propounds that the principle of gender equality takes into account such difference, rather than requiring women to meet standards set by a male model. Equality requires that we treat the same interests without discrimination, and also that we treat different interests in ways that respect those differences. Failure to take into account the special health needs of women, so as to ensure their access to appropriate health information and services, constitutes discrimination. Equality is not a formal matter of guaranteeing to women the same rights as men and combating purposeful discrimination, but rather a substantive matter of ensuring the effective enjoyment of equal outcome in health status and well being. Women's rights to health and health care on a basis of equality with men encompass both comparable health needs as well as sex-specific health needs. Failure to allocate resources or to ensure the provision of services for women's special health needs, in addition to those common to women and men, is discriminatory.

Illustrations—From the General to the Particular

This then is the legal context within which we are to address women's rights in relation to reproductive and sexual health. The text of the Convention is abstract, and expresses principles that are to serve as guides for conduct. What meaning do they have in actual practice? The Convention imposes a duty under international law to respect, protect and fulfil the human rights articulated thereunder. In an ideal world the aspirations of the legal norms would be observed, but the reality is such that they are not observed. Violations of these standards take different forms at different times and in different places. As mentioned, the following examples of some contemporary patterns of rights violations are taken from reports considered by the CEDAW Committee at its 18th session.

Non-Discrimination in Allocation of Resources

The issue of distributive justice in the allocation of resources for health is of major concern throughout the world, given the rising costs of medical technology and budget cuts often associated with programmes of structural adjustment. Too often women's health needs are the first to be affected. The bias against the allocation of resources necessary to provide health services to meet women's special needs, is a form of gender discrimination. This is illustrated well in those countries characterised as "economies in transition".

In Croatia, for example, contraception was the first medication to be removed from state funding in a comprehensive public health system within budget cuts resulting from economic constraints, as was abortion the first medical procedure to be removed from otherwise free health services. Similarly, in Bulgaria—where the government reported that the number of abortions was considerably higher than that of births—it was noted that family planning education was inefficient due to the economic situation in the country, with its free-of-charge health care system suffering from the economic crisis of the transition period.

Cuts in budgets in Azerbaijan resulted in a decrease in the number of maternity health centers. In addition, despite the fact that maternity care was officially provided free-of-charge by a state-funded health system, there had developed an informal fee-for-service practice which made hospital delivery unaffordable to many women and resulted in a rise in the number of home births. At the same time Azerbaijan reported that maternal mortality rates had increased five-fold between 1990 and 1995.

The Right to Life

Indeed, discrimination against women is a significant factor in the high numbers of deaths and complications related to pregnancy and childbirth. Failure to provide maternal health services often reflects the low priority attached to women's special needs in the allocation of resources. Maternal mortality and morbidity can largely be avoided through the provision of reproductive health services, including contraception, safe abortion, and essential and emergency obstetric care. The most obvious human right violated by avoidable death in pregnancy or childbirth is women's fundamental right to life itself. It is arguable that the core minimum content of governments' obligations under international human rights instruments is to provide access to affordable quality health services that would prevent maternal mortality.

In Indonesia, the government appeared to be in violation of its core responsibility to provide safe maternal health services: it attributed the high maternal mortality rate to deliveries by traditional birth attendants, which amount to almost 64 per cent of the total. The report explained that many women prefer home births "due to convenience, low cost and flexible payment arrangements, the aftercare offered and the comfortable atmosphere prevailing in home deliveries". But it is arguable that "customer preference" should not relieve government of its obligation to respect, protect and fulfil women's right to life.

While the case of Azerbaijan illustrates violation of the right to affordable services, in the Dominican Republic there appeared to be a violation of the right to quality of care. The actual rate of maternal mortality was not known until recently, due to the unreliability of health statistics in general and the lack of sex-disaggregated data in particular, but in latter years there had been an increase in maternal deaths, despite the prevalence of prenatal care and hospital births. According to non-governmental sources, the high level of maternal mortality was due to the low priority accorded to women's reproductive health.

Reproductive Choice—Abortion

Unsafe abortion is also a major cause of maternal mortality and morbidity. States Parties' reports to the Committee often fail to contain official data on this due to the illegal nature of abortion in many countries, but they consistently demonstrate a correlation between unsafe abortion and high rates of maternal mortality and morbidity, presented as haemorrhaging and complications of pregnancy.

Thus, Zimbabwe reported that haemorrhage and infection after abortion are major causes of death, though actual figures are not ascertainable given the illegality of abortion. The Dominican Republic, similarly, reported that "clandestine abortions" are the third leading cause of maternal death (following toxemia, and haemorrhages during childbirth), but noted "heavy underreporting".

There are grounds for the view that laws which criminalize health services that only women need, whether aimed at the persons who provide such services or the women who receive them, are discriminatory as such. The criminalization of abortion is particularly heinous, because it not only impairs women's right to reproductive choice to make free and responsible decisions concerning matters that are key to control of their lives but also exposes them to the serious health risks of unsafe abortion, violating their rights to bodily integrity and, in the most extreme cases, to life itself.

In many countries there are exceptions to the criminal norm, allowing for legal abortion in limited circumstances, such as in cases of danger to the life of the mother (or the fetus), or where pregnancy has resulted from rape. In Indonesia, however, rape does not constitute grounds for legal abortion, which means that the state is effectively compounding the sexual violence targeted at the woman by forcing her to carry the resultant pregnancy.

Reproductive Choice—Family Planning

The right to reproductive choice means that women have a right to choose whether or not to reproduce, including the right to decide whether to carry or terminate an unwanted pregnancy and the right to choose their preferred method of family planning and contraception. A violation of this right was revealed by a nongovernmental report on widespread pregnancy based discrimination against women employed in Mexico's export-processing (*maquiladore*) sector. A fact-finding mission investigating allegations of the practice, found that all women applying for work in this sector were routinely required to undergo pregnancy testing for screening, and that employed women were forced to resign when they became pregnant. In some factories women were obliged to show sanitary napkins to company nurses as a condition of ongoing employment. The report concluded that such practices penalize women for exercising reproductive choice, and inherently compromise their ability to decide freely on the number and spacing of their children, and that the government of Mexico was responsible to ensure that such employment practices cease.

The right to family planning education, information and services is key to reproductive choice, and central to women's sexual and reproductive health, especially given the risk of maternal mortality and the illegality of abortion in many countries.

Family planning services are particularly important where abortion is illegal. In the Dominican Republic, abortion is illegal, but birth control education is provided only by non-governmental organisations. Arguably, where the state does not allow for safe legal abortion, its core obligation is to at least provide itself those family planning services that guarantee women their right to exercise reproductive choice.

Even in countries where abortion is legal, prevention of pregnancy is preferable to termination in terms of women's health. However, in many instances the legal option of abortion is not supported by adequate family planning measures. In the Czech Republic, for example, the government noted the high incidence of induced abortions as a major public health problem, mirroring the inadequate use of contraception. However, the costs of contraception are only partly covered by the general health insurance scheme (reflecting, perhaps, discrimination in the allocation of resources, considering that these are services only women need). The Government also pointed out that health care personnel sometimes lack sufficient knowledge of contraception.

In other instances, there is a gap between the *de iure* (legal) protection of reproductive choice and the *de facto* (actual) situation, and governments might be held accountable for unauthorised violations of legal rights by health care personnel. In Zimbabwe, for example, where abortion is legal in only limited circumstances, the government subsidizes the costs of contraceptives and there are no legal restrictions on the provision of family planning services to minors. Yet the governmental report stated candidly that "it is not unusual for health personnel to turn away sexually active school girls requesting contraception on the grounds that the girls are still too young to indulge in sexual intercourse or that they are not married and therefore have no need for contraceptives." Teenage pregnancy appears to be, nonetheless, a major problem. It is worth noting further in this context, that the cumulative data on the incidence of HIV/AIDS in Zimbabwe show that in the 15-19 age group, infection among females accounts for 84 per cent of the cases. Clearly, sexual and reproductive health education, information and services is essential for adolescent girls. Mexico, in its report, expanded upon the negative health and social effects of a high rate of teenage pregnancy. It noted inadequate sex education and information as one of the causes, despite an official policy to provide information and high quality services for pregnant adolescent girls.

Informed Consent

The report from Mexico demonstrated another instance of the gap between the legal situation and actual practice, that is, between the *de iure* and the *de facto* implementation of the Convention. While the Federal Constitution recognises the right to reproductive choice, and while the law provides for family planning services as basic health services provided by the government, one study has shown that only two contraceptive methods are offered: IUD and surgical sterilization. Furthermore, while the law provides that consent to sterilization must be given freely and voluntarily in writing, according to one study, one fourth of sterilized women claimed not to have been informed of its irreversible nature or of alternative contraceptive methods, and two fifths claimed not to have signed a consent form. In addition, there was at least one case in which the ovaries of a woman suffering from an undiagnosed urinary tract infection were removed without her knowledge. Interestingly enough, the representative of the Government of Mexico stated in her oral presentation to the CEDAW Committee, that most of the complaints submitted to a newly established Medical Arbitration Board during the first year of its operation concerned gynecological care.

In extreme cases, violations of women are right to autonomy and informed consent in relation to reproductive health care amount to outright coercion. Indonesia provides an unfortunate example. There the government adopted a rigorous and effective family planning programme resulting in a significant decline in fertility rates, which was presented in the State Party's report as one of the most successful in the world. According to nongovernmental sources, however, women have not been allowed choice as to contraceptive method, nor have they been given information as to side effects of methods provided by the government. Moreover, there have been recurring reports of coercive practices employed by local officials attempting to meet target quotas set by government, often involving military and police officials in rounding up women in villages and forcing them to accept contraception. According to one study, IUDs were inserted at gunpoint for those who refused.

Equality before the Law

Indonesia also requires spousal authorisation for certain reproductive health procedures, in violation of women's right to full legal capacity in relation to informed consent and to confidentiality in health care. There a woman cannot choose to be sterilised without her spouse's consent. In addition, though abortion is illegal, it may be undergone where the mother's life is in danger, except that the agreement of "the husband or the members of the family" is required in addition to that of the pregnant woman. Failure to acknowledge women's competence to consent to health care is a violation of their right to equality before the law.

Another example of violation of women's right to equality before the law relates to procedures for legal abortion. Even where there do exist grounds for lawful abortion in limited circumstances, there may not be adequate legal procedures to ensure women's enjoyment of their legal rights. In Zimbabwe, for example, there was one case of a pregnancy resulting from rape, in which the request for permission to undergo abortion dragged on in court to such an extent that the permission was eventually granted one month after the woman had given birth. In Mexico, abortion is in the jurisdiction of the several states, with varying exceptions to the criminal rule, but there are no legal procedures whatsoever for establishing the circumstances that fall within the exceptions and would allow for a legal abortion. Moreover, even though the woman herself may be liable for punishment, it appears that prosecution may be avoided by the payment of a bribe.

Women in Vulnerable Situations

In recent years there has been a growing focus in human rights work on vulnerable groups. This has been a result of a new interest in economic and social rights and the concomitant concept of social justice. Whereas the previous emphasis on civil and political rights drew mainly from the concept of liberty and focussed on individuals as such, attention is now given to violations of rights of individuals as members of vulnerable groups within a given society. Thus, health practices and policies should be examined in light of the needs of the most disadvantaged groups in society. These include, among others, rural and marginal urban groups, women in situations of armed conflict, and women in prostitution.

Mexico indicated in its report the unmet need for contraception among rural women and the urban poor, while in Zimbabwe, according to a non-governmental source, twenty percent of the population in rural areas does not have access to family planning or maternal health services despite the government's political will to provide such.

Women in situations of armed conflict are particularly vulnerable to sexual violence and torture, with the health consequences of mental harm, susceptibility to sexually transmitted disease and related reproductive health problems, including unwanted pregnancy. As a result of such abuse, women may be isolated, stigmatized and rejected by their families and communities. Women are often reluctant to report these violations because they are felt to be shameful, as indicated by a non-governmental report on women in East Timor.

Women who are internally displaced as a result of armed conflict may have limited access to reproductive health services. Thus, a study of women in five internally displaced person settlements in Azerbaijan, conducted by a United Nations High Commissioner of Refugees reproductive health field worker, found that women overwhelmingly consider family planning as a primary health concern, but that there had been bureaucratic hurdles to supplying condoms. Similarly, in Croatia, it appeared that refugee women were not legally entitled to all the services provided under the comprehensive publicly funded health care scheme.

Women in prostitution are significantly marginalised in all societies and are at an extremely high risk of suffering rape and other forms of violence. This is of increasing concern, given the alarming growth in the international trafficking in women and girls. At the same time, they are often singled out for discriminatory treatment by public health programmes that fail to address the broader concerns and underlying determinants of the issue under concern. In Indonesia, for example, the Department of Social Affairs disseminates information on the danger of HIV/AIDS "in the vicinity of the location of prostitutes"; while there have been reports that under sporadic urban "cleansing" programmes, women detained as suspected prostitutes are at risk of being forced to undergo vaginal examinations during interrogation.

It should be noted that health professionals are often in a position to identify the health consequences of sexual violence, and should be able to respond effectively to the health needs of survivors. Bulgaria, for example, failed to include in its report any information on gender-based violence, but a non-governmental source received first hand evidence from health care professionals who considered it to be a serious problem, describing some cases as brutal.

Conclusion

All the above examples can be summarized as violations of one of three major human rights concepts—liberty, social justice and equality. The principle of liberty is key to notions of civil and political rights, while the principle of justice is key to notions of economic and social rights. The principle of equality is an overriding one. Questions of distributive justice arise in relation to the tragic economic choices that go to the fair allocation of scarce resources and the setting of priorities, and here we often find discrimination against women in the low priority given to their special sexual and reproductive health needs. But many of the issues raised by this paper go to the attitudes of policy makers and of health care providers in relation to their clients, and to the fundamental notion of respect for human dignity and the right to reproductive autonomy, which are not essentially a matter of economic cost.

Struggles over women's rights to sexual and reproductive health have been central in advancing women's human rights in general. Advocates of women's human rights have drawn attention to the ways in which women's status is fundamentally linked with the reduction of women, through social and political processes, to aspects of their physical selves. When reproductive health is understood to involve more than just the biological workings of a woman's womb, we arrive at "women centered" approaches to sexual and reproductive health. This means trusting women as autonomous beings, able to take control over their sexual and reproductive lives and to make decisions on these matters on the basis of access to adequate information. A woman's right to reproductive autonomy is often impaired because of her status in society. Enjoyment of this right depends on her right to act as an independent adult of full legal capacity to participate in civil society and to be free from discrimination in its various forms. Conversely, without the right of reproductive choice, all other human rights—civil and political, economic and social—have only limited power to advance the well-being of women.

Human rights are aspirations to full participation, equal membership and active involvement in society. Rights structure relationships of power, responsibility, trust and obligation. Rights empower people. They make us aware of our own power and of our responsibility to others less fortunate than us, especially to persons in the most vulnerable and disadvantaged groups and situations. When we look around us and listen to the stories people tell, we learn ways in which we can exercise our own power and position to improve the lot of others. Thus a human rights to sexual and reproductive health is pertinent in diverse ways to policy makers, programme designers, and providers.

The discourse of human rights does not provide any ready made answers to the problems and dilemmas that arise in any given context. Human rights are not absolute values in the sense that they trump all other considerations. Indeed, in some instances the rights of one person may be in conflict with the rights of another. But rights are absolute in the sense that they must be taken into consideration and balanced against other interests. In making and implementing law and policy, and in the delivery of services, the rule should be that violations of human rights may be justified only as measures of last resort; after all other possible means to achieve desired goals have been exhausted. Where several measures present themselves as comparably effective, there should be preference for that which is the least detrimental alternative in terms of its effect on the enjoyment of human rights. The process of deliberating among possible alternatives in terms of their effect on human rights, increases our sensitivity to the compromises we make in reality while aspiring to an ideal world in which human dignity is the paramount value.

6

Managing Reproductive Health Services with a Gender Perspective

Guidelines for Programme Managers

Why a Gender Perspective is Needed in Managing Reproductive Health Services

Community clinic or health programme managers may ask why they need to adopt a special gender perspective in managing their services for women. Haven't women already benefited from the reproductive revolution of the over 30 years and the expanding availability of modern contraceptive methods?

Yes, thanks to family planning programmes and reproductive health services, women around the world are able to pursue new activities and expand their roles. These services have helped improve the health of women and families, especially in low-income rural and urban communities. Also, thanks to many types of health and social action programmes, women's lives have improved in important, practical ways. Around the world, women now live longer than do men. Maternal mortality rates have been reduced by one half, and fertility rates by one third. Female literacy has also improved dramatically: from 54 per cent to 74 per cent of the male literacy rate, according to the World Health Organization.

Along with these improvements, many women are moving from the margins to the centers of community life in many countries, contributing labor, conducting business, earning cash income, and/or producing food, as well as taking care of the diverse needs of home and family.

Inequities have an Impact

Despite these advances, however, great discrepancies persist between women and men. In many places, most women are still marginalized. Their status—economic, social, and political—has hardly changed, and in some places it has deteriorated under worsening economic conditions. They often receive far fewer of the benefits from socioeconomic development than do men. The inequities make women more vulnerable to health risks. They are less likely to receive the right services and treatment.

Women are more important to their families and communities than ever before, as socioeconomic pressures increase throughout the developing world. Community health programmes are in the best position to deliver services that help close the gender gap in health, as a key to generating benefits in other areas of life for both women and men.

Equity in the area of human rights is also a central issue in gender considerations. The United Nations adopted the Universal Declaration of Human Rights in 1948, thereby recognizing that every human being has the right not to be discriminated against because of his or her sex. While both men and women suffer from breaches of their human rights, women are more vulnerable to abuse, much of which occurs in their homes and may be condoned by their communities.

A Global Commitment to Gender Equity

The agreements and plans of action from the global conferences call on all governments to contribute to the solutions, in part through health programmes. Most donors have developed or are developing requirements for gender-sensitive health services, obligating health professionals to do what they can to contribute to equity and human rights in providing their services.

As the manager of a health programme, you can support your government's commitments by enhancing the gender sensitivity of your programmes. You can analyze your services to find how they could become more responsive to both women's and men's needs. You can help your staff to examine how gender issues affect your ability to work together, manage your programmes, and achieve your shared goals. You can listen to the concerns of your staff and clients in considering programme modifications to respond to gender-related concerns.

Areas where a gender perspective could help improve your services include:

- Improving the satisfaction of both female and male clients with the way in which they are received and cared for;
- Improving provider practices, including communication and clinical skills;
- Using gender-relevant information to establish policies, set goals, develop strategies, and organize and evaluate operations;
- Strengthening management systems that support gender-sensitive services, including human resources, logistics, and information management; and
- Encouraging men to develop responsibility in respecting women's reproductive rights.

Adopting a Gender-Sensitive Perspective

Considering gender issues is like putting on new glasses. You look at the same reality, but you see it differently. Reviewing the organization and delivery of your health services from a gender perspective is like seeing them through a special lens that highlights the gender-related aspects.

You take a focused approach in thinking about your work, how you do it, and the different effects it has on your male and female clients. You see how gender issues affect providers, managers, and the operations of organizations and programmes, as well as the reproductive behaviour, attitudes, and practices in your client community.

Gender Concepts in Action

Approaches to gender in reproductive health services range along a continuum, from reinforcing existing gender roles and relationships to actions that work to change them:

- *Gender-biased approaches* tend to use and perpetuate stereotypes of men and women, such as presenting a "macho" image of male sexuality and treating women as powerless victims. An example is marketing of condoms with an image of male virility.
- *Gender-neutral approaches* do no harm to gender relations, but fail to respond to the gender needs and interests of individuals, such as offering generic educational messages that are not targeted to either women or men, or ignoring women's possible preference for female counselors and providers.
- *Gender-sensitive approaches* recognize and respond to the different needs and constraints of individuals based on their gender and sexuality, such as counseling women to negotiate condom use or addressing the reluctance of some men to use condoms.

By increasing the focus on gender-sensitive services, your programme is responding to the practical gender needs of female and male clients. Doing so may also indirectly contribute to meeting strategic gender needs. But you may decide to go further to meet strategic gender needs directly—to move towards gender equity by beginning to modify gender relations and power in your community.

Two other approaches can help a programme in this long-term task:

- *Transformative* approaches go beyond gender sensitivity, actually toward changing gender relations in society. Such approaches involve working over the long term with young men and women, or adolescent boys and girls, to redefine gender norms and encourage healthy sexuality. Other programmes seek to influence the development of constructive attitudes and behaviours of young boys and girls, through schools or community-based educational activities. *The Men as Partners (MAP) initiative is one example. Conducted by AVSC International, MAP examines the impact of gender and sexuality on male and female sexual health and relationships. MAP uses varied educational interventions to increase men's participation with women in making sound reproductive health decisions and reducing male violence towards women.*

- *Women's empowerment* approaches seek to balance the gender equation by giving women access to information, skills, services, and technology; encouraging their participation in decision making; and creating a group identity that becomes a source of power. These approaches recognize that targeted interventions are still needed in many settings to free women from a long tradition of restrictive social norms. *For example, through some reproductive health programmes, female outreach workers have enhanced their status and prestige in their families and communities, and gained opportunities for employment or access to micro-finance programmes.* An understanding of the elements of all these approaches will help you and your staff set goals that are realistic for your organization's current work. It will also contribute to longer-term gender equity among the people you serve.

A gender perspective starts with recognition that your range of services will always affect men and women differently. It enables you to see that relationships between women and men can vary depending on the context. Your clients and staff are not just representatives of the male or female sex—they are also part of their families and communities, with varied options, quality of life, experiences, attitudes, and perceptions.

A gender perspective takes into account gender roles, social and economic relationships and needs, access to resources, and other constraints and opportunities imposed by society or culture, age, religion, and/or ethnicity on both men and women.

In tackling the complex issues of gender, some people in your programme may feel threatened and resist change. Attitudes and actions vary from person to person, organization to organization, and country to country. In addressing the social and economic imbalances between the sexes, you may find that some people resist because they fear loss of power or change in the status quo. You may have to help them remember that the goal in addressing gender issues is not to substitute one group's interests for another's—it is to open up discussion and work toward a new, shared vision from which all can benefit.

Focusing on Reproductive Health Programmes

Reproductive health is a good starting point for addressing gender issues.

Synergy exists between reproductive health and the issues of women's and men's participation, empowerment, equity, and human rights. Human rights and dignity include the core of reproductive health programmes: the rights to establish a family, decide freely and responsibly the number and spacing of children, and have access to health information, education, and care.

Gender inequity profoundly affects those rights when it limits contraceptive use and choice. Traditional gender roles often deny women control over their own sexual decisions, and create pressures that compel some men to undertake risky sexual behaviours. This form of inequity has serious health implications because of the increased risk of unwanted pregnancy and sexually transmitted infections (STIs), particularly HIV/AIDS.

Gender inequity also has an impact on maternal morbidity and mortality. The value accorded a woman's life in some societies determines whether financial or other resources are available for prenatal care or emergency obstetric services.

Experience and research have shown that attention to gender issues can enhance the impact of reproductive health programmes. Local realities of reproductive behaviour, family structure, and gender relations need to be acknowledged and dealt with, for they can undermine the effectiveness and sustainability of a programme. Issues of gender inequity, for example, can be part of the reason why policies and programmes may work more effectively in some countries than in others, in helping women and men to achieve full reproductive choice.

By promoting an understanding of the links between gender roles and health, health programmes and service providers can help clients of both sexes to take appropriate action. Reproductive health services that do not address gender biases and obstacles lose valuable opportunities to reduce inequities, to contribute to positive relations between women and men, or to achieve service objectives. While many managers and providers are aware of these truths, they may not always know how to organize and offer services that reflect a gender perspective.

Addressing Gender Issues in Reproductive Health Services

Gender-sensitive services for reproductive health require a mindset based on a thorough and realistic understanding of male-female relationships within the social and economic settings of women's and men's everyday lives. Health programmes and providers can use this mindset to address two key elements of service: access and quality.

Access encompasses all the factors that enable or obstruct female and male clients in using health services: physical access, such as adequate transportation, as well as social, cultural, and economic factors. Gender can limit access to health services through:

- *Financial Costs*—families may be less willing to invest in health care for female family members than for males;
- *Opportunity Costs*—women or men may have responsibilities that prevent them from seeking services where health centers are distant, transport is difficult, or clinic hours are inconvenient; and
- *Socio-cultural Constraints*—women may be prohibited from traveling alone or being treated by male providers, or men may not feel comfortable being treated in health facilities where most clients are women and children.

The quality of reproductive health services encompasses choice of methods, information for clients, technical competence of providers, interaction between providers and clients, and mechanisms to encourage consistent and appropriate use of health services. However, gender-sensitive services go beyond those widely accepted components of quality of care. They address the different ways in which women and men experience health problems and illness.

A gender-sensitive provider tries to understand all the reasons for which a client seeks services, taking into account her or his medical history, work, social and cultural setting, daily life, sexuality, and personal feelings. In particular, the provider can contribute to every woman's sense of self-determination, her capacity to take control of her body, her dignity, and the exercise of her rights. In serving men, the provider can help counteract the destructive macho mentality with clear information about the consequences of certain sexual behaviours.

A gender-sensitive approach trains providers in issues pertaining to relationships between men and women, including domestic violence, sexual abuse, and negotiation of sexual activity and contraceptive use.

Mainstreaming the Gender-Sensitive Approach

Most organizations that try to bring a gender perspective to their reproductive health programmes do not generate a separate programme component or activity. Rather, they mainstream gender across all services by building:

- Awareness and understanding of gender issues and concepts among all staff;
- Managerial commitment to address gender issues;
- Managerial ability to adapt systems and procedures to accommodate a gender perspective; and
- Knowledge and skills for designing, implementing, and evaluating gender-sensitive programmes, services, and activities

Mainstreaming Gender-Sensitive Initiatives

There are five steps your programme can take to prepare for successful gender mainstreaming:

- Step 1: Introduce gender awareness and concepts at every level of the programme.
- Step 2: Conduct a gender analysis of your working environment.
- Step 3: Assess your programme's readiness for gender mainstreaming.
- Step 4: Determine the desired gender-related results: short-and long-term goals and objectives.
- Step 5: Identify the strategies and activities to help you meet those goals and objectives.

Step 1: Introduce Gender Awareness and Concepts

You can use this issue of *The Manager* to discuss and increase awareness about gender issues in your programme—to orient yourself and your colleagues to gender concepts and discuss how gender influences and impacts the delivery of your services. The conversation should include managers at the top level of the programme, because it is important to have committed leadership in making any kind of organizational change. Then the conversation should go on to include your entire staff, as well as other stakeholders—board members, community leaders, representatives of other agencies or organizations with whom you work.

As prevailing attitudes begin to change and receptivity grows across the programme, formal training in gender issues may further educate managers and providers about the impact of gender issues on health. Gender training workshops can introduce gender concepts and encourage the participants to explore their gender-related experiences, attitudes, and stereotypes. The workshops can provide staff members with skills for addressing gender issues. Gender training may be available from a local university, from a gender unit in your ministry of health or ministry of women's affairs, or from international technical assistance agencies.

The training may be free of charge or may be sponsored by such international donor agencies as the US Agency for International Development, the Canadian and Swedish international development agencies, and the World Bank, or such international organizations as the International Planned Parenthood Federation (IPPF) and the Center for Development and Population Activities (CEDPA). All these organizations are committed to addressing gender inequities in development programmes that they support.

Step 2: Conduct a Gender Analysis

Gender analysis is a method of systematically collecting data about the broader environment in which your programme works. It helps you to look carefully at the financial, economic, social/cultural, and political/legal factors that affect women's and men's roles and the balance of power in their relationships. It highlights their differing needs, constraints, and opportunities, and the impact of those differences on their lives. And it enables you to examine unfounded assumptions and uncover gaps in information.

In the context of reproductive health, gender analysis can reveal how gender norms affect reproductive health services, and how those norms determine differential exposure to risk, access to services and their benefits, to information, and to resources. Gender analysis provides a solid basis for gender-sensitive programme planning.

Gender analysis is based on questions about how gender affects key aspects of life and work. These questions fall into four broad areas: gender roles and activities, access to and control of resources, social and cultural patterns, and legal and political considerations. The following questions are examples of what you might ask in each area. As you and your colleagues conduct the analysis, you will likely think of other questions that reflect the particular environment in which you work.

- *Gender Roles and Activities*: How is the workload distributed—who does what in local households and in the wider community? What household and external tasks occupy women and men during the course of the day? During different seasons of the year? Who does the paid work? Who does the unpaid tasks?
- *Access to and Control of Resources*: Who is able to use the resources available to a household—time, disposable income, food, household goods, land, etc.? Who can use the resources available in the community? Who defines and makes decisions about the use of those resources in the household and wider community?
- *Social and Cultural Patterns*: What behaviours are valued for women in your community and nationally? What behaviours are valued for men? What traditional practices reflect these values? What social and cultural changes are taking place locally or nationally?
- *Legal and Political Considerations*: Is there a legal and political framework for women's equality in your country? What are women's rights regarding inheritance, ownership of property, work, access to education and freedom from violence and abuse? What human rights treaties has your government signed? What national or local human rights initiatives for gender equity are being pursued by your government or local women's groups? How do women and men learn about these rights?

You can consider each set of questions in the context of the use of your reproductive health services. For example, men's and women's workloads and incomes may have a strong impact on whether and how often they seek services. Their roles may also determine the extent to which they can participate in such activities as joining community health committees, advocating for reproductive health, or serving as paid or volunteer outreach workers. Access to and control of resources will also influence couples' decisions about the use of contraception, antenatal care, and attended deliveries. Social and cultural patterns may make certain groups reluctant to seek reproductive health care. For example, unmarried, sexually active women or adolescents of both sexes may fear the repercussions of asking for family planning services. Legal and political restrictions may hinder women from making fertility decisions on their own, or women and men may be unaware of legal and political rights that would support women's right to make such decisions. Your programme might want to find a way to inform women and men of their human rights, and the presence of local or national human rights initiatives may enable you to form strong alliances for gender-sensitive reproductive health.

A gender analysis, based on the questions above, might develop into a complicated and time-consuming effort. To avoid that, you can make an analysis along the lines of a rapid assessment. You can collect the information you need by involving colleagues, decision makers, and the community in individual or group interviews, or focus groups, to discuss the guiding questions. The challenge is to build a representative picture of how gender relationships function in your environment.

As you collect and discuss information during the gender analysis, you can present the results in a matrix like that of the "Summary Sheet" on the next page. The matrix encourages you to apply your general findings to reproductive health, while acknowledging the obstacles at individual, household, and community or national level. You should then think of factors at all levels to build on in overcoming some of the obstacles. The information you gather and enter on the matrix will help you to identify organizational goals, strategies, and priority activities that you can implement.

The constraints interact and reinforce each other. The "individual level" refers to constraints that exist because of a woman's or man's own combination of skills, experience, knowledge, and confidence. "Household" refers to the connection of social relations within a household.

The connections are often considered solely in relation to husbands and wives. In many societies, however, the household unit is broader and includes sons and daughters, parents, and other relatives who can limit the set of choices that men and (usually) women face. It is likewise important to recognize the limitations that the wider society imposes, in terms of norms of behaviour, legal rights, and perceptions of the value of what women and men do.

Step 3: Assess Your Programme's Readiness for Gender Mainstreaming

Your programme's readiness to adopt or strengthen a gender-sensitive approach depends largely on its leadership, mission, and structure, as well as on the management systems that support the delivery of your services. As with the gender analysis in Step 2, a few key questions will help you conduct this assessment. Again, these are illustrative questions; you may wish to add or change questions to reflect your own organizational culture, structure, and systems.

Organizational Leadership and Culture

a) Is the leadership of your programme aware of gender issues?
b) Are the leaders committed to changes in the organization and delivery of your reproductive health services, to address gender needs and interests among the population you serve?
c) Does the rest of the organization share this commitment to gender-related changes?

It is not essential for the leaders of your programme to be female for services to be gender-sensitive. Both male and female leaders who are determined to mainstream gender can listen to and respond to the concerns of staff, motivate them to commit to change, encourage learning and open communication, and manage the change process.

Programme Mission and Structure

a) Does your programme's mission statement affirm a commitment to both women and men in the communities you serve?
b) Are the management and decision-making roles of women and men in your programme distributed equitably?

The mission is a statement of the purpose(s) for which your programme exists. It establishes an identity that distinguishes your work from that of other groups. Gender mainstreaming may be implied in your mission statement, but if you hope to highlight the importance of gender for staff, board, clients, donors, and other stakeholders, you will want to express this commitment clearly and directly.

To bring the mission to life, your organizational structure should reflect the same commitment to gender mainstreaming. Although women tend to outnumber men as service providers in the formal health care system, they are often underrepresented at policy, management, and decision-making levels. If men predominate at those levels of your programme, then women's discussion groups (or well-facilitated mixed groups) and focused individual interviews can give women a voice on important issues.

A common question is whether an organization needs a special unit or staff person dedicated to gender concerns. That may not be practical at the local level, because of work demands and resource constraints. In any case, the goal is for all staff to be gender-sensitive. If a single person or small unit takes on that responsibility, it may never be shared or internalized by everyone.

Human Resource Management

a) Do human resource management policies and practices provide equal opportunities to female and male employees in recruitment, compensation, professional development, advancement, and promotion?

b) Has staff at all levels been trained in gender concerns? Are supervisors sensitive to gender issues?
c) Has an appropriate balance among outreach workers and clinic-based staff been established so that both male and female clients are able to access services and benefit from your activities?

Human resource management is an important testing ground for gender sensitivity regarding your programme's mission and structure. It may seem obvious that all employees should have the same human resource options, but gender-biased or gender-neutral policies, systems, and practices may work in subtle ways to undermine opportunities. It is useful to review actual experience, as well as written policies, to ensure that the policies are being carried out fairly.

Staff training in gender issues, as discussed above, will help to build a common understanding among staff at all levels and alert all staff to gender issues related to organizational structure and systems. To maintain the benefits of training, supportive supervision is critical as providers learn to use new communication or clinical skills and to solve problems. Gender-sensitive supervisors will reward staff for responsiveness to clients' concerns, to the social and cultural aspects of fertility decisions and sexual behaviour, and to privacy requirements.

The acceptability of male or female service personnel varies among different cultures. In some cultures, a man may not conduct a clinical examination of a woman. That can constitute a significant barrier for some women in accessing services. In other cultures, social norms are less stringent.

Research on the acceptability and effectiveness of female and male providers, whether clinicians, counselors, or outreach workers, has shown that, in many settings, the sex of the provider does not matter. The essential need is that the provider communicate information clearly, treat clients with dignity and respect, and demonstrate an understanding of the needs, interests, and constraints to accessing and using reproductive health services, whether the client is male or female.

Operations and Logistics Management

a) Are the location and timing of your services accessible to both men and women?
b) Is there a dependable distribution system to ensure that supplies are always available to serve the needs of both men and women?

Gender-sensitive services may necessitate extension of clinic hours in order to serve adolescents and working men and women, or offering outreach services by sending workers where men and women tend to congregate. If your programme tries to make services more accessible to certain groups of people, you will need to be sure that your logistics and inventory systems work smoothly, so that well-trained and competent staff, contraceptives, and other supplies are always available for the range of services you are offering.

Financing and Financial Management

a) Are funding levels adequate for mainstreaming gender into your programme?
b) Have fees been adjusted to avoid financial barriers to access and use by female or male clients, including adolescents?

These questions are difficult to address in this time of diminishing government and donor resources for public health. But you may find that not much money is needed to create a gender-sensitive programme. The first task for your programme is to become aware of the needs, interests, and barriers to services that exist among your clients and then to reorient the ways in which services are organized and delivered.

Most reproductive health organizations are under pressure to find their own means of financial sustainability, and charging fees is one obvious alternative—one with potential implications for the access of disadvantaged women and men. If you must charge for services, you might institute a sliding scale, or subsidize reproductive health services with revenues obtained through other health services. Another alternative might be to refer clients to other facilities that provide services free or at a lower cost.

Collection and Use of Information

a) Does your management information system allow you to disaggregate data—to collect separate data on services provided to women and men?
b) Are staff trained to interpret and use gender-disaggregated data for planning and other management purposes?

You will need separate data sets on female and male clients, in order to examine your progress in implementing gender mainstreaming and its impact. You can collect data on services provided to women and men while you are compiling information from your records for regular monthly or quarterly service reports. If your current reporting requirements do not include breakdowns by sex, you can probably obtain information on the sex and age of each client from medical records or registers.

Your identification of gender-sensitive indicators is critical to the measurement of gender-related changes in your activities over time. The selection of indicators will depend on the goals of your programme and the groups you are trying to reach. Following are illustrations of indicators that could be used:

a) Demonstrated knowledge of family planning and reproductive health among intended programme beneficiaries (for example, men, newly married women, adolescents, etc.);

b) Sex ratio of clients served by your clinic;
c) Demonstrated changes in providers' counseling content, style, and attitudes in dealing with women and men;
d) Providers' identification of and appropriate counseling for clients at risk for violence or STIs;
e) Demonstrated changes in community attitudes towards reproductive health;
f) Reported increases in discussion of reproductive health issues between wives and husbands;
g) Amounts and types of commodities used; and
h) Clinic hours and client waiting times.

Step 4: Determine the Desired Gender-related Results

Now you can use your gender analysis and organizational readiness assessment to consider the results you hope to achieve through your efforts at gender mainstreaming. These intended results—your goals and objectives—will guide you as you adjust or redesign your programme and services to incorporate a gender perspective. That will ensure that the roles, needs, and participation of women and men are thoroughly considered in planning and implementing your programme activities.

If you hope to achieve these goals and objectives, they should be consistent with broader organizational goals, adding a gender component to what the programme is already committed to. Gender-related goals might address improvements in the reproductive health status of both women and men in the population you serve. Building on your analysis of male-female differences in the use of services, they might specify subpopulations to reach in addition to those you already serve, such as adolescent males and females, men at risk of STIs, or women who have been subjected to domestic violence.

As with all goals, gender goals should be realistic and attainable. Reaching short-term goals will motivate staff to continue or increase their efforts to mainstream gender into their work, and pave the way to the achievement of long-term goals. These long-term goals can be broader—still realistic, but ambitious enough to encourage positive changes in the relations between women and men.

Selecting goals and objectives that are both realistic and challenging will require thoughtful discussion across the programme because of their major implications for everyone's work. These goals will bring a gender perspective to decisions about the population groups you will serve, based on sound information about the health, demographic, and socioeconomic characteristics of women and men in your community.

To set goals and objectives, it is important to consider the advantages of gender-sensitive services to your clients, as well as any social and financial burdens those services might impose on the women and men you serve.

Sometimes a goal that benefits one group has negative results for another. Even if you are sure your gender-related goals will benefit the entire community, some groups may perceive that they are losing some advantages as another group gains, and it will be important for all stakeholders to understand the reasons behind these new goals. You may find it useful to consult with local organizations and community leaders of both sexes as you incorporate gender into your goals.

If you look back at "Gender Concepts in Action", you can determine whether your goals match the approaches you would like to pursue. Short-term goals are likely to fulfill practical gender needs through gender-sensitive approaches, while you might select some long-term goals that will embody transformative or empowerment approaches.

Step 5: Identify Strategies, Activities, and the Indicators of Success

The selection of the most appropriate strategies depends on the results of your gender analysis, your resources, and the degree of commitment of your staff—the extent of all your willingness, interest, capacity, and capability. Strategies to meet gender-related goals and address obstacles are likely to fall into four broad categories, to satisfy different purposes:

- Strategies to enhance women's awareness and related skill development, such as providing educational materials for illiterate women.
- Strategies to influence men's attitudes and behaviour towards women within the household and the local community, and their use of reproductive health services, such as initiating efforts to reach men with services and information, and to encourage them to adopt, or support their partner's adoption, of contraceptive methods.
- Strategies to strengthen the gender sensitivity of your services, in order to expand access and improve quality, such as promoting the participation of female and male staff members in designing, implementing, and evaluating services, and building staff expertise in counseling clients of the opposite sex.
- Strategies to change social norms and legal frameworks that affect women's status and rights, such as building partnerships with other organizations to advocate for change in women's status and rights; supporting community-based initiatives that encourage men and women to discuss changing social norms and gender roles.

Some strategies could satisfy several of the four categories listed above:

a) *Promoting* the participation of both women and men in the community you serve in every stage of project development and implementation.
b) *Improving* your clients' knowledge of contraception and reducing fear or misunderstanding about methods.

c) *Implementing* programmes or offering services for female and male adolescents, in and out of school, to help them make the best life choices and protect themselves from unintended pregnancies and STIs.

As with any planning process, the next stage in planning for gender mainstreaming is identifying the activities needed to carry out your strategies and meet your goals and objectives. The challenge is to introduce activities that will bring the gender concepts to life, and address some of the obstacles without draining the energy of your staff and the resources of your programme. If the staff and other stakeholders have been involved throughout the planning process, these activities will be the next logical stage in a planning sequence to which they can claim ownership and to which they will be committed.

The last element of the plan will be to determine indicators of success and the sources of data with which you can measure those indicators. This monitoring and evaluation function is critical for assessing your performance against expected results at any point in time. You will need to build these functions into your existing monitoring and evaluation budget; in many instances, you may find it possible to combine the evaluation of gender mainstreaming with your current evaluation activities.

Implementing, Monitoring, and Evaluating Your Gender-Sensitive Services: Now you are ready to carry out your programme. You can use the planning matrix to help you stay on course as you carry out and regularly monitor your activities, assessing your performance against the expected results at a given point in time, and identifying key learning points. The indicators will help you to monitor progress regularly and adjust activities to reflect changing circumstances.

You and your staff may decide to meet informally at regular intervals to see how the programme is going and to share experiences. These periodic reviews will contribute to more formal evaluations of the extent to which the following occur:

a) Constraints are being overcome that were preventing women and men from using your services;
b) Men's needs for information about their own and their partners' sexual and reproductive health concerns are being addressed;
c) Men are being encouraged to take responsibility for their sexual and reproductive behaviour;
d) Resistance from the community or within your programme is fading; and
e) Mechanisms are in place to ensure that you hear both women's and men's views.

If your programme achieves the desired results, you can celebrate your successes and consider moving forward to more ambitious gender-related goals. If you do not achieve all the results you aimed for, you may find it useful to review the mainstreaming process and see whether some steps were skipped or only partially carried out. Then you may want to adjust the goals, objectives, strategies, or activities as needed.

Sustaining Services with a Gender Perspective

Being sensitive to gender roles and responsibilities is vital in operating participatory, client-focused services. It is essential for an enduring impact on the health status of your clients.

Once your programme has adopted a gender perspective and mainstreamed gender into its services, the obstacles will not simply disappear. You and your staff will need to continue to be alert to the external environment and internal culture, structure, and systems that can support or undermine your efforts. Whenever you review strategies and activities and develop new plans, it will be important to ask yourselves the same questions about the differing needs and status of women and men that steered you towards a gender-sensitive perspective.

As you improve your skills in designing and implementing gender-sensitive services, you can expect to increase your programme's commitment to gender issues, and the effectiveness of your services. Once you have had some success, you can share your results and the lessons you have learned with others, so that other organizations in your country, or in other countries, can benefit from your experience.

Reproductive health programmes around the world can feel encouraged by the success of family planning, which shows that traditional attitudes toward gender and health can change over time. Reproductive health programmes like yours can take advantage of the momentum to work within a gender perspective and achieve further goals of gender equity.

Working Solutions—Peru: Working with Men toward Women's Goals

Men have never been approached to cooperate in making responsible family planning decisions in quite the way pioneered by the *ReproSalud* project in Peru. And they were invited to do so by women. This innovative initiative has well repaid the participating women and their communities, making ReproSalud one of the first large-scale gender-sensitive projects to address the barriers to improving reproductive health.

- *Background*: *ReproSalud* is an ambitious venture between the Movimiento Manuela Ramos—a Peruvian, nongovernmental feminist organization—and the US Agency for International Development (USAID). (Manuela Ramos is a generic name for "Everywoman.") In the late 1980s, the "Manuelas" articulated their goals for hard-to-reach women in rural and peri-urban areas whose reproductive health needs fell outside the scope of conventional contraceptive delivery programmes. In the early 1990s USAID developed a five-year, $25 million project for low-income and rural women, in the new spirit of the "gender and development" agenda. From feedback at the end of the 1990s, the project has succeeded in addressing reproductive health needs in target communities. Crucial to its success has been its strategy of getting women and men to work together. *ReproSalud* was able to evolve a strategy of grass-roots wisdom because the "Manuelas" listened and learned from the women they sought to help.

- *Approach*: In the *ReproSalud* approach, women's groups identify their reproductive health problems and related socioeconomic issues, and determine how to tackle them. At the outset, in designing their first activities, the women wanted to involve men, because their husbands were curious about their activities and the women wanted to minimize male opposition. Their long-term goal was to moderate the patriarchal attitudes and behaviours that were obstacles to women's reproductive health goals.

ReproSalud's "Gender and Health Workshops for Men" open men to critical reflection on their cultural roles. An introductory exercise called "The Male Body" explores the relation between concepts of masculinity and their consequences for the body and health. The participants consider the relationship between being male (boss/worker/other male icons) and the physical and emotional impacts that result (such as loneliness, stress, heart disease, alcohol abuse, and domestic violence). They discuss the association between being a "lady's man" and sexually transmitted infections. They probe what their own experiences have done to them in the perspective of their current family relationships as husband and fathers. The goal is to encourage them to adopt responsible behaviours, and to impart their evolving health-oriented values to their peers. The process of training men to educate others in their own communities has become key to *ReproSalud's* overall success.

- *Results*: Men have been eager to learn about sexuality, the ways they use (and abuse) their bodies, and reproductive health of both sexes. The men have taken their lessons home, going on to explore ways to foster harmonious family relations and to educate their peers in the value of accepting domestic and reproductive responsibilities. A key result has been improvements in spousal communication. As one of the women said, "My husband and I had talked about using birth control before, but he was against it. He said that it was bad for you and that women could go with other men. But after the training, he understood and he agreed to family planning."

ReproSalud, in the words of USAID consultant Barbara Feringa, "is proving that working with men on women's terms is an extremely powerful concept that offers tremendous opportunity to family planning programmes." Its success shows that "gender is constructed locally, and that women are therefore much more able to determine their needs in gender than are programme managers".

7

Reproductive, Child and Women's Health

WHO's Activities in the Western Pacific Region

The importance of reproductive, child and women's health issues was recognized from the very start of WHO's activities in the Western Pacific Region. The Regional Director's Report to the second session of the Regional Committee in 1951 pointed out that: "The protection of the health of mothers and children is now considered as one of the most, if not the most, important functions of a health service in any country".

Thirty-eight years later, the Regional Director's Report to the thirty-ninth sessions argued that maternal and child health (MCH) remained as important as ever: "*Because of the sheer magnitude of the target population, who constitute two thirds of the total population in developing countries, the MCH/ family planning programme clearly plays a decisive role in attaining the health-for-all goal in the Region*".

Study on Domestic Violence

The first-ever World Health Organization (WHO) study on domestic violence reveals that intimate partner violence is the most common form of violence in women's lives—much more so than assault or rape by strangers or acquaintances. The study reports on the enormous toll physical and sexual violence by husbands and partners has on the health and well-being of women around the world and the extent to which partner violence is still largely hidden.

"This study shows that women are more at risk from violence at home than in the street and this has serious repercussions for women's health," said Dr. LEE Jong-wook, Director-General of WHO at the study release in Geneva. "The study also shows how important it is to shine a spotlight on domestic violence globally and treat it as a major public health issue."

The study is based on interviews with more than 24 000 women from rural and urban areas in 10 countries: Bangladesh, Brazil, Ethiopia, Japan, Namibia,

Peru, Samoa, Serbia and Montenegro, Thailand, and the United Republic of Tanzania. The Women's Health and Domestic Violence Against Women study makes recommendations and calls for action by policy makers and the public health sector to address the human and health costs, including by integrating violence prevention programming into a range of social programmes.

The study finds that one quarter to one half of all women who had been physically assaulted by their partners said that they had suffered physical injuries as a direct result. The abused women were also twice as likely as non-abused women to have poor health and physical and mental problems, even if the violence occurred years before. This includes suicidal thoughts and attempts, mental distress, and physical symptoms like pain, dizziness and vaginal discharge. The study was carried out in collaboration with the London School of Hygiene and Tropical Medicine, PATH and national research institutions and women's organizations in the participating countries.

"The degree to which the health consequences of partner violence in the WHO study are consistent across sites, both within and between countries, is striking," noted Dr. Charlotte Watts, from the London School of Hygiene and Tropical Medicine, a member of the core research team for the study. "Partner violence appears to have a similar impact on women's health and well-being regardless of where she lives, the prevalence of violence in her setting, or her cultural or economic background."

Domestic violence is known to affect women's sexual and reproductive health and may contribute to increased risk of sexually transmitted infections, including HIV. In this study, women who were in physically or sexually abusive relationships were more likely to report that their partner had multiple sexual partners and had refused to use a condom than women in non violent relationships. Women who reported physical or sexual violence by a partner were also more likely to report having had at least one induced abortion or miscarriage than those who did not report violence.

Although pregnancy is often thought of as a time when women should be protected, in most study locations, between 4 per cent and 12 per cent of women who had been pregnant reported being beaten during pregnancy. More than 90 per cent of these women had been abused by the father of the unborn child and between one quarter and one half of them had been kicked or punched in the abdomen.

For policy makers, the greatest challenge is that abuse remains hidden. At least 20 per cent of women reporting physical violence in the study had never told anyone before being interviewed. Despite the health consequences, very few women reported seeking help from formal services like health and police, or from individuals in positions of authority, preferring instead to reach out to friends, neighbours and family members. Those who did seek formal support tended to be the most severely abused.

The report recommends a range of vital interventions to change attitudes and challenge the inequities and social norms that perpetuate abuse. It further recommends integrating violence prevention programming into ongoing initiatives aimed at children, youth, HIV/AIDS, and sexual and reproductive health. Health service providers should be trained to identify women experiencing violence and to respond appropriately. Prenatal care, family planning or post abortion care is potential entry points to provide care, support, and referral to other services. Schools need to be safe places, support systems for victims must be strengthened and prevention programmes put in place. Raising awareness of the problem among the general public is critical. "Domestic violence can be prevented and governments and communities need to mobilize to fight this widespread public health problem," said WHO's Study Coordinator, Dr. Claudia Garcia Moreno. "WHO will continue to raise awareness about violence and the important role that public health can play to address its causes and consequences. Globally, we need to stop the violence from happening in the first place, and to provide help and support to women who are in abusive relationships."

WHO's Global Campaign for the Prevention of Violence supports governments to develop comprehensive violence prevention programmes to address domestic violence alongside other types of violence.

Some Quotes from Women Interviewed for the Study

- "I suffered for a long time and swallowed all my pain. That's why I am constantly visiting doctors and using medicines. No one should do this." Woman interviewed in Serbia and Montenegro.
- "He got this gun, I don't know from who... And he would tell the girls: "I'm going to kill your mother... The day will break and your mother will be dead right here..." I would sleep in a locked bedroom and with a dog inside the room with me. My dog. So he would not kill me". Woman interviewed in Brazil.
- "He hit me in the belly and made me miscarry two babies—identical or fraternal twins, I don't know. I went to the Loayza hospital with heavy bleeding and they cleaned me up." Woman interviewed in urban Peru.

How Physical and Sexual Violence was Measured

For physical violence, women were asked whether a current or former partner had ever:

- slapped her, or thrown something at her that could hurt her;
- pushed or shoved her;
- hit her with a fist or something else that could hurt;
- kicked, dragged or beaten her up;

- choked or burnt her on purpose; and
- threatened her with, or actually used a gun, knife or other weapon against her.

Sexual violence was defined by the following three behaviours: Being physically forced to have a sexual intercourse against her will; having sexual intercourse because she was afraid of what her partner might do; being forced to do something sexual she found degrading or humiliating.

Then and Now

Regional Data and Reproductive Health Trends (1948-1998)

Data from the early years of WHO operations in the Region are scarce and often comparisons cannot easily be made. Early reports from some Member States to sessions of the Regional Committee give some indication of MCH in the Region, but not all Members were able to provide data. As data collection began to improve, and methods became more standardized across the Region, a clearer picture of the health of women and children in the Region began to emerge. The data also showed a clear distinction in many of the indicators between the developed and the developing countries in the Region.

Maternal Mortality Ratios and Infant Mortality Rates

- Brunei Darussalam reported an infant mortality rate (IMR) of 93.07 per 1000 births in 1959; this had fallen to 69.18 per 1000 in 1960. The drop in infant mortality was attributed to 'Operation Kinabalu', an anti-infant death campaign introduced in 1959. On the other hand, Fiji reported an IMR of 38.94 in 1957, but this had risen to 42.59 in 1959. As of 1995, Brunei Darussalam had an IMR of 7.9 per 1000 live births, while Fiji reported an IMR of 21.0 in 1996, both representing drops in their previous rates.
- Hong Kong's data on IMR showed a decrease from 60.9 per 1000 births in 1956 to 26.4 in 1964. By 1970, IMR had fallen further to 21.8 and by 1974 to 17.4. However, between 1956 and 1969 the maternal mortality ratio (MMR) rose from 90 per 100 000 live births to 150 per 100 000 live births. It rose slightly over the next five years and in 1974 it stood at 160.
- Japan had more extensive data than many of the other Member States of the Region, and could show a decrease in IMR from 61.7 per 1000 births in 1948 to 30.7 in 1960, and down to 13.1 in 1970.
- The MMR per 100 000 live births had also falle from 157 to 1948 to 116 in 1960.
- The IMR in Malaysia per 1000 live births fell from 76 per 1000 in 1957 to 45 in 1967, and MMR per 100 000 live births fell from 320 in

1957 to 168 in 1967. North Borneo reported an infant mortality of 74 per 1000 births in 1960.
- The Philippines had the highest reported IMR in the Region of 101.6 per 1000 live births in 1950. This had fallen to 72.4 by 1959, still the highest known IMR in the Region. MMR fell from 370 per 100 000 live births in 1950 to 260 in 1959. In its report to the twelfth session of the WHO Regional Committee for the Western Pacific, the Philippines indicated that annually, over 2000 died in child-bearing, and the population of women of child-bearing age was estimated to be approximately 3.3 million in 1958.
- The disparity between developed and developing countries is highlighted by data from the early 1980s.

By the fortieth session of the Regional Committee in 1989, the Regional Director could report that 25 out of the then 31 countries and areas reporting on infant mortality had achieved a rate of below 50 per 1000 live births, and there had been a progressive decline in the IMR of almost all the countries and areas in the Region.

Total Population, Growth, Birth and Total Fertility Rates

Since 1950, the population of many countries and areas in the Region has more than doubled. The populations of Hong Kong, Mongolia and the Philippines have tripled. That of Brunei Darussalam has grown from 40 657 in 1947 to 296 000 in 1995.

Growth rates throughout the Region ranged from just over 1 per cent per annum for the Republic of Korea to 4.9 per cent per annum for Singapore in 1950. Current percentage growth rates range from negative for Niue and Tokelau (mainly due to out migration) to 3 per cent or over for Brunei Darussalam, the Federated States of Micronesia, Macao, the Marshall Islands and Solomon Islands. Based on the 1997 World Population Date Sheet, at current growth rates, population doubling time is 30 years or less for Brunei Darussalam, Cambodia, the Lao People's Democratic Republic, the Philippines and several of the Pacific island countries and areas. Longer population doubling times are estimated for the more developed countries, from 64 years for Singapore to 289 years for Japan.

Birth rates in Hong Kong and Japan fell considerably from 39.7 per 1000 population in 1956 to 19.9 in 1970 for Hong Kong, and from 33.5 in 1948 to 18.8 in 1970 for Japan. However, Japan's birth rate per 1000 population had dropped as low as 17.2 by 1957, and had begun to rise again slightly by 1970. The current crude birth rate for Japan is 10.0, the lowest in the Region. Low current birth rates are also reported for:

a) Australia (14.1),
b) China (17.7),

c) Hong Kong (11.8),
d) Republic of Korea (15.9),
e) Macao (14.0),
f) New Zealand (16.4), and
g) Niue (15.12), and Singapore (15.7).

The highest crude birth rate is Cambodia, at 45 per 1000 population. Many Pacific island countries and areas have birth rates between 22 (e.g. New Caledonia 22.04, Palau 22.6) and 37 (Solomon Islands).

Total fertility rates in the Region have decreased for most countries and areas for which data since 1950 are available. Fiji's total fertility rate was one of the highest reported, at 6.59, in 1950, but had dropped to 2.62 by 1995. Likewise, total fertility rates for China, Fiji, Malaysia, Mongolia, the Republic of Korea and Singapore have halved over the past 45 years. The picture is different for Papua New Guinea, where total fertility rate has only fallen from 6.21 to 4.7 over the same period. Viet Nam has seen a drop from 5.48 to 3.1, and the Federated States of Micronesia from 5.9 to 4.6. The total fertility rate for the Lao People's Democratic Republic has decreased from 5.9 to 5.6.

Life Expectancy at Birth for Women

The lowest life expectancies at birth for women reported for the Region in 1950 were Cambodia (40.8 years), China (47.5), Laos (39.2), Mongolia (46.5), Papua New Guinea (34.5), the Philippines (47.5), the Republic of Korea (49) and Viet Name (39.2). Papua New Guinea was unique among the countries for which data is known, in that it was the only country where women's life expectancy at birth was shorter than that of men. The more developed countries typically had much higher life expectancies at birth for women, the highest being New Zealand at 72.9 years. Others where life expectancy at birth was over 60 years for women included Australia, Fiji, Hong Kong, Japan and Singapore.

Recent figures from the country health profiles in the 1997 revision indicate that life expectancy at birth for women in the Region is now over 70 years for 22 countries and areas, and between 60 and 70 for a further 10 countries and areas. The improvement in life expectancy has not been so marked in Cambodia (55 years) and Lao People's Democratic Republic (55 years).

WHO Activities

Improvement of Midwifery Skills and Delivery Practices

The provisions that existed for the health care of mothers and children in the countries of the Region varies greatly when the Regional Office was set up in 1950. Very few government health administrations included a MCH administrative unit at the national level. In some countries, the limited services provided for mothers and children did not include preventive care, as practically all available resources had been directed to meet the pressing need for increased facilities for curative treatment. Other countries had established basic MCH facilities, but these were limited in scope. A few countries had well-developed health services where many of the chief dangers to MCH had been largely brought under control and attention was directed at special problems.

It was evident that, in most countries, one of the greatest handicaps to developing effective MCH programmes was lack of trained personnel. This deficiency was seen at all levels and in all aspects of the programme, administration, supervision, service, and training. Some countries require full training and licensing of all practising midwives. Others were planning training activities. Domiciliary midwifery was still in the early stages of development in Cambodia and the Republic of Korea. In addition, many countries lacked the facilities for expanding MCH activities and were unable to provide the necessary equipment and supplies.

Training of Traditional Birth Attendants and Fostering Safe Deliveries in Medical Institutions

Although in some parts of the Region in the early 1950s over 90 per cent of confinements took place in hospital, with either a physician and an obstetrical nurse or a midwife in attendance, in large areas of the less developed countries, the only attendant on whom a mother could rely was a relative or an untrained traditional birth attendant (TBA).

The TBA has long been recognized as an integral part of MCH care in the Region. Using and involving the TBA is essential in many areas where more skilled midwifery services are unavailable or access to such services is difficult. The TBA may be a women who has experience of many births, or simply a neighbour or relative who happens to be on the spot at the time of delivery and renders whatever assistance she can. The TBA may follow traditional practices that can be harmful to the mother or newborn, or she may have some knowledge of safer procedures. In addition to improving their standards of care at childbirth, the training of TBAs as auxiliary midwives means that TBAs are able to educate women and help to develop MCH programmes.

WHO's work on traditional midwives has demonstrated that "uneducated" people can make valuable contributions if they are given the training, the incentives and the confidence to do so. These traditional practitioners used to be ignored, maligned, even considered dangerous. As a result of WHO's catalytic and promotional work, they are increasingly looked on as a great resource for bringing selected primary health care to all.

An Expert Committee on Midwifery Training was convened in August 1954 to consider the training of midwifery personnel at all levels, with particular reference to those areas where maternity care services were less well developed and where auxiliary midwifery personnel were required. The committee discussed the importance of understanding the customs, beliefs and traditional practices of the people for whom midwifery services were to be provided.

Progress in training TBAs has continued wherever they form an important part of the local MCH care. For instance, in Samoa, 125 traditional birth attendants were trained on Upolu Island during 1977. By the end of 1978, all traditional birth attendants in the country were trained and provided with midwifery kits for use in the villages.

In the primary health care era, Member States approached the task of developing primary health care in different ways. However, training at the grass-roots level remained fundamental. Traditional practices related to reproductive health were reviewed by the Regional Office in 1995-1996, and the need to take traditional practices into account when designing reproductive health programmes was recognized. However, it has also been recognized that the role of the TBAs has to be correctly assessed, taking into account local conditions, traditions and legislation. There have been a number of successful attempts to integrate the services of TBAs into the overall MCH services in the Region, e.g. in Malaysia.

Promotion of Maternal and Child Health Care through Primary Health Care Activities and Community Awareness

There was early recognition that more effective care could be provided through closer coordination of preventive and curative health services for mothers and children and through integration of MCH services into the general health programme. This integration was one of the main subjects discussed at a Conference on Maternity Care in Manila, the Philippines, 1959. By making women aware of the simple things they could do themselves to improve their health and that of their children, pressures on health services for curative interventions could be lessened. An active programme of information and education to the public would help give women the health knowledge they needed.

MCH care was specified as one of the eight components of primary health care in the Declaration of Alma-ata in 1978. The Regional Office had already begun working on MCH in the primary health care context:

Development of primary health care is at various stages in different countries or areas of the Region. Strong endorsement by UNICEF and WHO spurred governments to intensify their efforts in extending health services coverage through affordable means.

Development and Dissemination of Fertility Regulation Methods

Population issues began to gain prominence in the 1960s. The Technical Discussions at the eighteenth session of the Regional Committee in 1967 looked at this issue in relation to MCH and other aspects of health:

Throughout the broad spectrum of public health concern, ranging from disease control to clinical services, the achievement of our ultimate goal has been considerably offset by too rapid population growth.... The problem of population growth is acute, and the need is most urgent in most of the countries which need family planning.

The Regional Director's Report to the same session of the Regional Committee noted that: "There is almost everywhere a growing interest in family planning...", and during the Technical Discussions it was also noted that "... for the first time, efforts were being made at the regional level to organize family planning activities. The topic of the discussions was significant since the interaction between health and population dynamics had become a universal concern.

Recent activities outside the Special Programme included supporting the formulation of a birth spacing policy for Cambodia, stressing the message that the correct timing and proper planning and spacing of pregnancies are the key interventions in reproductive health programmes to reduce morbidity and mortality of mothers and children, and underlining the fact that the overall decline in many countries total fertility rates has generally helped to improve women's health. WHO has also been providing technical support to UNFPA-funded country projects and programmes since the mid-1970s.

Improvements to the Status of Women and Freedom of Reproductive Choices

The status of women in society is affected by political, economical, social and cultural norms. These factors influence women's health directly or indirectly, through poor nutrition, lack of access to health care, lack of control over number of pregnancies, lack of education, among others.

Lack of education is a key determinant of MCH. Maternal education strongly enhances the chances of child survival as measured by nutritional status, infant mortality and child mortality. A child whose mother has not gone to school is 2.5 times more likely to die than a child whose mother has had seven or more years of schooling.

Collaboration with the Expanded Programme on Immunization on Tetanus Toxoid Immunization

UNICEF and WHO have collaborated extensively through the Expanded Programme on Immunization (EPI), in particular to provide technical and financial support to overcoming difficulties of expanding immunization to underserved areas. All developing countries of the Region had adopted the WHO-recommended immunization schedule by 1987, aimed at fully immunizing all children under one year of age. Provision of tetanus toxoid was identified by a regional workshop on innovative approaches to maternal and child health and family planning, held in Manila in September 1986 as an appropriate technology to be used by MCH and FP health workers at all levels. In 1996, the Regional Director's Report noted that one of the contributing factors to the remarkable improvements in the health status of children that had been achieved in most countries and areas of the Region was the expanded coverage of immunization programmes, including tetanus toxoid given to mothers during pregnancy.

Expansion of Maternal and Child Health Care to Women, Family and Reproductive Health

The importance of seeing MCH issue sin their broadest context was clearly brought out in the technical discussions at the eleventh session of the Regional Committee in 1960:

> "MCH should not be considered as a specialized, separately administrative service, but as an integral part of the total health service organization and operation. This is especially true where such hazards exist as poor sanitation, malnutrition and communicable diseases. These underlie many of the conditions insufficiently death with when individual care is given to a mother or infant. A home visit of a mother or child should be made as a *family visit.* The health needs of the whole family should be observed and catered to instead of such visits being allowed to become a routine maternity or child care observation for recording purposes. In providing MCH services, one should be on guard against the tendency to concentrate activities of antenatal work and conduct of deliveries to the neglect of infant and child care. Infant and child care should, therefore, be extended beyond the neonatal period to at least the time when the infant is weaned and when communicable diseases seem most prevalent."

The concept of family health inter-linking MCH, FP, nutrition and health education had gained wide acceptance by the twenty-fourth session of the Regional Committee in 1973. Family health was considered an "*approach whereby an effort is made to improve the health of the various individuals in the family through multidisciplinary services and thus influence society as a whole*".

Production of Educational Material

A large variety of information, education and communication (IEC) material is continuously being developed by the Regional Office and widely disseminated, along with material received from other agencies or WHO Headquarters. Approximately 600 reproductive health managers and service providers in the Region receive regular publications and advocacy material. Production of IEC material has contributed to an additional involvement of the male partner and to increased community awareness. IEC material was developed to provide women with more self-determination and with wider reproductive choices. Aware that sexuality is a taboo issue in many communities, the Regional Office developed and printed *Teaching Modules for Education in Human Sexuality* and *Teaching Modules for Continuing Education in Human Sexuality* as part of the *HIV/AIDS Reference Library of Nurses.*

WHO's Contribution to the Major International Conferences

The International Conference on Population and Development was held in Cairo, Egypt, in 1994. WHO had already started promoting reproductive health from a broader perspective as opposed to purely mother and child health services before the conference. In 1992, WHO published *Reproductive health: a key to a brighter future*, in which fertility regulation was recognized as important for reducing population growth rates. The document also stressed the link between reducing population growth and achieving sustainable development.

In preparation for the Fourth International Conference on Women, held in Beijing, China, in 1995, the Regional Office prepared eight monographs covering a wide variety of women's issues; 2500 copies of each were distributed at the conference. The topics covered included reproductive health, ageing, maternal education and child health, abortion, lifestyle changes and their impact on women's health and women's health profiles of Australia, the Philippines and Viet Nam. Focal points for women's issues were identified in several countries and a panel discussion on the health of women in the Region was held during the conference.

Collaboration with the United Nations Children Fund, United Nations Population Fund and International Planned Parenthood Foundation

Close collaboration between UNICEF and WHO has been a feature of practically all MCH programmes in the Region. Collaboration has taken several forms, for example in some projects undertaken by governments and supported by UNICEF, WHO has provided technical services. The International Planned Parenthood Foundation (IPPF) and the United Nations Population Fund (UNFPA) have been active partners in many aspects of FPA and fertility regulation projects.

Achievements

Reductions in Maternal Mortality Ratios, Infant Mortality Rates, Total Fertility Rates and Population Growth Rate

When WHO's work began, most countries of the Region were still suffering from the effects of the Second World War. Infant mortality was high, and in some less developed countries, half of all children died before they reached their first birthday.

IMR's have improved dramatically. In 1970, Cambodia has IMRs of 176 per 1000 and 142 per 1000 for female infants and for male infants, respectively. These IMRs fell to 120 and 103 in the 1990s. Similar decreases have occurred in the Pacific Islands, which have reported reductions over 20 years; Fiji from 65 to 17 for females and from 97 to 50 for females and from 115 to 53 for males; and Papua New Guinea, from 102 to 67 for females and from 101 to 66 for males. Such improvements may be attributed largely to public health measures such as immunization, education about dehydration and promotion of breast-feeding.

Improvements in Obstetric Practices

One of the major functions of the Regional Office continues to be the establishment of norms, guidelines and protocols for the delivery of reproductive health.

Through the primary health care approach, the Regional Office has been promoting delivery of health care for mothers and children at community level, with an increased community participation and in an integrated and comprehensive manner. Other essential elements of care, such as provision of essential drugs, water supply and sanitation, education and information, availability of safe and modern contraceptive methods, development of the health system, identification of cases at risk and referral etc. continue to be at the forefront of activities promoted by the Regional Office.

Introduction of Safe Contraceptive Methods in Several Countries

The expansion of FP programmes has increased access to contraceptives overall in the Region. Use of contraceptives has increased in China; Hong Kong; and the Republic of Korea to more than 50 per cent of women in the reproductive age group. Access to contraceptives is considered to be very good in China; Hong Kong, Malaysia; the Republic of Korea; and Singapore. Access is considered fair for:

a) Mongolia,
b) the Philippines, and
c) Viet Nam.

Advancement of Women's Status (Education, Nutrition, Equal Opportunities)

Women's status can be influenced and improved through advocacy. The Regional Office has published and widely distributed documents and monographs that point out how low status affects women's health and that of their children. Activities on advocacy on women and gender issues are directed inside, as well as outside, the Organization. Within WHO, concerns on gender issues are being considered or increasingly taken up in every programme of work, as highlighted in the publication *Women in Development—a position paper.* In addition, efforts are being exerted to develop gender-specific, gender-disaggregated and gender-sensitive health and social indicators, to collect better information on women's status and to improve analysis of the situation of women with more objective and appropriate instruments and more reliable data. Seminars on gender issues are being planned for the staff at the Regional Office. As well as using education as a means to improve women's status throughout the Region, WHO has also made commitments to expand the involvement of women in the work of WHO itself. A leading advocacy role has been played by the Global Commission on Women's Health and by the Women, Health and Development Programme. The World Health Assembly has revised its target for employment of women to professional categories to 50 per cent of new appointments to professional categories by 2002.

Underachievement

High Maternal Mortality Ratios and Infant Mortality Rates in Some Countries

Not all countries and areas in the Region have benefited equally from reproductive health programmes, as shown in the continuing disparity between some of the developing countries in the Region and the developed countries. The highest reported MMRs are in Cambodia at 473 per 100 000 live births, the Lao People's Democratic Republic (656), Papua New Guinea (930) and Solomon Islands (549). The regional target for maternal mortality is 300 deaths per 100 000 live births. The data for parts of the Region are still not considered accurate because maternal mortality suffers from considerable underreporting, as maternal deaths are often ascribed to other causes, such as septicaemia or heart disease, particularly so if the death is not close to the delivery period or is the result of a termination. Thus the overall picture for maternal mortality may be much worse than these figures indicate. IMRs show a similar disparity although the range is not as wide. The highest rates reported are in Cambodia and the Lao People's Democratic Republic. Regionwide, however, mortality is higher for male than for female infants.

Domestic violence perpetrated against women is a major contributor to the global burden of disease and an important element of the status issue. It has been estimated that: "*At least one in five of the world's female population has been physically or sexually abused by a man or men at some time in their life*".

Barriers to Wider Contraceptive Use

There are many cultural and social barriers that still prevent women from being able to exercise their freedom of reproductive choices. Religious beliefs, price constraints and other issues affecting access to contraceptives continue to hinder the use of modern contraceptive methods in some countries and areas in the Region. Limited choice or poor availability of contraceptives often makes adoption of fertility-regulating methods difficult. Access to contraceptives is considered poor in Cambodia, the Lao People's Democratic Republic and Papua New Guinea. Unwanted pregnancies are still prevalent and no doubt lead to many unsafe terminations. Regional data on terminations are woefully inadequate due to lack of reporting or national policies that make termination legal.

Low Women's Status in Several Countries

Improved data collection and analysis demonstrates the low status of women in parts of the Region. Information on schooling, for instance, shows that in some countries and areas boys are more likely to be educated than girls and that girls have a higher drop-out rate after primary schooling. Women's status affects their health in many ways and education forms one of the links between status and health.

Future

Further Improvement in Obstetric Practices

Work will continue on improving obstetric practices and stopping the occurrence of harmful traditional practices, while acknowledging that other traditional practices may have their place in a society. Promoting the adoption of safe practices such as clean hands, a clean delivery area and clean instruments for cutting the cord, will be one way of eliminating harmful traditional techniques.

Promotion of Use and Wider Choice of Fertility Regulation Methods

Making a wider range of safe contraceptives available, accessible and affordable will have an important effect on maternal mortality and morbidity not only by reducing the number of births and facilitating birth spacing, but by reducing the number of high-risk pregnancies and unsafe terminations.

Development of Information, Education, and Communication and Advocacy/Awareness Material

The status of women is linked to access to and use of health facilities. Advocacy will be directed towards political, religious and community leaders who can make a difference to women's status in their communities. Improved public knowledge through schools, mass media and training of local health personnel, will also increase the use of health facilities. WHO is not the only agency within the United Nations system to take part in this campaign; for example, many UNFPA and UNICEF projects have a media component.

Integrations of Population/Environment Concerns into Health Sector

Population issues will receive more focus as rapid population growth, particularly in the smaller Pacific island countries, will put pressure on dwindling natural resources and threaten sustainable development. The population doubling time for at least 10 countries or areas in the Region is 30 years or less, barely time to develop the extra health and other resources needed to cope with twice as many people. Already, several countries are unable to provide for universal primary or secondary education. The known links between girls' education and female reproductive health make this doubly alarming.

Population issues in the Western Pacific Region will not only be concerned with freedom of reproductive choice and availability of contraceptives, but also with cultural issues that may have a more important influence on the size of families than contraceptive availability.

8

A Human Rights Approach to Promoting and Protecting Reproductive and Sexual Health Rights

The Role of Treaty Bodies, United Nations Agencies and NGO Partnerships

Rationale

Over the last five years, human rights treaty bodies, UN agencies and bodies and NGOs have paid increasing attention to reproductive and sexual health. However, the acceptance of the application of a human rights framework to reproductive and sexual health rights is still quite recent. Despite the advances and commitments made in Cairo and Beijing, the UN human rights system has yet to include or effectively utilize adequate monitoring language and mechanisms for the human rights associated with reproductive and sexual health rights.

Clearly, there is a pressing need for this to happen soon. The 1997 UNFPA report *Closing the Gap between Women's Aspirations and their Reproductive Experiences* noted that an estimated 228 million women who want to delay or cease childbearing are in need of effective contraceptive methods. The Report of the 1996 Round Table of Human Rights Treaty Bodies on Human Rights Approaches to Women's Health, with a Focus on Sexual and Reproductive Health and Rights, noted that in many countries few women are able to exercise their right to reproductive health. Every year, more than 585,000 women die from pregnancy and maternity-related causes. Two million girl children are subjected to some form of female genital mutilation (FGM). Twenty million women undergo unsafe abortions, of which 70,000 die as a result. Moreover, inadequate standards exist in the urgent situations of women and child refugees, many of whom are subjected to systematic rape and violence, in situations of emergency or armed conflict.

The ICPD +5 Process provides Canada with a key opportunity to take the lead on urging the international community to implement effective strategies and mechanisms to monitor progress of state commitments made in the Cairo Programme and the Beijing Platform on reproductive and sexual rights. Key steps must be taken to hold states accountable for reproductive and sexual health rights violations. Canada must act as a driving force behind the move towards integrating the principles espoused in the Cairo Programme and the Beijing Platform, as well as effectively utilizing the expertise of and collaborating with UN agencies and NGOs, into the treaty body monitoring and implementation process.

Background

Although several human rights treaties have recognized the right to non-discrimination on the basis of sex, violations of women's rights were, until recently, largely marginal to human rights within the UN human rights system. During the last decade, however, positive developments within the UN human rights system, national laws and policies and in NGO initiatives have advanced the understanding of women's human rights. This development was apparent at the 1993 World Conference on Human Rights (the Vienna Conference) at which there was a clear recognition that women's rights are an integral and inalienable part of all human rights.

Moreover, the Vienna Declaration and Programme of Action paved the way for women's human rights, and in particular women's health rights, to be more fully integrated as a priority concern for the UN human rights system and UN agencies. The importance of human rights principles in advancing women's health rights, including reproductive and sexual health, was clarified in the language of 1) the Programme of Action (the Cairo Programme), which was adopted by 184 UN Member States at the 1994 International Conference on Population and Development (ICPD); and in 2) the Declaration and Platform of Action (Beijing Platform) adopted by 187 UN member states at the 1995 Fourth World Conference on Women. In Cairo and Beijing, there was a clear affirmation that reproductive and sexual health rights are integral to human rights.

Both the Cairo Programme and the Beijing Platform recognize not only the importance of taking programmatic steps to implement the agreements made in Cairo and Beijing, but also the need to apply international human rights instruments to protect women from human rights violations as well as to hold state parties accountable for ensuring women's health, in particular reproductive and sexual health. The Beijing Platform specifically calls for treaty bodies and state parties to take into account the Platform commitments during the state reporting process.

Moreover, the ICPD and the Beijing Platform clearly noted that reproductive rights consist of separate human rights that "are already recognized in national laws, international laws and international human rights documents and other consensus documents". Each human rights treaty, convention or covenant includes human rights provisions which should be interpreted to include the various aspects of reproductive and sexual health. Examples of this purposive approach to interpreting the relevant human rights provisions are as follows:

- The right to life and survival is interpreted to include obligations to seriously reduce maternal mortality which is a core objective in both the Cairo Programme and Beijing Platform.
- The right to liberty and security of the person can be applied to obligations to eliminate compelled sterilization and unsafe/inaccessible abortion, FGM and sexual violence.
- The rights to the benefits of scientific progress includes obligations to promote research on women's health, including contraception, HIV infection and STDs.
- The right to family and private life includes obligations to provide relevant information, education and services to protect the formation of families.

Violations of reproductive and sexual health rights can be categorized as:

- those resulting from direct action on the part of a state, such as coercive sterilization;
- those relating to a state's failure to meet the minimum core obligations of human rights, such as neglecting to reduce maternal mortality rates; and
- those relating to patterns of discrimination, such as persistent and gross discrepancies in access to health services, that cumulatively disadvantage the reproductive health of groups, such as adolescents.

The Cairo Programme and the Beijing Platform symbolize the consensus of the world community on the importance of the protection and promotion of reproductive and sexual health rights. The conclusions made in the report of the 1996 Round Table of Human Rights Treaty Bodies on Human Rights Approaches to Women's Health, with a Focus on Sexual and Reproductive Health and Rights, go so far as to state that, given this global consensus, the Cairo Programme and the Beijing Platform contribute the to the evolution of customary international law norms and obligations by clarifying the evolving meaning, or progressive development, of human rights norms as well as by indicating widely approved steps or means to further their implementation

Thus, while the Cairo Programme and the Beijing Platform help interpret the meaning of, and provide indicators on reproductive and sexual health, it is through the use of international human rights laws and their relevant treaty bodies, with the collaboration of UN agencies and NGOs, that states can be held to their commitments to protecting and promoting reproductive and sexual health rights. As such, it is clear that this issue should be a top priority for Canada and other nations.

Analysis

Role of Treaty Monitoring Bodies

The treaty monitoring system is key to the promotion and protection of human rights standards relating to women's right to health, including reproductive and sexual health rights. Treaty body mechanisms to enforce these rights include state reporting obligations, such the Committee on the Elimination of Discrimination against Women (CEDAW), established under the Women's Convention to monitor its implementation. Mechanisms also exist under some conventions, such as the European Convention on Human Rights and the International Covenant on Civil and Political Rights, that enable individuals from consenting countries to bring complaints against them for violations of their rights.

Treaty bodies have begun the process of reflecting upon the role that women's human rights play within their mandate of state monitoring. This is apparent in some of their guidelines for reports and questions to state parties, General Comments, recommendations and concluding observations. Some of the General Comments already refer to aspects of reproductive and sexual health or can be interpreted as doing so (for example the Committee under the Convention on the Elimination of All Forms of Violence against Women (CEDAW) General Recommendation No. 21 which deals with women's reproductive health in the context of the protection of equality in marriage and family relations; or CEDAW's Suggestion No. 8 which expressed the Committee's intention to follow the implementation of Cairo Programme with respect to women's human rights and to develop a jurisprudence of international legal standards with respect to women's health through the reporting mechanism under CEDAW).

Few of the treaty bodies, however, have developed their approaches to incorporate gender dimensions to human rights, particularly in the area of reproductive and sexual health. Canada must take the lead on urging the world community and the UN human rights system to facilitate the capacity and commitment of human rights treaty bodies to fully integrate reproductive and sexual health into their mandate and processes.

In particular, Canada must promote, within the international community, the importance of developing and implementing systematic performance standards which can be utilized by treaty bodies to measure the extent to which states discharge their obligations for the protection and promotion of reproductive and sexual rights. These standards can then be used to monitor state compliance with their obligations under human rights conventions and covenants, such as the UN Convention on the Rights of the Child (the Children's Convention), the International Covenant on Civil and Political Rights (ICCPR), the International Covenant on Economic, Social and Cultural Rights (ICESCR), the Convention Against Torture (CAT), and the UN Convention on All Forms of Discrimination Against Women (the Women's Convention), in the area of reproductive and sexual rights.

The following strategies are recommended for promoting the role that treaty bodies can play in advancing reproductive and sexual health rights:

- Treaty bodies must develop and implement systematic standards of performance for the protection and promotion of reproductive and sexual heath right. These standards should be developed with the below in mind:
    - a clear conception of the specific components of each right and the concomitant obligations of states;
    - the delineation of performance standards for each component, including the identification of violations;
    - collection of relevant data, appropriately desegregated by sex and other significant variables;
    - development of information management systems for data that facilitate analysis of trends over time and comparison of the reproductive rights of groups within a country; and
    - analysis of collected data.
- Treaty bodies should take into account the Cairo Programme and the Beijing Platform as providing a useful source of standards, indicators, and questions for monitoring state compliance on reproductive and sexual health.
- Treaty bodies should require full and clear disclosure in state parties' reporting obligations and require that a plan of action be developed by state parties where the treaty body has expressed concerns about the levels of progress, commitment or effectiveness in the area of reproductive and sexual health.
- Treaty bodies should draw upon the expertise of UN agencies and UN bodies, such as UNFPA and WHO, in compiling information on fact-finding, monitoring and reporting of reproductive and sexual rights violations as well as in developing human rights indicators, standards, practices and priorities in relation to reproductive and sexual rights.
- The key to the development of systematic performance standards and effective mechanisms is the regular flow of reliable information with the UN human rights system and the co-ordination of joint activities. To this end, there should be increased coordination between UN Special Rapporteurs and Treaty Bodies. Timing their annual meetings to coincide, and the regular sharing of information, analysis, and findings can facilitate this.

- There should be greater collaboration and coordination between treaty bodies in order to effectively implement the rights set out in the covenants and conventions. For example, greater collaboration between treaty bodies under the Children's Convention and the Women's Convention could lead to sharing of data, development of joint recommendations and implementation strategies with respect to the sale and trafficking of women and girl children, early or forced marriage and FGM.
- CEDAW should take definitive steps to implement and apply their General Recommendation No. 24 on Health. This Recommendation can be used by treaty bodies to interpret human rights provisions and develop systematic performance standards that relate to reproductive and sexual rights in order to monitor State compliance with their obligations under CEDAW.
- Treaty bodies should begin to apply reproductive and sexual health to the interpretation of specific rights provided for in their respective treaty. For example the Human Rights Committee under the ICCPR should apply the right to life to maternal mortality (article 6); CEDAW should apply the right to non-discrimination on the ground of gender to the criminalization of medical procedures needed only by women, such as abortion (article 1 and 12); The Committee under the Torture Convention should apply the right to be free from torture, in respect of women being raped in custodial-type situations and wars (article 1 and 4).
- Treaty bodies should be encouraged to explicitly incorporate women's health concerns in the revision and development of General Comments, recommendations and guidelines while emphasizing the obligation of state parties to adopt positive measures to ensure the related rights. These should then be publicized and disseminated through the appropriate media, including the Internet.
- Since women's right to health, including reproductive and sexual health, is encompassed within the meaning of human rights provisions of the principal international human rights conventions and covenants, treaty monitoring bodies should require state parties to address the status of these rights, provide and respond to reliable gender-sensitive data, as well as comprehensively examine the implementation of these rights during the reporting process.
    - It is essential to urge treaty bodies to direct states to comply with their obligations relating to the protection and promotion of reproductive and sexual rights under international human rights treaties. Some key steps include requiring states to:
    - ensure that their national legislation conforms with the relevant human rights provisions;

- enact laws, polices, and programmes to ensure universal affordable access to a full range of high quality health care, including reproductive and sexual health services;
- implement a gender perspective in all policies and programmes affecting women's health;
- involve women and NGOs in the implementation and monitoring of such policies and programmes;
- allocate the overall budgetary, human and administrative health resources to women's health in a manner comparable to resources allocated to men, taking into account the particular health needs of various groups of women including the most vulnerable such as refugee, disabled, aboriginal and visible minority women.

- Given that many human rights conventions and covenants oblige states to provide human rights education on the relevant human rights, treaty bodies should be urged to monitor the extent to which states comply with such treaty provisions. Treaty bodies should also emphasize state obligations to increase the understanding and knowledge of all actors within civil society of the scope of and entitlements related to reproductive and sexual health rights.
- Urge the UN human rights system to implement system-wide human rights training for all treaty body members and UN staff to:
  - increase and improve their knowledge and understanding of the scope and significance of, as well the state obligations on, reproductive and sexual rights;
  - develop a consistent system-wide approach to reproductive and sexual rights based upon international human rights standards; and
  - promote formal and informal human rights education in its initiatives.
- Treaty bodies should be encouraged to set specific time frames during their Annual Meeting to consider particular thematic issues, including reproductive and sexual health, and invite the participation of appropriate UN agencies and NGOs in these discussions.
- Treaty bodies should encourage greater cooperation among the UN human rights system and NGOs by appointing one member of each treaty body to liase with UN agencies, other related UN bodies and NGOs on thematic issues, in particular women's health issues, including reproductive and sexual health.
- Treaty bodies should implement a procedure whereby UN agencies and NGOs promptly receive state party reports and concluding observations, and are afforded the full opportunity to analyze and respond to the reports. Such a process would enable UN agencies and NGOs to alert treaty bodies of gaps and conflicts between state reports and collected country-specific data.

- Treaty bodies should facilitate greater NGO participation in the work of treaty bodies by setting up annual information/education sessions between treaty body members and NGOs

Additional measures that Canada should promote among the world community and UN human rights system to strengthen the role of treaty bodies and the impact of human rights conventions and covenants in the protection and promotion of reproductive and sexual health rights are as follows:

- Given that Paragraph 4.5 in the Programme of Action sets out states' commitment to sign, ratify and implement all existing agreements that promote women's rights, states that have adopted the Cairo Programme should be urged to universally ratify all international human rights conventions and covenants that include women and children's human rights, as well as withdraw any reservations to human rights provisions in international human rights treaties relating to reproductive and sexual health rights.
- Canada must develop, and assist the international community in developing, accessible mechanisms for individuals to enforce their reproductive rights set out in human rights treaties and conventions, such as assisting with the development and implementation of Optional Protocols and effective complaints mechanisms open to individuals and NGOs.
- The UN human rights system should be urged to immediately adopt and implement optional protocols to the International Covenant on Economic, Social and Cultural Rights, the Convention against Torture, the Convention on the Rights of the Child and the Convention on the Elimination of All Forms of Discrimination against Women. Such protocols should include, where appropriate, procedures for the treaty bodies to receive complaints from individuals and NGOs.

The Role of UN Agencies and Other UN Bodies

Both the Cairo Programme and the Beijing Platform note the importance of strengthening cooperation and coordination between treaty bodies and UN agencies. It goes without saying that UN Agencies can provide immeasurable value to the treaty body monitoring process, while their work can also be better informed by the principles developed by treaty bodies.

Given the long-standing role that UN Agencies have played in fact-finding, monitoring and reporting human rights violations within the UN human rights systems, UN agencies, in collaboration with NGOs should play a key role in providing sound and reliable country-specific data, indicators and information on sexual and reproductive health to all treaty bodies that monitor state compliance of international human rights covenants and conventions.

This data could be events-based, for example, the incidence of rape of women; standards-based, for example, rates of maternal mortality; or norms-based, for example, the absence of a law on the minimum age of marriage. This data and information should be make available to treaty bodies in relation to the reporting process, the standard-setting process and the compliance process. Furthermore, such data and information should also be used as a basis for initiating complaints and for calling for particular remedies, for reparations, or for the amendment of laws and practices.

Canada must take the lead on, within the international community, promoting the expanded role that UN Agencies and other UN bodies can take in assisting and working with treaty bodies with their mandate in the area of reproductive and sexual health rights. Strategies for this initiative include:

- UN agencies should assist treaty bodies in elaborating the content of the core minimum obligations of state parties, setting out steps that can be taken to comply with treaty provisions, and developing inquiries for State parties regarding the inclusion of relevant quantitative and qualitative information in their reports with respect to reproductive and sexual health rights.
- UN agencies should consult with treaty bodies to identify the areas in which the agencies could provide the greatest assistance in collecting, developing and analyzing data, indicators (both quantitative and qualitative) and information in order to enhance the capacity of treaty bodies to monitor state parties' obligations on reproductive and sexual health rights. Meticulously documented data can demonstrate that human rights abuses represent systematic state policies, rather than merely individual aberrations.
- Given UNFPA's high credibility among governments and NGOs, strong field presence, clout within the UN system, and commitment to and involvement in the ICPD + 5 process in relation to reproductive and sexual health rights, UNFPA would be an ideal agency to be given the mandate to lead the collection and analysis of data, standards, indicators and information on reproductive and sexual health.
- In particular, UNFPA's conclusions and recommendations reached during their regional reviews on the progress in implementing the Cairo Programme, global field inquiries and round table and technical meetings and can be used as a starting point for this initiative.
- The approach taken by WHO in its reproductive health strategies, a participatory and community-based approach with an emphasis on respect for women's autonomy and equality, as well as their established health indicators, should be considered by treaty bodies to assist them in developing systematic performance standards and implementation strategies for state parties.
- UN agencies should act on the treaty bodies' concluding comments

and suggestions by working with countries to assist them in implementing such recommendations.

- All UN Agencies and UN bodies should be required to conduct a human rights, including reproductive and sexual health rights, impact assessment prior to implementing any project or programme; make these assessments available to, and consult with, those affected by the project or programme, related United Nations human rights agencies and local and international NGOs; and implement procedures whereby this assessment must be used in the planning, design, implementation and evaluation of the project or programmes.
- All UN Agencies and UN bodies should be required to report to human rights treaty bodies on how their projects or programmes have affected the reproductive and sexual rights of the persons in the countries in which they operate. Urge UN Agencies to implement any recommendations made by these treaty bodies into their projects or programmes.
- UN agencies should provide and assist with human rights education, training and technical assistance within the UN system, including treaty bodies, on understanding, developing and applying standards and processes for monitoring women's health issues, in particular reproductive and sexual health rights
- There should be greater collaboration between UN agencies and UN bodies working in the area of reproductive and sexual health rights such as the close cooperation on project initiatives and technical exchange between UNFPA and WHO.
- Based upon their capacity to elicit participation and support, UNFPA and other specialized UN agencies are in a position to play a key role in facilitating and advancing dialogue between governments and NGOs in the areas of reproductive and sexual health rights.
- UN agencies should establish strong strategic partnerships, as well as facilitate and support and collaborate, with NGOs working in the area of promoting or protecting reproductive and sexual health rights and in particular assist NGOs in their capacity to use information from the treaty monitoring process to protect human rights. A model of effective cooperation may be found in UNFPA's ongoing initiatives, through the sponsoring of regional projects and conferences, with NGOs and women's groups in the areas of women's health, including reproductive and sexual health.
- With the support of the UN human rights system, UN agencies and UN bodies should collaborate with NGOs to take steps to implement the Beijing Platform recommendation of the creation of independent Ombudspersons, Rights Advocates or Defenders, with power to investigate alleged violations of reproductive rights, issue periodic

reports, advise governmental and other agencies and make recommendations for reforms. Such advocates can assist in the development and implementation of strategies that ensure women in Canada and abroad have access to legal services that educate them about their rights, and counsel them if their rights have been violated. Moreover, legal service advocates can recommend individual and collective remedies for violations of rights, and preventative action that governments can take in anticipation of rights. An example of an effective model is the Profamilia, the largest provider of reproductive health services in Colombia, which has successfully integrated legal programmes into its organization.

The Role of NGOs

NGOs are critical participants in the international human rights system. The importance and value of collaboration and partnering with NGOs in order to effectively monitor reproductive and sexual health right violations and apply human rights standards to women's health is also firmly recognized in the Cairo Programme and the Beijing Platform. In particular, NGOs play a key role in outlining the regional status of human rights for treaty bodies through their provision of credible and reliable data and information on human rights in Shadow Reports which supplement state reports during the state reporting process. As such, Canada must take the lead on promoting international support for the implementation of the following strategies related to the role of NGOs within the UN human rights system:

- When states are due to report to the various treaty bodies, they should be encouraged to include NGOs in the process of preparing reports and NGOs should be encouraged to prepare shadow reports.
- NGOs should be encouraged and supported to develop and disseminate shadow reports that emulate the exemplary model formulated by the Center for Reproductive Law and Policy (CLRP), in collaboration with local NGOs, for CEDAW. The CLRP shadow reports clearly sets out the national laws and polices affecting women's reproductive lives and contrasts this to the reality of women's reproductive lives in that country. For example, their 1998 shadow report on Peru sets out statistical and contextual information on sexual and reproductive health, the economic and social situation and conclusions on the serious gaps and lack of effective mechanisms in areas such as violence against women, family planning, sexual education and maternity benefits. These shadow reports also clearly note CLRP's belief that "reproductive rights are fundamental to women's health and equality and that state parties' commitment to ensuring them should receive serious attention" and that these rights are already recognized by international human rights laws and documents. Moreover, these

reports strive to bring to the attention of treaty monitoring bodies the human rights dimensions of reproductive and sexual health. In order to do this, there are explicit links made in the shadow reports between various fundamental reproductive rights issues, and relevant provisions of the Women's Convention. Clearly, the value of these types of shadow reports in bringing meaningful data, indicators and information to treaty bodies is immeasurable and should be fully supported and facilitated by state parties and the UN human rights system.

- NGOs should be encouraged to provide and analyze meaningful quantitative and qualitative criteria and data, which will assist treaty bodies in developing General Comments and recommendations as well as states in preparing their reports.
- The participation of NGOs in the treaty monitoring and conference implementation processes should be facilitated and supported.
- NGOs and other civil society actors that are involved in monitoring the implementation of reproductive and sexual rights must be provided with resources adequate to their mandate, which should include human rights education and women's legal rights under human rights covenants and convent.

9

Benefits of Investing in Sexual and Reproductive Health and Rights

Background

"The developmental, ethical and economic arguments for promoting reproductive choice are overwhelming. There remains a considerable gap between desired and actual family sizes. Lower fertility is associated with better child health and lower lifetime risk of pregnancy-related death and disability. Large family size (especially at the stage when children are young) is closely associated with poverty. There is strong macroeconomic evidence for the "demographic gift" as lower dependency ratios feed through to higher per capita income, savings and investment."—Better Health For Poor People, Department For International Development (DFID), United Kingdom, November 2000, Page 18.

Achieving sexual and reproductive health and rights for all is an end in itself; it needs no further justification. But it also confers great benefits on the economic and social life of the community.

Meeting the Needs of Women and Men Worldwide

Investing in this area serves to *meet the needs of the women and men worldwide* who wish to make their own decisions about how many children to have and when to have them. At least 120 million couples in the developing world still want to space or limit childbearing but do not have access to contraception. Much work remains to be done if we wish to attain universal access to reproductive health services by 2015, the target set by the international community.

Improving the Health of Men and Women and Saving Lives

Providing comprehensive reproductive health services to all improves the health of men and women and saves lives. Reproductive illnesses and unintended pregnancies weaken and kill women and men. There are as many as 100 million unwanted pregnancies each year. A fifth of these end in unsafe abortion. More than half a million women die each year from pregnancy related causes, and millions more suffer from serious complications related to pregnancy.

Comprehensive reproductive health care services, including family planning, would prevent many of the maternal deaths that occur each year—as well as dramatically reduce the number of reproductive health illnesses that weaken men and women.

Such services are essential if we are to reduce the maternal mortality rate by three-quarters by 2015, the internationally-agreed target.

Saving Children's Lives

Providing high quality sexual and reproductive health services to men and women saves children's lives. *To reduce the rate of infant and child mortality by two-thirds by the year 2015—which is the internationally-agreed target—providing comprehensive reproductive health services must be part of the plan.*

Reproductive health services, including family planning, help women to avoid high-risk pregnancies and increase the time between births. Babies born less than two years apart are twice as likely to die in the first year as those born after an interval of at least two years. In many countries, the risk of death during the first year of life is up to 1.5 times higher for infants born to mothers under the age 20 than for those born to mothers aged 20 to 29.

Also, when a mother dies in childbirth, her newborn's chance of survival is greatly reduced. And the siblings of that child are less likely to receive adequate nourishment and health care and are more likely to die. Further, children that survive the death of a mother—particularly girls—are much more likely to drop out of school to care for younger siblings and do household chores.

Education for All

With respect to education, comprehensive reproductive health services are essential if we wish *to ensure that all children have access to and complete a primary education of good quality by 2015*—the internationally-agreed target. As Minister Minna stated at the September 20th consultation on Financing for Development in Ottawa, "I don't see success in development unless we educate all children, especially girls". But getting pregnant too early is one of the surest ways to cut short a girl's schooling and limit her prospects in life. For many teenage girls, childbirth and child-rearing become virtually insurmountable obstacles to school attendance and advancement. Girls who give birth are far less likely to complete high school than their childless peers. Without sufficient schooling, women find it difficult to improve their economic and social life.

Improving the Quality of Women's Lives

Sexual and reproductive health services are *central to women's empowerment and improve the quality of women's lives.* With fewer children, more time between births, and better reproductive health, women find it easier to work outside the home, raise their incomes and provide for their families. They also have more time to participate in the social and political life of their communities.

Combating HIV/AIDS

HIV/AIDS is devastating the developing world. Comprehensive sexual and reproductive health services—including family planning, maternal health care, and STI/HIV prevention and care—*are clearly central in the global effort to contain the HIV/AIDS pandemic.* It is common knowledge that HIV/AIDS is devastating entire generations of children in much of the world.

Nearly half of all new HIV infections occur in people under the age of 18. Studies in HIV-prevalent countries show that most adolescents are unaware of even a single way to protect themselves from the disease.

Cairo called for a number of interrelated actions to address the HIV/AIDS pandemic including: explicitly addressing the gender inequalities that fuel the epidemic; empowering girls and young women to control their own lives, and, in particular, their sexual relations; and, providing comprehensive sexual and reproductive health information, education and services to young people, both in and out of school, before and after they become sexually active. If we are to *reduce the number of HIV-infected youth by 25 per cent in the worst affected countries by 2005 and globally by 2015—which are the targets set by the international community*—comprehensive sexual and reproductive health information and services—like the kind promised at Cairo—are essential.

Fighting Poverty

Eliminating poverty is the single greatest challenge that the world faces. And empowering women and men to make key decisions about their lives—such as the decision about whether to have children, when and how often to do so—is essential to poverty eradication efforts. At the family level, high fertility can have a substantial impact on household income and can, in the extreme, makes the difference to a household being above the poverty line and being below it. If women have access to reproductive health information and services, they can take control of their fertility and break the cycle of repeated pregnancies, enabling them to seek employment or training and increase their family income. The burden of poor reproductive health affects women and men in their most productive years. Given the amount of disability and premature death caused by reproductive health problems in the poorest nations, it is difficult to imagine young adults—especially women—lifting themselves and their families from poverty without full access to basic reproductive health information and services. *Reproductive illness and death help to perpetuate a vicious cycle of poverty among the poor.* Poor and uneducated women are far more likely than other women to die or be disabled during pregnancy, or to bear the cost and consequences of clandestine abortions. Poverty is highly correlated with other variables, including early age at marriage and first birth, low contraceptive prevalence rates, short birth intervals, low birth weight, and relatively high risks of maternal and infant mortality. *On a larger scale*, there is new and more convincing evidence that high fertility at the economy-wide level makes poverty reduction more difficult and less likely. Rapid population growth exercises a negative impact on the pace of aggregate economic growth in developing countries.

Crucial to National Development

Good reproductive health is crucial to national development. Half of the world's 6.1 billion people are under age 25; more than one billion are between the ages of 10 and 19. Within 15 years—less than one generation—all 3 billion will have reached reproductive age. Societies will need to make massive investments to prepare young people for economic and social participation, indeed, for all aspects of national development. Countries that fail to provide girls and boys with the means to remain healthy and in school will not benefit as fully from other investment they make in young people. What we do today will have far-reaching implications for the world in years to come.

10

The Impact of Family Planning and Reproductive Health on Women's Lives

Historically, social science research associated with family planning has focused on predicting contraceptive use or non-use. Because most modern contraceptive methods are designed for use by women, and because most programmes assume that women are primarily responsible for family planning, women have been the primary subjects of contraceptive and family planning research. Researchers have asked the question, "How do various aspects of women's lives (e.g., residence, educational status, age at marriage, employment) affect the likelihood, or level, of family planning use?" (Bulatao and Lee, 1983; Mason, 1984). An exception to this line of inquiry was raised by Dixon, who, in 1975, theorized that the status of women both determines and is a consequence of variations in fertility. She suggested that the ability to plan childbearing "may be examined separately for its effect on a woman's health, the health of her children and the exercise of her economic, social and political rights" (p. 3). The question was subsequently phrased, "How does family planning affect various aspects of women's lives?"

Recently, programmatic research has addressed the need for population policies and family planning programmes to become more client-centered and to address women's rights (Bruce, 1990; Dixon-Mueller, 1993). Jacobson (1992:44) writes, "In assigning 'rights and duties,' the emphasis [of population policies] is too often placed on the obligations of couples to have smaller families, and too rarely on the duties of governments to ensure that their people have the resources required to meet basic needs." According to de Barbieri (1993:87), "population policies appear to want to reduce the population growth rate without any fundamental alteration in existing social relations and inequalities."

Critics of past family planning policies have challenged researchers to enlarge their vision and to focus on women's perceptions and experiences with family planning, women's reproductive health needs and the effect family planning use has had on their lives (Hong and Seltzer, 1994). For example, Berer (1993:8) states that often women are caught in the middle of both pro- and anti-natalism—"encouraged to say no to sex and early marriage on the one hand, but denied the alternatives that education, paid employment and social independence would bring on the other hand." Women's advocates and researchers around the world are raising new questions as to whether—and under what circumstances—greater contraceptive use and reduced fertility improve women's lives. To what extent is contraceptive use an important ingredient for a more personally, socially or economically rewarding life for women, beyond the well-documented benefits of family planning to the health of women and the welfare of their children? In other words, both groups want to understand the effect of family planning on the *quality* of women's lives. The purpose of this paper is to outline a conceptual framework developed to study the impact of family planning on women's lives and to present a number of studies being undertaken based on the framework.

The Women's Studies Project

In order to help expand the research agenda on family planning and women's lives, Family Health International (FHI) began a five-year Women's Studies Project (WSP) in 1993, with funding from the United States Agency for International Development (USAID). The objectives of the WSP are, first, to support social and behavioural research on the consequences for women of family planning decisions and, second, to provide information to help strengthen reproductive health policies and programmes through better understanding of women's needs and perspectives.

These two basic objectives are guiding the WSP in 12 countries. Six countries are considered emphasis countries because they are the site of more than one study, and research is being directed by in-country advisory committees. These countries are Brazil, Bolivia, Egypt, the Philippines, Indonesia, and Zimbabwe. In addition, China, Jamaica and Mali are the sites of one WSP study each. The study in China is being supported with funding from the Rockefeller Foundation. Finally, in three countries—Nigeria, Bangladesh and Malaysia—the WSP has supported secondary analysis of existing data.

In each of the WSP countries, the research agenda differs somewhat depending on how stakeholders in the country have prioritized specific reproductive health issues. The common denominator, however, remains the effect of family planning on women's lives.

WSP Conceptual Framework

To guide WSP research, FHI has developed a conceptual framework that adds the day-to-day experiences of women to traditional outcomes of fertility control. The framework takes into account the larger context of social, cultural, economic and other factors associated with the quality of women's lives as defined by women themselves. While this conceptual framework is not being rigidly applied to all WSP research and is being adapted to different content areas, the conceptual framework is useful in describing the WSP in general and in guiding our work. The framework also helps researchers in WSP countries conceptualize their studies and allows them to achieve a measure of comparability among the studies. In addition, the conceptual framework can be used to help identify gaps in research.

In developing a framework to assess the impact of family planning on women's lives, understanding both the concept of gender and the roles of women are important. While sex is a biological distinction, gender is defined as the socially constructed roles ascribed to males and females. "This means that from birth, males and females are reared to occupy different social positions having different rights and obligations". (Mason, 1994:2). Socialization varies from individual to individual, and gender norms can change over time and vary widely within and among cultures (UNFPA, 1992). Gender, while important, is a social classifier that operates in conjunction with other classifiers, such as social class, culture, race and religion (Charlton, 1988).

While Gender ascribes certain roles to women, an important consideration in research is the roles women play in a society, compared to those of men. Rather than the dual roles of reproduction and production that are generally ascribed to women, Moser (1989:1801) notes that women have three roles. "In most low-income households, 'women's work' includes not only reproductive work (the childbearing and rearing responsibilities)... but also productive work, often as secondary income earners.) ... [In addition,] women, within their gender-ascribed role of wives and mothers, struggle to manage their neighbourhoods." At the community level, men often have a leadership role reflected in political participation, whereas women have a community management role, based on the provision of items of collective consumption. Demographic change, both at the individual and national level, can affect gender norms, women's roles and the time devoted to each role (Freedman and Blanc, 1991; McCauley *et al.*, 1994).

In proposing a WSP conceptual framework, we have benefited in our thinking from Oppong's framework on the seven roles of women (1980); Hong and Seltzer's framework of family planning and the six domains of women's lives (1994); Schuler and Hashemi's framework of women's empowerment (1993); quality of life studies (Spilker, 1990; Waszak *et al.*, 1994); Stycos' model of the psychosocial consequences of contraceptive use for women (1995), and the International Reproductive Rights Research Action Group's conceptualization of women's perception of their reproductive rights (IRRRAG, 1994; 1995).

The WSP conceptual framework has four main clusters of variables. Within the large box, two clusters of variables focus on the woman herself. One cluster contains the variables on family planning provision and use and women's experiences with pregnancy and childbearing. The other focuses on three domains of women's lives: the individual domain, the household and family sphere, and societal and economic roles. These two clusters, which are the primary outcomes of interest to the WSP, are influenced by two sets of societal factors and another set of individual factors. Societal factors include the social, political and economic context in which a woman lives and the gender norms that shape her life. Finally, a woman's life cycle stage and other socio-demographic characteristics shape her family planning use, her childbearing experience and the three domains of her life (individual, family and community).

Family Planning Experience: The starting point of the WSP conceptual framework is women's experience as users of family planning programmes. This cluster of variables includes types of programmes (e.g., public or private, integrated with other development activities or non-integrated), types of service providers (e.g., physicians or other service providers, male or female providers), and the quality of services. Aspects of services that may have an impact on a woman's experience with contraception include the sex of the provider, the organization of the service (integrated or vertical), the availability of services and methods, and the quality of interaction with service personnel and amount of counseling and information received by the client.

Increasingly, countries are moving beyond family planning to a more encompassing view of the role of reproductive health in women's lives; thus, the framework includes use of other reproductive health services as another dimension that may affect contraceptive use and childbearing experience. Reproductive health services will vary by country but might include sexually transmitted disease (STD) diagnosis and treatment, general gynecological care, infertility counseling and treatment, maternal health services and abortion services, among others.

The model also draws attention to both use and non-use of contraceptives. In addition to the standard notion of use of contraceptive methods, we have included non-use by women who do not desire pregnancy, as well as by women who may desire pregnancy but are unable to achieve it. What is behind a woman's active or passive decision not to use a method, or to discontinue a method once she has started it? What are the consequences of unwanted pregnancy? If she uses contraception, other questions arise: What side effects do different methods have? And does the person who determines the method a woman gets make a difference in her experience with that method?

Use of reproductive health services may influence contraceptive use (e.g., if a women hears of family planning during a postnatal visit to a maternal and child health clinic) or it may affect childbearing experience (e.g., if a woman receives infertility treatment). Reproductive health services can be obtained through the family planning programme or through a different programme (e.g., an STD diagnosis and treatment center). The availability of general primary care for women or STD diagnosis and treatment may influence how a woman experiences family planning.

Since the use of contraception has a direct impact on a woman's childbearing experience, pregnancy and childbearing are pivotal concepts in the conceptual framework. Along with the number of births or live children a woman has, fertility variables also may include a woman's ability to space, delay or limit children, as well as her experience with infertility, child loss or planned or unplanned childlessness.

Domains of Women's Lives: In this framework, the outcomes of contraceptive use are expressed as consequences for various aspects of women's lives. These concepts are the dependent variables in most of the WSP studies and have been combined into three dimensions of a woman's life: societal and economic, family and household, and the woman as individual. Together these dimensions reflect the quality of a woman's life. Quality of life is an elusive concept, which combines objective elements with subjective perceptions and interpretations of personal experience. As such, it is observable only through an individual's self-reporting and is influenced by the social and cultural context of norms, values and expectations that give meaning to everyday life.

It is difficult to fit the complexity and richness of a woman's life into a classificatory scheme. However, although cultural and individual differences challenge generalization, the WSP has attempted to construct a framework that reflects aspects of women's lives most likely to be affected by family planning and reproductive health. Below we discuss these three dimensions of women's lives and give examples of WSP studies designed to assess each dimension.

Societal and Economic Roles: A woman who uses contraception may have more opportunities to become involved in the workforce and in community-based activities, because having fewer children may relieve some of the domestic burden inherent in raising a large family. On the other hand, the same woman may be negatively perceived by the community for failing to produce as many children as expected. Thus, the impact of contraceptive use on the public lives of women is variable, depending on numerous contextual and mediating factors.

Women's social and economic lives may be operationalized in terms of their participation in community activities; access to community resources, education and employment opportunities; and access to health care services, security in old age and the status accorded to women by others in their communities. Economic productivity is an important aspect of this dimension. Through both formal and non-formal work roles, women contribute to the economy.

The extent to which contraceptive use and fertility influence the nature of women's work has not been well studied; hence, WSP researchers at the Carolina Population Center, FHI and the University of San Carlos in Cebu, Philippines, chose to examine the complex relationships between women's use of family planning and their participation in the workforce, including type of work, salary, mobility and job satisfaction. Similarly, WSP research in Bolivia is exploring women's access to credit and the effect of a recent pregnancy on work characteristics/economic activities. Focusing on the early adult years, researchers at the University of Zimbabwe are investigating how early sexual experience and access to contraception may have shaped the vocational goals of young women and influenced their ability to pursue desired careers.

A woman's ability to choose how she will allocate her time to work, family, community activity, political action or leisure is critical to this dimension. In the WSP study being carried out at Xavier University in the Philippines, time allocation is a key variable, operationalized as how women balance their time across several domains, including family roles and interpersonal relations, employment, community participation and personal leisure. The Demographic Institute of the University of Indonesia is assessing whether use of contraception influences women's decisions to join the labor market, and whether labor market activities and earning power affect household decision-making and plans for children's futures. A study at the University of Zimbabwe has added a political change component to their explanation of this dimension of societal and economic roles—the participation of its women in community advocacy, as well as local elections, political campaigns and even running for office themselves. At issue in these and other WSP studies is the extent to which a woman who has taken control of her own fertility is empowered to act independently in other domains as well.

Household and Family Roles: Women's household and family roles include those of spouse/partner, household head, parent/guardian, and nuclear and/or extended family member (including being one wife of a polygamous husband). In many cultures, the status of women is derived from their performance in these roles, along with cultural expectations of how women "should" behave relative to others in the household unit. A woman's interaction with her spouse and other family members concerning decisions about family size may improve communication and strengthen relationships. On the other hand, it may result in negative sanctions, including domestic violence. Although the nature of women's domestic roles varies across cultures, common denominators may be found in partner relations (including issues of sexuality and sexual relations), family communication and dynamics, household decision-making, role strain and violence against women. A WSP study in Indonesia is addressing women's empowerment in the family as a result of family planning use and work experience. A follow-up study of the Cebu longitudinal survey in the

Philippines includes a module on household decision-making. This module examines who makes decisions and what women do if they disagree with their partners or other household members.

Among several aspects of women's household and family roles being examined in a study of the consequences of tubal legation in Brazil, marital stability and affective relations with partners and children have been emphazised. Family relations are also a focus of studies in Egypt and Bolivia. In a secondary analysis of data from the Malaysia Family Life Study, WSP research at Cornell University found that, compared to non-users, women who used any method of family planning in the 1970s were less likely to be divorced or separated by the late 1980s (Kritz & Gurak, 1995).

In the extended family that values high fertility, a woman who uses contraception and produces fewer children may find herself in a state of conflict with her husband's relatives. The Center for Research on Population and Development in Mali is conducting a prospective qualitative study of new users of contraception. One outcome of interest in this study is the dynamic of family communication and its relationship to women's subsequent decisions to continue, change or abandon the method they have adopted. In this study, as in a study at the University of Zimbabwe of the mediating effects of gender on women's participation in development, researchers are focusing on the normative context in which empowerment emanating from a woman's decision to take control of her own fertility may be encouraged or discouraged, depending on the gender-based expectations of male partners and affinal family members. Similarly, researchers in Cochabamba, Bolivia, are examining the effects of fertility regulation on the quality of conjugal relationships as perceived by both spouses, highlighting aspects such as satisfaction with communication and the influence of extended family members on couples' decisions regarding use of economic resources and family planning.

Individual Psychological and Physical Factors: Numerous studies in the past 15 years have documented the impact of family planning on women's physical health and well-being, offering strong evidence that the health benefits of contraception outweigh the risks. In contrast, a woman's psychological well-being, or the personal satisfaction she may or may not derive from critical decisions that affect her fertility and reproductive life, remain largely unexplored. Use of contraception may have positive psychological effects if it relieves women of anxiety about pregnancy and abortion. Negative effects may occur for a woman if she is using contraception secretly, or if she experiences or fears side effects or the disapproval of her spouse and others.

The meanings of psychosocial concepts such as self-esteem, self-efficacy, satisfaction, control, personal autonomy (or their opposites in alienation, subordination, fear or guilt) are variable across cultures and subcultures but no less critical to understanding the effects of family planning decisions on women's lives. For example, one might speculate that use of contraception would promote a woman's sense of autonomy and increase her ability to make decisions in other areas of her life. But, in countries with strict family planning programmes, such as China and Indonesia, women may feel their autonomy is limited by strong government promotion of the use of contraception. In another example, a woman who is unable to bear children may experience loss of self-esteem and severe role strain in relations with her spouse or family. Or, conversely, she may find a sense of personal empowerment, considering childlessness an opportunity to become more active in the workforce or the community. Sexual health, including sexuality, is an equally important and unexamined component of psychological well-being and is closely related to a woman's relationship with her spouse or partner.

Psychosocial factors tend to be difficult to measure and, hence, are often neglected in family planning research. However, several WSP studies are focusing on this dimension, attempting to operationalize women's sense of themselves as women, conditioned by the cultural milieu of which they are a part. A study in El Alto, Bolivia, is exploring the effects of both modern and traditional contraceptive use on women's self-esteem and locus of control (i.e., whether she feels events in her life are controlled by her or by external forces) and asks, in addition, whether use of contraception enhances or diminishes sexual satisfaction for women and men. At the American University in Cairo, researchers also are examining the effects of family planning use on Egyptian women's self-esteem and personal autonomy. WSP researchers at Atma Jaya University in Indonesia regard the impact of family planning on women's self-image as an important focus of study, hypothesizing that positive self-image leads to greater empowerment for women, which in turn may be the foundation for a better quality of life. Using primarily qualitative techniques to explore individual perspectives, the quality of women's lives is being studied in several countries. For example, University of Zimbabwe researchers will conduct focus group discussions to explore cultural constructions of quality of life and how the consequences of fertility may influence the quality of a woman's life positively or negatively.

The framework includes three additional sets of factors. These factors affect the family planning/contraceptive use/childbearing experience of women, as well as the three domains of their lives and, therefore, must be controlled in studies. The first set includes *social, political and macro-economic factors* that affect all aspects of women's lives and the impact of family planning. These include, among others, political system and climate, economic environment, prevailing religious climate, legal system and availability of educational and employment opportunities. Also relevant in this context is a country's population policy, which might call for compulsory use of family planning or, conversely, might be pro-natalist.

Gender norms, which interact with social, political and economic factors, affect all aspects of women's lives. Mason has theorized that when assessing demographic change, it is more important to understand "institutionalized gender stratification in society's allocative processes... [than] the position of individual women on various measurable social hierarchies... (1994:1)." She notes the need to study, at a macro-level, both gender norms and the processes by which valued goods are distributed among individuals, including access to and control over material resources; decision-making autonomy and freedom of movement; sexual norms and women's sexual freedom; legal rights; and public roles. For example, the system of *purdah,* which operates in many Islamic countries, greatly constrains women's movement outside their homes and family environment and the opportunities available to women (Schuler and Hashemi, 1994). Gender inequality can affect reproductive decisions made at the household level, as well as the nature of services that are provided and the individual who decides how services are provided. For example, family planning programmes have traditionally targeted women for contraceptive use. Recently, the need for male responsibility has been articulated around the world, but thus far, with little change in service provision.

Along with this institutional and normative context, a woman's *life cycle stage* forms part of the background against which we will try to understand the perspectives of the women who participate in our studies. Life cycle stage of the woman and *other personal factors* can affect fertility regardless of contraceptive use, as well as the three dimensions of women's lives noted in the framework. Adolescents, single and married women of reproductive age, and older women will be affected differently by family planning and childbearing experiences. For example, the intensity of a woman's feelings about her situation may change over time. A woman in her 20s who finds she cannot have children may express stronger feelings than the same woman in her 40s. Likewise, a woman with small children may experience more role strain than the same woman whose children are grown. Life cycle stage itself can affect women's lives, irrespective of family planning use. Other personal attributes such as ethnicity, social class and residence can also affect contraceptive use and its impact on women's lives. Social class can mediate the effects of gender in that women of different social classes are often held to different standards. In some cases, women of a higher social class have greater mobility and the ability to work, while in other cases, women of higher social class have more constraints in their movements outside the home.

As noted by Hong and Seltzer (1994) in their framework on the impact of family planning on six domains of women's lives, we acknowledge the difficulty in distinguishing direction of causality. We have included arrows indicating multiple lines of causality in this conceptual framework to reflect the complexity of women's lives. The studies outlined in the next section are one step in helping to establish directions of causality in the relationship between family planning and women's lives.

WSP Studies and the Conceptual Framework

Each WSP study fits into the conceptual framework. Some studies are more comprehensive, addressing multiple aspects of the framework, while others are more focused. All of the studies, with the exception of one in Egypt that focuses on family planning providers, include contraceptive use/non-use and pregnancy/childbearing experience. Nine studies address all three dimensions of women's lives, five address the household/family and community/society roles, and three address primarily individual, psychosocial and physical factors, and family/household factors. Two studies focus on individual, psychosocial and physical factors, and one focuses on individual and community/society roles.

Following is a brief description of each WSP study collecting primary data, along with an illustration of how the project fits into the conceptual framework:

- *Bolivia—Impact of Men's Knowledge, Attitudes and Behaviour Regarding Fertility Regulation on Women's Lives*: A study in Cochabamba by the Cooperazione Internazionale and the University of San Sim explores men's and women's knowledge, attitudes and behaviour regarding family planning, reproductive health, information sources on reproductive health, ideal family size, sex preferences, and socioeconomic and demographic characteristics. It seeks to determine the influence of these factors on family planning use and satisfaction. Men's knowledge, attitudes and behaviours are also examined as mediating the effect of family planning use on women's self-esteem, locus of control and economic activity. A cross-sectional survey is being conducted, using a multistage probability sample of 600 couples, with women's ages ranging from 20 to 49. The primary independent and dependent variables being examined in this study are: gender norms, contraceptive use/non-use, use of other reproductive health services, household and family roles and psychological and physical factors. The variables of secondary interest are:
  - family planning programmes,
  - pregnancy and childbearing experience, and·
  - societal and economic roles.
- *Bolivia—Psychosocial Impact of Fertility Regulation of Women*: The Proyecto Integral en Salud in El Alto is examining the psychosocial impact of fertility regulation, both on the couple (in terms of couple stability, sexual relations and standard of living) and on the individual level (in terms of sexuality, self-esteem and locus of control). The study is carrying out in-depth interviews with three groups of 35 women: those currently using modern contraception, those who have quit using a modern method for reasons other than a desire to become

pregnant and those who know about modern methods but never have used one. Men make up a fourth group. The primary variables in this study are:

- contraceptive use/non-use,
- pregnancy and childbearing experience,
- household/family roles, and
- psychological and physical factors.

- *Brazil—Adolescent Longitudinal Study*: In Fortaleza, Brazil, a three-year study is being undertaken among two groups of adolescents, ages 12 to 18, who have sought medical attention at the Maternidade Escola Assis Chateaubriand (MEAC). The first group is composed of 400 pregnant teens seeking prenatal care; the second consists of 200 teens who have undergone an incomplete abortion and are seeking treatment. The study seeks to discern whether there are differences between these two groups in terms of socioeconomic status, psychological measures, personal and professional aspirations, and whether the pregnancy had been planned. The study is following the adolescents to determine if there are changes over time in their family planning use, acceptance of the pregnancy, school attendance and relationships with their parents and male partners. A sample of the teens' mothers is being interviewed, to look at mother-daughter patterns of reproductive decision-making. The study also asks the participants about their perceptions of the advantages and disadvantages of their choice to continue or abort the pregnancy, both for their lives and those of their partners. In this longitudinal study, pregnant teens are being interviewed four times:
  - when they arrive at MEAC for their first prenatal visit,
  - at approximately week 35 of their pregnancy,
  - at day 45 postpartum, and
  - at one year postpartum.

  Abortion patients will be interviewed three times: 1) before hospital discharge, 2) day 45 post-abortion and 3) one year post-abortion. While not reflected in the conceptual framework, an additional objective of the study is to measure impact of pregnancy intendedness and acceptance on the child's development at age one. The primary variables being examined in this study are: pregnancy and childbearing experience, household/family roles, psychological and physical factors, and societal/economic roles. The secondary variable is contraceptive use/non-use.
- *Brazil—Comparative Study of the Consequences of Tubal Legation for Women's Lives*: This study, conducted by the Centro de Pesquisas das Doen? Materno-Infantis (CEMICAMP) in Campinas, examines the experiences and perceptions of women who have undergone tubal legation. The study centers on how sterilization affects the course of

women's lives in terms of work history, time allocation, marital stability, educational attainment and psychosocial variables, such as self-esteem and affective relationships with partners and children. Using a probability sample, 388 women who have undergone tubal legation at least five years prior to the study and 388 women (of the same age and community) who have not been sterilized are being interviewed. The interviews are being conducted in the women's homes. The surveys include open-ended questions on psychosocial variables and women's perceptions of their life experiences within the last five years. Focus groups were used to develop the questionnaires for both groups. The primary variables in this study are: contraceptive use/non-use, household/family roles, psychological and physical factors, and societal/economic roles. The secondary variable is pregnancy/childbearing experience.

- *People's Republic of China—Impact of Family Planning on Women's Lives*: The Chinese Population Information and Research Center is investigating how family planning has affected the various roles women play and the opportunities they have had. The study addresses the changing roles and positions of women in the household and family, family relations and the value of children, changing roles of women in society and the community, and changing individual psychological and physical factors that have resulted from the use of family planning and subsequent childbearing experience. The study is being carried out in Jiangsu Province, which has a booming economy and a rapid decline in fertility, and in Anhui Province, which has an agrarian economy and a less effective family planning programme. A survey and focus group discussions are being conducted among women and men, and case studies of 40 four-generation families will be undertaken. The primary variables in this study are: contraceptive use/non-use, family planning programmes, pregnancy/childbearing experience, household/family roles, psychological and physical factors, and societal/economic roles. The secondary variable is use of other reproductive health services.
- *Egypt—Impact of Family Planning on the Lives of Egyptian Women*: The American University in Cairo is examining family planning's effects on women's self-esteem, personal autonomy, family relationships, public standing, educational level, work for cash outside the home, economic resources and physical and psychological health. Formative qualitative research, focus group discussions and in-depth interviews, in rural and urban areas of Upper and Lower Egypt will identify the relationships as perceived by Egyptian women between use of family planning and other aspects of their lives. Hypotheses generated by these discussions will be tested in a household survey of

a representative sample of women drawn from six (of 26) governorates. Some 4,500 women overall will be interviewed, including 800 women who will be re-interviewed in a sample of two villages in Menoufia Governorate in a retrospective longitudinal study. Data from the sub-sample of these 800 women will be linked to data from a 1990-91 survey among the same group. This previous survey dealt with women's and children's health and family planning. The primary variables in this study are: contraceptive use/non-use, household/family roles, psychological and physical factors, and societal/economic roles. The secondary variables are: family planning programmes and pregnancy/childbearing experience.

- *Egypt—Role of Women as Family Planning Employees*: The Cairo Demographic Center is implementing a study to test the Hong-Seltzer conceptual framework by assessing the role of women (as physicians, nurses, social workers and dayas) in the Egyptian family planning programme. The study consists of two phases: quantitative and qualitative. The quantitative phase involves collecting data on female employees in family planning programmes from official records. The qualitative research will explore perceptions among approximately 600 female family planning employees in four governorates in Upper and Lower Egypt of how their jobs have affected other aspects of their lives. Findings from this study will provide greater understanding of the contributions women make to the family planning programme in Egypt and will identify strengths and weaknesses of the programme for its female employees from their own points of view and its effect on their own lives (e.g., autonomy, self-esteem) as well as their husbands'.
- *Indonesia—Impact of Family Planning on Women's Economic Activity and Household Autonomy*: The Demographic Institute of the University of Indonesia is focusing on Indonesian women's labor force participation. The study will examine whether family planning use affects a woman's decision to enter the labor force and whether labor force participation, in turn, influences a woman's bargaining power in household decision-making, specifically with respect to family spending, contraceptive use and plans for children's futures. Secondary analysis of the 1993/1994 Indonesian Family Life Survey (IFLS) is looking at the relationships between reproductive histories, including contraceptive use, and work histories. A qualitative research component, using in-depth interviews, is exploring more fully the relationships among contraceptive use, labor force participation and autonomy in household decision-making. The qualitative component of the study is being conducted in North Sumatra and West Java. The primary variables are: contraceptive use/non-use, pregnancy/

childbearing experience, household/family roles, societal/economic roles. The secondary variable is family planning programmes.

- *Indonesia—Impact of Contraceptive Use and Fertility on Family Welfare and Women's Activities*: The Population Studies Center of Gadjah Mada University is analyzing the effect that family planning practice and number of children have on family welfare and women's social and economic activities. "Family welfare" is defined by the Indonesian family planning programme (BKKBN) as, "legal marriage, capable of adequately fulfilling spiritual and material needs, devoted to God Almighty, possessing harmonious, proportionate and balanced relations among its members and between the family and society." A survey is being conducted among 800 women in Central and East Java. Additionally, a sub-sample of about 2 percent of the women and their husbands is participating in in-depth interviews. In-depth interviews also are being conducted with community leaders. The primary variables are: contraceptive use/non-use, pregnancy/childbearing experience, household/family roles, societal/economic roles. The secondary variable is family planning programmes.
- *Indonesia—Impact of Family Planning on Women's Empowerment in the Family*: The Women's Studies Center of the University of Indonesia is investigating women's use of contraception and economic autonomy, social autonomy and empowerment in the family. The study examines the husband's support of women's economic and social autonomy among working and non-working wives who are users and non-users of family planning. A secondary goal of the project is to assess, from the client's perspective, the extent to which the family planning programme is gender-sensitive. Approximately 800 women, ages 30 to 45, in Jakarta and Udung Pandang, South Sulawesi, will be surveyed. In order to obtain more detailed information, the survey results will be supported by an in-depth study of 18 couples in each city. In situations where a woman lives in an extended family household, other family members may be interviewed in addition to her husband. Local leaders also are being interviewed to collect information on the status of women in the communities in which they live. The primary variables are: contraceptive use/non-use, pregnancy/childbearing experience, household/family roles, psychological and physical factors, and societal/economic roles. The secondary variable is family planning programmes.
- *Indonesia—Women's Reproductive Decision-Making and Its Relation to Psychological Well-Being*: The Atma Jaya Research Center of Atma Jaya University and the Women's Studies Programme of the University of Indonesia are examining who is involved in the decision to use or not use family planning, how the woman views her position in this process in relation to others' positions, what happens when opinions differ (including

whose decision usually is dominant) and what kind of support women receive from family planning programmes for reproductive decision-making. The study also explores whether family planning decisions are related to career choices and whether the woman's experience with the process of making those decisions influences her level of self-esteem and the couple's marital adjustment. Women's reactions to family planning failures (especially abortion and its consequences) are being related to their self-image and their views of others. Approximately 800 married women, ages 25 to 49, are being surveyed in Lampung and South Sumatra. In addition, focus group discussions are being conducted with women, their spouses and service providers to explore issues facing women in family planning, and in-depth interviews will be held with 24 couples to collect general information about women's experiences in family planning and the decision-making process. The primary variables are: contraceptive use/non-use, pregnancy/childbearing experience, household/family roles, and psychological and physical factors. The secondary variable is family planning programmes.

- *Jamaica—The Jamaica Adolescent Study (Evaluation of a Project to Delay First Pregnancy)*: The Fertility Management Unit of the University of the West Indies is conducting a study on young adolescents at high risk of unplanned pregnancy and fatherhood. The Grade 7 Project, being implemented by the Women's Centre of Jamaica Foundation, is a new in-school family life education programme designed to increase 7th graders' knowledge of sexuality issues, improve decision-making skills and increase self-esteem. These changes are hypothesized to make students more likely to postpone first intercourse and use family planning methods. The Jamaica Adolescent Study is documenting the implementation of the Grade 7 Project and assessing prospectively its effects over a three-year period. In addition, the study explores the sexual and reproductive attitudes and behaviours of Jamaican adolescents as they make the transition into adulthood. Approximately 500 students in the Grade 7 Project and 500 students in a comparison group completed a knowledge, attitudes and practices (KAP) questionnaire in September 1995, before the Grade 7 Project began. The same students again completed the questionnaire from May to June 1996, when the Grade 7 Project ended, and will complete the questionnaire again one year later. The students participating in the study attend 10 different schools, both urban and rural, in five Jamaican parishes. Additionally, eight groups of students, with boys and girls in separate groups, are participating in focus groups at two points in time during the study period. The family life education programme should be considered part of the "family planning programmes" box in the conceptual framework. The primary variables are: contraceptive use/non-use, family planning programmes, pregnancy/childbearing experience, psychological and physical factors, and life cycle stage and other personal factors. The secondary variable is societal/economic roles.

- *Mali—Impact of Family Planning Use on the Lives of New Contraceptive Users in Bamako*: The Centre d'Etudes et de Recherche sur la Population pour le D?loppement (CERPOD) in Mali is looking at how family planning use influences a woman's communication with her spouse and in-laws, her employment status and her power in household decision-making. The study explores, among new users, experiences consequent to their decision to adopt family planning and identifies strategies women use to achieve their reproductive objectives and enhance their economic status in the household and the community. Investigators are following 55 new family planning users over a 15-month period, using in-depth interviews and focus group discussions. Interviews focus on the dynamics of communication in the family concerning reproductive decisions, including control, persuasion and conflict resolution; support/non-support for family planning decisions; the woman's role in household economic decisions, and the woman's economic activity. The primary variables are: contraceptive use/non-use, household/family roles, and societal/economic roles. The secondary variable is pregnancy/childbearing experience.
- *Philippines—Cebu Longitudinal Follow-Up Survey and In-Depth Interviews*: Researchers from the University of San Carlos in Cebu, Philippines, and the University of North Carolina, with assistance from FHI, are conducting a follow-up study to the Cebu Longitudinal Health and Nutrition Survey (CLHNS). The original survey was administered in 1983-86, and the first follow-up study was conducted in 1991-92. The new survey adds a third set of individual, household and community data to the existing data from the prospective survey begun in 1983, thereby providing the time depth needed for a comprehensive view over a significant portion of women's reproductive lives. The new survey collects data on women's lives, particularly work and income histories; health and nutritional status; education, and issues relating to women's status and decision-making. The study sample includes approximately 2,300 women from the original CLHNS who are still living in the Metro Cebu area. In addition, a new sample of 500 women, ages 15 to 25, has been added. The main survey is being supplemented by a series of three in-depth ethnographic interviews with a subset of 60 women. These in-depth interviews provide detailed data on the process of decision-making and women's perceptions about family planning and their childbearing experience. The primary variables are: contraceptive use/non-use, household/family roles,

psychological and physical factors, and societal/economic roles. The secondary variable is pregnancy/childbearing experience.

- *Philippines—Economic and Psychosocial Influences of Family Planning on Lives of Women in Western Visayas*: Central Philippines University is collaborating with local women's groups and family planning organizations to conduct a study of about 1,100 ever-married women from urban and rural communities in the province of Negros Oriental. The study combines information from survey interviews, focus group discussions and in-depth interviews to examine the association between family planning practice and selected psychosocial and economic characteristics of women's lives. Pre-survey focus group discussions were used to establish appropriate measures of psychosocial indicators, such as "quality of life," "self-esteem" and "self-image." Post-survey focus groups will examine perceptions and views on the impact of family planning on women's lives among women who were not survey respondents, women who are members of women's groups and non-governmental organizations, and selected husbands. In-depth interviews are being conducted with key informants who are expected to have knowledge about the influence of family planning on the lives of women. These informants include family planning providers, members of women's groups involved in family planning, family planning motivators, community volunteers and husbands of family planning users and non-users. Results of the in-depth interviews also will be used to validate, supplement and complement survey results and/or elaborate on the influences of family planning practice on women's lives. The primary variables are: contraceptive use/non-use, psychological and physical factors, and societal/economic roles. The secondary variables are: family planning programmes and pregnancy/childbearing experience.
- *Philippines—Social and Economic Consequences of Family Planning Use in the Southern Philippines*: Data from two surveys and a set of focus group discussions are being used to examine the effects of family planning use on the lives of about 1,250 urban and rural women in Mindanao. Special emphasis is given to psychosocial well-being, employment and time allocation, including time for leisure and rest. The first survey interviewed a sample of about 250 rural ever-married women, ages 15 to 49, who were previously surveyed in 1994 for a UNICEF-funded maternal and child health study. The rural sample consists of women from higher-and lower-income communities and from tribal communities. The longitudinal data on the rural women allows examination of short-term effects of family planning use on selected outcomes. The second sample of 1,000 urban women was selected using a two-stage clustered sampling procedure, in which the

first stage consists of all urban communities in Cagayan de Oro and the second stage consists of married women ages 15 to 49. To supplement the quantitative data, focus group discussions are being conducted with a subset of the women and their husbands. The primary variables are: contraceptive use/non-use, household/family roles, and societal/economic roles. The secondary variables are: pregnancy/childbearing experience and psychological and physical factors.

- *Zimbabwe—Impact of Family Planning on Women's Participation in the Development Process*: The University of Zimbabwe's Department of Sociology is looking broadly at the extent to which women who control their fertility also control other important aspects of their lives. By analyzing key social, economic and political events in women's lives in relation to their reproductive history, investigators are examining the relationships between contraceptive use/non-use and the roles that women play in household, educational, economic and political domains. The study examines the link between family planning use or non-use and women's condition (defined as employment, land ownership and/or use of credit facilities), their position in the household (defined as their role in decision-making about family size, use of income, children's education, their own employment and whether they are allowed to travel outside the home) and their position in the community (defined as their involvement in public demonstrations and/or politics). The study also asks women about their levels of knowledge regarding local and national government and marriage and inheritance laws. Background information will be analyzed from the 1987 and 1994 DHS data sets and from the Socio-Cultural Study, which was conducted in 1992. Original data will be collected in a household survey of a national sample of 2,500 women, using the Zimbabwe Revised Master Sample. The primary variables are: contraceptive use/non-use, pregnancy/childbearing experience, household/family roles, and societal/economic roles.
- *Zimbabwe—Impact of Family Planning on Academic Achievement and Vocational Goals of Young Women*: The University of Zimbabwe's Sociology Department is gathering information on women's early experiences with sexuality and reproductive health and the ways that access to contraception has shaped their academic and vocational goals. Many young women drop out of the educational system when they become pregnant, jeopardizing the opportunity to acquire the knowledge and status they need to pursue social and economic goals associated with lower fertility. The study is tracing reproductive, academic and vocational events in the lives of sexually active young women who have left school due to pregnancy and comparing them with students who have remained in or returned to school. It is identifying factors that may be associated with the ability of sexually active young women to continue

on a course that will enable them to achieve their academic and vocational aspirations. All currently enrolled female students, ages 18 to 25, in three teacher training colleges are being surveyed. Additionally, in-depth interviews will be held with 30 women under the age of 26 who have just given birth and who indicate that they quit school because of this most recent pregnancy, as well as with 30 mothers in the community who dropped out of school for pregnancy at an earlier point in their lives. The primary variables are: contraceptive use/non-use, pregnancy/childbearing experience, and psychological and physical factors. The secondary variable is societal/economic roles.

- *Zimbabwe—Attitudes of Significant Others and their Mediating Effects on Impact of Family Planning on Women's Participation in Development*: The University of Zimbabwe's Institute for Development Studies is examining the roles of husbands and affinal family members in determining the extent to which women contraceptive users participate in development activities. Family planning has been promoted as a means of reducing the domestic burden, freeing women to participate in economic and other status-enhancing activities. There is little scientific evidence, however, to document whether family members encourage women in these activities or whether strong family ties in a patriarchal society discourage women from taking strategic advantage of opportunities for personal advancement. This study uses qualitative methods to gain insight into the influence of significant others (husbands and older affinal female family members) on the ability of women with large and small families to participate in three domains: household decision-making, economic activity and political action. In-depth interviews are being held in both rural and urban communities with four types of participants: married women ages 25 to 40 using contraception and having one to four children; married women ages 25 to 40 using contraception and having five or more children; married men ages 25 to 50, and women over age 40 whose extended families include daughters-in-law. Focus group discussions also will be held to gather normative data on attitudes, values and expectations of men and older women regarding women's participation in development activities and the role that family members play in determining how women with larger and smaller families allocate their time. The primary variables are: societal, political and economic factors; contraceptive use/non-use; pregnancy/childbearing experience; gender norms; household/family roles; and societal/economic roles.
- *Zimbabwe—Consequences of Family Planning for Women's Quality of Life, Self-Esteem and Empowerment to Act*: The Department of Community Medicine at the University of Zimbabwe is asking Zimbabwean women to define what "quality of life" means to them,

including how this concept is shaped by factors such as their roles in household decision-making about family size; use of income and children's education; the time they have to devote to work versus leisure activities; their participation in the labor force, and the nature of the paid labor they do and their level of political involvement. The women also are being asked about consequences of family planning for their quality of life, as they define it, and the strategies they have developed to overcome potentially negative consequences. Data will be collected through focus group discussions, comparing women on the basis of age, education, and residence (rural/urban). The primary variables are: pregnancy/childbearing experience, household/family roles, psychological and physical factors, and societal/economic roles. The secondary variable is contraceptive use/non-use.

Summary

Women's lives are complex and multidimensional; thus representing women's lives in a simple framework is difficult. FHI's Women's Studies Project has developed a framework that we think captures the dynamic sequence (and feedback) of the impact that family planning can have on the lives of women, from adolescence to the older ages. While many of the elements of this framework are similar to earlier models, three additional concepts have been added:

a) the life cycle;
b) the notion of childbearing experience, which includes unfulfilled pregnancy desires and infant and child mortality, rather than just the use of family planning to delay, space or limit births, and
c) the role that other reproductive health services play both in family planning use and in women's lives more generally.

In addition, the framework includes the three broad dimensions of women's lives:

a) the personal,
b) the familial, and
c) the societal.

This framework has been useful in helping to conceptualize and design the many studies described in this paper. Although issues in women's reproductive health—and, hence, the research agenda itself—differ among the countries, the framework provides a common focus for the studies. The framework will be especially useful at the end of the WSP, to help to look at lessons learned from all the research studies. This conceptual framework then can be modified to reflect the findings from the diverse studies being undertaken, to provide the field with a deeper understanding of the impact of family planning on women's lives.

11

Delivering Reproductive Health Promises Through Integrated Services

The current emphasis on reproductive health (RH) in population programmes began years ago when human rights and women's health advocates began to question the rationale of traditional policies that mainly focused on reducing population growth through the provision of family planning services. The increasing prevalence of sexually transmitted diseases (STDs) and AIDS sparked further discussion about the best ways to provide family planning services and treatment for STDs and HIV. Client expectations began to change, often as a result of work by organized groups of health care advocates, and women began to ask more from family planning than contraception (Sciarra, 1993). The 1994 International Conference on Population and Development (ICPD) in Cairo further focused the international community's attention on reproductive health. At the ICPD, there was consensus among national delegations on the need for a more comprehensive, client-centered view of reproductive health and for implementation of reproductive health programmes in addition to family planning.

To translate broad and ambitious reproductive health goals into programmes that meet clients' needs, policy-makers working with programme managers, health care advocates, service providers and others must determine, from an array of proposed reproductive health options, what package of services to provide. They must also decide on the structure of expanded reproductive health programmes, funding requirements and the sources of funding. These decisions will be difficult, since programmes will require coordinated efforts and will compete with other priorities for limited domestic and international funding.

To meet clients' broader needs for reproductive health, programmes will have to expand the range of services offered. At the same time, there is an unfinished agenda to increase access to and improve the quality of existing services. While there have long been discussions of the merits of integrated services, the 1994 ICPD intensified the interest in implementing reproductive health services through integrated programmes. As governmental and non-governmental organizations (NGOs) begin to develop strategies for implementing ICPD recommendations at the local level, an important question remains: Will integrated programmes be a successful mechanism for meeting reproductive health needs?

Definitions of Reproductive Health and Proposed Service Delivery Packages

The consensus definition of reproductive health ratified at the 1994 ICPD represents an important initial step in the process of health service transformation is as follows:

> "Reproductive health is a state of complete physical, mental and social well-being and not merely the absence of disease or infirmity, in all matters relating to the reproductive system and to its functions and processes. Reproductive health therefore implies that people are able to have a satisfying and safe sex life and that they have the capability to reproduce and the freedom to decide if, when and how often to do so. Implicit in this last condition are the rights of men and women to be informed and to have access to safe, effective, affordable and acceptable methods of family planning of their choice, as well as other methods of their choice for regulation of fertility which are not against the law, and the right of access to appropriate health care services that will enable women to go safely through pregnancy and childbirth and provide couples with the best chance of having a healthy infant".

In line with the above definition of reproductive health, reproductive health care is defined as the constellation of methods, techniques and services that contribute to reproductive health and well-being through preventing and solving reproductive health problems. It also includes sexual health, the purpose of which is the enhancement of life and personal relations, and not merely counseling and care related to reproduction and sexually transmitted diseases (ICPD, 1994).

There are general similarities among proposed packages, which list 16 broad categories and 76 specific services or related activities. In terms of health services, in addition to family planning, all groups support the provision of maternity care services, including the subcomponents of prenatal care, safe delivery, and postpartum care.

All groups support the provision of STD/AIDS services, with more organizations mentioning treatment than prevention. While all groups support the provision of counseling, there is little agreement on substantive issues. The majority of groups have recognized a need for infertility services, but few organizations have specified the nature of the services. Most organizations support some type of pregnancy termination care (mostly management of complications and post-abortion family planning).

In terms of related activities, which include, for example, linkages with other sectors and public education, there is less agreement among organizations. Related activities should differentiate between those activities that can be undertaken through the health system and those that will require the participation of other ministries and organizations.

National programmes also will have to consider numerous questions: To what degree should programmes be fully integrated; under which government ministry or ministries should programme responsibility lie; should a National Reproductive Health Commission, similar to the National Population Commissions common in many countries, be appointed to oversee and coordinate activities at the policy level; if a country was able to implement all 76 services and related activities which ministries would be involved. It is conceivable that several government ministries would need to play a role – for example, the Ministry of Health, the Ministry of Population (for service delivery), the Ministry of Education (for sex education), the Ministry of Social Affairs (for introducing parenting skills and household management education), the Ministry of Justice (for insuring gender equality and addressing domestic violence), the Ministry of Planning, and the Ministry of Foreign Affairs. If one ministry has a coordinating role, how would it coordinate programme components implemented by other ministries?

Rationales for Integrated Services

An integrated approach represents the most commonly proposed strategy for implementing reproductive health services, although a broader range of services and improvements might also be achieved through enhanced single-purpose programmes (e.g., expanded STD clinics and improved enforcement of laws against domestic violence), as well as through legal and policy reforms. Given the broad range of potential options, it is unlikely that many countries will introduce new vertical reproductive health programmes unless such programmes focused almost exclusively on medical activities and could be placed under the auspices of one ministry.

Definitions of Integration

In family planning, the term "integration" has a long and controversial history. It has been used to describe the interaction between population and development, the incorporation of demographic variables into development plans, the addition of family planning activities to other service sectors or vice versa, the union of family planning and primary care or other health programmes, the formation of umbrella coordinating committees, and the simultaneous introduction of different service packages. In family planning, "integration" has referred to various types of "administrative," "service," and "role" integration.

Administrative and Service Integration

Integration of various policy and programme components may occur in varying degrees at the national, provincial, district, local, and other administrative levels. Administrative and service integration are not mutually exclusive; attempts to integrate services without an effective administrative structure (integrated or not integrated at the various levels) may be counterproductive. The relationships between administrative and service integration are complex, and undertaking reproductive health service delivery requires an improved understanding of the conceptual and practical linkages between administration and service delivery to utilize effectively a limited pool of resources.

Two Rationales for Integration

While there are many ethical issues related to reproductive health—for example, can septic abortion treatment be provided without family planning, or can pills be provided without counseling on the risks of acquiring STDs and the potential need for dual method protection?—the authors focus on two rationales that have been offered for integrated service delivery of reproductive health services: Integrated services may better meet clients' needs, and integrated services may improve the efficiency and effectiveness of service delivery.

Better Meeting Clients' Needs

The most fundamental rationale for integrated services is the likelihood that programmes will be better able to help clients meet their reproductive needs. While programmes may separate services for administrative or financial reasons, from a client's perspective, it may be difficult to separate different reproductive health needs. The client may feel or actually be disadvantaged if offered an IUD without diagnosis and treatment of a reproductive tract infection, or if provided with antenatal and delivery care but no information on family planning or the signs and symptoms of reproductive health problems.

Some clients expect a broad array of reproductive health services when they have contact with a provider. Queen *et al.* (1991), for example, found that the clients from separate family planning and STD clinics in London assumed that providers would counsel them on all aspects of sexual health. Some clients, however, might not want all reproductive health services delivered at the same location. For example, family planning clients might consider it inappropriate to receive services at the same clinic attended by

STD clients, or they might consider that they have to wait too long for family planning if family planning is offered together with MCH services.

A central premise of the reproductive health movement is the need to provide clients with high quality care by considering the client's perspective in the selection and delivery of services. The framework for family planning that outlines six elements of quality of care that programmes should provide (Bruce, 1990) can be extended to other reproductive health services (Mora *et al.*, 1993). More research is needed on the array of reproductive health care services clients would value most and the service delivery mechanisms through which they would like the services offered (e.g., through integrated or vertical programmes). There are several links between reproductive health interventions and health outcomes. A framework developed by the Pan American Health Organization, FHI, and the International Projects Assistance Service (PAHO/FHI, 1993) outlines the linkages of desired health outcomes to three reproductive health components. Empirical evidence supports this framework. Cuca and Pierce (1977, 1977) discussed results of 15 service experiments that integrated either maternal and child health and family planning, postpartum care and family planning, or post-abortion care and family planning, or that used multipurpose workers. They found a synergistic relation between family planning and other health programmes.

The challenge is not just to add services but to reach new populations. Family planning programmes have traditionally focused on married women of reproductive age. Dixon-Mueller and Germain (1992) have proposed broadening definitions of "unmet need" for contraception to include additional groups: unmarried and married nonusers; users needing another method; users and nonusers needing a method to terminate unwanted pregnancies; and users and nonusers needing other reproductive health services. Men and adolescents generally have not been recipients of reproductive health services, nor have postmenopausal women. Integrated reproductive health services could fill the family planning needs of some of these underserved groups, as well as address other health concerns.

Improving Efficiency and Effectiveness of Services

Integration of reproductive health services under some conditions, but not all, can improve the efficiency and effectiveness of the delivery system in relation to specified outcomes, such as increases in contraceptive prevalence or reductions in unintended pregnancies, maternal mortality, or incidence of sexually transmitted diseases. The terms "effectiveness" and "efficiency" could also be used to define outcomes regarding clients' health, for example, the effectiveness of treatments and efficiency with which clients receive care (Finkle and Crane, 1976). Here we focus on effectiveness and efficiency as they relate to the service delivery system.

Greater efficiency could be achieved by requiring fewer worker-client contacts, minimizing duplication, sharing facilities, and training selected workers to perform multiple tasks. Some agree that service integration enhances programme effectiveness, while others fear that service integration will cause one component to suffer at the expense of another. Walley *et al.* (1991) note in Ethiopia that despite an increase in visits of mothers and children to the multipurpose health worker (trained to provide growth monitoring/nutrition advice, immunizations, antenatal/postnatal care, family planning, and health education) certain services received more attention than others: Immunizations were offered regularly, growth monitoring was offered irregularly, and family planning and antenatal care were not offered but were provided when requested. On the other hand, integration of services can increase the interest and participation of a variety of service providers by enhancing their skills and level of responsibility (Files, 1982; Population Council, 1991).

Grouping similar services may help influence the effectiveness of service integration. Degraff *et al.* (1986) found that the addition of oral dehydration therapy to the Matlab family planning and health services project had a significant negative effect on contraceptive prevalence, whereas the addition of child care at the family welfare centers increased contraceptive prevalence. A study in Colombia, in which family planning employees of PROFAMILIA conducted AIDS outreach and prevention activities, showed that the new activities did not cause contraceptive sales to decline (Vernon *et al.*, 1990).

Integrated service delivery can yield a lower cost per output than non-integrated programmes (Gibbs, 1973; Rosen *et al.*, 1989). Service integration can facilitate the use of existing health infrastructures and programme staff, thus avoiding the costs of creating a new programme infrastructure (Ness, 1981), as shown in the postpartum family planning programmes and integrated maternity and family planning care in Honduras, Peru, and India (Faruqee, 1982a; Seward and Fong, 1983; Population Council, 1991). The assurance of a smooth flow of funds (Laing, 1981), the choice of populations served (Vernon, 1990), and the type of delivery strategy within the context of integrated programming (Rosenfield, 1984) distinguish between programmes that are cost-effective (depending on the programme and outcomes of interest) and those that are not.

Depending upon choice of measures and analytical approach, however, two cost-effectiveness analyses of the same integrated service can vary markedly, depending on assumptions made in the analysis (Simmons *et al.*, 1991). Furthermore, analyses rarely consider outcomes from the standpoint of longer-term client satisfaction or behaviour:

- Did clients continue to use family planning effectively for birth spacing and limiting over a significant portion of their reproductive lifetimes?
- Did clients treated for STDs avoid contracting them again?

- Did clients who were taught good prenatal practices adhere to them in later pregnancies, and with what effect on morbidity as well as mortality?
- What costs did the client experience in utilizing the services that may not have been captured in measuring budgetary costs to the programme?
- Were desired outcomes more likely with integrated or vertical reproductive health services?

Challenges to the Integration and Delivery of Reproductive Health Services

Establishing a structure for service integration can facilitate, but does not guarantee, implementation of reproductive health services, due to the complexity of reproductive health service packages, the existence of established vertical programmes, and weak administrative capacity in some countries. This section draws on past experiences to address challenges facing integrated service interventions, looking first at the donor level, then at the national programme environment, and finally, at the service delivery environment. We base these results on a review of more than 50 published and unpublished impact evaluations, operations research projects, demonstration projects, and other studies of national public-sector programmes over the past 25 years. Many of these challenges are common to any service delivery programme, but all are exacerbated in an integrated programme setting.

Donor Level Environment

Effective donor collaboration will greatly facilitate the implementation of reproductive health service delivery. International agencies can influence national programmes in various ways (World Bank, 1993; Mitchell *et al.*, 1994). The expanding number of donors subjects recipients, as well as other donors, to increasing pressures of competing priorities. The orientation of the donor may result in an unbalanced evaluation of integrated services. Managers, for example, may worry about the response of a family planning donor to an integrated programme that fails to raise contraceptive acceptance rates but improves maternal or child health. Finally, separate donor monitoring and reporting requirements can overburden in-country administrators with unnecessary duplication of reports.

Donors must address these concerns as well as those of resource sharing, assuming joint responsibility for successes and failures, and balancing local priorities with agency interests. One means to achieve this end could involve the establishment of a coordinating body with relevant ministries in recipient countries to ensure that donor inputs are complementary and that regular meetings between donors and governments occur. Donors may also form consortia to fund national programmes or at least create informal groups to review progress and problems in reproductive health.

National Programme Environment

National Policies

Translating the broad goals of reproductive health into national policy through an implementation strategy requires political will and motivation by high-level government officials. There has been much debate about the content of expanded population policies that incorporate reproductive health. Cook (1993), for example, proposes a comprehensive view of public policy that incorporates women's rights, addresses reproductive health explicitly, and condemns all forms of discrimination.

Reproductive health policies will be most likely to succeed if the national policy development process includes a wide range of constituencies; for example, policy-makers, women's advocacy groups, grass-roots organizers, service providers, and client representatives, among others. Some policy-makers may resist addressing ideas such as women's empowerment and domestic violence. Lack of support from religious, political, or community groups can also frustrate policy efforts. Since some of the proposed reproductive health interventions have not been widely tested, community ideas must be elicited. Broad-based participation in the design, planning, and management of reproductive health programmes will facilitate the creation of sustainable programmes.

An assessment of reproductive health care services currently available will provide a useful basis for policy discussions on service gaps. Many national programmes have data from the Demographic and Health Surveys (DHS) and from studies such as the situation analysis of family planning service delivery points that can be used to inform decision-making. While quantitative techniques have been useful tools for setting targets, the goal of meeting clients' needs will benefit from increased use of qualitative research, particularly to discover which services clients themselves consider high priority components of reproductive health care.

Budgetary planning should accompany policy development, particularly if the policy will be implemented through an integrated programme (World Bank, 1993). According to Mitchell (1994), "*when integration proceeds without changing the budgeting process, it does not work*". Policy-makers, through balanced allocations, can implement mechanisms at the planning stages that de-emphasize capital-intensive projects, discourage competition for scarce resources, and encourage the formation of programmematic and sectoral linkages.

Setting Priorities and Phasing Implementation

In many countries, access to currently available services is limited. The relative deficiency of services in rural areas has long been a problem for integrated and non-integrated programmes (Taylor and Berelson, 1971; Rosenfield, 1982; Simmons and Phillips, 1987; Thaddeus and Maine, 1994). For example, despite efforts to integrate mother and child health services in Ethiopia, health units have remained inaccessible to much of the population in the Wollo region (Walley *et al.*, 1991). Village women, who must walk many kilometers over mountainous terrain to reach the clinic, tend to visit the clinic only for emergencies. Geographic access was also reported to be a problem in the rural Maternal and Child Health and Family Planning Project in Calabar, Nigeria (Weiss, 1982). Rosenfield (1982, 1984a) attributes the gaps in MCH and family planning in rural areas to the introduction of costly, highly technical, and physician-oriented urban strategies that drained national health budgets. Problems of access will be more critical as programmes work to expand availability of other reproductive health services.

A limited programme focusing on priority needs can have a greater impact on health outcomes and can achieve higher quality of care than a comprehensive programme that becomes overextended. Additional field support should accompany each new component so that new activities do not overburden workers and divert their energy from existing tasks (Phillips *et al.*, 1984a). The UNFPA (1984) programme report for Malawi, for example, suggests that as services are added (e.g., child spacing to MCH), programme managers should assess the additional needs for supervisors and service personnel.

A delicate balance exists between the expansion of reproductive health services and the improvement of quality of care for every service component. Evidence from programmes in Indonesia and Bangladesh demonstrates that the addition of new technologies does not necessarily expand choice; in fact, the removal of technologies that overburden a delivery system may improve quality of care. Likewise, introduction of new reproductive health services may tax an existing health care system. Reproductive health programme planners and evaluators must remain cognizant of the costs to quality of care that will accrue if health providers are asked to assume new tasks without adequate resources, training, equipment, and other prerequisites. The introduction of one service that is desired by a community may foster the community's acceptance of additional service components. Phased implementation of service components would allow programmes time to adjust the logistical and service delivery systems to accommodate programme growth. Given the complex nature of proposed programmes, national leaders and other constituents should provide explicit and realistic goals for the phase-in of new services and geographic programme expansion.

Interministerial and Intraministerial Level Issues

Even with consistent national policies, the organization of government ministries makes integration challenging (NCIH, 1982). When ministerial personnel, resources, and policies are organized vertically, a programme subsumed under one ministry receives that ministry's focus. Fear of takeover and loss of status or career prospects create barriers to effective collaboration (Laing, 1981). Despite political support, integration under such circumstances can threaten established channels of command over scarce resources.

Service Delivery Environment

Infrastructure and Service Referral

In the short-run, the feasibility of integrated health service delivery is contingent on the adequacy of the existing health infrastructure. In the long-run, advocates are proposing that investment be made to strengthen infrastructure. Referral systems represent a potential linkage where health infrastructures are particularly weak. Referral systems can be established vertically to provide higher levels of care (e.g., referral for female or male sterilization) or horizontally to link programmes (e.g., family planning, STD).

Referral between services and providers can be an effective intermediate or long-term strategy for improving coverage and quality of care without moving services to the same delivery point. First, components serving similar populations and using similar service delivery strategies can be identified and linked through. One or both of the programmes should be functioning at the desired level of performance before linkage. Ladipo and Delano (1984) proposed the establishment of "health teams" consisting of a variety of providers with clearly defined roles. Their health teams parallel the Maternity Care Pyramid, which illustrates provider roles and linkages between the three levels of a country's district health system.

The absence of functional facilities at the first and second referral levels, however, makes referral from the periphery an empty gesture (Simmons *et al.*, 1990). Unfamiliarity among providers about the benefits of referral may require supervisory visits and discussion before the practice is adopted. Clinicians may require training to develop skills in merging discrete activities through referral, which can be accomplished with on-site supervision and short training programmes for clinic staff and community workers.

Medical Support, Supplies and Logistics

A continuous supply of drugs and equipment to all service delivery levels is essential to enhance reproductive health. Yet many health posts lack basic equipment. Sixty-one percent of health posts in the Guatemalan highlands, for example, were without refrigerators for drug and vaccine storage, 44 percent lacked a work table, and 90 percent did not have educational materials (Annis, 1981 in Thaddeus and Maine, 1990).

Deficiencies in essential supplies have serious implications for several reproductive health components, especially STD diagnosis and treatment, maternity care, and management of abortion complications. Barriers to the regular provision of medical support and supplies, not only found in integrated programmes, include resource limitations, the lack of supplies at the central level, poor national or local systems of distribution, inadequate local storage capacity, untimely or inaccurate projections for needed supplies, irregular monitoring of supply use, and poor management of available resources. Simmons *et al.* (1990) show in Bangladesh that as a result of deficiencies in medical support and distribution of supplies, a field worker can identify a basic medical need, such as iron for anemia, but she must rely on hospital referral because there is no field distribution of iron tablets. Mitchell *et al.* (1994) have suggested that logistics systems should be integrated only when services are operating at similar levels of efficiency.

Updated Service Delivery Guidelines

Work has been undertaken to analyze guidelines that would accomplish three goals: to reduce barriers hindering access to family planning, to broaden access to contraceptive methods, and to improve the quality of care with which contraceptives are provided. Similar work will be required to ensure that guidelines exist for all reproductive health services offered in a country and that the guidelines are based on current scientific information. The guidelines must be disseminated to all service providers who offer reproductive health services.

Integrated Records Systems

Integration of reproductive health services will require changes in record-keeping and reporting. Experts have recommended the integration of records systems at the district level and below to avoid overburdening the programme with separate reporting and evaluation systems if collaboration among agencies is involved.

Delegation

Potential advantages of delegation of activities from higher to lower level staff include overcoming a shortage of trained workers, freeing physicians from routine tasks, conserving the specialist's time for emergencies, avoiding long delays in care caused by a centralized system, and promoting worker satisfaction. These advantages can affect programme performance, as shown in the Katibougou family health project in Mali: "[A]s the responsibilities of the health workers expanded, more information and services became available at the village level".

Barriers to effective delegation include resistance among medical professionals, delegation without adequate training, unclear job descriptions, and ineffective communication sparking team rivalries. Despite the potential pitfalls, local literate or illiterate health workers, given proper training and supervision, can successfully perform a variety of tasks normally reserved for more highly trained professionals (Tom *et al*., 1984-5; Koblinsky *et al*., 1994). Delegation of some medical responsibilities (e.g., prescribing antibiotics) to paramedical workers may require legal and regulatory changes. In some cases, staff in local health centers carry out tasks they were not assigned, simply because they are the only staff available. They lack training, ironically, because the tasks fall outside of their job description. Ultimately, "[p]olicy decisions about the delegation of tasks need ... to be based upon ... the potential for reducing morbidity and mortality, the level of skills involved, the ability to maintain that level of skill, and the possibility of alternatives" (WHO, 1994).

Adequacy and Competence of Personnel

Availability of trained personnel, worker density, worker competence, and the geographic distribution of workers have been issues of concern in integrated programmes for decades. In general, Fathalla (in Khanna *et al*., 1992) notes that fewer than 20 percent of births in some developing countries are attended by trained personnel. The UNFPA (1991) notes, in a review of the integrated maternal and child health/family planning programme in Botswana, that 140 health posts lacked enrolled nurses. As a result, family welfare educators were unable to carry out community-level activities and had to assume clinic nursing functions. High turnover due to job reassignment and the absence of temporary replacements also affected management capacity. Integrated reproductive health programmes, having invested resources in training staff, will have to find ways to reduce staff turnover and make maximum use of existing staff.

The overburdening of workers and supervisors may be more pronounced as reproductive health services are expanded. Both the number of assigned tasks and the geographic area for which workers are responsible can contribute to the problem. Expecting field workers to complete an unmanageable number of tasks over a large geographic area can reduce workers' morale, motivation, and productive work time, and can ultimately hinder the quality of care of the programme or of selective components. Some field workers in Bangladesh, for example, do not provide maternal and child health services because it adds to an already heavy work burden, and high worker/client ratios increase the difficulty of client contact (Simmons *et al*., 1990). Programmes should assess how many tasks different levels of staff can learn and carry out.

Staff Training

Adequacy of staff training has been cited repeatedly as an issue for integrated services. Several characteristics of training personnel in integrated programmes repeatedly appeared in the literature. All levels of workers should be trained in accountability and quality of care, including technical competence, sensitivity to the needs of clients, continuity of care, commitment to informed choice, and listening to clients (Dixon-Mueller, 1993). Phased training, where health workers are taught new skills after they are competent in other skills, is recommended. Refresher training can maintain a positive rapport among staff and the interest of providers and supervisors in the quality and intensity of work (Bhatia *et al.*, 1980; NCIH, 1982; Rosenfield, 1984; UNFPA, 1984; Pratt *et al.*, 1989; WHO, 1994). Training of supervisors is critical, as well. If supervisors are not trained in the new skills of their staff, they will not be able to adequately supervise the new activities. They will also be less likely to encourage staff to use their newly acquired skills.

An expanded package of reproductive health services, however, is likely to complicate the retraining of supervisors and service providers. In addition to having more topics to teach, programmes will have to organize either on-site training in potentially remote areas or interrupt the availability of services to retrain staff away from the service delivery point.

Supervision

Supervision will play a key role in ensuring that workers are able to perform their expanded duties. Workers need to understand their new roles in reproductive health programmes to enable them to perform their new jobs effectively and to discourage them from reverting to their former practices. Barriers to adequate supervision have included deficiencies in supervisory training, inadequate transportation, unclear definition of supervisory responsibilities, inadequate materials and checklists, and the absence of a reporting system at the peripheral level. Weak supervision in Danfa, Ghana, contributed to lowered activity of the field staff and loss of new skills. Such barriers can also affect the nature of the supervisor-supervisee relationship. Fong *et al.* (1982), found in South Korea that the frequency of interaction between workers and the clinic chief explained 50 percent of the variance in clinic-level performance. In the public sector in Bangladesh, the bureaucratic hierarchical nature of public-sector programmes hampered supportive, problem-solving supervision.

Supervisors can encourage positive staff interaction. In Malaysia, collective problem-solving had a positive impact on programme performance (Fong *et al.*, 1982). Building effective working relationships at the local level, paying attention to norms of service, and effective external interaction are programme characteristics under the direct control of managers. Under supportive conditions, supervisors should be able to conduct regular site visits, observe worker activities directly, train workers, and facilitate effective programming.

Evaluating Integrated Programmes

Assessing whether the Intervention Works

In the long-run, experimentation with various combinations of reproductive health services can help programmes develop their optimal package of services. Demonstration projects can test the feasibility of integrating reproductive health services (NCIH, 1982; Germain and Antrobus, 1989). For example, current demonstration projects in Bangladesh and Navrongo, Ghana, could be used to study the interventions that have emerged in recent discussions of reproductive health and from the 1994 ICPD. Certain national characteristics can be incorporated in the design of a demonstration project to ensure its replicability and applicability. In Bangladesh, the Matlab Extension Project has transferred innovations far beyond the original service area.

One critique of demonstration projects is that issues and policy-makers change during the course of an extensive demonstration project, which may hinder the use of the findings in the end. Another concern is whether the findings will be replicable beyond the demonstration project, which often benefits from well-trained staff and abundant financial resources. The high costs of demonstration projects and impact evaluation also must be balanced with the benefits of learning whether or not an intervention can work.

Programme Evaluation

Future evaluations of reproductive health programmes will benefit from the development of conceptual frameworks and indicators that apply to various national and local contexts, that incorporate a broader range of outcomes—including longitudinal and community-level outcomes—and that consider the views of stakeholders in reproductive health outcomes, most notably clients.

Tsui (1994) conceptualizes the demand-side, supply-side, life-cycle, behavioural-epidemiological, and donor views of reproductive health through a framework for understanding the common implementation features of different combinations of reproductive health components.

Mora *et al.* (1993) have developed a framework for evaluating quality of care in reproductive health that focuses on the integration of maternal health, STDs, and family planning, and outlines three levels of care (community, clinic and hospital). They have provided an array of indicators useful for evaluating programme components by type of service delivery point.

FHI's Women's Studies Project has designed a framework to assess the impact of family planning and reproductive health programmes on a number of aspects of women's lives, including individual psychological and physical factors, women's household and family roles, and their community and social roles (FHI, 1994). Because the Project is designed to collect information on women's perceptions of family planning services, a logical extension might be use of the framework to guide evaluation of reproductive health programmes and to understand the impact of these new activities on the lives of women.

Evaluations will require use of multiple indicators of success based on expanded target populations. A USAID working group has identified more than 180 indicators to measure various components of reproductive health (Bertrand and Stewart, 1995). Definitions of positive impact may vary among different constituencies for projects (for example, donors, policy-makers, health care advocates, and clients may all perceive different indicators of success). Jain and Bruce (1993) suggest the use of a modified HARI index (Helping Individuals Achieve their Reproductive Intentions), which is 100 if the programme is completely successful and 0 if the programme fails to prevent unwanted pregnancy and unnecessary morbidity. The HARI index allows clients to define the reproductive health needs to be met and implies the logical intervening steps of quality of care. A challenge to the use of a modified HARI index is the current difficulty of measuring reproductive health morbidity in the developing world. Murray and Chen (1992) have developed a conceptual framework for measuring morbidity that includes both perceptions of the client and observations of the health worker. Family Health International currently is undertaking a five-country study and preliminary results show that the incidence of maternal morbidity is higher than previously estimated 240 to 330 maternal morbidities to each maternal death compared to 15 to 100, as previously estimated.

Policy Actions

Countries have an unique opportunity to capitalize on the historic consensus reached at the 1994 ICPD: to expand beyond family planning to broader and more client-centered approaches to reproductive health care. Taking advantage of the excitement and momentum created in Cairo, countries must now translate broad goals into specific service delivery programmes to meet the reproductive health needs of women and men worldwide. While the 1994 ICPD has set the agenda, many tasks remain. Policy-makers, programme planners, reproductive health advocates, and donors, among others, must first set national goals for reproductive health and translate them into policies. Countries then need to decide on the package of services to be offered, in light of services currently available, to reach the goals for improving reproductive health. Next, countries must determine funding requirements and sources of funding, both national and international. Finally, they need to plan an implementation strategy, including integration of services or service linkages, organizational responsibilities and a timeline for phasing in the services, given financial and infrastructure constraints. Programmes will need to monitor the implementation of reproductive health services and to be flexible about making appropriate shifts in programmes.

Summing Up

The 1994 International Conference on Population and Development (ICPD) Programme of Action calls for a comprehensive, client-centered view of reproductive health and for the promotion of reproductive health in addition to family planning. If countries are to translate these broad and ambitious reproductive health goals into programmes that meet clients' needs, they will have to select those services that provide the widest reproductive health benefits for the most people, taking into consideration epidemiological trends, services currently offered, client demand, and resources available.

12

Strategies for Effective Family Planning Programmes

Family planning programmes help millions of people, providing reproductive health care that saves lives, avoids unintended pregnancies, and offers more choices. National leadership commitment and adequate funding for family planning programmes are essential to assure widespread access to good-quality reproductive health care. Support from health care officials, policy-makers, donor agencies, women's organizations, the news media, and religious and community leaders also is important.

Advocacy for family planning is becoming crucial as demand for reproductive health care grows. Worldwide, as many as 600 million people use contraception, and millions more would do so with better access to good-quality services. Although fertility levels are falling in much of the world, rapid population growth remains a critical issue in most developing countries, where needs are great and resources are scarce.

For many programmes advocacy is a new and challenging responsibility. Advocates must attract and hold the attention of key audiences with powerful arguments and persuasive communication. In particular, research-based evidence of the benefits of family planning helps leaders justify their support.

Benefits of Family Planning:

- *Saving Women's Lives*: Avoiding unintended pregnancies could prevent about one-fourth of all maternal deaths in developing countries. Especially, using contraception helps avoid unsafe abortions to end unintended pregnancies. It also enables women to limit births to their healthiest childbearing years and to avoid giving birth more times than is good for their health.
- *Saving Children's Lives*: Spacing pregnancies at least two years apart helps women have healthier children and improves the odds of infants' survival by about 50 per cent. Limiting births to a woman's healthiest

childbearing years also improves her children's chances of surviving and remaining healthy.

- *Offering Women More Choices*: For many women, controlling their own childbearing, by using effective contraception, can open the door to education, employment, and community involvement. Also, couples who have fewer children are more likely to send their daughters as well as sons to school.
- *Encouraging Adoption of Safer Sexual Behaviour*: All sexually active people need to protect against sexually transmitted infections (STIs), including HIV/AIDS. Always using condoms correctly or avoiding sex except in a mutually monogamous relationship are the best ways. With enough support, family planning programmes—along with parents, schools, and peers—could help more young people make sexual decisions responsibly, avoiding STIs and unintended pregnancies.
- As more people choose family planning, fertility falls and population growth slows. Although fertility has fallen throughout the world, further declines would make a crucial difference in many developing countries. World population has reached 6 billion and is growing by nearly 80 million people each year.
- *Slower population Growth Helps Protect the Environment*: It conserves resources, preserves clean air and water, improves health, eases pressures on cities, and helps avoid conflict.
- *Slower Population Growth Aids Development*: It buys time and, with more of the population in their productive years, provides a demographic bonus that can be invested in education, job creation, health care, and other efforts to raise living standards.

The sooner fertility falls to low levels, the better most countries will be able to achieve sustainable development. Even small declines in fertility today will make a substantial difference in population size in the future. Acting now to obtain support for reproductive health care helps meet people's needs today and improves prospects for the 21st century.

The Importance of Advocacy

Adequate funding, favourable policies, and popular support are important to the success of family planning programmes. Programmes need support not only from clients but also from the general public and, especially, from health officials, policy-makers, funding agencies, the news media, employers, health care providers, women's organizations, and religious and community leaders.

Such support cannot be taken for granted. Developing country reproductive health programmes and their allies often must appeal for support. They must use powerful evidence and persuasive arguments to make the case for family planning and other reproductive health care, in ways that attract and hold an audience's attention

For many programmes advocacy may be a new responsibility. Few health care professionals have experience at advocacy. If programmes and their clients do not advocate good-quality family planning, however, who else will do so? Advocacy encourages others who support family planning to speak up, too. Where family planning programmes face vocal opposition, expressing the majority's support for family planning is especially important.

The Need for Advocacy

Advocacy is becoming crucial as demand for good-quality reproductive health services rises. In most developing countries national family planning programmes have been instrumental in providing contraception to women who want it, improving health and reducing fertility levels. Now, leadership commitment and financial support are essential if programmes are to be able to meet rising demand.

Toward Better Reproductive Health: Today, many family planning programmes focus on providing clients good-quality reproductive health care. Good-quality care includes a range of contraceptive methods, sensitive counseling, and meeting other important reproductive health needs as well as providing family planning. As quality improves, clients are healthier, more satisfied, and better able to make informed choices, to use contraception effectively, and to continue using it.

Recognizing the need for good-quality family planning and other reproductive health care, representatives of 179 countries, meeting in 1994 at the United Nations International Conference on Population and Development (ICPD) in Cairo, agreed to improve reproductive health care and better meet people's needs.

Progress toward ICPD goals has been uneven, however. A 1999 study of eight countries, representing all developing regions, found that half are adopting policies that reflect the Cairo consensus, but some are facing difficulties obtaining the support needed to carry out the new policies. "Continued efforts in advocacy and in broadening policy-making are needed to speed the process," the study concluded.

To meet ICPD goals, countries in Cairo agreed to contribute to the US$17 billion needed each year, with donor countries providing one-third and developing countries providing two-thirds. Few developing countries or donor countries, however, have lived up to the commitments that they made in Cairo. The consequences of failing to meet ICPD funding goals are serious—an estimated 42 million unintended pregnancies, 17 million induced abortions, and 99,000 maternal deaths each year.

In 1999, after reviewing the five-year record of efforts to meet the Cairo commitments, countries endorsed the Cairo consensus again, called on developing countries to take the steps needed to improve reproductive health care and cut unmet need for family planning in half by 2005. They urged donor countries to "reverse the current decline" in development assistance. Unless donors make a new, expanded commitment, however, "it remains an open question" whether international assistance for family planning programmes will increase substantially.

Population Growth is Still a Crucial Issue: Worldwide declines in fertility rates have led some people to declare, incorrectly, that population growth is no longer a global concern. In fact, every 12 or 13 years another billion people are added to the world's population, almost all in developing countries. The 20th century is ending with more than 6 billion people on earth compared with 2.3 billion at mid-century. The world's population has doubled in a single lifetime. World population has grown more in the past 50 years "than during the 4 million preceding years since our early ancestors first stood upright".

In some places, meeting the needs of so many people already threatens the natural resource base on which the future depends, and the situation will get worse. For example, 31 countries, accounting for 8 per cent of the world's population, currently face chronic shortages of freshwater. In 2025, because of population growth, 48 countries, containing 2.8 billion people, or 35 per cent of the world's projected population, will face chronic water shortages.

The United Nations has projected that world population will be 8.9 billion in 2050, nearly a 50 per cent increase over the current 6 billion. As the Population Reference Bureau has observed, even that scenario "rests upon a sweeping assumption: that family planning will continue to spread in less developed countries, including those where it is now little used". Advocacy for family planning can help turn this assumption into fact.

Evidence for Advocacy

How can family planning programmes win more support? At the core of advocacy is objective evidence to help answer the question, "Why should I support family planning and other reproductive health care?" Decision-makers are more likely to give their endorsement if convinced that it will make a difference and that the policies and programmes advocated deserve high priority and will benefit many people.

While arguments based on factual evidence alone seldom are enough to persuade leaders, they are important and necessary because they provide reasons that leaders need to justify support of family planning. Many surveys, studies, and expert analyses show that individuals and countries benefit from family planning and family planning programmes. Furthermore, survey statistics and case studies can help show that constituents want and need services.

Effective advocacy often also involves a "human element"—presenting stories of people's personal experiences to illustrate the meaning of facts and statistics and to show how family planning improves individual lives. Like people in general, leaders are interested most in information that is timely, affects them directly, and offers solutions as well as describes problems.

Advocacy for family planning must deal with—and sometimes can thrive on—opposition. Family planning programmes often are controversial and face attacks from opponents. Effective advocacy deals fairly and frankly with controversial issues, neither exaggerating claims nor ignoring criticisms. Using reasoned arguments to refute opponents' incorrect or misleading claims can draw more attention to family planning, attract supporters, and may even overcome some opponents' objections.

The Advocacy Campaign

Advocacy is a process. The first step in an advocacy campaign is analysis to define purposes and set goals. An advocacy campaign identifies the potential audiences to be reached and decides what and who will influence them. It develops a strategy for mobilizing opinion, organizing resources, and reaching key audiences effectively. Often, supporters in the community can become involved in designing and carrying out advocacy activities. A network or coalition of community members and organizations can create powerful advocacy. Satisfied clients, for example, often express personal commitment that leads the way to public advocacy.

Advocacy messages, materials, and activities are designed to respond to the intended audience's interests, using arguments that will appeal most. Messages are most effective when they also specify what actions the audience is expected to take and emphasize their urgency. Advocates should monitor and evaluate the campaign to gauge progress and to measure the changes that the campaign has caused. This information can help programmes reinforce and extend their successes while learning from mistakes. Each advocacy campaign must find the combination of activities that is appropriate for its specific objectives and audiences.

Effective Advocacy: Examples from Around the World

As the following examples show, organizations have advocated family planning and reproductive health effectively in a variety of ways:

- *Kenya*: In Kenya the Youth Initiatives Project developed an advocacy strategy to reach policy-makers and community decision makers after a study found that many leaders did not believe in or support programmes and organizations to help youth. The advocacy campaign was intended to show leaders that providing youth with health care information and services could address many of their reproductive health concerns.

The first step was to analyze government policies and legislation toward youth and to interview over 100 political and community leaders. The project trained over 40 advocates from districts throughout Kenya in how to reach leaders in their area. Following training, these advocates held public meetings with community groups, distributed an information kit to selected leaders, and discussed with them the need for more focus on youth. Following the campaign over 80 per cent of district development committees, parents, church groups, and social workers approved of measures to address adolescent reproductive health.

- *Turkey*: In Turkey, to promote equality for women, 17 women's organizations developed an advocacy strategy based on networks of supporters and collaboration among organizations. By joining together and adopting a common goal and theme, the organizations had far more influence on policy-makers than if each had made a case separately. As a coalition, they were able to obtain new government funding for contraceptive supplies, which helped compensate for a reduction in funding from the United States Agency for International Development.
- *The Philippines*: In 1995, when religious groups publicly attacked family planning as "anti-child, anti-family, and anti-life," the Family Planning Organization of the Philippines (FPOP) developed an advocacy strategy to refute their criticism. The strategy focused on providing persuasive information about how family planning benefits children and families, demonstrating that in fact, family planning is "*pro-child, pro-family and pro-life*". In public messages the FPOP also stressed the key role that family planning programmes play in increasing reproductive choices for couples and improving their reproductive health. In addition, the FPOP persuaded President Fidel Ramos to declare his full support for family planning.
- *Bolivia*: In 1991 a coalition of Bolivian family planning organizations developed an advocacy strategy that focused on the family health benefits of family planning. The goal was to make the topic of family planning less taboo and to encourage public discussion. Campaign messages emphasized family planning as part of a larger reproductive health agenda and highlighted the need to achieve goals related to safe motherhood and women's health. The Bolivian campaign organizers obtained endorsements from President Sanchez de Lozada, Vice President Victor Hugo de Cardenas, and their wives, who stressed how family planning benefits mothers and their children.
- *Jordan*: As part of an advocacy campaign to increase men's approval of modern contraception, the Jordan National Population Commission focused on male religious leaders, physicians, social workers, and other

community opinion leaders. The campaign particularly sought to increase religious leaders' approval of contraception because their approval would strongly influence Jordanian men. To win their support, the commission sponsored community meetings, providing information about family planning and assuring the religious leaders that contraceptive use is safe and effective and in concordance with Islam. The meetings succeeded in motivating the leaders to discuss family health issues with their wives and to use health services. Participants agreed to return to their communities as advocates for family planning—creating a ripple effect that could reach as many as 50,000 people.

Meeting Demand for Family Planning

Meeting Current Needs

Worldwide in 1998, 570 million couples, were using contraception, according to an estimate by the United Nations. Family planning programmes are meeting current demand better by expanding the range of contraceptive choices, reaching more clients in rural areas, providing empathic counseling, and addressing the concerns of their clients.

Nonetheless, according to a study of 20 developing countries in 1990, an average of 22 per cent of all births are unwanted. This estimate is probably low because many parents do not want to acknowledge that a child was unwanted. Also, of the estimated 182 million pregnancies each year in developing countries, some 66 million—about 36 per cent—are unintended. About 36 million of these are estimated to end in abortion. Almost half of these induced abortions are unsafe.

Meeting Unmet Need

Millions of people who might be interested in family planning are not being served at all. In developing countries over 100 million married women of reproductive age—one woman in every five outside China—are estimated to have an "unmet need" for family planning. Unmet need, which is estimated from survey data, refers to married women who say that they would prefer to avoid or postpone childbearing but who are not using any method of contraception. Many sexually active unmarried women probably have an unmet need as well.

There are many reasons for unmet need and for unintended pregnancies. For instance, women and men often worry about side effects of contraceptive use. Other women lack accurate information about reproductive health or access to appropriate services. Family planning programmes could address most of these reasons. Such an effort, however, will require more financial support and stronger leadership commitment to the importance of avoiding unintended childbearing.

Serving contraceptive users better also could reduce the number of unintended pregnancies substantially. Many unintended pregnancies result from contraceptive failures, which are often caused by inconsistent or incorrect use. Offering counseling and choices helps clients use contraception correctly and consistently.

Worldwide over 350 million couples—more than one-third of all couples—do not have access to a full range of modern family planning information and services, the United Nations Population Fund (UNFPA) has estimated. As programmes make more contraceptive methods available, more people are able to find methods that meet their needs.

Meeting Rising Demand

In developing countries the percentage of married couples using contraception has risen substantially, from less than 10 per cent in the 1960s to 55 per cent in 1998, and it continues to rise. Family planning programmes have played a key role in this increase by turning "latent demand"—people's desire to space and limit births—into actual demand for contraceptive information and services. In most developing countries many people have been able to space and limit their births because—and somctimes *only* because—widely supported family planning programmes have provided contraception and made it increasingly understood, accepted, and accessible.

As contraceptive use has spread, the average number of births per woman has declined. Each 15 per cent increase in contraceptive prevalence results in approximately one less birth per woman on average. Reflecting people's growing interest in having fewer children, the number of births in developing countries has fallen from over six children per woman in the 1960s to about three children today.

Improving Access and Quality

Programmes help people use contraception by maximizing access to good-quality services. Good-quality care makes contraception safer and more effective by: offering a range of methods; informing clients fully about them, including side effects; screening clients for medical eligibility; helping clients choose for themselves methods that suit their own circumstances; showing clients how to use methods properly; and supporting clients when they encounter problems or decide to switch methods.

As quality improves and more methods become available, more couples use contraception. For example, for each additional method that is widely available in a country, contraceptive prevalence—the percentage of married women using contraception—increases by an average 3.3 percentage points, according to data from Demographic and Health Surveys (DHS) in 44 countries.

Given a range of contraceptive methods and other good-quality care, virtually any person can find a method that is safe and appropriate. When used appropriately and correctly, family planning methods pose almost no health risk. Using contraception typically is much safer than giving birth. The average lifetime risk of dying from maternal causes worldwide is 1 in 60 and much higher in many developing countries. Use of modern contraception is rarely a cause of death.

Nor does contraception cause undesired permanent infertility, as some people incorrectly believe. Male and female sterilization are the only contraceptive methods that result in permanent infertility—which is their purpose. All other methods are temporary, as they are intended to be, and fertility returns either immediately or with-in some months after discontinuation of use.

Some contraceptive methods have positive health benefits in addition to those of preventing pregnancy. For example, condoms protect men and women from sexually transmitted infections (STIs) including HIV/AIDS. Combined oral contraceptives can reduce a woman's risk of developing cancers, anemia, benign breast disease, ectopic pregnancy, and pelvic inflammatory disease (PID).

Ensuring a Human Right

Increasingly, governments around the world are embracing the concept of reproductive rights. The concept is reflected in national laws and international agreements.

At the 1994 ICPD in Cairo, 179 countries agreed to the Programme of Action, which states that everyone has the right to "the enjoyment of the highest attainable standard of physical and mental health" and the right "to decide freely and responsibly the number, spacing, and timing of their children and to have the information and means to do so". The ICPD programme of action urges:

> States should take all appropriate measures to ensure, on a basis of equality of men and women, universal access to health-care services, including those related to reproductive health care, which includes family planning and sexual health. Reproductive health care programmes should provide the widest range of services without any form of coercion.

For over 20 years family planning has been widely recognized as a human right. To make the right to reproductive health a reality, however, requires national commitment.

Reaching Out to Youth

By providing facts and guidance, family planning programmes can help young people make responsible sexual decisions. For youth who need them, programmes also can provide better access to reproductive health services, including contraception.

A Large Group, a Growing Need

Sex among unmarried young people often attracts widespread attention—and usually disapproval. Policies toward youth often reflect the view that sexual activity should not occur before marriage. Increasingly, however, people are recognizing the need to reach out to all youth with appropriate care.

Almost 1 billion people are between ages 10 and 19—one-sixth of the world's total population. Most sexual activity among young people takes place within marriage. A minority of unmarried young men and women are sexually active, typically episodically and infrequently. Premarital sexual experience has become more common, however, as the age at first marriage has risen and age at puberty has fallen.

Substantial numbers of young men and women have their first sexual experience outside marriage. In sub-Saharan Africa surveys show that, by age 20, on average 38 per cent of women had sex for the first time before marriage. In Latin America and the Caribbean an estimated 28 per cent did so. Elsewhere, few surveys have asked whether first sex before age 20 was before or after marriage.

Consequences

Young men often face peer pressures to take sexual risks—for example, visiting sex workers and not using condoms. Risk-taking often has fatal consequences. Half of all people who have become infected with HIV became infected between ages 15 and 24. Currently, about one-third of all people with HIV are ages 15 to 24.

Having an unintended pregnancy often hastens or even forces marriage at a young age. While data are unavailable for Asia, in sub-Saharan Africa and Latin America births to unmarried adolescents are common; in many countries, one-third of the births to women ages 15 to 19 occur among unmarried women.

Many unintended pregnancies and STIs occur because few young people use condoms or any other contraception the first time that they have sex. The most common reason that young people give for not using contraception is that they did not expect to have sex; the second most reported reason is that they did not know about contraception.

Focusing on Young People

Today, countries are focusing more on helping young people improve their reproductive health. In 1999 the UN General Assembly, as part of a broader resolution reflecting on progress since the 1994 ICPD in Cairo, urged governments to recognize that "sexually active adolescents will require special family planning information, counseling, and health services," as well as prevention and treatment of STIs.

Because life-long attitudes and behaviour patterns form during youth, addressing the needs of young people will have positive consequences for them now and throughout their lives. Young people need to learn about sexuality and reproductive health from everyone in a position to provide accurate information and counseling—family planning and other health care providers as well as parents, teachers, peers, and the mass media. Peers and the entertainment media are particularly powerful influences on young people. They can provide models of healthy behaviour.

Sex Education

Sex education programmes help young people remain healthy. Most studies find that sex education does not encourage young people to be promiscuous. In fact, of 53 studies of various sex education programmes reviewed by UNAIDS, 22 found that sex education delayed the onset of sexual activity, reduced the number of sexual partners, or reduced unplanned pregnancy and STI rates. Another 27 found that a sex education programme neither increased nor decreased sexual activity. Only three studies reported increases in sexual behaviour associated with receiving sex education.

For many unmarried young people, sexual abstinence may be a good choice. Studies have not found, however, that programmes advocating only abstinence have reduced levels of sexual activity among young people.

Box 1: Family Planning—Contribution of Association of Maternal and Child Health Programmes (AMCHP)

Family planning is a vital part of assuring healthy women, babies and families. When women plan their pregnancies, they are more likely to seek prenatal care, improving their own health and the health of the baby. Family planning helps women and their partners have children when they are physically, emotionally and financially prepared to take on the responsibility of a child.

Roughly half of all pregnancies in the United States are unplanned. While pregnancy intendedness is not the only factor that determines healthy outcomes for moms and babies, unintended and unwanted pregnancies do have important health, economic and social consequences. Unplanned pregnancies tend to result in lower birth weights, premature births, and higher rates of infant illness and death. The infant mortality rate in the United States is higher than 28 other industrialized nations, and the number of low birth weight babies has increased over the last decade. The rate of fetal alcohol syndrome has risen sharply, and the maternal mortality rate has not declined for 10 years.

The Association of Maternal and Child Health Programmes (AMCHP) has built a solid foundation in women's health by promoting best practices and conducting advocacy and education on issues related to pregnant women, new mothers, and their infants. The Women's and Perinatal Health Programme emphasizes disease prevention and wellness promotion throughout the primary reproductive years to ensure better birth outcomes and good health for women as they grow older. As we move forward, we aim to further strengthen our members' capacity in women's health by working to assure positive health outcomes for women regardless of intent or ability to have children, and by addressing issues such as chronic disease and injury, healthy lifestyles, and health disparities.

Family planning is much more than birth control. The AMCHP supports family planning in its broadest sense. Planning for a family means making conscious and informed decisions about the initiation of sexual activity and the safe and effective use of contraceptives to time a healthy pregnancy.

Comprehensive family planning should include a broad range of clinical and social options for adults and adolescents before, during and after pregnancy, such as abstinence, comprehensive sexuality education, contraception, parenting education and adoption. AMCHP believes that family planning should be a standard part of basic health care for all women of childbearing age and their partners. All adults and adolescents should have universal access to family planning services that are culturally competent and age-appropriate. AMCHP believes that all private and public health insurance should cover all FDA-approved birth control, including devices and procedures used for emergency contraception.

Comprehensive family planning also includes educating patients about future pregnancies to ensure their physical and mental health and that of their babies. Information about the importance of good nutrition, particularly folic acid, and the adverse effects of using alcohol and tobacco during pregnancy can enable women, adolescents and their partners to make decisions for a healthier pregnancy and a healthier baby. Preconception counseling is integral to reducing low birth weight and infant mortality and in improving women's health.

Involving Men

While men share responsibility for reproductive health, lack of attention to them in the past has conveyed a message that family planning is not their concern. The more that programmes can reach men, the healthier the consequences will be-for men, women, and children.

Communication and Decision-Making

Men are more interested in family planning than is usually assumed. Today, family planning programmes increasingly are focusing on involving men. Yet much remains to be done to turn interest into healthy behaviour.

In particular, encouraging men to discuss reproductive health, including family planning, with their partners and to share responsibility for reproductive decisions is a good health care strategy. Also, in the era of HIV/AIDS, it is urgent for men's own protection and that of their partners that programmes address the problem of sexual risk-taking.

Men play powerful—even dominant roles in reproductive decisions.

Without considering their partners' wishes or the health consequences for themselves or their partners, however, their actions can have unhealthy and even dangerous results. In contrast, couples who talk to each other about family planning and reproductive health reach healthier decisions. For example, they are more likely to use contraception and use it effectively.

Surveys show that many husbands and wives do not know each others' views about family planning. When men and women do not know their partners' fertility desires, family planning attitudes, or contraceptive preferences, the consequences can include unintended pregnancies and unsafe abortions.

Men's Attitudes and Behaviour

Men's contraceptive use is lower than might be expected, given their levels of knowledge and approval of family planning, according to surveys of men in developing countries, mostly in sub-Saharan Africa.

For example, between one-quarter and two-thirds of these men say that they do not want to have more children, but neither they nor their wives are using contraception. By comparison, in countries surveyed about one-fifth of married women say they do not want to become pregnant but are not using any method of contraception.

With more information and encouragement, more men would be able to play positive roles in reproductive health. For example, a husband can help his wife have safe pregnancies and give birth to healthy babies if he becomes better informed about maternal and child health. Reproductive health care programmes can help men play supportive roles during pregnancy and delivery and during breastfeeding. Increasing men's participation can be a promising strategy for achieving good reproductive health for all.

Encouraging Healthier Sexual Behaviour

Most men, and particularly sexually active unmarried men, have a lot to learn to become responsible sex partners. Most need to know more about preventing pregnancy and about avoiding and preventing HIV/AIDS and other STIs. In some countries only a minority of never-married men who have heard of AIDS know that condoms prevent AIDS.

Even when men know that unprotected sex is risky, many still take the risk. Yet among men there is much demand for condoms that family planning can meet. In sub-Saharan countries surveyed 7 per cent to 50 per cent of unmarried men report using condoms. In Latin America condom use reported by unmarried men ranges from 27 per cent to 64 per cent. Few data on sexually active unmarried men are available elsewhere.

Family planning programmes can address many of the obstacles that men face to learning about and adopting safer sexual behaviour. For example, programmes have organized community activities and meetings where men can discuss their concerns about sexual behaviour comfortably and openly.

Young men are particularly difficult to reach, but some youth programmes have found that peer educators in particular can provide information and counseling about healthy behaviour. By reaching men of all ages now, family planning programmes can do more for the health of all people.

Protecting the Environment

Every country can do something now to assure a liveable environment for generations to come. To varying degrees, all countries can conserve natural resources, use cleaner production technologies, manage resource supply and demand better, and slow population growth.

Slowing Population Growth

In any country population size helps determine demand for resources and levels of pollution. The other important factors affecting the environment are consumption levels per capita and technology. Industrialized countries consume far more resources per capita than developing countries. Almost all future population growth, however, will occur in developing countries. Rapid increases in population, along with rising per capita demand for natural resources, can put tremendous pressures on the environment.

In developing countries family planning programmes have played an important role in slowing population growth. Without access to modern contraception most people are unable to space or limit their births effectively. By providing good-quality family planning information and services, programmes have helped people have the smaller families they prefer, fertility has fallen, and population growth has slowed.

There is no way to predict how large the population could become before it overwhelmed the planet, but few people would want to find out the hard way. At current levels of population and technology, human activities are already causing "rapid, novel, and substantial changes" to the environment, biologists Peter Vitousek and colleagues argue. Two basic ways of easing humanity's impact on the environment, they note, are to use resources more efficiently and to slow population growth.

Preserving the Environment

Slowing population growth would help ease demand for freshwater supplies and arable land, avoid air and water pollution, lighten the burden on cities, and, by reducing competition for scarce resources, avert conflict and civil strife.

13

Male Involvement in Family Planning

Selected Programme Initiatives in Africa

Male involvement in family planning (FP) means more than increasing the number of men using condoms and having vasectomies; male involvement also includes the number of men who encourage and support their partner and their peers to use FP and who influence the policy environment to be more conducive to developing male-related programmes. In this context "male involvement" should be understood in a much broader sense than male contraception, and should refer to all organizational activities aimed at men as a discrete group which have the objective of increasing the acceptability and prevalence of family-planning practice of either sex.

In the past, family-planning programmes have focused attention primarily on women, because of the need to free women from excessive child-bearing, and to reduce maternal and infant mortality through the use of modern methods of contraception. Most of the family-planning services were offered within maternal and child health (MCH) centers, most research and information campaigns focused on women. This focus on women has reinforced the belief that family planning is largely a woman's business, with the man playing a very peripheral role.

Involving men and obtaining their support and commitment to family planning is of crucial importance in the Africa region, given their elevated position in the African society. Most decisions that affect family life are made by men. Most decisions that affect political life are made by men. Men hold positions of leadership and influence from the family unit right through the national level (IPPF, 1984). The involvement of men in family planning would therefore not only ease the responsibility borne by women in terms of decision-making for family-planning matters, but would also accelerate the understanding and practice of family planning in general.

Only recently have family-planning associations recognized the importance of men's role and motivation in fertility decision making, particularly in Africa. But now that this has been recognized, the question is "what can family-planning and reproductive-health programmes do to encourage men's cooperation?"

Some programmes have developed IEC campaigns aimed at increasing the awareness and knowledge of men. However, one of the crucial questions now facing these programmes is how to move beyond increasing knowledge to changing attitudes and practice. How to address the needs of men through different service-delivery strategies is also an important question.

Various service-delivery strategies to meet those needs can be provided in a variety of ways, including primary health care facilities, special hours for men in MCH/FP clinics, male-only clinics, STDs clinics, integration of FP promotion in AIDS prevention programmes, mobile units, organized groups, income generating schemes, employment-based programmes, youth programmes and peer counseling, male-to-male community-based distribution of condoms, social marketing, involvement of private agencies and medical practitioners.

Contributing Factors

Many factors, of course, affect women's and men's contraceptive use, but there are three key elements which deserve to be highlighted:

First, men's support or opposition to their partners' practice of family planning has a strong impact on contraceptive use in many parts of the world, including Africa. Within marriage in Africa, men typically have more say than women in the decision to use contraception and in the number of children that the couple will have.

For example, according to the 1984 Zimbabwe Reproductive Health Survey, 42 percent of married women stated that it was the husband's responsibility to decide whether his wife should use FP methods. Focus groups conducted by Zimbabwe National Family Planning Council (ZNFPC) and a private research agency suggested "that men were the ultimate decision makers on family size and FP matters in Zimbabwe".

In Ghana, "despite the independent nature of some marital relationships, recent evidence indicates that men have the primary decision-making power in matters of FP." Both DHS data and focus-group research reveal that the husband is usually the effective decision-maker about fertility. Furthermore, husbands' family-planning attitudes and fertility goals usually are not influenced by those of their wives. And, when partners disagree on whether to use family planning, the man's preference usually dominates (Population Reports, 1994). Also, "There is a reason to suspect that men comprehend FP messages differently than women do. Men felt that financial considerations were the primary motivation for FP use, whereas women reported that health and the need for women to 'rest' were the primary motivations for use". According to an analysis from DHS surveys, the mean ideal family size for currently married men is higher than for married women. This difference is significant in West Africa, ranging from about two children in Burkina Faso to more than four children in Niger and Senegal (exception is Ghana, 0.6). In East and North Africa, no significant difference in fertility desire was found. This shows the importance of targeting men with FP programmes.

The husband's support is found to be a good predictor of future practice and continued use. There are studies done in the Philippines which indicate that the continuation rate among women whose husbands support their contraceptive practice is much higher than those whose husbands do not give support to their wives (IPPF, 1984). In South Korea researchers found that 71 percent of women whose husbands approved family planning had used contraception at some time, compared with 23 percent of women whose husbands did not approve (Population Reports, 1994). In Madagascar, Norplant continuation rates were higher after one year among couples in which the husband had been involved in the decision-making process, and among these couples both wives and husbands were more satisfied with Norplant than those in which only the wife was counseled.

Second, spouse communication is positively associated with contraceptive use: DHS data from seven African countries (Botswana, Burundi, Ghana, Kenya, Senegal, Sudan, and Togo) show that the percentage of women using modern contraceptives is consistently higher in the group that had discussed FP with their husbands in the year before the interview than in the group that had not (JHU/PIP, 1994).

Because of lack of communication, many women do not know what their husbands think about FP. Many women think that their husbands disapprove of FP, when in fact the husband approves. In West Africa, about three quarters of the men and women had not discussed family planning with their spouse in the year preceding the survey, except in Ghana and Cameroon where the proportions were about one-half and two-thirds respectively. In East Africa, the figure is less than 40 percent, except in Burundi and Tanzania (Ezeh *et al.*, 1996). In Burundi, 94 percent of men surveyed approved of contraceptive use, but only 48 percent had discussed it with their wives in the preceding year. (Population Reports, 1994). According to a 1993 DHS survey, 45 percent of married women in Tanzania either did not know what their husbands thought about FP or thought their husbands disapproved of family planning, when in fact many of the husbands approved.

Third, men's lack of access to services has been a barrier to family-planning use. Men cannot share responsibility for reproductive health and family planning if services and information do not reach them. Most FP clinics cater to women, so men are uncomfortable about going to these clinics. Men must be reached in other ways. This testimony from a Kenyan man is a good illustration of that need: "After having three children, my wife went on the pill for her contraception because we could no longer afford an accident with the natural methods we were using. Her blood pressure immediately shot up, and she was advised to discontinue. She tried other methods, but they had complications too. I felt I was unfair and it was my duty, too, to take part in family planning. One morning we went together to our local family-planning clinic. I will never forget how embarrassed I felt. There was not even a single man there, just queues of women and their babies. This was a woman's world and I felt totally lost". This confirms the assumption that no matter how many men want to know about and utilize contraception, most family-planning programmes have not yet given adequate attention to serving them.

There are some examples of experience and initiatives in various forms which illustrate a genuine concern and creative approach toward achieving greater male involvement in family planning in Africa. Programmes to encourage men's involvement in family planning are expanding, especially through interventions to increase knowledge and interest of men, such as information, education, and communication campaigns using mass media, and interventions to increase access and use of FP services by men such as community-based distribution, condom sales and promotion, workplace programmes, and a few male clinics and vasectomy services. Some of the field experiences have shown that well-targeted, focused male-involvement programmes can have an impact on both male and female behaviours related to reproductive health.

Promotional Campaigns

Zimbabwe

In 1988-89, the Zimbabwe National Family Planning Council (ZNFPC) conducted a national education project targeting men, the first of its kind for sub-Saharan Africa. Funded by USAID with technical assistance from the Johns Hopkins University Population Communication Services (JHU/PCS) programme, the project was designed to increase men's knowledge of, and promote more favourable attitudes toward, family planning, increase modern family-planning methods, and promote joint decision making.

The project used a radio serial drama, educational talks for men, and family-planning leaflets to promote these messages. An extensive evaluation found the radio drama to be the most effective method for reaching about two of every five men in both urban and rural areas. Of the other methods, the talks reached 11 percent of men, and the leaflets reached 5 percent. The proportion of men who reported joint decision making in family planning rose from 25 percent to 35 percent from 1988 to 1989.

Analysis of survey results from the first study (which controlled for demographic variables and radio ownership) found that men who were exposed to the campaign were 1.4 times as likely to use a modern family-planning method as were other men, 1.7 times as likely to use condoms, and 1.4 times as likely to believe that both husband and wife should participate in deciding how many children to have. However, the campaign was not entirely successful in promoting the idea of joint decision-making, because men who were exposed to the campaign were 2.4 times more likely than others to state that the husband alone decides whether to practice family planning (Kim, *et al.*, 1996). But positive lessons from this first campaign were that Zimbabwean men want to learn more about family planning, and that communication materials directed at men can change men's attitudes towards family planning, stimulate discussion between husbands and wives, and motivate men to support the practice of family planning.

A second male-motivation campaign was launched in 1993, drawing heavily on the lessons learned during the first campaign, again to encourage male involvement in family planning and to encourage use of long-term methods to limit family size. This second campaign used a wide variety of media to reach more men and to expose them to multiple, reinforcing sources of information: radio, television, posters, newspapers, motivational talks, family festivals, a football tournament with giant puppet shows at half-time, live dramas, and musical shows. This campaign also focused on improving the quality of services by developing a new training curriculum and a video on counseling and interpersonal communication, and trained clinic-based health workers and community-based distribution agents.

A post-campaign evaluation showed that 88 percent of adults living in the campaign areas were exposed to at least one campaign material or activity. Again radio had the greatest reach, 62 percent of men, followed by print materials (posters, newspapers and magazines, and pamphlets reached 57 percent, 48 percent, and 46 percent of men, respectively). Football matches drew far larger audiences (18 percent of men) than any other type of community event. Exposure to the campaign was associated with a rise in use of modern contraceptives. Before the campaign, contraceptive demand was declining as a result of increases in contraceptive prices and primary health care fees. With the launch of the campaign, this trend reversed, and contraceptive demand, especially for long-term methods, began to rise. People exposed to three or more campaign components were 1.6 times as likely as others to use a modern contraceptive method.

According to the surveys, knowledge of long-term and permanent methods rose over the campaign period as did the number of people holding positive attitudes toward them. The campaign also encouraged couples to communicate more about family planning and to decide jointly on a contraceptive method. The proportion who reported discussing family planning with their spouses or partners rose from 37 percent to 57 percent. Twenty-nine percent of men who were exposed to four or more campaign components reported that they had discussed family planning with their partners, consulted service providers, or adopted modern contraceptive methods, compared with 16 percent of men exposed to two or three components, and 2 percent of men exposed to just one component or none. As men became more interested in family planning, many wanted to play an active role in the decision-making process. Rather than leaving family planning decisions to their wives or partners, men were more likely after the campaign to believe that they alone should be responsible for making such decisions or that decisions should be made jointly. The rise in interest in solely male decision-making recorded by the surveys suggests that the campaign's reliance on traditional masculine images may have reinforced stereotypes about male decision-making and blurred campaign messages about the value of joint decision-making (Kim, *et al.*, 1996).

Ghana

In September 1987, the Health Education Division of Ghana's Ministry of Health (MOH/HED) began a systematic family-planning IEC project with funding from USAID and technical assistance from JHU/PCS. The goals of the first phase of the project were to 1) increase knowledge of, and improve attitudes toward, family planning and promote contraceptive use among men and women of reproductive age, 2) enhance family-planning counseling skills among MOH service providers, and 3) strengthen the MOH's ability to develop, implement, monitor, and evaluate communication programmes in health. The project used situational analysis, service provider training, and IEC material development and mobilization for two campaigns in three regions before expanding the campaign to remaining areas. The project used a wide variety of IEC material, media, and activities, including leaflets and booklets, motivational posters, national radio and television broadcasts, drama, a theme song, community audiovisual material, and community activities.

The second phase of the project highlighted male involvement in family planning. A November 1991 study of the project found that almost all males surveyed in six regions had seen or heard at least one IEC family planning campaign medium. In the Ashanti, Brong-Ahafo, and Central Regions where more intensive campaigns were run, more men were reached than in other regions. Findings indicate a significant increase in men's family planning knowledge and practice, and improvement in attitude with the increasing length of the project. Also, among those men exposed to the intensive campaign, 47 percent had discussed family planning with their partners, and 26 percent stated that they or their partners were using a more modern contraceptive method.

Niger

In 1987, Niger's Ministry of Health and Social Affairs (MOHSA) of the Directorate of Family Planning initiated a communication project in collaboration with the JHU/PCS. The project included an IEC campaign with three objectives:

a) to increase public awareness of modern methods of child spacing,
b) to reinforce positive attitudes toward contraceptive use, and
c) to motivate potential clients to seek family-planning services.

Project activities took place over a two year period in Niger's capital, Niamey, and in the two urban centers of Maradi and Zinder. Project activities included a communication workshop for programme managers, a national family-planning logo design, focus group discussions, two awareness seminars for opinion and political leaders, a series of radio and television broadcast dramas with family-planning themes, and contraceptive sample kits for health agents.

The project was not targeted to men exclusively. However, a post-project survey found that the project had contributed to positive changes in men's knowledge and attitudes: a 21 percent improvement in their ability to name one or more contraceptive methods without assistance; an 11 percent increase in approval of the use of contraceptives for birth spacing; men's exposure to television programmes with family-planning themes increased by 94 percent; men's reports of hearing a radio programme with a family-planning theme increased by 47 percent.

Recommendations for the project included, among others, targeting men as a primary audience for family-planning messages; developing messages targeted to men that emphasize the economic benefit of having fewer children; creating a new role model for men that portrays responsible men as those who discuss family planning with their partners; expanding awareness-raising into organized male networks, such as the political parties, employers, unions, the military, and paramilitary; using male Social Affairs agents to reassure men that society views family planning as desirable and responsible.

Nigeria

The Planned Parenthood Federation of Nigeria (PPFN) conducted programmes to enhance male motivation. These included educational outreach to leaders, family life education for youth, and reaching men through existing groups. Government officials, traditional rulers, and religious leaders were among those targeted, as were journalists, health educators, teachers, social workers, and agricultural extension workers. PPFN also made contacts with Nigerian Army units and the police. PPFN saw significant progress in developing programme guidelines and initiating collaboration with other organizations (IPPF, 1984).

Campaign for Vasectomy Promotion

The Kenya Vasectomy Promotion Project, sponsored by JHU/PCS and the

Association for Voluntary and Safe Contraception (AVSC), was designed to increase potential acceptors' knowledge of vasectomy. Messages stress that the vasectomy procedure is simple and safe, that men who have vasectomies remain healthy and virile, and that "wives love it because they no longer fear an accidental pregnancy." Wives in the television commercials: "He's strong really ... We have great sex!" Radio, television, and newspaper ads also direct men to visit Kencom House, the male-only clinic in Nairobi, where specially trained male service providers and counselors make men feel welcome. Potential clients can also write or access a special telephone hotline for more information.

Campaign for Employer-Based Programmes

In 1987, the Planned Parenthood Association of Zambia (PPAZ) launched a male-involvement campaign that included a campaign for industrial workers, targeting the working man. Since that time, PPAZ has held discussions with employers to encourage them to include family-planning services in work-site clinics. PPAZ has also been invited to give talks by the labor and social security ministry and at labor union meetings. In 1984, John Snow, Inc., in conjunction with the National Council for Population and Development and funded by USAID, began the Family Planning Private Sector Programme in Kenya to help private companies and NGOs expand health services to their employees by including family planning. Health workers conducted education sessions in the workplace, as well as providing health services. The programme also encouraged employers to form their own community-based committees that included representatives from management, unions, and workers to plan information and education programmes. Cashew, tea, and sugar companies and paper mills were among the 30 employers involved in the programme, all of which employ mainly men. The programme aimed to recruit at least 30,000 new family-planning clients. No results were given for this programme (Population Reports, 1986).

In 1989, with the support of AVSC, Mulanje Mission Hospital in rural Malawi took a leading role in increasing male participation in family planning by initiating a "child spacing club" for men. This club—modeled on the Man to Man programme in Blantyre, an initiative of the NGO Banja La Mtsogolo—initiated educational seminars for male hospital staff ranging from grounds keepers to nurses; the club also took their child-spacing messages to two rural villages and a tea estate. One of the villages and the tea estate had asked to be involved after hearing about the project. Workshops were held at village meeting places, and over a seven-month period, 320 men actively participated in workshops, with many men requesting further learning opportunities. Many of the men cited their exclusion from previous education and counseling opportunities as the reason for their lack of involvement in the past. As a result of the Mulanje Mission Hospital effort, the Mulanje staff have had more requests for visits than they can handle from other villages. The project has operated at very low cost to AVSC—only for educational materials and gasoline—while the staff have contributed their time and enthusiasm. As of November 1992, a second mission hospital was due to start a similar club (Mason, 1992).

Fathers' Clubs

In 1981, the Ministry of Health and Social Affairs in Mauritania launched a school for fathers to sensitize men to women's health problems and family planning. Fathers meet monthly to discuss issues that impact children and women. In 1984, the project expanded to include a weekly school for husbands, aimed at informing young men who do not yet have children about family health. No information is given about the results or effectiveness of the programme (Population Reports, 1986). A fathers' club initiated by the family health clinic of the Institute of Child Health and Primary Care of the University of Lagos, Nigeria, is credited with increasing awareness of family planning between 1975 and 1982. The fathers' club was one of the clinic's strategies for gaining support for family-planning and child health programmes (Olukoya, 1985). The Planned Parenthood Association of Ghana (PPAG) sponsored three pilot "Daddies Clubs" through its special Male Motivation and Planned Parenthood project in 1980. These clubs were employer-based, located at the Pretsea Oil-Palm Plantation (Western Region), among Dungu Amasachina Young Farmers (Northern Region) and at the Tafo Cocoa Research Institute of Ghana (CRIG). Of these, the Pretsea project was the most successful. In 1982 alone, about 5,000 people were contacted, about 4,000 of them through lectures and discussion groups. About 1,620 were contacted through 450 follow-up visits to their homes. A total of 1,519 acceptors were recruited, of whom 1,310 were for non-clinical contraceptives and 209 for clinical services. The clinical acceptors were mostly women encouraged by their husbands to seek services. In addition to contraceptive services, the Pretsea programme offered services regarding sub-fertility and infertility. Of the eight cases receiving treatment at the PPAG clinic, two women became pregnant. News about this side of family planning helped spread the word about the programme, gained it further credibility, and attracted more people to the Daddies Club. These successes are credited with raising membership in the club from 25 to 100 (IPPF, 1984).

Sporting Events

"Ghanaian family-planning professionals have hit upon an innovative new scheme to get men and women talking about family planning. They sponsor tournaments of games that men like to play, such as soccer, tug-of-war, and checkers. Then they recruit the wives to oppose the men, altering the rules where necessary to make a fair match. Male soccer players are only allowed to use their left foot, for instance, and the female tug-of-war team is allowed extra members. The couples enjoy the matches, and the winners are given a gallon of condoms, or another prize that will spark conversation about family planning. Results seem to be good. Couples are talking, and family planning is losing its wicked connotations. Half of the reduction in fertility in one rural area in Ghana appears due to the acceptance of family planning by men".

In Zimbabwe, a "Family Planning Challenge Cup" soccer match is used to mobilize men and attract them to the family-planning message. Each of the three tournament games played by four of Zimbabwe's top soccer teams attracted over 30,000 spectators, mostly men. Soccer was used as the image for the campaign along with the slogans "Play the Game Right" and "The Dream Team" (the latter being the nickname Zimbabweans give their national soccer team), which were used for billboards, t-shirts, and newspaper and television ads.

Male Clinic

In March 1993, the first Family Planning Centre for Men (as part of the Population and Health Services/Marie Stopes Clinics) opened in Nairobi, Kenya, to provide vasectomy services, counseling, and other male reproductive health services in a confidential environment. In June 1993, the second Centre for Men was opened in Mombasa. This center offers two evening sessions of two hours per week. The need for these centers was identified during formative research conducted by Innovative Communication Systems as part of a campaign to increase vasectomy awareness and acceptance in Kenya. Since these first two centers opened, four more have been added. AVSC has provided training for Kenyan surgeons in no-scalpel vasectomy in connection with these centers. In addition, AVSC conducted IEC activities, largely through mass-media advertising, particularly via radio, to get basic information about vasectomy out to men. They also ran newspaper ads with coupons that could be returned to get more information. AVSC found that the number of men who used the Centre for Men rose sharply following each ad campaign. Through the experiences with the centers for men, AVSC has learned that men are interested in family planning. The majority of men don't want children they cannot care for. Men need good counseling and reproductive health services.

Community-Based Programmes

Kenya

A March 1995 report by the Population Council's Africa Operations Research and Technical Assistance project, funded by USAID, describes a study undertaken in Kenya to gain programmatic experience in using community-based distribution agents trained to focus specifically on reaching males. In addition, insights were gained on the relative effectiveness of using trained teams of only men, trained teams of only women, and trained teams of both men and women in promoting and providing family-planning services and in educating men and women about HIV/AIDS. Previously, the assumption had prevailed that female CBD agents can discuss family planning or distribute contraceptives to women more effectively than male CBD agents. Evidence from this study held that this may not necessarily be true and that there is much to gain by using male CBD agents, particularly given that men who do not have regular jobs can devote more time to CBD activities, whereas women agents have household and other chores in addition to their CBD activities.

The following were among the findings of the study: all agents interviewed recommended a mixed group of male and female agents; involving males, both as distributors and as targets for family-planning activities and services resulted in a greater use of family planning by men and increased communication between spouses; education for HIV/AIDS prevention resulted in a sharp increase in positive behaviour change among males, with little change for women; and HIV/AIDS education did not lead to greater discussion of the subject among partners (Population Council & FPAK, 1995).

Beginning in 1983, the Nairobi-based African Medical and Research Foundation (AMREF), with funding from USAID, ran training programmes for shopkeepers in distributing non-prescription contraceptives to their customers. The scheme took advantage of community trust in the shopkeepers and the shopkeepers' experience in distributing drugs. To help shopkeepers learn to supply contraceptives and dispense commercial drugs more effectively, training focused on such topics as communications and client management, primary health, modern and traditional contraceptive methods, background instruction about Kenya's population growth, the importance of seeing the husband and wife together, and when to refer customers to a health center. In this scheme, most of the shopkeepers were men. The shopkeepers worked on a volunteer basis and gave free contraceptives without commission, citing their willingness to do something for their communities as their motivation.

Ghana

As part of the Ghana National Family Planning Programme, GNFPP, mobile family-planning teams were organized to provide birth-control services to villages in the Danfa region. The staff of MCH centers and village-based primary health care workers supplemented the work of the GNFPP. Early in this effort, it was clear that family-planning services for men would be an important element, since nearly half the clients of these services were men. The programme had several notable results: men proved to be better family-planning advocates than women; more men tried to persuade their friends to use contraceptives than did women; men who chose birth control for either themselves or their partners reported that their partners had fewer pregnancies than did women who participated directly in the programme. An evaluation of the GNFPP by the School of Public Health at the University of California at Los Angeles attributes at least one-half of the fertility reduction in Danfa to male acceptance of contraception. Lessons learned showed that men in Danfa preferred visiting the mobile clinics for obtaining condoms, rather than buying them in a store, which required their traveling outside the village. However, this must be balanced against tying programmes to formal health services that in other cases may be less mobile and more costly in terms of personnel. Community-based programmes were seen as having the greatest opportunity for increasing men's use of birth control (IPPF, 1984).

Between 1980 and 1982, the Planned Parenthood Association of Ghana (PPAG) conducted community-based distribution through 203 outlets, 133 of which were in urban and 70 in rural communities. One hundred twenty were administered by PPAG and 83 were administered by CBD agents who received token incentives for their involvement. Agents were often recruited from other PPAG programmes. For example, agents at the Tafo Cocoa Research Institute of Ghana (CRIG) and the Pretsea Oil Palm Plantation were the secretaries of Daddies Clubs at those companies. Agents worked through pharmacies, maternity homes, groceries, banks, police and military barracks, and other points throughout the community in collaboration with PPAG to deliver non-clinical contraceptives. PPAG also has worked with local traditional birth attendants, some of whom are men, and given them training as CBD agents. TBAs were found to be very effective because of their credibility in their communities and their frequent contact with community members, whom they serve as traditional doctors. PPAG recruited about 100,000 acceptors through its CBD projects. Seven hundred boxes of condoms, 174,700 tubes of Neo-Sampoon, and 23,300 cycles of pills were distributed (IPPF, 1984). Planned Parenthood of Ghana offered a "cafeteria style" series of lectures on topics of interest and concern to men. The most popular lectures selected were on AIDS, impotence, the breakdown of relationships, and male and female physiology. Delivering the lectures to existing groups of men such as workers' committees, clubs, or other groups has led to PPAG's success with the programme. PPAG workers stress that family planning is to help couples have the number of children they want, which is up to each couple. They also emphasize the infertility services that family-planning associations offer. CBD programmes back up the PPAG effort by making contraceptives available, for which family-planning field workers earn a 10 percent commission on the supplies they sell.

Swaziland

"Man Talk" was a programme in Swaziland in which men who have been trained in communication talk with other men one-to-one in bars, pool halls, clubs, and factories. Other activities include distributing educational leaflets, motivational materials, and condoms and working with local business owners. An example of a result from this effort is that the owner of a nightclub was persuaded to install a condom dispensing machine in the men's restroom. At the time this activity was documented, negotiations were underway for a condom machine in the women's restroom.

Social Marketing

In Ghana in 1986, the SOMARC project of the Futures Group, funded by USAID, undertook a condom-marketing project aimed at middle-and lower-middle-class married men between 26 and 35 years old who had a secondary-school education. Panther condoms, the brand marketed, already had some name recognition from previous availability, though the condoms had not been sold since 1978. The theme for the campaign was "Panther Condoms Are Back." Television, radio, print, and point of purchase advertising were rolled out in four phases, with progressively more specific messages regarding family planning, generic condom advertising, trade advertising, and brand-specific advertising. Research was conducted to evaluate the effectiveness of these interventions in improving male attitudes toward the condom and in stimulating acceptance and use. More than 80 percent of the men in a 1991 urban sample knew the brand name, up from 50 percent in 1988. Men who had ever used a Panther condom increased from 12 percent in 1988 to nearly 50 percent in 1991, and nearly 60 percent of men who recalled a condom ad remembered Panther. Over 25 percent of all men in the sample claimed they were using a condom regularly, up from 9 percent of men in 1988. A 1990 consumer profile showed that over 42 percent of Panther users had never used contraception before they started using Panther. Thirty-six percent had switched from a less effective method, and 16 percent had switched from another brand or a more effective contraceptive. Ninety-eight percent of users were middle or lower-middle class, 89 percent had some secondary education, 57 percent were married, and 31 percent were younger than 25 years old. The majority of users were satisfied with the product overall and intended to continue using it. Availability, quality, low price, and the advertising were the main reasons users chose Panther.

Roles of Male Opinion Leaders

From 1991 to 1993, an operations-research study was conducted by the Population Council and the Ministry of Public Health of Cameroon on the role of male opinion leaders in promoting and delivering family-planning services in rural areas. In this study, which was supported by USAID, KAP surveys were conducted before and after the intervention period of 12 months. During the 12-month period, male opinion leaders (MOLs) were trained in a variety of health interventions, including family planning, treatment of diarrhea, and antenatal and vaccination referrals, and completed IEC activities in rural areas surrounding Nkambe in Cameroon's northwest province. The MOLs received one-week initial training and three refresher courses during the intervention period. MOLs were supervised at the district level and worked in tandem with traditional birth attendants.

The results of the study indicate that MOLs were very active in delivering health interventions in rural areas, as shown by an average of 90 percent submission of monthly activity reports by MOLs. The effectiveness of their performance improved with successive refresher courses.

In the populations served, the pre-intervention KAP survey indicated that knowledge of specific family-planning methods was relatively low for both men and women. After the MOLs' intervention, levels of knowledge for all methods rose, with a dramatic change in knowledge of condoms and spermicides specifically. In the male sample, knowledge of condoms increased from 52 percent to 81 percent; for women, knowledge increased from 47 percent to 72 percent. For spermicides, men's knowledge increased from 12 percent to 44 percent, and women's knowledge increased from 17 percent to 42 percent. More than 6,000 condoms and nearly 4,500 spermicides were distributed in villages during the intervention period.

Approval of family planning only rose slightly, attributable to already positive attitudes noted in the pre-intervention survey. However, there remained a meaningful percentage of men (14.1 percent) and women (13.5 percent) who disapproved of family planning after the intervention period. In the post-intervention KAP survey, 34.6 percent of men and 40.1 percent of women had benefitted from MOL service provision. The target population was generally satisfied with the IEC activities the MOLs conducted (Population Council, 1993).

Family Life Education Programmes for Youth

Between 1980 and 1982, the Planned Parenthood Association of Ghana (PPAG) reached out to about 200 schools and youth organizations, and contacted nearly 90,000 people through Family Life Education (FLE) programmes, referring about 15,000 acceptors for clinical and non-clinical services. This was achieved through specially organized lectures, film shows and educational materials. The programmes were individualized to the needs of each institution and the group targeted, based on their age and experience. The programme has raised some important issues on curriculum development and the whole question of how FLE should be effectively organized and introduced into the school system. As a result, the Ministry of Education began pilot FLE programmes in selected schools, for a later introduction of FLE in due course into all second-cycle institutions in Ghana.

Counseling was found to be an important component of FLE, and PPAG was joined by another organization, the Christian Council of Ghana, for the training of 103 counselors. The YMCA of Ghana also joined the initiative, and trained more FLE counselors to be used at the grass-roots level to produce a multiplier effect. In 1981-1982 about 19,000 people were contacted with nearly 9,000 referrals made to the nearest Family Planning Clinics for service (IPPF, 1984).

- A well-designed and well-focused IEC campaign can have a positive impact on men by increasing their knowledge and improving their attitudes toward FP; this impact, in turn, will increase joint decision-making and promote contraceptive use for men and women. Well-designed family-planning campaigns can reach men by using multiple communication channels that appeal to them (such as radio dramas and sporting events) and by developing messages that relate FP support/use to responsible fatherhood and virile images. But one needs to be particularly careful not to reinforce the stereotype of male decision makers, and thereby reduce women's roles in making decisions, since women will still be the main users of contraception, given the diversity of female methods.
- Campaigns focused on work-site clinics are usually well perceived, as employers quickly pick up the benefits of FP programmes for the company: fewer sick and maternity leaves, fewer child allowances. Also these campaigns can be cost-effective, given the high concentration of the target population in a relatively small area, as proven by the Malawi Mulanje Hospital's example.
- Innovative programmes, such as the use of support groups, sporting events, fathers' clubs, and male opinion leaders, are excellent and give the opportunity to involve more men in programme design and implementation. They demystify FP, and remove its negative connotations. The successes from Malawi's "Man to Man" and Swaziland's "Man Talk" initiatives show that using men to inform and educate other men about family-planning works. Male opinion leaders are underutilized and often ignored in family-planning programmes. Given the strong credibility and respect they have within their communities, they can be very effective in promoting and delivering family-planning services in rural areas (especially condoms and spermicides) for both men and women.
- CBD programmes have a great potential for increasing men's use of contraceptives. Men trained as CBD agents can be very effective in reaching both men and women, and can be more sustained advocates than women, because they can devote more time to CBD activities, as proven by the OR study in Kenya. But, it is very important to chose CBD agents from people who already enjoy community trust and respect. There is no standard rule for involving CBD agents that we

can learn from the programmes. Kenya shopkeepers and Cameroon male opinion leaders chose to be volunteers, while agents from the Ghana CBD programme earned a 10 percent commission on the supplies they sell. The most important element is motivation.

- Social marketing is a strong channel to sell a contraceptive method, specifically condoms, if good advertising is coupled with availability, quality, and low price of the product. But one needs to be careful about the messages. In the SOMARC programme, 16 percent of men acceptors had switched from another brand or a more effective contraceptive, which was not the intended impact. This supports the conclusion from some programme managers that, while AIDS appears to have caused an increase in the use of condoms, it has not necessarily increased the usage of the condom as a family-planning measure.
- Vasectomy can be accepted in Africa if good counseling and quality services are associated with a strong information and sensitization campaign, as proven by the success of the Nairobi male clinic. But two important elements to be considered are confidentiality, and integration with other male reproductive health services.
- Males generally prefer clinics that offer a range of reproductive-health services for men. In several examples, we have seen that integration or availability of other services on site, such as infertility, STD management, and sexual-disorder management, had a positive impact on male FP services, and gave further credibility to programmes, which in turn increased the number of acceptors.
- Programmes targeting young males, particularly those dealing with contraception, are very rare. The Planned Parenthood Association of Ghana's model should be encouraged and disseminated in other countries.
- Close the knowledge-practice gap: As in so many population programmes that seek to change behaviour, male-involvement programmes display a classic KAP-gap; that is, there is a gap between knowledge and practice, between what people know they should do and what they actually do. Motivational campaigns, IEC activities, print media, operations research, workplace programmes, Daddies Clubs, sporting events—all these approaches have been used to increase men's share in parental responsibility. Condom social marketing has been used, leading often to increased in condom use mostly for STDs/AIDS prevention. Male clinics succeeded in increasing vasectomy acceptors by offering good counseling and comprehensive reproductive health services. All of them have led to high level of awareness of family planning; however acceptance rates have remained relatively low. Therefore addressing this gap should be the next step in future programmes.

- Include evaluation in programme design: There is a need for better programme design including evaluation. Most of the programmes presented in this paper did not have an appropriate evaluation component. Those which did evaluate the effectiveness of their programmes, such as the second Zimbabwe male motivation project, should be encouraged to use the results to adjust programmes to achieve these desired goals.
- Exchange experiences: Programme officers and managers working in the field should be brought together in order to exchange their experiences with current approaches, evaluate their relative successes and failure, highlight the success stories, and identify new strategies and directions for current and future programmes. During that gathering, answers should be found to two key questions: a) How do we move from high level of awareness to high level of support and acceptance? b) How can we improve communication between couples about reproductive-health issues?
- Target messages to men: Special messages, targeted to men, should encourage them to be responsible and caring, and to discuss FP with their partners. There is a need to target men as a primary audience with family-planning messages that emphasize the economic benefit of having fewer children, and create a new role model for men that portrays responsible men as those who discuss family size and contraception with their partners. In future campaigns, care should be taken to emphasize the need for the husband and the wife to share decisions.
- Pay attention to education and services for young men: It is important to introduce family-planning knowledge into the secondary schools and university as preparation for young people for future responsible parenthood. The most successful programmes seem to be those which see sexuality education as a life-long process, beginning with programmes to help parents teach their children, male and female alike, throughout their developmental years. Research has concluded that programmes working with parents and children, first in separate groupings and later together, are by far the most successful in ensuring ongoing dialogue and the most meaningful behavioural change (IPPF, 1984).
- Provide advocacy training: There is a need for strong advocacy training for programme managers, service providers, teachers, and male opinion leaders, in order to enable them to advocate and propagate family planning in their respective communities.
- Move urban lessons to rural areas: Most of the male-involvement initiatives are in big cities (urban areas). However, the inhabitants of the big cities are only a small proportion of the African population in

most countries, most of whom live in the villages and rural areas. Moreover, the dependency of women on men is stronger in rural areas than in big cities. Therefore, there is a need to look at ways to expand or replicate these initiatives in the rural areas in order to reach this majority and have a greater impact.

- Learn about the male audience: There is a need for additional research. The first lesson of audience research is to "know your audience." Information on male attitudes, needs, and preferences is essential, also, understanding the needs and attitudes of men relating to sexuality is essential for the development of programmes. Qualitative research should be carried out to look for answers to these questions:
  - What are the factors for further acceptance of family-planning programmes by men?
  - What is men's role in fertility decision making?
  - How does a couple reach consensus on the choice and use of a contraceptive methods?
  - What are the determining factors for the acceptance or refusal by a woman to involve her partner in her reproductive health decision?
  - What are service providers' thinking and attitudes towards men's and adolescent boys' involvement in reproductive health?

In addition, research on male methods should be pushed forward. There are only two major modern male contraceptive methods. This is often used by men as a good argument for not being involved in family planning, and can reinforce the image of a family programme too often thought of as exclusively female. The practice of contraception cannot and should not the sole responsibility of women. The responsibility for contraception should be shared equally between men and women. In order to make this a reality, more vigorous attempts should be made to develop a more acceptable male contraceptive.

14

Outreach Reproductive Health Programmes for Young Adults

The delivery of reproductive health information, counseling and services to young people is an emerging area. Many efforts involve schools, although courses typically avoid sensitive sexual issues and often—especially in Africa and Asia—refrain from discussing sexuality altogether. Compounding the difficulty is that not all young people attend school. Health facilities, too, are beginning to establish youth services, but many adolescents are reluctant to take advantage of this option.

What Types of Programmes can be Used to Reach Youth in the Community?

Outreach has emerged as an innovative way to reach young people. This summary describes how education and services are offered at special youth sites or through the efforts of roving health educators who bring information and services directly to adolescents. Outreach programmes can be grouped into the following categories:

- Youth centers include those that seek to prevent too-early pregnancy along with other risky behaviours while helping to enhance life skills, and those that assist pregnant and parenting teens to pursue educational and vocational objectives.
- Peer promotion programmes deliver information and services in the community and workplace through peers similar in age and background. These programmes are successful in difficult-to-reach populations such as out-of-school youth, street children and commercial sex workers.
- Community outreach programmes reach youth in the community, but services are typically delivered by adult health professionals. One

example is a workplace model, where information and services are provided by the employer or health agency at the place of employment.

- Reproductive health programmes provided by youth-oriented organizations for their constituents are often characterized by a high degree of youth involvement in their operations.

What are the Key Elements of Outreach Programme Design and Planning?

Establishing reproductive health outreach programmes for young people can be tremendously challenging. According to professionals who have managed, funded or observed outreach programmes, several elements are instrumental in reaching youth. They include:

- *Strategic Planning.* A common mistake is promising more than a project can deliver, whether through optimism, inexperience or the desire to please stakeholders. Clearly stating process and behavioural objectives before the project begins is a prerequisite to measuring project success. What is feasible also depends on the cultural and political environment. An AIDSCAP study conducted in Haiti found that providing a variety of prevention options, from abstinence to condom use, offered target audiences a choice and allowed gatekeepers to remain neutral or supportive of certain activities.
- *Target Audience Identification.* Young people are a diverse population and respond to different approaches and messages. The same socioeconomic or cultural group may need different messages at different stages of their young adulthood. It is important, therefore, to identify the specific target group in regard to age, marital status, school status, gender and other factors relevant to planned activities. Not only does this process facilitate development of a feasible workplan and appropriate strategy, it avoids the trap of reaching an accessible group, such as in-school youth, at the expense of more needy young people. Targeting younger, pre-sexually active teens was a successful strategy for a Peruvian family planning association's youth center, and has the great advantage of teaching responsible behaviours before unsafe and unhealthy habits become entrenched.
- *Needs Assessment.* Once a target audience has been identified, it is important to conduct a needs assessment to plan relevant outreach activities. The World Health Organization underscores the importance of repeating this process at various times once the programme is underway. Particularly in HIV/AIDS prevention, understanding the target group's specific needs may be key to designing an effective intervention. A Brazilian project for street children began its design by conducting in-depth interviews to understand their high-risk

behaviours, especially the role of sex in their lives and what is important to them.

- *Youth Involvement.* Common sense dictates that the target group can best identify its own needs, and it may feel more a part of an effort if it has the opportunity to be substantively involved. Experts recommend that young people be involved in many, if not all, stages of their programmes. They regard this concept as an important guiding principles in work with youth. Trends support the growing strategic emphasis on youth involvement. A study of 103 adolescent reproductive health projects, conducted by the Center for Population Options, reported that more than half of the projects involve youth in a significant way.
- *Community Involvement.* There is wide agreement that community involvement plays a role in programme success. Depending on a programme's objectives and sensitivities, specific groups should be identified for targeted activities, including policymakers, health professionals and religious and other community leaders. At the same time, the community as a whole needs to be engaged to come up with solutions to harmful gender-related practices, such as forced sex and female genital mutilation, that serve as barriers to improving adolescent reproductive health. A review of AIDS-prevention activities in Haiti concluded that seeking the expert advice of community leaders before implementing a project helped foster a sense of local ownership, with the sense that the community has a stake in the process.
- *Parental Involvement.* The acceptance and support of parents is important to the success of youth outreach programmes. One way to gain this support is to convince parents of the consequences of not dealing with adolescent reproductive health. The UMATI project in Tanzania concluded that it was especially important for programmes like theirs to gain parental support because absenteeism on the part of young women is typically caused by household obligations. Young people have indicated a desire that their parents be better informed and, where possible, that they participate in activities of youth programmes.
- *Evaluation Design and Monitoring.* Project staff are becoming increasingly aware of the importance of effective monitoring and evaluation mechanisms to improve their programmatic activities. Organizers of the Red Cross AIDS-prevention project in Jamaica, for example, improved their project design through individual feedback, regular debriefings and quantitative reports. Young people themselves are becoming more involved in evaluation tasks, facilitating their cooperation in providing needed information and also in the resulting activities.

What are the Key Elements of Implementing Peer Projects?

Young people have always sought and received information from one another, and they are doing so today in increasing numbers. Having especially-trained peers provide information helps to ensure its accuracy and usefulness, and peers are often better at contacting their own age and social groups. There is also evidence that outreach programmes using peer educators are less costly per contraceptive user. The following are characteristics of successful peer programmes:

- *Careful Peer Selection.* Peer promoters should be selected based on important characteristics and interests. Peers should be capable of being respectful and able to hold confidences; credible role models, especially for the behaviours they advocate; admired and respected for their social skills; committed to good reproductive health, including contraception and STD prevention; and good at communicating. They also need to share characteristics of their target audience (such as age, language and ethnicity) so they are true "peers" and can relate well.
- *Training.* Training of peer educators and adult counselors is a critical element in all young adult programmes, given the special needs of this age group. Some analysts suggest that all staff involved in youth projects, including administrators, should receive training in order to be better managers, know what to expect, and be supportive. Training should be participatory and offered over time as refresher courses.
- *Clearly Defined Responsibilities*: Peer promoters need a clear understanding of what is expected of them. If managers hope to achieve a certain level of accomplishment, specific objectives and tasks must be identified and agreed upon by peer promoters.
- *Effective Supervision and Support*: Peer promoters require close supervision of their activities and reinforcement of their efforts. This oversight must continue throughout the life of the project. Supervisors must work with peers to identify their task-related needs and areas for upgrading—and then address those gaps.
- *Availability of Relevant Materials*: Materials that peer educators use with their peers should be accurate, clear, interesting and relevant. It is especially important for materials to address sexuality fits into young people's relationships and lives. Presentation of the materials should allow for participation and interaction, such as question-and-answer periods, group discussions, drama presentations and role-playing.
- *Planning for Turnover*: Young people will naturally grow older, leaving the age range appropriate for peer programmes. But they will also move on to other pursuits faster than adults, given their need to establish personal lives and careers. Projects can minimize turnover with good supervision and by rewarding peer promoters. Planning for the

inevitable need for replacements, such as by training more promoters than needed to provide alternates for absentees and/or dropouts, can lessen the impact of peer turnover.

Reproductive Health Programmes for Young Adults—Social Marketing and Mass Media Approaches

During the last several decades, social marketing interventions have successfully addressed such diverse topics as smoking cessation, breastfeeding, safe motherhood practices and the prevention and control of diarrhoeal disease. Today the use of social marketing strategies and mass media campaigns are increasingly being used to promote the reproductive health of young people.

Social marketing refers to a process for designing health-promotion interventions that utilizes techniques drawn from commercial advertising, market research and the social sciences. Social marketing defines its objectives in terms of beliefs, practices and values of its target audiences. Extensive audience research guides the ways in which social marketers position projects objectives in terms of the benefits they offer a target audience.

Mass media are frequently used as one of the major channels of communication in social marketing intervention strategies. The term mass media refers to self-contained audio, visual or print distribution systems that can simultaneously reach large numbers of people with the same message. Examples include radio, television, computers, newspapers, magazines, billboards, direct mail and telemarketing systems.

Social marketing strategies can be used to achieve a variety of health promotion objectives including: increased use of health-related products, such as condoms; increased access to health services; and such changes in health behaviours and practices as the practice of abstinence or having sex with a single partner.

What are the Challenges of Designing Social Marketing Campaigns to Reach Young Adults?

The most successful programmes recognize that addressing the reproductive health needs of adolescents, particularly in the developing world, pose special challenges for the discipline of social marketing and its use of media communications. These challenges include:

- Given their developmental stage, the behavioural practices of many young adults are still in the process of being formed, and consequently are often difficult to define or predict. This "developmental transition" stage of young adulthood calls for extensive use of social marketing methods such as audience segmentation and behavioural analysis so that communications and marketing interventions can be designed and implements.

- At risk young people are often difficult to reach. Many are illiterate, not in school and unemployed. Mass media can be a useful vehicle for transmitting basic messages to this audience, but social marketers also need to find channels of communication and develop marketing systems that can connect hard-to-reach young people with supportive reproductive health services and counseling.
- Young people are particularly vulnerable to a wide range of variables (e.g., opinions of peers, media images of sexuality, access to contraceptives), which inform and shape their behaviour. In the development of intervention strategies, social marketers need to take into account these variables.

What are the Key Elements of Effective Social Marketing to Reach Young People?

Well-designed social marketing strategies and media campaigns are having a positive influence on the reproductive health practices of young people around the world. According to the literature, several elements are critical to good project design:

- *Effective Interventions Address the Behavioural Issues of Young Adults Themselves as Well as the Environmental Factors and Social Norms Influencing Their Behaviour*: There is a strong correlation between environmental factors and social norms and the attitudes and behaviours of young people. Social marketing programmes, therefore, need to target diverse audiences. These include young people themselves, their parents, service providers, media planners, peer educators, business and civic leaders and policymakers. The Philippines Foundation for Adolescent Development, for example, produced an educational video for parents about the impact of their communication skills on their children.
- *Involving Key Gatekeepers and Stakeholders at the Outset is a Critical Factor in Project Success*: Given the controversial nature of youth-specific reproductive health programmes, it is important to get key leaders and stakeholders behind the project as early as possible. Meetings with these individuals should be held to obtain agreement on what project goals and objectives can be mutually supported. Programme planners in Oyo and Enugu States, Nigeria built support for social marketing and mass media activities by forming technical advisory councils made up of decision-makers and technical experts. Prior to the launch of television programming containing potentially controversial material, council members reviewed programmes and made comments. Programme planners addressed their concerns which led council members to become advocates for the mass media campaign.

- *Young People Need to be Involved in all Aspects of the Interventions*: The impact of social marketing inventions can be greatly enhanced if young adults themselves are included in project design, implementation and evaluation. The participation of youth enables project staff to better understand their needs and wishes, design more effective messages and materials, and gain greater insights into the effectiveness of specific interventions. Programmes in a wide range of countries actively involve young people in all components of social marketing and mass media campaigns. In Côte d'Ivoire, for example, high school students wrote a drama that was turned into a 40-minute promotional video. The video, which captures young adult realities as they see them, was disseminated throughout the country. It was broadcast on national television and used by schools as a tool to stimulate frank discussion of sexual issues.
- *Media Advocacy Activities are an Important Complement to Social Marketing Interventions*: To reduce the transmittal of images and themes of sexuality that conflict with messages promoting safe sex and sexual responsibility, youth advocates engage media representatives in dialogue about reproductive health programming themes and values. Their goal is to encourage positive messages that address the reproductive health needs of young people. The media, they feel, have the potential to play an important role by creating visibility for sexuality issues, providing legitimacy for their discussion, and modeling words and phrases to make discussion more comfortable. The Kenya Association for the Promotion of Adolescent Health provides an example of how this process works. Through content analysis, its staff reviews how the media are addressing the needs of youth, meets with media representatives to discuss what they observed, and suggests ways in which distorted images and statements can be corrected. The association also develops fact sheets to help the media create accurate reproductive health messages.
- *Pre-Testing Messages is Essential*: Effective social marketing messages promoting behaviour change should address a carefully-targeted objective and be culturally relevant, credible and practical. Pre-testing messages is essential in a field that is as sensitive as youth adult reproductive health and where messages transmitted by the mass media instantaneously reach large numbers of people. Youth advocates pretest materials with young people as well as key stakeholders, including parents. In Indonesia, for example, producers of *Alang-Alang*, a mini-series promoting education for girls and discouraging multiple pregnancies, held focus group discussions with parents and their daughters in elementary and secondary school. Participants approved of the drama, considering it to be believable, informative and suitable for all ages. As part of the "Keep On Keeping It On" condom campaign

in Jamaica, social marketers conducted focus group discussions to test the concept and investigate young people's attitudes and behaviours regarding condoms. The test allowed researchers to measure message comprehension, credibility and likelihood of behaviour change. Adjustments were then made prior to the launch of the campaign, which contributed to its success.

- *Supportive Networking and Training Activities Need to be Carried Out throughout the Life of the Project*: Networks among and between relevant policymakers, media professionals, health service providers, counselors and peer educators are essential in helping to shape young people's reproductive health social norms. Relevant and ongoing training activities for the many groups involved is another component of project success.
- *Projects should Include a Well-designed Evaluation Component*: In a competitive climate for development resources, it is essential that the impact of reproductive health social marketing interventions for youth be fully documented. Implementing organizations need to know which interventions succeed in changing the reproductive health knowledge, attitudes and behaviours of beneficiaries. Data on project impact help contribute to project sustainability and expansion, advance the state-of-the-art of project design, and build a receptive climate for investment in similar projects.

By designing effective evaluation mechanisms, youth advocates are demonstrating the impact of their activities on target audiences. In Ghana, for example, designers of an AIDS-prevention campaign conducted a baseline survey and followed it up a year later with a knowledge, attitude and practice study to assess the impact of social marketing/mass-media activities on 15-30 year olds in two regions of the country. According to research results, the percentage of sexually active 15 year olds declined from 44 to 27 percent; awareness of AIDS as a serious disease for youth increased from 28 to 50 percent; and among unmarried, multiple-partner respondents, reported condom use during last sexual intercourse increased from 14 to 23 percent.

15

Capacity Building in Reproductive Health Programmes—Few Experiences

Defining Capacity Building

Capacity building or capacity development is defined as "the process by which individuals, organizations, institutions, and societies develop abilities (individually and collectively) to perform functions, solve problems, set, and achieve objectives". Capacity development is seen as having three cornerstones:

- it is a continuing learning and changing process;
- it emphasizes better use and empowerment of individuals and organizations; and
- it requires systematic approaches be considered in devising capacity development strategies and programmes.

UNFPA'S Contribution to National Capacity Building for Reproductive Health

The United Nations Development Programme (UNDP) has proposed a framework for sustainable capacity development based on four interrelated dimensions:

- Individual. Education, on-the-job training, and formal and informal skills development to accomplish tasks and solve problems are core requirements.
- Entity. A well-trained productive person needs access to finance information, technology, infrastructure, and other resources. This often means working within an entity that has an organizational structure with a clear mission and clear goals, functions, systems and resources.
- Interrelationship Between Entities. Organizations and groups interact with others for a common purpose. Themes, sections, institutions and

geographic divisions comprise one or more systems where entities interact for a common purpose.

- Enabling Environment. Sustainable capacities for individuals, entities, and systems require an enabling environment for addressing cross-sectoral issues relevant to all parts of society—the state, civil society and the private sector.

Capacity building activities generally fall into the first two elements of the above definition; i.e., individual and entity, and may include the following activities:

- *Individual*: building institutional capacities through human resource development, training, transfer of skills and technology with a view to creating indigenous capability in leadership and visioning, teamwork and cooperation, and research and analysis;
- *Entity*:
    a) building information-processing capacity in terms of procedures, systems and a knowledge/information base;
    b) building infrastructural capacity and the ability to maintain the infrastructure; and
    c) building financial management and budgetary control capacity and the ability to financially sustain the institution.

National Execution and Capacity Building

UNFPA is currently going through a transition from a heavy emphasis on execution by United Nations agencies to national execution. National execution in this context means that the host government takes on much of the responsibility for the formulation and management/implementation of projects. Therefore, capacity development takes on both a new meaning and new urgency if UNFPA is to be successful in delivering its programme.

National execution has the potential to greatly improve the capacity of institutions to manage development programmes under the right conditions. The learning-by-doing experience of actively executing and implementing projects rather than serving as counterparts and recipients of Agencies' projects has been salutary.

In addition, it should be noted that our review of the UNFPA documentation revealed a lack of specific results, indicators, or performance measures for capacity building. In addition, there was very little indication of the overall level of organizational capacity development at previous points in the evolution of UNFPA programmes. As a result, we relied very much on anecdotal evidence of capacity building from thematic evaluations and documents available at the country level. In addition, there is very little evidence of sustainability of past capacity building.

- UNFPA has supported the building of regional and country level capacity through its Country Support Teams.
- In establishing the Country Support Teams, UNFPA has assembled a regional group of experts who now have the capability to support country programmes.
- UNFPA is also promoting the utilization of national consultants in place of international consultants.
- UNFPA's transition to national execution is also contributing to capacity building.
- In many countries, UNFPA has provided computer equipment (including software) and training for staff working in reproductive health.
- UNFPA has supported the upgrading/building of facilities used for delivering reproductive health services including clinics, health centres, and operating rooms.
- UNFPA has provided medical equipment and furniture required for reproductive services.
- UNFPA has helped in the transfer of contraceptive production technology to a number of countries and in the construction of contraceptive factories.

Building of Institutional Capacity

- UNFPA has helped support a number of governments in developing population policies and programmes by working behind the scenes in the early stages of policy development and in laying the groundwork for the initiation of large-scale family planning programmes.
- UNFPA has strengthened the MCH/FP (reproductive health) delivery system in a number of countries through:
- The provision of technical advisory support for the establishment of management procedures, systems and practices for the Ministry of Health;
- The provision of training for health professionals including doctors, nurses, and TBAs in reproductive health and gender training; and,
- Support for the development of IEC units in government health and education ministries.
- UNFPA has been instrumental in the incorporation of population and sex education into school curriculum and teacher training. Integration of sex education topics into the school curricula is an important aspect of institutional capacity building.

Building Information-processing Capacity

UNFPA has supported capacity building in demographic data collection and analysis and has supported research into linkages between population and development. The data so collected is often used as a source for the planning of reproductive health programmes. *In addition*, UNFPA has provided technical support for the conduct of demographic and health surveys and their analyses. Demographic and Health Surveys (DHS) are the cornerstone for both the planning and evaluation of the effectiveness of reproductive health programmes.

Capacity Building—Role of USAID

USAID is one of the few donors working to improve the capabilities of people, institutions, and governments in order to enhance local expertise and pave the way for countries to achieve their development objectives in family planning and reproductive health. Capacity building allows national programmes—government, public, private, nongovernmental organizations (NGOs), and community-based institutions—to design, implement, finance, and evaluate sustainable family planning programmes. When successful, these local entities have become the premier family planning delivery organization in the country, with some now providing technical assistance and training to their countries' Ministries of Health, other in-country private organizations, and organizations in other countries.

Population and Reproductive Health Capacity Building Programme—World Bank

The Population and Reproductive Health Capacity Building Programme (PRHCBP), a programme of the World Bank's Development Grant Facility, supports innovative ways to stimulate and sustain local responses to population and reproductive health needs. The Population and Reproductive Health Capacity Building Programme works with development partners and countries working in the health sector—usually through organizations actively engaging and leveraging grassroots NGOs in the development and implementation of their strategies, programmes and projects—to:

- support community and peer groups in responding to reproductive health needs, pilot new approaches,
- carry out small-scale operations research,
- disseminate relevant materials in local languages,
- build local organizational capacity and networks, and
- facilitate the participation of community-based organizations in major global and regional conferences and initiatives.

16

New Reproductive Health Focus

Migrants, refugees, and internally displaced persons are among the world's most vulnerable people. Clustered on the margins of cities or culturally isolated within them, housed in camps meant to be temporary, or without homes at all, they often have urgent health needs, including reproductive health. Programmes and relief agencies are beginning to respond to this need.

People move for many different reasons, and their circumstances vary widely. Still, they are alike in three important ways:

- *Disruption*: Most have left behind the support of traditional values, extended families, friends, and familiar ways of life. With limited means, they face new and uncertain situations.
- *Differences*: Culture and language often set them apart from their new neighbours. Reproductive attitudes and behaviour often differ as well.
- *Difficulties of access*: Many are ineligible for health care benefits, unfamiliar with family planning programmes, and unable to obtain information easily.

Growing Numbers, Growing Needs

An estimated 16 million people migrate each year from rural to urban areas of developing countries, excluding China, accounting for about half of recent urban growth. In addition, about 2 to 4 million people migrate internationally each year. Another 18 million people—over five times the number 20 years ago—have fled their own countries, as refugees. Also, about 20 million people are internally displaced. They have fled their communities and sought safety elsewhere within their own countries. The reproductive health of many migrants, refugees, and internally displaced persons suggests several concerns:

- *Contraceptive Access and Use are Limited*: Recent migrants are less likely than other urban residents to use family planning. Attitudes explain part of the difference, but access is often a problem. Among contraceptive users, rural-to-urban migrants are more likely than urban non-migrants to travel at least an hour to reach the nearest source of modern contraceptives.

- *Risks of HIV/AIDS and Other Sexually Transmitted Diseases are High*: The disruption of family and community life during moves, especially in situations of poverty and crisis, increases risky sexual behaviour and exposure to STDs.
- *Safe Motherhood is Difficult*: Among refugees and internally displaced persons, childbearing can be life-threatening. During emergencies women often lack adequate food, shelter, and sanitation. Prenatal and delivery care often are minimal, and emergency care may be hours away.
- *Violence against Women is Frequent*: Women who move are especially vulnerable to sexual abuse. Among refugees, rapes occur frequently. Some women may have no choice but to trade sex for protection, money, and food.

Reaching Out with Information and Services

While reproductive health programmes often serve migrants along with others living in urban areas, few have recognized rural-to-urban migrants as a specific group with special needs. In urban areas health care providers need to reach out to new migrants. The first step is to assess migrants' needs and how they differ from others' needs. Then information and services must be tailored to meet these needs, made appropriate in language and culture, and provided with the involvement and often the help of the community.

In refugee emergencies the burdens of caring for huge numbers of people on short notice have prevented relief agencies from paying much attention to reproductive health needs. Although camps are meant to be temporary, most refugees no longer are in emergency situations. Therefore, relief agencies and reproductive health care providers are starting to find ways to address the continuing reproductive health needs of refugees and internally displaced persons—including prenatal, delivery, and postnatal services; STD prevention and treatment and HIV prevention; and family planning information, counseling, and services.

People Who Move: New Focus for Reproductive Health Care

Today millions of people are moving—some from rural to urban areas, others across national borders, some in search of opportunities and others fleeing disorder and danger at home, seeking refuge wherever possible. Clustered on the margins of cities or culturally isolated within them, housed in camps that were intended to be temporary, or without homes at all, migrants, refugees, and internally displaced persons are among society's most vulnerable people.

Although estimates of the total number of rural-to-urban migrants in the world are uncertain, perhaps about 16 million people migrate each year from rural to urban areas of developing countries, excluding China. This figure is derived from a recent United Nations assessment of the percentage contribution to urban growth of migration plus reclassification of territory from rural to urban status in 27 developing countries in the 1980s. The estimate of 16 million by *Population Reports* assumes that this percentage held true for the developing world as a whole and continued into the 1990s.

Also, an estimated 2 to 4 million people migrate internationally each year. An estimated 125 million people or more, about one in every 50 people, are living outside their country of birth.

In addition, some 18 million people, almost all in developing countries, have fled their home countries. About 15 million are formally recognized as refugees. An estimated 20 million more are considered to be internally displaced persons: they have fled their homes but remain within their own countries.

A New Focus

As their numbers grow, migrants, refugees, and internally displaced persons are becoming a new focus for reproductive health care programmes in developing countries. In particular, three aspects of their situation call for a special focus:

- *Disruption*: Whatever their reasons for moving, to varying degrees the lives and circumstances of virtually all migrants, refugees, and internally displaced persons have been disrupted. They have left behind the support of traditional values, extended families, friends, and familiar ways of life and must deal with a host of new challenges. Refugees and internally displaced persons, in addition, have often lost their possessions, their jobs and income, their social status, and even their human dignity in the move. People who have been dislocated face many risks to their health, including their reproductive health.
- *Different Characteristics*: People who move often differ from the people in places to which they move—in their age, socioeconomic status, financial circumstances, and sometimes even culture and language. Not all mobile groups are alike, of course, nor do their characteristics necessarily mean that their need for reproductive health services is greater than that of other groups. Nevertheless, it is important that programmes know more about migrants, refugees, and internally displaced persons in order to tailor information and services to meet their specific needs.
- *Difficulties Gaining Access*: People who move need reproductive health care but often lack access to services. For example, they may

be ineligible for health care benefits, unfamiliar with family planning programmes and other services, unable to obtain information easily, and uncertain where to turn.

Few reproductive health and family planning programmes have focused on migrants as a specific group, although urban reproductive health care programmes—especially those that serve squatter settlements—often reach migrants along with other urban residents. Observers generally agree that few programmes recognize migrants as a distinct group. Even fewer design services with migrants' specific needs in mind.

Some countries have recognized the presence of large numbers of migrants and have moved to provide reproductive health services. For example, China has acknowledged the need to provide better family planning services to its migrant "floating population" of some 80 million people, while in the Dominican Republic an AIDS prevention programme and in Portugal a family planning programme have focused on migrant groups.

The reproductive health needs of refugees and internally displaced persons have received little attention until recently. The burdens of providing for huge numbers of dislocated people on short notice, often with limited funds, have largely precluded attention to anything except emergency needs for food, shelter, and sanitation. Recently, however, the reproductive health needs of refugees are being recognized. Similarly, in Azerbaijan, Sri Lanka, and elsewhere, recent reproductive health care projects have focused on internally displaced persons.

Migration and Urbanization

For several decades in developing countries, urban areas have been growing much faster than the general population because of massive migration from rural areas. The United Nations, on the basis of 36 developing countries, calculated that 40 per cent of urban growth in the 1960s was due to net rural-to-urban migration plus reclassification of rural areas as urban. The UN estimate climbed to over 50 per cent for the 1980s, largely because 72 per cent of urban growth in China during the 1980s was attributable to migration and reclassification. Estimates for China are unavailable for the 1960s and 1970s. Outside China, the average proportion of urban growth due to migration and reclassification increased from 40 per cent in the 1960s to 44 per cent in the 1970s and then dropped back to 40 per cent in the 1980s.

In Africa migration from rural areas accounted for as much as half of all urban growth during the 1960s and 1970s and about 25 per cent of urban growth in the 1980s and 1990s. In Asia, excluding China, about 40 per cent of urban growth in the 1960s, and over 45 per cent in the 1970s and 1980s, has been due to migration and reclassification of territory from rural to urban. In Latin America migration from the countryside, along with reclassification, caused about 40 per cent of urban population growth from the 1950s to the 1970s and about 35 per cent in the 1980s.

Given the steady flow of migrants over the past several decades, it is not surprising that migrants and their families now comprise a substantial percentage of urban residents. A study using data from the Demographic and Health Surveys (DHS) for 14 countries in Africa found that, among married women of childbearing age living in urban areas, between 22 per cent and 55 per cent had migrated from villages and towns within the past 10 years.

Urbanization has been a powerful trend in developing countries. Just over 25 per cent urban in 1975, developing countries were nearly 40 per cent urban by 1995. The number of people in urban areas of developing countries has risen from about 800 million in 1975 to about 1.7 billion today. Some developing-country populations have already become largely urban. In Latin America and the Caribbean seven countries are at least three-fourths urban—Venezuela (92%), Uruguay (90%), Argentina (88%), Chile (84%), Brazil (78%), Cuba (76%), and Mexico (75%). In North Africa and the Near East, Libya is about 85 per cent urban, and Saudi Arabia, about 80 per cent urban.

The world's population, estimated by the United Nations to be 45 per cent urban in 1995, is projected to be nearly 60 per cent urban by 2015. By 2015 over half of people in developing countries will live in urban areas. By then the estimated urban population of the developing world will exceed 3 billion. Of these, over 1.2 billion will be living in "million-plus" cities. Between 2015 and 2025, for the first time ever, the rural areas of developing countries will begin to decline in population. The population of the developed countries, already about three-quarters urban, will become even more urban, rising to a projected 80 per cent in 2015.

International Migration

Of the world's 125 million international migrants—people who voluntarily left their countries of origin for other countries—about half are living in developing countries. The major flows of international migrants are from developing countries in Africa, Latin America, and Asia to Western Europe, North America, Australia, and other developed regions. Migration from one developed country to another, which was substantial in the earlier part of this century, has become minimal today. Migration from one developing country to another is thought to be substantial, but there are few reliable estimates. In the developing world most international migrants move within the same region.

Refugees and Internally Displaced Persons

In recent years the number of refugees and internally displaced persons in the world has grown rapidly, raising concerns among governments and international agencies about the need to shelter and protect these unfortunate people. Worldwide, in 1995 the number of refugees was estimated at about

15 million, five times their number in 1976. Another estimated 3 million people have fled their home countries but are not formally recognized by governments as refugees (but are included in this category in this report). These include an estimated 700,000 Palestinians in Jordan and 350,000 Burmese in Thailand. As noted, internally displaced persons probably number at least 20 million, although estimates are unreliable.

- *Refugees*: At least three-fourths of the world's refugees are in developing countries. Africa and the Near East each contain over 30 per cent of the total—more than 5 million in each region. Africa had only about 400,000 refugees in 1960, but the continent has seen large-scale refugee movements in recent years. Refugees sometimes move in both directions between neighbouring African countries. For example, in 1995, 15,000 refugees from Mauritania lived in Mali, while 35,000 from Mali lived in Mauritania.
  Among refugees in the Near East, Palestinians are the largest group. Most have settled in Jordan, Lebanon, Syria, Gaza, or the West Bank. The second largest refugee group consists of Afghanis who fled to Iran and Pakistan when the Soviet Union intervened militarily in Afghanistan in 1979. In 1995 Iran had about 2 million refugees, more than any other country. Two-thirds of them were Afghanis.
  Other regions have fewer refugees, but several countries have substantial numbers, nonetheless. In Asia, for example, Pakistan has an estimated 870,000 refugees, mostly from Afghanistan. Of the estimated 320,000 refugees in India, over one-third are from China. Most of the 100,000 refugees in Nepal are from Bhutan.
- *Internally Displaced Persons*: Many countries have substantial numbers of people who have fled ethnic or religious strife, civil disorder, and other threats in their communities and sought safety elsewhere within their own country. Sudan, after years of civil war, contains more internally displaced persons than any other country, an estimated 4 million people, or about one-seventh of its total population. Other countries that are estimated to have at least 1 million internally displaced persons are Angola, Iraq, Liberia, Sierra Leone, Turkey, and Bosnia and Herzegovina, where an estimated one-quarter of the population are either refugees or internally displaced persons. In 1993 an estimated 12 per cent of Rwanda's people were displaced within the country.

Meeting Different Needs

Rural-to-urban migrants, international migrants, refugees, and displaced persons differ from place to place in many ways, reflecting the circumstances surrounding their moves. They vary in culture, language, and demographic and socioeconomic characteristics. At the same time, these groups have much in common. Understanding these differences and commonalities will help programmes provide reproductive health care to the millions of people who move from one place to another.

Fertility and Family Planning

When people migrate from rural to urban areas, their fertility and family planning behaviour at first is likely to differ from that of long-term urban residents. The longer they remain in urban areas, however, the more their behaviour becomes like that of other urban residents. Similarly, the fertility and family planning status of refugees and internally displaced persons is likely to differ, especially at first, from that of people in their new areas.

Reproductive Health Care

The reproductive health status of many migrants, refugees, and internally displaced persons suggests several reasons for concern:

- *AIDS and other sexually transmitted diseases (STDs)* spread more rapidly as populations become more mobile.
- *Safe motherhood* is nearly impossible for refugees and displaced persons, especially in the early phases of an emergency, because people live in conditions of extreme dislocation, minimal shelter and food, poor sanitation, and physical danger.
- *Violence against women* is widespread during refugee and internal displacement movements. When women and children move, they are often alone and powerless and thus at risk of becoming sexual prey.
- *Unsafe abortions* are common among refugees and internally displaced persons. Service providers can help avoid abortions by providing effective contraception and should be ready to deal with complications of unsafe abortion.

Personal Characteristics

Knowing more about refugees, displaced persons, and migrants—including their demographic characteristics, social and economic status, and culture—can help service providers meet their needs Reliable information about these groups is scarce, however.

Many migrants cluster in certain neighbourhoods of large cities, primarily in squatter settlements at the edges of the cities. People who live in urban slums and squatter settlements often have little access to health care and other services. Clustering, however, offers an opportunity for reproductive health care providers to focus information and services on migrant communities. Other migrants live together at their places of work—for example, in factory dormitories, where service providers may be able to reach them.

New migrants from rural areas often settle among earlier migrants. They are drawn together by common ethnicity, the presence of family or friends, or by the fact that they are joining others from the same village or region. How this pattern affects migrants' adaptation is not clear. On one hand, the tendency for recent migrants to live among earlier migrants might slow adaptation to urban attitudes and reproductive behaviour by sheltering new arrivals from urban influences. On the other hand, it could speed their adaptation, because earlier migrants have already "learned the ropes" and can help new arrivals adapt.

Surveys such as the DHS can provide some information about characteristics of rural-to-urban migrants. Almost all information about characteristics of refugees and displaced persons are based on assessments by relief agencies. Because refugee situations change quickly, even accurate information can soon become inaccurate. Reproductive health programmes need to collect and analyze data themselves to learn more about the people who have recently arrived in their service.

Taking Reproductive Health Care to People who have Moved

How can reproductive health care be improved for people who move? The first step is to assess their status, especially how they differ from other people in the area. Knowing their intended clientele, programmes can find better ways to reach out to them and can serve them better.

Assessment

An assessment of how to improve reproductive health care for people who have recently moved begins with gauging their level of integration into the general population. What differences between migrants and existing clients are likely to affect service delivery? How fast do groups of migrants adapt to urban norms? What has been their previous experience with reproductive health care? Also, especially for refugees and displaced persons, does their vulnerability call for special support and counseling?

Planning for Care

Reproductive health programmes and urban planners typically do not anticipate providing services to an influx of migrants from rural areas or from other countries. When a large new group arrives, services and supplies often are not available to meet the increased demand. Nor are staff prepared to deal with people who may speak different languages and have different cultural preferences.

Nevertheless, as much as possible, health programmes should anticipate migration and plan to provide services to the migrants. At the beginning of an irrigation project in the Kou Valley of Burkina Faso, for example, planners concluded that social and health services should be in place before the project began.

Then migrants attracted by the project would have services available when they arrived. Similarly, to deal with movements of refugees and internally displaced persons, service protocols, training manuals, service delivery guidelines, and informational materials should be prepared in advance and made available as quickly as possible.

Rural-to-urban migrants often have poor access to reproductive health care. DHS data suggest that migrant communities are not as well served as other areas. Among contraceptive users, rural-to-urban migrants are more likely than urban non-migrants to travel an hour or more to reach the nearest source of modern.

Reaching Out with Services

People who move often can be served better if health care programmes reach out to them where they work and live. Often this can be done by adapting existing services. In other cases new services are needed. For example, a programme in the Adana region of Turkey reached some 24,000 seasonal migrant farm workers and their families by operating from mobile vans. Special clinics stayed open during evening hours to accommodate the workers. Use of modern contraceptives rose from 10 per cent to 50 per cent among migrant married women of reproductive age. The programme followed up after migrants returned home, making sure that they had continued access to family planning.

In South Africa projects have provided reproductive health services specifically for temporary migrant workers and their families in mining areas. In Azerbaijan mobile teams periodically visit settlements where internally displaced persons are living In Pakistan and China programmes have offered nomads unique services, such as audio tapes about reproductive health that women could listen to while herding.

Programmes also can reach out to refugees living in camps. For example, use of health services often increases when services are located more conveniently. In Pakistan, when refugee women were not allowed to leave their homes, health workers went to their homes.

International Efforts for Refugees and Internally Displaced Persons

International efforts to provide reproductive health services to refugees and internally displaced persons have greatly strengthened in recent years. In 1997 about 40 agencies operate over 100 such reproductive health projects in 35 countries, according to the United Nations High Commissioner on Refugees (UNHCR), which spearheads efforts to provide reproductive health care for refugees.

UNHCR support for comprehensive primary health care programmes in refugee camps now often includes reproductive health services, as in the Caucasus, Ethiopia, Nepal, Rwanda, Sudan, Uganda, and West Africa. UNHCR and the International Federation of Red Cross and Red Crescent Societies have provided reproductive health materials and supplies as well as technical assistance to nongovernmental organizations working in Rwanda, Tanzania, Uganda, and the former Zaire.

The United Nations Fund for Population Activities (UNFPA) is not, by definition, a relief agency. Since 1995, however, UNFPA policy has been to assist in providing support for reproductive health services in emergency situations, providing equipment, supplies, and drugs. In 1997 UNFPA is supporting reproductive health programmes for refugees in more than 40 countries, including Ethiopia, Kenya, Tanzania, Uganda, and Zambia, as well as camps in the Caucasus and Palestine.

17

Fertility Regulation and Reproductive Health in the Millennium Development Goals

Reproductive health refers to the diseases, disorders and conditions that affect the functioning of the male and female reproductive systems during all stages of life. Disorders of reproduction include birth defects, developmental disorders, low birth weight, preterm birth, reduced fertility, impotence, and menstrual disorders. Research has shown that exposure to environmental pollutants may pose the greatest threat to reproductive health. Exposure to lead is associated with reduced fertility in both men and women, while mercury exposure has been linked to birth defects and neurological disorders. A growing body of evidence suggests that exposure to endocrine disruptors, chemicals that appear to disrupt hormonal activity in humans and animals, may contribute to problems with fertility, pregnancy, and other aspects of reproduction.

The reproductive health needs of women and men change over time and are influenced by a variety of biological and situational factors. It is estimated that a woman spends approximately three decades of her life attempting not to become pregnant. During this time, physical, behavioural and environmental factors may impact a woman's or couple's ability to become pregnant in the future. Additionally, the number of women and men choosing to delay having children continues to rise, increasing the demand for infertility treatments.

Although several key elements of sexual and reproductive health are included in the United Nations Millennium Development Goals, a measure of women's capacity to regulate their fertility safely and effectively is missing. We considered the usefulness of 3 pairs of indicators in monitoring this component of reproductive health: contraceptive prevalence and total fertility; unmet need for contraception and unplanned births; and unsafe abortion and abortion mortality.

A single measure of contraceptive use is insufficient. The risks women face from unplanned births and unsafe abortion should also be incorporated into the monitoring process, either directly within the Millennium Development Goals framework or as a parallel effort by reporting governments and other agencies.

POA and the MGDs

The Programme of Action adopted at the 1994 International Conference on Population and Development (ICPD) in Cairo stresses the importance to social and economic development and to individual and family well-being of achieving reproductive health for all. he United Nations Millennium Development Goals (MDGs) adopted by heads of government in 2000 embrace much of the ICPD Programme of Action in their emphasis on eradicating extreme poverty, achieving universal primary education, promoting gender equality and empowering women, reducing child mortality, improving maternal health, combating HIV/AIDS, malaria, and other diseases, ensuring environmental sustainability, and forging a global partnership for development. Although reproductive health is not specifically named (the narrower term "maternal health" is used instead), it is widely recognized that ensuring universal access to reproductive health care, including family planning and sexual health, is essential for the achievement of all of the MDGs, and vice versa.

Two benchmark indicators of reproductive health adopted by the UN General Assembly at its 1999 review of progress in implementing ICPD agreements (ICPD+5) are included in the MDG framework:

- the percentage of births that are attended by skilled health personnel (together with the maternal mortality ratio [MMR]); and
- the knowledge of how to prevent HIV/AIDS among young people aged 15-24 years (or HIV prevalence among young pregnant women).

However, the fertility regulation indicator from ICPD+5—the percentage of women with an unmet need for contraception—is missing, despite its clear relevance to the goal of improving maternal health. Also missing from the MDGs is the consensus from ICPD+5 that all primary health care and family planning facilities should be able to provide a full range of reproductive health services. In response, the Millennium Project Task Force on Child Health and Maternal Health has recommended that a target of "universal access to reproductive health services by 2015" be added to the maternal health goal, with appropriate indicators.

The task force has also recommended the addition of a fertility regulation indicator of maternal health: the percentage of the total demand (or desire) for contraception that is satisfied by current use, which is a variant of unmet need. In considering this and other recommendations, we ask: is there a perfect indicator? Is any single measure of contraceptive use or fertility outcomes sufficient to capture the health-and rights-based concept of fertility regulation articulated at Cairo? If not, what additional measures are needed to create a more inclusive set of monitoring tools for this purpose?

To answer these questions, the study has assessed 3 pairs of process and outcome indicators with respect to their utility in tracking women's capacity (i.e., the exercise of their right) to regulate their fertility safely and effectively in accordance with their reproductive intentions: contraceptive prevalence and total fertility rates (TFRs); unmet need for contraception (or proportion of demand or desire satisfied) and unplanned births; and unsafe abortion and abortion mortality. Reported here as aggregates for countries (a data table is available on request), each indicator is amenable to analysis by age, marital status, socioeconomic status, rural-urban residence, and other characteristics of interest, because each is (or can be) derived from population-based surveys. Indeed, disaggregating the data is essential for identifying the nature and degree of within-country inequalities and for designing approaches to overcome them, especially for adolescents, marginalized ethnic groups, and the poor.

Contraceptive Prevalence and Total Fertility

In 2000, a WHO/UNICEF/United Nations Population Fund (UNFPA) working group selected the contraceptive prevalence rate (CPR) as one of 17 core indicators of reproductive health for global monitoring. The CPR enumerates current contraceptive users (of modern and traditional methods, separately or combined) as a percentage of all women of reproductive age who are in a marital or consensual union and, in the Caribbean, in a regular visiting union, whether or not they are currently sexually active and at risk of pregnancy (i.e., fecund and not currently pregnant). Some demographic and health surveys (DHSs) and related studies also solicit information on method use from sexually active adolescents and unmarried adults.

Although classifying women or couples as contraceptive users or nonusers involves widely recognized measurement problems, the CPR and its subcategories of particular method use offer a number of advantages for global monitoring. Familiar and widely reported, CPRs at the aggregate level are a good predictor of the TFR across countries, that is, the average number of children a woman would have in her lifetime on the basis of current age-specific birth rates. Among 102 countries in less-developed regions for which data are available, the correlation between contraceptive prevalence and total fertility is strongly negative (-0.875; $P = .00$), with fairly consistent patterns across regions.

An additional advantage is that the distribution of users across categories of modern and traditional contraceptive practices can serve as a proxy index of method "choice," which has been shown to contribute to higher contraceptive uptake, continuation, and safety for the user. When combined with data on the user-effectiveness of each method, such distributions can be used to estimate rates of contraceptive efficacy within populations and subgroups. Related measures, such as contraceptive knowledge, past use of a method, and awareness of where to obtain modern contraceptives, are also useful markers of the capacity of nonusers to regulate their fertility if and when they wish to do so.

Limitations of the CPR

The CPR has limitations as a monitoring tool, however. The first relates to the assumption that women's contraceptive needs are somehow "met" when they are classified as users. Yet women may not be choosing the safest method with respect to their individual health status, or using the most effective method with respect to the nature and intensity of their fertility intentions (e.g., avoiding conception altogether vs. delaying the next pregnancy), or practicing the method correctly or consistently. An estimated 34 per cent of all mistimed and unwanted births worldwide are to women who claim that they or their partners were using some preventive method(s) during the month that conception occurred, and self-reported contraceptive users also account for a substantial proportion of abortion clients in most settings. Thus, despite the high cross-country correlation, contraceptive prevalence in the aggregate is a rather poor gauge of women's ability, at the individual level, to match their reproductive outcomes with their intentions.

A second problem with the CPR is the setting of goals and targets. How should progress be measured, and against what endpoint? Given that contraceptive use or nonuse depends so heavily on individuals' or couples' reproductive preferences, it makes little sense to set a target rate in the absence of a specific demographic rationale for doing so. Yet it is exactly this linkage with the "demographic imperative" and its associated policies of population control that made contraceptive prevalence and related measures such as "*couple years of protection*" and "*births averted*" so vulnerable to criticism in the past. Contraceptive prevalence, with its assumption that "*higher is better*", does not adequately reflect either women's reproductive preferences or their difficulties in achieving them. This is especially problematic in countries with low levels of modern or traditional contraceptive use that are difficult to interpret without additional information.

Total Fertility as an Indicator of Reproductive Health

The WHO/UNICEF/UNFPA Working Group in 2000 also selected the TFR as a core indicator for global monitoring. Like the CPR, the TFR by itself tells us little about women's reproductive preferences (especially at high fertility levels) or their effectiveness in achieving them. Instead, it serves, for our purposes, primarily as a marker of the frequency of women's exposure to the prevailing risks of pregnancy and childbirth. In this context, it is not the TFR per se, but rather, its *interaction* with the MMR that tells the relevant story.

In the abstract, high fertility would not represent a significant threat to women's health if the ratio of pregnancy-related deaths to live births were very low. But because high fertility is typically found in the same resource-poor settings as is high maternal mortality, their combined effects are explosive. A woman's lifetime risk of dying during pregnancy, abortion, childbirth, or its aftermath is perhaps the single best indicator of the profound inequities in maternal health across and within populations. According to estimates from the WHO, women living in developed regions have 1 chance in 4085 during their lifetime of dying from pregnancy-related causes compared with 1 chance in 61 in developing regions as a whole, and 1 in 16 in sub-Saharan Africa. At the extremes, the risks for Swedish women are 1 in 29 800 compared with 1 in 7 for women in:

a) Angola,
b) Malawi, and
c) Niger.

The age-and parity-specific fertility rates from which TFRs are derived are indispensable for identifying potentially high-risk population profiles, such as first births to young adolescents, high-parity births to older women, and closely spaced pregnancies, many of which might otherwise be prevented with effective contraceptive use. But the extent to which these potential risks translate into poor maternal mortality and morbidity outcomes depends on the accessibility and quality of antenatal, delivery, and postpartum care. Where quality and accessibility are favourable, age-and parity-specific differentials tend to diminish or even disappear. In addition, the majority of maternal deaths in most populations occur in women who would *not* be identified as high risk according to these age-parity criteria. For this reason, some investigators have concluded that family planning strategies that try to persuade women to avoid potentially high-risk categories of pregnancies are likely to be less effective in reducing MMRs than are health system strategies designed to provide essential obstetric care and emergency referral services for *all* women during childbirth and the immediate postpartum period. (An indicator of access to emergency obstetric care is proposed in the recommended "universal access to reproductive health services" target for the MDGs.) What family planning programmes *can* do better is to enable women who are already motivated to postpone, avoid, or stop childbearing to do so more effectively, thus circumventing the avoidable risks of unsafe abortion or delivery posed by conceptions or births that they did not intend to have.

Unmet Need for Contraception and Unplanned Births

The concept of unmet need for contraception has the considerable advantage of taking into account women's expressed interest in postponing or avoiding a pregnancy in assessing her "need" for a contraceptive method. In its 5-year review of ICPD, the UN General Assembly at ICPD + 5 adopted a target of eliminating the global unmet need for family planning by 2015—that is, closing "the gap between contraceptive use and the proportion of individuals expressing a desire to space or limit their families."

Unmet need is conventionally defined as the percentage of women in marital or consensual unions who (or whose partners) are not using any contraceptive method even though they are at risk of conceiving (that is, are sexually active, fecund, not currently pregnant) and do not want to be pregnant any time soon. Unmet need can be calculated for spacing purposes (to postpone pregnancy by at least 2 years) and limiting (stopping or avoiding childbearing entirely) according to women's reports of their reproductive intentions at the time of the interview. On the basis of the conventional definition, the proportions of women with an unmet need for some form of contraception range from under 10 per cent in countries such as Kazakhstan, Indonesia, Viet Nam, Brazil, and Colombia, up to 35 per cent or more in:

a) Rwanda,
b) Uganda,
c) Senegal,
d) Yemen, and
e) Haiti.

To obtain a more realistic picture of the scope of unmet need, many surveys now interview sexually active adolescent and adult women who are not currently in a marital or consensual union. Some also count users of traditional methods, such as withdrawal, periodic abstinence, or postpartum amenorrhea, as having an unmet need for *modern* (that is, presumably, "better") contraception. This second definitional shift raises the estimates of unmet need in the developing world from 113.6 million to 201 million couples, the latter representing 3 in every 10 women at risk of conceiving unintentionally.

Are high CPRs associated with low levels of unmet need for contraception across countries? Not necessarily. Unmet need is not a mirror image of the CPR, for each taps a slightly different dimension. Whereas the overall correlation between contraceptive prevalence and unmet need among all 56 countries in developing regions for which data are available on both measures is in the expected negative direction ($r = -0.71$; $P = .00$), the association is *positive* and the points are more dispersed among the majority of sub-Saharan African countries, plus Yemen, Haiti and Cambodia. This is a familiar reverse U-shaped pattern (one finds the same result with contraceptive prevalence and unplanned births), in which women's rising aspirations for postponing the next pregnancy (if not to avoid it altogether) in the early stages of a population's adoption of contraception are, for various programmatic and personal reasons, not yet accompanied by an equivalent uptake in contraceptive practice. It is only at higher levels of prevalence that the expected negative relation appears, and then imperfectly.

What Does "Unmet Need" Reflect?

The concept of unmet need—whether for any contraception or for a modern method—clearly taps into the ICPD concept of fertility regulation as a matter of sexual and reproductive health and rights. It takes into account a woman's reproductive desires and has—at least hypothetically, if not realistically—a zero end-point.

Despite its relative advantages as a monitoring tool, however, unmet need also has its limitations. Primary among these is the interpretation of its underlying causes. Like contraceptive use, unmet need in a population can be low because most women want to become pregnant, for example, and not because their contraceptive needs have been satisfied. Alternatively, high levels of unmet need do not necessarily reflect a lack of access to information and services. Surveys that ask women why they are not using contraception even though they say they do not want to get pregnant right away do cite such reasons, but more frequently they mention causes such as health concerns and fears of side effects, husband's or community opposition, and other personal and cultural explanations that are, by and large, not amenable to direct programmatic intervention. In addition, a woman's reproductive intentions may be changeable, unclear, situation-specific ("it depends"), or not shared by her partner. Qualitative, in-depth investigations of unmet need usually identify complex mixtures of feelings and behaviours relating to a possible pregnancy, such as ambivalence, miscommunication, denial, uncertainties about the sexual relationship, and lucky (or unlucky) experiences with the use or nonuse of contraception in the past.

Because the need for contraception is defined by the research design and not by the woman herself, unmet need may or may not represent an active *demand* or desire for contraception. In this sense, the indicator proposed for the MDGs by the Task Force on Child Health and Maternal Health, the "percentage of demand (or 'desire for family planning') satisfied," is somewhat misleading in its implication. Indeed, it is this very elusiveness of the multiple factors underlying unmet need that have led some observers to suggest that a programme strategy that focuses on serving current contraceptive users better (e.g., with methods that are more appropriate to their needs and that support correct use and continuity) may be more effective in avoiding unintended pregnancies than one that attempts to reduce or eliminate unmet need, which in some settings may be quite resistant to change.

The Relationship between Unmet Need and Unplanned Births

The birth of a child that a woman says was unplanned—either mistimed or unwanted—at the time of its conception is a clear indication of a mismatch between reproductive intentions and outcomes. DHSs ask every woman who had any live births during the past 5 years to think back to the time she became pregnant and to say if she had wanted to become pregnant then, did not want to until later, or did not want to have any (more) children at all. Because interviewers refer to the child by name when asking about each pregnancy, women may redefine pregnancies that were unwanted at the time they occurred as having been wanted (perhaps less so for those that were mistimed). Even so, despite this almost certain bias, the proportions of births that women say were *unwanted* at conception range from 5 per cent or fewer in 13 sub-Saharan African countries and in Kyrgyzstan, Turkmenistan, and Uzbekistan, up to 20 per cent or more in Malawi, Yemen, Nepal, Cambodia, Haiti, Mexico, Bolivia, Brazil, Colombia, and Peru. Proportions of births *unplanned* (unwanted plus mistimed) are far higher, exceeding half of all births in 9 of the 67 countries in developing regions for which data are available.

The limited value of unmet need for contraception as a predictor of proportions of births unplanned among 56 developing countries with data for both variables is revealed in the low correlation between these 2 measures ($r = 0.26$; $P = .06$). In addition, the proportions of births that are unplanned almost always exceed the proportions of women with an unmet need for some form of contraception. This occurs most dramatically among countries in which 10 per cent or fewer of women have an unmet need for contraception as conventionally measured. Among these is Turkey, where women terminate 20 per cent of their pregnancies by legal abortion, and define an additional 30 per cent of their births as unplanned. Legal abortion ratios are also high in Kazakhstan (41%), Turkmenistan (23%), and Viet Nam (44%), even though unmet need is below 10 per cent. In Brazil, Colombia, and Peru, where similarly low levels of unmet need are combined with CPRs of 70 per cent or more, women terminate perhaps 30 per cent of their pregnancies with induced clandestine abortion (a regional estimate), and report *half or more* of their births as unplanned. Thus, low levels of unmet need are not necessarily associated with low proportions of births being unplanned.

Unplanned pregnancies and births represent unanticipated and largely avoidable social, economic, and health costs to women, couples, and families that are relevant to all of the MDGs—not just maternal health. A review of surveys of abortion clients in 23 countries found that economic reasons ("cannot afford a baby") were second only to the nonspecific reasons of "want to postpone childbearing" or "want no (more) children" given by women seeking legal terminations in the 1990s. Poverty alleviation—the overriding concern of the MDGs—is a prime motivation. Other reasons include the disruption of education or work, relationship problems, partner does not want the pregnancy, the woman is too young or is unmarried, and risks to the health of the woman or the fetus.

Unplanned births tap into other dimensions of maternal and child health as well. In some but not all settings, they are associated with adverse child health outcomes that begin with delayed antenatal care and continue through a sequence of depressed levels of maternal investment in the newborn, such as breast-feeding and other expressions of physical and emotional care. Moreover, unplanned pregnancies and births may be related to unwanted intercourse (within or outside marriage) or difficulties that girls and women face in negotiating protection from unwanted pregnancy, as well as lack of access to information and services for terminating an unwanted pregnancy safely and humanely, especially among unmarried adolescents and the poor.

Unsafe Abortion and Abortion Mortality

When all else fails (or, for various reasons, is not attempted), the ultimate decision for safe and effective fertility regulation centers on the possible interruption of an unintended or unwanted pregnancy. Although promoting more effective contraceptive use with good information and wider access to high-quality care can go a long way toward reducing the numbers of abortions, it will not eliminate the need or demand for safe services.

An estimated 26 per cent of all pregnancies worldwide are terminated by induced abortion: 41 per cent in developed regions and 23 per cent in developing regions. Of the estimated 76 million unintended pregnancies that occur annually in developing countries, perhaps 34 million result in unplanned births. Among the rest, an estimated 10 million end in miscarriage and 32 million are interrupted by induced abortion. Reliable data from the developing world on the ratio of abortions to pregnancies are limited almost entirely to those Asian countries in which abortion is permitted on broad grounds, ranging from 10 per cent in Uzbekistan to 40 per cent in Armenia, Kazakhstan, and Viet Nam. For other regions, the estimated ratio of abortions to pregnancies is 15 per cent in sub-Saharan Africa (of which 99% are probably illegal); 21 per cent and 30 per cent, respectively, in Central and South America (of which virtually 100% are illegal, except in Cuba); and 18 per cent and 20 per cent, respectively, for Central and Southern Asia and for Southeast and Eastern Asia (of which an estimated 78 per cent and 60 per cent are illegal).

Eliminating Unsafe Abortion and Abortion Mortality

The ICPD Programme of Action urges governments and intergovernmental and nongovernmental organizations to strengthen their commitment to women's health by addressing the impact of unsafe abortion as a major public health concern. Delegates agreed that women with unwanted pregnancies should have access to reliable information and compassionate counseling; to quality services for the management of complications arising from (unsafe) abortion; and—crucially—where abortion is not against the law, that such abortion should be safe. At ICPD + 5, governments further agreed that health systems should train and equip health service providers to ensure that such (legal) abortion is safe and accessible. Because abortion is permitted by law, on at least some grounds, in 189 of the 193 countries of the world, this mandate to provide safe services within health and family planning facilities for those who are eligible applies virtually everywhere.

Accurate statistics on the incidence of abortion and on related morbidity and mortality are notoriously difficult to collect, however, whether from institutional sources, indirect estimation techniques, or from women themselves. The exception is in countries where services are available on request and where most procedures are performed in the public health system or in private clinics—that is, in approved facilities by trained personnel—with good reporting systems. In these countries, one can calculate abortion ratios (per 100 pregnancies or, alternatively, live births) and abortion rates (per 1000 women of the relevant age group or marital status) as well as abortion mortality ratios, recognizing that there may still be some underreporting.

In estimating the percentages of all abortions that are performed under unsafe conditions where data are scarce or unreliable, however, both the numerator and denominator are problematic. On the basis of complex assumptions and a variety of complete and incomplete country-specific data sources, the WHO estimates that 19 million of the approximately 45 million abortions performed annually worldwide are unsafe according to their definition, with 97 per cent of all unsafe procedures being performed in developing countries. Perhaps 68 000 women die each year from the complications of unsafe abortions, including those that are self-induced, and untold numbers suffer from infections and other damage to the reproductive tract. Preventable deaths from improperly performed procedures constitute 13 per cent of maternal mortality globally, and 25 per cent or more in some countries where maternal mortality from other causes is relatively low (e.g., Eastern Europe and South America), making unsafe abortion the leading single cause of maternal mortality worldwide.

In developed countries in which safe services are broadly accessible, abortion deaths average about 1 per 100 000 procedures compared with 6 to 25 deaths during pregnancy, delivery, or its aftermath per 100 000 live births. Risks are hundreds of times higher in countries where women turn to untrained providers, quacks, or self-induced methods. Abortion deaths average 330 per 100 000 procedures in all developing regions (excluding China) and as high as 680 per 100 000 in sub-Saharan Africa. Ensuring the safety of *all* voluntary pregnancy terminations and not just those that are acceptable on narrow legal grounds is clearly central to the reduction of maternal mortality as proposed in the MDGs. The persistence of restrictive policies in many countries should be a major cause for alarm, however. These policies impede women's access to high-quality services, often with disastrous results, in addition to impeding the collection of reliable data for the global monitoring of maternal health.

Can Population Surveys Collect Information About Abortion?

Although the abortion mortality ratio (like the MMR) requires either a complete reporting system or a good indirect method of estimating deaths from this cause, we believe that an approximation of the percentage of all procedures that are *unsafe*—like the percentage of births attended by skilled health personnel—could be obtained from population surveys. The standard DHS questionnaire does not ask women about abortions, except in the general question "have you ever had a pregnancy that miscarried, was aborted, or ended in a stillbirth?" (respondents are also asked when the pregnancy ended and at how many months). Appropriately worded follow-up questions could distinguish among these outcomes (as in the 2000 DHS of Armenia, for example) and ask about the conditions of abortion as they do about childbirth. Abortion methods, providers, and settings could also be routinely identified, as they are in the 2000 Cambodia DHS, and the percentages of unsafe procedures reported overall and for subgroups, such as adolescents, ethnic minorities, and the rural and urban poor.

In addition, in the family planning section of the questionnaire, women could be asked, as they are asked now about delaying or avoiding pregnancy, "have you ever used anything or tried in any way to induce a late menstrual period or terminate a pregnancy? If yes, what have you used or done? Was it successful or not? What else have you tried?" They could be asked if they know of a method for doing so (traditional or modern, the latter referring to medical inductions, vacuum aspiration, or dilation and curettage) and of a service provider or facility. There will be underreporting, of course, as there is for questions about other sensitive issues, such as sexual partnerships and exposure to HIV/AIDS.

Conclusions

- Contraceptive prevalence and TFRs are useful primarily as background information for analyzing levels of unmet need and unplanned births. By themselves, they do not capture women's capacity to manage their fertility safely and effectively because they do not take reproductive preferences into account. Nor are the safety aspects apparent on the surface; rather, these manifest themselves in relation to women's capacity to avoid a high-risk abortion or delivery in resource-poor settings with high MMRs.
- Indicators of the proportions of women having an unmet need for contraception and proportions of births that are unplanned have the strong advantage of taking women's reproductive intentions at the time of the interview (unmet need) or at the time of a previous conception (unplanned births) into account. Both are subject to some measurement error, however, and to difficulties in interpreting underlying causes. Their hypothetical "zero" target—that of *eliminating* unmet need and unplanned births—is unrealistic for these reasons. Perhaps the most

that could be accomplished is to reduce their aggregate levels to under 10 per cent and to eliminate within-country inequalities.

- Access to safe services for the voluntary termination of a mistimed, unwanted, or otherwise problematic pregnancy represents the ultimate measure of safe and effective fertility regulation in accordance with women's reproductive intentions. The indicators of unsafe abortion and abortion mortality are intended to monitor progress in this area. Both measures have a feasible zero target that can be reached in supportive policy and programme environments. Reliable cross-country data that could otherwise be obtained are critically lacking, however, in large part because of political restrictions by some governments that block not only reproductive health advocacy and safe services, but also the necessary data collection and research. These restrictions need to be removed.

In summation, no single measure of contraceptive use (or nonuse) or of total fertility is sufficient without addressing both the high proportions of births in the developing world that women (both users and nonusers of contraception) say were unplanned at the time of conception and the percentages of induced abortions that are performed under unsafe conditions. Because the narrative of women's attempts to manage their fertility safely and effectively—especially in conditions of poverty—inevitably embraces their experiences with unintended pregnancies and potentially life-threatening deliveries or clandestine abortions, these processes and outcomes should be monitored for the maternal health goal of the MDGs.

The major prerequisite for both the data collection and analysis and for the design of responsive policies and programmes is the strengthening of political commitment at national and international levels to the ICPD Programme of Action in all of its manifestations. Reinforced by the Fourth World Conference on Women held in Beijing in 1995, reaffirmed many times since, and supported in 2004 by a declaration of world leaders and by the adoption of a global reproductive health strategy by the World Health Assembly, the ICPD agenda for sexual and reproductive health and rights remains a vital force.

At the 2005 World Summit, governments made the strongest commitment yet to reproductive health, recognizing that it is essential for the accomplishment of the MDGs. Within this context, there is a crucial need for bilateral and multilateral donors and foundations to fund the data collection and analysis recommended here, as well as the broader policy and programmatic changes and health system capacity-building required to fulfill the Cairo consensus on sexual and reproductive health and rights. The UN needs to play its part by adding a target—universal access to reproductive health—under the maternal health goal, along with a more inclusive set of indicators, so that countries can plan and monitor their progress more effectively.

18

Considerations in Selecting Birth/Fertility Regulation Methods

Existing contraceptive methods are of five types-hormonal, intrauterine devices, sterilization, barrier, and natural or traditional methods. Both surgical and medical techniques exist for inducing abortion.

Each method has intrinsic characteristics which must be considered when governments or agencies choose a method for particular countries or programmes. Women's health advocates emphasized, however, that the selection process must also take into account the sexual, reproductive, social and economic realities of women's lives; their health; and the quality of family planning and health services in particular settings. That is, the technologies should not be selected in isolation from the conditions in which they are to be used.

Women are concerned that, in many in stances, this principle has not been followed. As a result, methods that should, in women's view, be provided only by well-trained personnel in settings with strong health infrastructure that can ensure informed choice have been misused or abused. Scientists usually consider that they are contributing to knowledge about a particular technology and that they rarely have the possibility of influencing how and where a method is used.

Researchers have discussed at length the standards that should be set for selection and use of contraceptives, and the efforts needed to encourage adoption of these standards. It was agreed that women's health advocates and scientists, working together, might design more appropriate standards and also monitor selection and use, at least in some settings.

Researchers have agreed that a woman's selection of a method of fertility regulation is affected by many considerations. These include such personal circumstances as her health, sexual relationship(s) and point in her reproductive life cycle; the societal conditions that affect her sexuality such as her status in society, risk of violence, and possible exposure to infected partners; her prior experience with fertility regulation methods; and her access to information. Her choice will also be affected by the availability of health and family planning services, their quality and accessibility, the mix of methods offered as well as the availability of safe abortion.

Box 1: Quote

"*Access is not only a question of how distant her home is, or how much the transportation costs or who will take care of the baby if she goes to the clinic. We have to ask what is the attitude of the husband what is the attitude of the mother-in-law what is the attitude of the neighbourhood, of the family, of the city, of the society at large with respect to that woman using that method? What are the sources of information? ...Much more emphasis should be put on this field*".—Aníbal Faundes

It has also been agreed that no one method can work for all women at all times in their lives, and that therefore, the broadest possible number of fertility regulation methods should be offered. Some scientists see greater hope for improving choice through development of highly effective, reversible, long-acting methods. Many women's health advocates see a greater need for the promotion of already existing methods that have minimal side effects, are user-controlled, and are protective against infection, such as barrier methods. Behind these preferences lie differences in the definitions and relative weight assigned to four fundamental characteristics of fertility regulation technologies: safety, efficacy, acceptability and availability.

Safety, Efficacy, Acceptability and Availability

Safety

Scientists want to ensure that a method they develop causes no dangerous or permanent side effects. Through toxicological and clinical studies they assess whether a method might be carcinogenic, or might have severe effects on physiological functions such as those of the heart, the kidneys or the reproductive organs, or might have other potentially severe outcomes. The women who use methods that have passed these tests are also concerned about how these methods might affect their overall health, including their sexual interest, physical stamina, or emotional well-being-aspects of health that generally have been given lower priority by researchers and service providers. Side effects such as menstrual bleeding disturbances, which scientists consider unimportant medically, can be of extreme concern to women, and may affect how they perceive the safety of any method. For a woman, safety of use of a method during lactation, and the long-term effects of method use, are of particular concern, and her concept of safety may also require that the method is immediately reversible. Because safety is impossible to measure in absolute terms, and accurate technical information is still insufficient, a broad spectrum of society, certainly women, should participate in the process of weighing risks and benefits of technologies to be introduced.

Some women feel that certain natural substances, such as herbs and plants used as contraceptives may be safer than modern methods and some women's health advocates felt that more emphasis should be put on researching traditional herbs and plants. Scientists pointed out that the Special Programme had funded a major international research programme in this area, albeit restricted to plants alleged to have properties preventing implantation of a fertilized egg in the uterus or to inhibit male fertility. No new chemical entities suitable for method development were identified. However, this area of research has by no means been exhausted.

Box 2: Quote

"*Natural is not always simple and safe. On the other hand, there are many traditional methods which I'm sure haven't been adequately explored and could very well turn out to have the advantage of simplicity and safety*".—Henry Gabelnick

Women's health advocates felt that attention needs to be given to the safety of particular methods in settings where disease and malnutrition are very substantial. They emphasized the need to examine interactions between fertility regulation methods and sexually transmitted diseases, especially AIDS. They suggested, for example, that a community with endemic reproductive tract infections, especially where they are undiagnosed and untreated, is an inappropriate environment in which to introduce IUDs. Scientists pointed out that some agencies do carry out studies on the wider health implications of method use. The Special Programme, for example, is conducting cross-cultural research in more than 20 countries to examine the effect of various contraceptives on a range of problems including HIV transmission, neoplasia, infant development, anemia, hepatitis B and cardiovascular diseases. It was recognized, however, that more needs to be done, and that the results of such studies need to be made available much more widely than is presently the case.

Scientists indicated that they need to know more about how clients perceive and define safety. However, they also urged that what is known medically about safety should be more adequately conveyed to women. For instance, a once-a-month injectable contraceptive sold over the counter in Latin American countries has been very popular among women because bleeding remains regular. However, the drug contains a high dose of estrogen which increases the risk of metabolic and cardiovascular diseases—a long-term problem which is not noticed on a daily basis by the user. This example underlines the essential need for communication between scientists and users. As a result of this situation the Special Programme has supported the development of an alternative, once a-month injectable with a lower dose of estrogen, which is currently being introduced into six countries.

Both scientists and women's health advocates agreed that cultural and service delivery factors influence the actual safety of any method. The safety of sterilization or IUDs, for instance, depends largely on the care with which they are delivered. Furthermore, for certain methods, the service provider determines a dimension of safety critical to most women: immediate and effective reversibility on demand.

A fundamental difference in perspectives on the relative safety of methods remains. Scientists tend to argue that the health risks of any method should be measured against the risks of a clandestine abortion or of a full-term pregnancy (wanted or unwanted). Their priority is to develop the most effective contraceptive methods to reduce the likelihood that women will resort to dangerous abortions or go through a high-risk pregnancy. Women's health advocates, on the other hand, often see the risks of some methods, whether inherent or caused by poor services, to be too high. Many argue for the provision of methods that have minimal side effects, along with safe abortion as a back-up. They also point out that emphasis on family planning services should not detract from efforts to improve pregnancy and delivery care.

Efficacy

Scientists measure the efficacy of a contraceptive method by quantifying how often it fails to prevent pregnancy. The measures applied are rates of "method failure" and of "user failure". Women, however, may define efficacy by how well a method "works for them in their lives". Their measures include not only pregnancy prevention but also "satisfaction". The latter may encompass the effects the method has on the woman's sexual relationship, her sense of control over the method, the freedom to use it when she pleases, and its efficacy in preventing infection. For many women, these aspects of effectiveness, along with safety as defined above, may be as or more important than contraceptive efficacy. Women's health advocates felt that the scientific community tends to give too much weight to contraceptiye efficacy. Scientists stressed that safety is their first concern and indicated that women's perception of their priorities in this regard is incorrect. Scientists and women's health advocates agreed that this is evidence of a serious communication gap that should be closed through continuing dialogue.

Women's health advocates questioned scientists' bias toward systemic or provider-dependent methods that have less likelihood of user failure. They suggested that this emphasis has led researchers to overlook low user acceptability or significant dissatisfaction with the method which may be masked by high continuation rates when assessing the efficacy of methods such as the IUD or sub-dermal implants. At the same time, what appears to be the lower effectiveness of barrier methods may be due not so much to the methods them selves as to failure to provide adequate information and support to women who use them. Furthermore, service providers have often simply asserted that the diaphragm is inappropriate for low income women who do not have privacy, water, education or other resources. It has been assumed, rightly or wrongly, that instruction in the proper use of barrier methods places undue demands on understaffed, overworked clinics. The meeting participants agreed that such assumptions need to be tested and the use-effectiveness of barrier methods further studied. They also agreed that clinical studies of effectiveness are not sufficient, since efficacy also depends on the social and health environment, on service providers, and on users, not just on the method itself. Women's health advocates also suggested that the safety-efficacy balance of barrier methods, backed up by safe abortion facilities, should be compared to the safety efficacy balance of systemic, provider dependent methods.

Acceptability

This concept permeated discussions throughout the meeting. The measures commonly used by scientists and policy makers are rates of acceptance (agreeing to start using a contraceptive method) and rates of continuing a method. Women's health advocates argued for indicators of acceptability that also measure in formed choice and user satisfaction. Research on the reasons not only for acceptance, but also for satisfaction and dissatisfaction, could help to increase understanding of what acceptability really means to women. Scientists pointed out that the Special Programme carries out research on these and other aspects of acceptability, particularly on reasons for discontinuation.

It was agreed that acceptance and acceptability are influenced by many factors. For example, if health service providers judge one method better than another, then the counseling and information they provide is likely to reflect that bias and affect acceptance and use of that method. Similarly, policy-makers and providers may make incorrect assumptions about what is acceptable to women and men. A common assumption is that women will not touch their genitals. In Thailand, a clinical trial of a vaginal ring run by clinicians was unsuccessful be cause of this assumption on the part of the male clinicians, whereas a trial of a similar ring run by midwives met with considerable success, because they spent time demonstrating how the method works. A similar experience occurred in the Dominican Republic. In Brazil, donors, health authorities and gynecologists have regarded the diaphragm as in effective and unusable, particularly for low-income women. Yet, a feminist health centre in Sao Paulo has shown that, if women are given information and counseling about a range of methods including the diaphragm, many of them, regardless of income level, choose the diaphragm and find it easy to use. In an other instance in Turkey, family planning officials assumed that women were their primary clients, even though the main method used up to that time was withdrawal. Early family planning efforts failed because men, who control contraceptive practice in Turkey, were not fully involved.

Women's health advocates indicated that women's definitions of acceptability change over time with changes in their circumstances. As women become more concerned with their rights and have more knowledge of their bodies, for example, they may be less willing to accept methods that can adversely affect their health. Many of the participants felt strongly that not only risks but also more responsibility for fertility regulation should be shared by men and that resources for the development of male methods should be increased. Some participants nonetheless expressed concern that even women in stable relationships may not trust their partners to use contraceptives effectively and, therefore, female methods should continue to have priority.

Finally, acceptability is also conditioned by the availability of methods. The participants agreed that if only one or two methods are available, it is not meaningful to speak of acceptability because there is no choice.

Availability

For a method to be truly *'available'*, a number of conditions must be met, including easily accessible distribution points (clinics, commercial outlets, etc.), where the supplies are consistent, staff are properly trained, and opening hours are convenient for clients. A key aspect of availability discussed at length is afford ability, both for the service provider (e.g., a national government programme) and for the consumer. Participants expressed considerable concern that some recently developed methods, such as implants, are costly. This also raised the question of manufacture. Participants from Africa and Asia in particular, stressed that many countries in their regions have no control over manufacture and supply of fertility regulation products, and that this affects availability.

Other Critical Factors in Selection of Methods

Health and Family Planning Infrastructure

Women's health advocates and scientists agreed that, in an ideal world, women and men should have the freedom to choose any method, the right to change methods, and the ability to afford any method. This requires properly staffed and maintained health and family planning services and the provision of safe abortion services. In reality, health and family planning services tend to be over worked, understaffed and under financed. Adding fertility regulation methods, especially those that require sophisticated delivery and follow-up, may simply compound existing service weaknesses.

Box 3: Quote

"*We get the feeling now and then that the method gets the blame whilst it is the services that should be the target of complaints*".—Olav Meirik

There was general agreement that the health and family planning infrastructure has a very significant impact on the safety and efficacy of fertility regulation methods. Those responsible for selecting methods therefore must determine whether the infrastructure is well enough staffed and equipped to ensure safety and efficacy. Are necessary supplies available consistently, along with trained staff who have both the skills and the time required to deliver the various methods safely? Can the staff ensure informed choice, provide counseling and follow up clients? Are services readily available to deal adequately with method complications, method removal, side effects or unwanted pregnancy?

There were different views on the criteria that might be used in answering these questions. Some participants argued that certain methods should simply not be selected by countries with very weak infrastructure. Others suggested that methods dependent on sophisticated facilities should perhaps be provided first (or only) at higher levels of the health system or in urban areas. Clearly, this is an area of on going debate which may be best resolved in particular countries through dialogue among policy makers, service providers and women's health advocates.

Quality of Services

Women's health advocates suggested that qualitative aspects of existing health and family planning programmes should be taken into account in selecting fertility regulation methods to introduce into those systems. A service that emphasizes quantitative targets:

- is unlikely to provide or reward counseling,
- may have coercive elements (e.g., denies women abortions unless they agree to accept a particular method of contraception or sterilization), and
- may not maintain privacy or treat clients with respect.

Box 4: Quote

"*Any type of new technology that we introduce in any country of the world will fail if you don't have good service delivery and good counseling*".—Kerstin Hagenfeld

Such systems will not provide any method appropriately, but especially those that are not reversible (sterilization), are reversible only with the cooperation of the service provider (IUDs, implants) or are not immediately reversible (e.g. long-acting injectables).

Many of these aspects of quality of care could be improved at little or no cost by adjusting objectives to emphasize choice among methods and respect for the client. Others, like counseling, demand time from already over-worked staff—a demand that will increase with the introduction of each additional method. One way to address this problem is to broaden personnel to include non-physicians in the delivery of services—an approach that has proved to be very successful in a number of countries. Participants generally agreed that, regardless of the method to be selected or introduced, family planning services must do more to ensure respect for the user and for her or his cultural, sexual and religious values.

Government and Donor Criteria for Method Selection

Women's health advocates expressed a need for more information on the definition and application of criteria for method selection at national levels. Since many countries are dependent upon supplies from donors, the criteria used by the donors are especially important. For example, a recent attempt to manufacture diaphragms in Brazil has been thwarted by lack of donor support, while in Bangladesh, until very recently, only high-dose contraceptive pills have been available.

Government policies can also be very restrictive. Natural methods of fertility regulation are often not included in the official list of contraceptive methods and thus services are not provided. Health ministries sometimes set supply quotas for certain methods such as condoms, and this can result in serious shortages. Although some public sector agencies are beginning to accept the need for barrier methods, a general prejudice still exists among donors and government programmes against providing methods that require spermicides be cause of the difficulty of maintaining supplies of spermicides in developing countries.

Unwanted Pregnancy and Abortion

The primary purpose of very large investments in contraceptive technologies and services to date has been to prevent unwanted, ill-timed or otherwise inappropriate pregnancies. In some countries, nonetheless, induced abortions equal or surpass the number of live births. Worldwide, it is estimated that between 36 and 53 million induced abortions occur every year, and as many as 200,000 women may die each year due to unsafe abortion. Clearly, as yet contraceptive technologies and services neither meet the needs of, nor are accessible to, millions of women who want to control their fertility.

Box 5: Quote

"Abortion has to be seen as an important integral aspect of reproductive rights which cannot be neglected. In my two years as coordinator of the women's health programme in Sao Paulo, I have been involved in research in 25 municipal hospitals in poor areas and have seen the increase in abortion and abortion complications as a great issue. The total number of complicated abortions presented at the hospital in 1989 exceeded the number of births. It is therefore impossible for researchers not to involve themselves publicly in the abortion issue in their countries".—Maria Jose Araujo

Recognizing that it will be some time be fore all women's contraceptive needs can be met, and that some women will always need safe abortion services, most participants felt strongly that women's groups and scientists should actively collaborate to encourage understanding of unwanted pregnancy and to prevent and eliminate unsafe abortion.

A limited number of institutions and organizations (such as the Special Programme) currently support research activities on particular aspects of abortion, including the very serious health effects of unsafe abortion, the factors that lead to unwanted pregnancy and unsafe abortion, and assessment of new technologies for safe induced abortion. These and other aspects of abortion urgently need more research, on which scientists and women's health advocates should collaborate.

Women's health advocates also emphasized that public education and advocacy are needed to decriminalize abortion. Women's health advocacy groups usually work for safe and accessible abortion services, but initiatives are needed from others as well. In a number of countries, physicians and other health professionals have taken the lead, some times in alliance with women's organizations. It was suggested that researchers could provide an additional strong and effective voice in national and international efforts to ensure women's access to safe services in all countries.

It was pointed out that the World Health Organization, as an inter-governmental organization, serves the needs of its Member States, who have divergent policies on the issue of abortion. In accordance with the recommendation of the 1984 International Conference on Population, WHO does not promote abortion as a method of family planning, but is concerned with the health aspects, particularly of unsafe abortion.

Box 6: Suggested actions

- *Re-examine* the basic concepts of safety, efficacy, acceptability and availability to incorporate women's perceptions and experiences in the definition of each and to define an appropriate balance among them as criteria for method selection and introduction.
- *Review* criteria used by national governments and donors in the selection of fertility regulation methods and, where appropriate, recommend modifications.
- *Promote* health and family planning systems that emphasize high quality care.
- *Undertake* further research on women's and men's attitudes, beliefs and practices about sexuality and fertility regulation in particular settings.
- *Increase* investment in male contraceptive methods and involve men in taking personal responsibility for reproductive health and fertility regulation.
- *Support* collaboration between scientists and women's health advocates on initiatives to eliminate unsafe abortion.

The Availability of Methods and the Reality of Choice: Bangladesh and Brazil

In theory, a wide range of fertility regulation methods is available in Bangladesh but, at most, one third of reproductive age couples use a contraceptive method, and many women resort to abortion. The methods available through governmental and non-governmental channels include high dose oral contraceptives, condoms, vaginal foam tablets, IUDs (copper T380A), two- and three-month injectables, Norplant subdermal implants, tubal legation and vasectomy, and menstrual regulation. Other methods used include natural family planning, breast feeding, withdrawal, ayurvedic and homeopathic methods.

Most women in Bangladesh do not have the wide choices that this list implies. The majority has no access to information about methods and only limited access to services, which are of poor quality. Many women are compelled to obey their husbands and in-laws, and, as a result, practice fertility regulation in secret, if at all. Consequently, methods requiring male cooperation are difficult or impossible for many women to adopt. Injectable contraceptives have become increasingly popular, in part because women can obtain them under the guise of taking their children to a clinic for immunization. Methods which cause menstrual disruption are problematic, however, because bleeding interferes with praying, fasting, sexual intercourse, and a woman's feeling of health and well-being. Women also want to avoid methods believed to cause cancer and methods which might cause infections such as an IUD inserted under unsterile conditions.

Given all these limitations, along with problems of service delivery, it is estimated that every year 750,000 women in Bangladesh have an abortion. Perhaps one-fifth of these have access to safe menstrual regulation through Government clinics; the rest risk their lives in clandestine procedures. For many women, a vasectomy for their partner is the ideal choice, but most men reject it. Most sterilization in Bangladesh is there fore undertaken by women, even though vasectomy is easier, safer and less expensive than tubal legation.

In Brazil, though the range of legal fertility regulation methods is extremely narrow, about two-thirds of women in marital or consensual unions use some method of contraception or are sterilized. Although the government has adopted an integrated women's health programme which mandates the provision of a wide range of contraceptive methods, in fact, the only fertility regulation methods accessible to most women are oral contraceptives provided through the private sector, clandestine abortion (legal abortion is severely restricted), and tubal legation. The lack of choice of contraceptive methods and the legal restrictions on abortion mean that women pay a very high price for fertility regulation.

For low-income women, the recurring cost of pills, along with costs of obtaining them, such as transportation, loss of earnings, and child care are deterrents to oral contraceptive use. Side effects of oral contraceptives, such as menstrual disturbances, weight gain, headaches, or loss of libido are reported often, and these kinds of effects frequently result in:

a) incorrect use,
b) discontinuation of the method and, ultimately,
c) unwanted pregnancy.

It is estimated that three million abortions occur each year in the country, compared to four million births. In a survey of low-income women in the state of Santa Catarina, 18 methods to induce abortion were reported, including catheters and knitting needles. In 1989, the number of cases with complications from induced abortion in the municipal hospital of Sao Paulo exceeded the number of deliveries.

With no temporary means of contraception available to them, many women undergo tubal legation. Not surprisingly, studies show that up to 50 percent of Brazilian women sterilized before 25 years of age regret it. Tubal legation is not officially provided in the public sector, but it is frequently done clandestinely at the time of Cesarean section. This helps explain the extremely high rate of "unnecessary" Cesarean sections and associated complications in Brazil.

Given the negative experience many Brazilian women have had with hormonal methods and with the service system, the greatest weight should perhaps now be given to methods that have minimal health risks or side effects, are reversible, inexpensive and easv to use. Careful introduction of barrier methods and the IUD may be more appropriate than the introduction of new methods which have systemic effects, require a physician's involvement, and therefore are not under the user's control.

By comparison, an ideal contraceptive in Bangladesh would be one that is easy to use with privacy, is inexpensive, and is not connected with sexual intercourse. It would not require leaving the home, would have minimal side effects and would be socially and culturally acceptable. But the issue in Bangladesh may be less selection of additional methods than improvement in service quality and availability along with broader changes in women's lives that would enable them to make choices for themselves.

19

Post-ICPD Progress in the Reproductive Health

Case Study from the Pacific

Reproductive health services provide men and women with the knowledge they need to protect their health and the health of their families. This includes methods for planning their families, preventing and treating sexually transmitted diseases, including HIV/AIDS, and discouraging harmful practices against women. The use of contraception is influenced by many factors, especially access to and knowledge of affordable and quality reproductive health services. And because gender relations affect reproductive health, men need to take greater responsibility for their own sexual behaviour as well as respect and support their partners' rights and health. Motivation towards the achievement of reproductive rights and reproductive health as a fundamental human right was integral to the proceedings, Programme of Action (PoA) and sequelae of the International Conference on Population and Development (ICPD).

The ICPD framework for attaining reproductive rights and reproductive health states that all countries should aim to:

- ensure that comprehensive reproductive health services, including family planning, are accessible, affordable and acceptable to all;
- enable and support responsible voluntary decisions about family planning and other legal fertility regulation methods and to have the information and means to do so; and
- meet the changing reproductive health needs over a person's life span.

All countries were urged to make accessible, through the Primary Health Care System, quality reproductive health services to all individuals of appropriate ages. These services included: family-planning counseling, information, education, communications and services; education and services for prenatal care; safe delivery and postnatal care; prevention and appropriate treatment of infertility; prevention and management of consequences of abortion; treatment of reproductive tract infections; sexually transmitted diseases and other reproductive health conditions; information, education and counseling, as appropriate, on human sexuality, reproductive health and responsible parenthood; and the prevention and management of harmful practices that impact sexual health. Countries were encouraged to implement innovative reproductive health programmes for adolescents and adult men, primarily aimed at improving decision making in sexual and reproductive health matters, specifically family planning and prevention of STIs, including HIV/AIDS.

The global paradigm shift, that occurred at ICPD, in the way population policies and programmes were perceived and reproductive health services were conceptualized, signified a major change in the mechanisms through which population and development goals would be achieved. Instead of a population-control development approach, a people-centred, rights-based approach was set forth as a means for meeting people's needs for sexual and reproductive health. Personal choice and the right to sexual and reproductive health, including voluntary decisions about childbearing, were perceived as fundamental to the process of achieving better quality of life throughout the relevant life span of men and women. This shift in global thinking had major policy and programming implications for Reproductive Health in the Pacific.

The ICPD PoA's framework, which recognised the importance of integrating family planning and sexually transmitted infections services into maternal care, within the current health care systems, also had implications for health sector reform in most Pacific Island Countries and Territories (PICTs).

At the ICPD+5, a special session to review progress towards meeting the ICPD goals, the United Nations General Assembly agreed on a new set of benchmarks which included reproductive health care and unmet need for contraception as well as maternal mortality reduction. Within the ICPD/ICPD+5 framework, mechanisms were presented for governments and civil society to implement so as to acknowledge reproductive health as a basic human right and to improve reproductive health services for all people of appropriate ages. Since ICPD, many PICTs have committed to improving the status of reproductive health of their people. Integration of reproductive health, including family planning and sexual health, within primary health care services has been implemented to varying degrees in PICTs.

A major objective of the Global Survey Field Inquiry was to determine progress made by some countries in the areas of reproductive rights and reproductive health. Thirteen Pacific Island countries responded to the field inquiry and documented progress towards the ICPD goals. The thirteen Pacific Island countries that responded to the Global Survey Field Inquiry were:

- Cook Islands,
- Fiji,
- Kiribati,
- Marshall Islands,
- Federated States of Micronesia (FSM),
- Niue,
- Palau,
- Papua New Guinea (PNG),
- Samoa,
- Solomon Islands,
- Tonga,
- Tuvalu, and
- Vanuatu.

Here, the responses to the ICPD+10 Global Survey for these countries are summarized for the following areas of reproductive rights and reproductive health:

- Promoting reproductive rights;
- Monitoring and reporting implementation of reproductive rights;
- Recognising reproductive health needs as priorities in health sector reform;
- Integrating reproductive health into the primary health care system;
- Increasing access to quality reproductive health services;
- Reducing maternal morbidity and mortality;
- Achieving Reproductive Health Commodities Security;
- Expanding contraceptive choice;
- Preventing and managing complications of unsafe abortion;
- Reducing and managing STIs, including HIV;
- Involving the beneficiaries of reproductive health services;
- Major constraints to implementing the reproductive health approach; and
- Cultural context contributing and constraining promotion of reproductive rights and reproductive health.

Promoting Reproductive Rights

ICPD PoA states that "reproductive rights rest on the recognition of the basic right of all couples and individuals to decide freely and responsibly the number, spacing and timing of their children and to have the information and means to do so, and the right to attain the highest standard of sexual and reproductive health. It also includes their right to make decisions concerning reproduction free of discrimination, coercion and violence, as expressed in human rights documents. The promotion of the responsible exercise of these rights for all people should be the fundamental basis for government and community-supported policies and programmes in the area of reproductive health, including family planning".

In the Global Survey Field Inquiry, Pacific Island governments were asked *if they had taken any policy measures, legislative/institutional changes or other national level measures to enforce reproductive rights (such as free informed choice and informed consent, abolition of quotas, incentives, etc).* Ten of the twelve countries responded affirmatively whilst three countries reported not taking any measures to enforce reproductive rights. Table 1 shows the measures undertaken to enforce reproductive rights by these ten countries.

Table 1: Pacific Island Countries' Responses of Policy, Legislative or Institutional Measures Taken to Promote Reproductive Rights

Description of Measures	*Countries*
Formulated a new policy on reproductive rights and reproductive health	Marshall Islands, PNG, Samoa, Solomon Islands, Vanuatu
Implemented Institutional Changes/training in reproductive rights	FSM
IEC/Advocacy on reproductive rights and reproductive health	Kiribati, PNG, Solomon Islands, Vanuatu
Formulated national plans/programmes/strategies for reproductive rights and reproductive health	Cook Islands
Other measures	Cook Islands, Fiji, FSM, PNG, Tuvalu

Several countries, including Marshall Islands, Papua New Guinea (PNG), Samoa, Solomon Islands and Vanuatu reported the formulation of new policies on reproductive rights and reproductive health. In the Marshall Islands, the National Population Policy states each citizen has reproductive rights; the Bureau of Primary Health Care includes reproductive rights; and the Women's Policy supports women's right to reproductive health care. Samoa responded that ICPD principles including reproductive rights were included in Samoa's Population Policy. In the Solomon Islands, similar Women and Youth Policies developed two years ago incorporated reproductive rights. In PNG and Vanuatu, policy changes have included the provision of free family planning, antenatal and delivery services in an attempt to improving access and utilisation. The basic principle that reproductive rights are essential human rights of all citizens was at the basis of decisions related to the provision of free services for all. Most PICTs have adopted policies, based on the principle of free and informed choice for all couples and individuals, and provide services without financial charges.

Federated States of Micronesia (FSM) reported ..nplementing institutional changes in their educational system, which permitted pregnant students to continue their education. Furthermore, FSM reported removing the requirement that parental consent was necessary for students receiving reproductive health services.

Kiribati, PNG, Solomon Islands and Vanuatu reported that advocacy campaigns and training programmes included promoting the reproductive rights of individuals. Although not reported in the Field Enquiry, it is well recognised that reproductive rights for youth have been included in advocacy and training programmes for adolescent reproductive health in Fiji.

The Cook Islands reported that national strategies for promoting reproductive health services and information/education and communication regarding reproductive rights were promoted by the government. Five of the Pacific Island countries reported taking "limited" policies or legislative changes while five countries reported taking "some" policies or legislative changes to promoting reproductive rights. Of the countries that responded negatively, reasons cited were that "reproductive rights have always been considered as services that are free"; "reproductive health is not a national priority"; and "reproductive rights is culturally sensitive".

The concept of reproductive rights may not be fully understood in some PICTs where government reports include reproductive health but few mention reproductive rights or report on them. However, in many PICTs, since ICPD, there have been developments in policies and programmes that should contribute to an enabling environment in which the reproductive rights of women can be fully recognized and exercised. Many countries in the Pacific have incorporated some form of legislative or institutional change, which enhances the reproductive rights of women and men; whether it is explicit policy or the introduction of new family planning methods, which facilitate better options for couples. However, despite this progress, where education and social status of women remain low, enhancing reproductive rights of women cannot be fully achieved. Ensuring gender mainstreaming in policies and programmes in Pacific island countries is considered vital for achieving reproductive rights of women.

Monitoring and Reporting Implementation of Reproductive Rights

ICPD PoA states that "governments at all levels are urged to institute systems of monitoring and evaluation of user-centred services and to ensure a continuing improvement in the quality of services. To this end, Governments should secure conformity to human rights and to ethical and professional standards in the delivery of family planning and related reproductive health services aimed at ensuring responsible, voluntary and informed consent and also regarding service provision".

In the Global Survey Field Inquiry, countries were asked *whether reproductive rights were included in the monitoring of the implementation of human rights.* Only five of the thirteen Pacific Island countries responded that reproductive rights were included in the monitoring of human rights. Pacific Island Countries' Responses to monitoring the implementation of reproductive rights are summarized in Table 2.

Table 2: Pacific Island Countries' Responses of the Inclusion of Reproductive Rights in the Monitoring of the Implementation of Human Rights

Description of Measures	*Countries*
Monitoring through international conventions and reporting mechanisms	Cook Islands, Marshall Islands, Samoa
Monitoring through cooperation with NGO reporting mechanisms	Solomon Islands
Monitoring through various national and regional monitoring institutions	Cook Islands, Samoa

Cook Islands stated that monitoring the implementation of reproductive rights was part of human rights reports regularly submitted. Marshall Islands stated that monitoring was undertaken through reports to Convention on the Rights of the Child (CRC). Samoa stated that monitoring was undertaken through international conventions such as CRC, Convention on the Elimination of All Forms of Discrimination Against Women (CEDAW), ICPD and Beijing Platform of Action. Samoa reported taking leadership in driving and coordinating CEDAW activities in the South Pacific region. A regional CEDAW meeting was held in Samoa in April 2003. Samoa also reported monitoring through national and regional monitoring institutions. Solomon Islands reported getting assistance from UNDP and non-governmental organisations to monitor reproductive rights. Of the countries that reported not monitoring the implementation of human rights, some countries stated a lack of capacity while others stated it was not currently considered a priority. The concept of monitoring reproductive rights was not fully understood by some of the questionnaire respondents.

Countries were also asked specifically *whether Reproductive Rights and Reproductive Health were included in these countries reporting to human rights treaty bodies, including CEDAW.*

A summary of relevant responses to this question is summarized in Table 3. Of the thirteen countries, nine countries responded that their countries' reporting to human rights treaty bodies, including CEDAW, included reproductive rights.

Cook Islands, Fiji, Kiribati, PNG and Samoa reported that reproductive rights and reproductive health reporting is included in the human rights treaty bodies and that they regularly submit country reports to CEDAW. The majority of these reports were handled through Ministries/Departments of Women.

Table 3: Pacific Island Countries' Responses of the Inclusion of Reproductive Rights in the Country's Reporting to Human Rights Treaty Bodies

Description of Measures	*Countries*
Country regularly submits country reports to CEDAW	Cook Islands, Fiji, Kiribati, PNG, Samoa
Country is a signatory of CEDAW	Cook Islands, Fiji, Kiribati, PNG, Samoa, Tonga
Country submits reports to other Human Rights Treaty Bodies	Marshall Islands, Samoa, Tuvalu

In addition to these countries, Tonga reported it was amongst the signatories to CEDAW. Tuvalu, Solomon Islands and Vanuatu have also ratified CEDAW. Countries that have ratified CEDAW but did not respond that they regularly submitted reports to CEDAW stated that these plans were in progress.

Marshall Islands, Samoa and Tuvalu Governments reported other channels of reporting to human rights bodies such as CRC. While several countries responded affirmatively to countries reporting to human treaty bodies, none of them discussed relevant mechanisms of reporting.

Clearly, greater advocacy for inclusion of a reproductive rights framework is necessary to fully implement the ICPD PoA. There remains the need to link reproductive rights to population policies in many PICTs in which policies have not been updated. Furthermore, while there has been progress in women's empowerment programmes, much work needs to be accomplished to achieve gender equity and the realization of reproductive rights in the Pacific.

Recognizing Reproductive Health Needs of Women and Children as Priorities in Health Sector Reform

Among the key actions for further implementation of the ICPD PoA, adapted at the General Assembly in 1999, it was stated that "governments, in collaboration with civil society, including non-governmental organisations, donors and the United Nations system should give high priority to reproductive and sexual health in the broader context of health-sector reform, including strengthening basic health systems, from which people living in poverty in particular can benefit. Reproductive health-care programmes should be designed to serve the needs of women, including adolescents, and must involve women in the leadership, planning, decision-making, management, implementation, organisation and evaluation of services. Governments and other organisations should take positive steps to include women at all levels of the health-care system".

In the Global Survey, countries were asked *whether reproductive health needs of women, men, adolescent and youth were explicitly recognised as priorities in the Health Sector Reform Package*. Eight countries responded affirmatively. These countries were Cook Islands, Kiribati, Marshall Islands,

FSM, PNG, Samoa, Solomon Islands and Vanuatu. The description of inclusion of reproductive health needs of women, men, adolescent and youth in the Health Sector Reform are included in Table 4.

Table 4: Pacific Island Countries' Responses to whether Reproductive Health Needs were Part of a Health Sector Reform Package

Description of Nature of Inclusion	*Countries*
Reform recognises health needs of adolescent/youth	Cook Islands, FSM, Kiribati, Marshall Islands, PNG, Samoa
Reform recognises health needs of women (obstetric care)	Marshall Islands, PNG
Reform recognises health needs of women, men, adolescents/youths	Cook Islands, FSM, Kiribati, Marshall Islands, PNG

Some countries reported that while it seemed that minimal attention was paid to women's obstetric care, reproductive health needs were reflected in various ways in the Health Sector Reform Packages, the revitalized National Development Plans and the Health Sector Strategic Plans..

The reasons cited by the countries, that stated reproductive health needs are not explicitly mentioned as priorities in the health sector reform package, were that reproductive health was not recognised as a national priority or there were no health sector reform packages.

Throughout the Pacific (with the exception of two countries), Health Sector Reform is in various stages of planning and implementation. Integral to these packages is the recognition that reproductive health is a priority issue. However, the real challenge lies in implementing these health sector reforms in an environment of limited resources and, in some countries, political instability. Ensuring quality of reproductive health services are delivered to all rural and outer island communities will be difficult if infrastructure and supplies are inadequate. Hence, the translation of political commitment into sustained change remains elusive in some PICTs.

Integrating Reproductive Health Components into the Primary Health Care System

ICPD PoA states that "countries should strive to make accessible through the primary health care system, reproductive health to all individuals of appropriate ages as soon as possible and no later than the year 2015. Reproductive health care in the context of primary heath care should, inter alia, include: family planning counselling, information, education, communication and services; education and services for prenatal care, safe delivery and post-natal care, especially breastfeeding and infant and women's health care; prevention of appropriate treatment of infertility; abortion as specified in PoA paragraph 8.25, including prevention of abortion and the management of the consequences of abortion; treatment of reproductive tract infections; sexually transmitted diseases and other reproductive health conditions; and information, education and counselling, as appropriate, on human sexuality, reproductive health and responsible parenthood".

Countries were asked about the integration of Reproductive Health Components into the Primary Health Care System before and subsequent to ICPD in 1994. Of the thirteen Pacific Island countries, seven countries reported that Reproductive Health Services had been integrated into the Primary Health Care System before ICPD. All thirteen countries responded affirmatively that measures had been taken to further *integrate reproductive services components into the Primary Health Care System (subsequent to ICPD).* A summary of these measures is summarized in Table 5.

Table 5: Pacific Island Countries' Responses of Specific Measures taken by Countries to Integrate Reproductive Health Service Components into the Primary Health Care System

Description of measures	*Countries*
Reproductive Health services expanded to include family planning	Fiji, FSM, Marshall Islands, PNG, Solomon Islands, Tonga, Vanuatu
Integration through institutional changes in reproductive health	PNG, Samoa
National plans/programmes/strategies in reproductive health	Palau
National policies integrate reproductive health	PNG
Information on STI and/or HIV/AIDS prevention integrated	Niue, Vanuatu
Information on treatment of infertility integrated	Vanuatu
Information on teenagers and youth integrated	Solomon Islands, Vanuatu
Integration through training of reproductive health providers	Solomon Islands, PNG, Vanuatu

While ten of the twelve countries discussed "limited" measures, two countries discussed "some" measures and only one country, Vanuatu, discussed "many" measures to integrate Reproductive Health Service components into the Primary Health Care System.

Most of the countries responded that Primary Health Care (PHC), before ICPD, had included maternal and child health as well as family planning. Subsequent to ICPD, reproductive health was integrated into PHC of which Family Planning was a key component. Tonga and Federated States of Micronesia reported promoting family planning through integrated service delivery and IEC awareness.

PNG reported how reproductive health and safe motherhood had been promoted since ICPD to replace traditional maternal and child health (MCH) through institutional changes. In-service training of health workers and curriculum reform for pre-service health workers also included focus on emergency obstetrics care. PNG also discussed the integration of reproductive health into PHC through the renewed focus on upgrading health center facilities to offer emergency obstetric care services.

Palau discussed the integration of reproductive health into PHC within the context of their national structure and programmes in Public Health.

Vanuatu's integration of Reproductive Health into PHC has also involved meetings, workshops and training. Their reproductive health framework, conceptualised as a wheel, includes the key areas of family planning, counselling, adolescent reproductive health, reproductive tract infections/ sexually transmitted infections, infertility, men's partnership in reproductive health, a life cycle approach to maternal and child health, reproductive tract cancers, domestic violence and management of the consequences of abortion.

In the response from Solomon Islands, the integration of a rights-based approach and the promotion of men's participation in Reproductive Health were cited as key areas of reproductive health that occurred subsequent to ICPD.

The challenges to integration of reproductive health components into PHC are formidable throughout the Pacific. In US associated territories such as the Federated States of Micronesia (FSM), Marshall Islands and Palau, although the concept of reproductive health is well understood, reality dictates maintaining separate national Family Planning, Maternal and Child Health and Sexually Transmitted Infections (STI)/HIV/AIDS programmes due to the requirements dictated by federal funding sources. While at the dispensary or clinic level these services are often provided in an integrated comprehensive fashion by a single health care provider, administration of these programmes remain vertical within the national and state departments of health.

Similar situations exist in other PICTs where vertical programmes persist at tertiary centers and national and provincial/subdivisional levels while PHC services at service delivery points are integrated. Managers of vertical programmes often are reluctant to take on additional responsibilities related to integrated Reproductive Health Services as often they fear such responsibilities may further burden their workload and encroach on their colleagues' domains. On the other hand, at youth clinics in some countries, Solomon Islands comprehensive services are provided within the context of a recreation facility where IEC, treatment of STIs and provision of family planning services are provided to the youth.

In most PICTs, mechanisms currently exist for facilitating referrals at various levels of the health care system. Integrating infertility care, reproductive cancer services, and management of complications of abortions at various levels of the health care system are limited by the number and capacity of health care providers, supplies and facilities and economies of scale in small island settings. In most PICTs further training of health care providers in dealing with violence against women is needed to facilitate integration of these services at the peripheral levels.

Pacific Island countries have developed a particular hybrid of integration, appropriate to the various scales of small island populations. This model allows countries to respond to the needs for RH services in various settings, incorporating mechanisms for coordination and referrals to higher levels.

Increasing Access to Quality Reproductive Health Services

One of the goals of ICPD is "universal access to reproductive health services through the primary health care system, with referrals to higher levels as appropriate, by the year 2015". *Reproductive health services were considered integral to basic health services.* The Global Survey asked countries *whether the governments had taken specific measures to increase access to quality reproductive health services.* All thirteen Pacific Island countries stated that governments had taken measures to increase access to quality reproductive health services. Some of the measures discussed are presented in Table 6.

Table 6: Pacific Island Countries' Responses of Specific Measures taken for Increasing Access to Quality Reproductive Health Services

Description of Measures	*Countries*
Free reproductive health services in all public health facilities	Cook Islands, Niue, PNG
Increase in number of Service Delivery Points	Cook Islands, FSM, Fiji, Marshall Islands, Samoa, Solomon Islands, Tonga
Allocation of more resources including equipment for reproductive health	PNG, Solomon Islands, Vanuatu
Decentralised health care and service delivery system	Fiji, Palau
Improvement of management and logistics in reproductive health	Cook Islands, Vanuatu
Provision of youth friendly services	FSM, Kiribati, Solomon Islands
Mobile reproductive health services	Fiji
Partnerships with NGOs, international organizations and private sector	PNG, Samoa, Tonga
Increased staff and training	Cook Islands, Kiribati, Marshall Islands, Palau, PNG, Samoa, Solomon Islands, Tonga, Tuvalu, Vanuatu

While only three countries, namely Cook Islands, Niue and PNG, mentioned free reproductive health services in all public health facilities, most PICTs provide free or very minimally charged basic health care services including reproductive health.

As expected, most PICTs had increased the number of service delivery points to accommodate the needs of their populations. There was increased allocation of resources for Reproductive Health Care equipment; particularly in Fiji. Unlike the rest of the PICTs, Fiji in an effort to move towards self-sufficiency, now provides its own Reproductive Health (RH) commodities. UNFPA provides RH commodities for thirteen other PICTs.

While most PICTs have some form of decentralized health care, only Fiji and Palau stated this in their response. It is interesting to note that many PICTs had decentralized health care systems even prior to ICPD in 1994.

Youth friendly services are being provided in many PICTs, including Federated States of Micronesia, Kiribati and Solomon Islands.

In an attempt to increase access in rural areas where there are no reproductive health care providers, Fiji stated it has a mobile RH clinic. This clinic provides integrated FP/STI/RH services.

Many countries have developed partnerships with NGOs, international organizations and the private sector for provision of FP services, prevention and management of STIs and other RH services.

Valid information, particularly the percent of the populations that have access to comprehensive and integrated RH information and services, is not available in many PICTs. Data related to percentage of SDPs providing 3 or more RH services is not available in many countries. Not only are the RH Management Information Services (RHMIS) in many countries inadequate, the indicators used, to determine the access and quality of RH services, are sometimes inappropriate. Hence, determining progress made since ICPD in improving access to RH services is difficult. Determining the quality of RH care provided can be a formidable task in situations where the health information system is rudimentary.

Access to RH services is uneven; basic RH services are not always available to populations residing in outer islands, atolls or rural areas despite the presence of SDPs. While upgrading of facilities and capacity building of health staff have occurred in all PICTs to varying degrees, health care providers in many settings are often not well equipped to deal with basic emergency obstetric care or other RH services.

Quality of RH care varies substantially between and within PICTs. Difficulties faced in providing high quality of care stem from the varying levels of technical competence of health care providers, a lack of adequate supplies/facilities, a lack of follow up or continuity of care and a lack of ongoing supervision. Factors that hinder access to quality RH care include geographical dispersion of small populations on outer islands as well as cultural/social inhibitions/barriers to RH services for disadvantaged groups such as adolescents and unmarried women. Despite these factors, progress in improving access to quality RH care continues to be made in most PICTs.

Reducing Maternal Morbidity and Mortality

The ICPD PoA states that "countries should aim to promote women's health and safe motherhood; to achieve a rapid and substantial reduction in maternal morbidity and mortality and reduce the differences observed between developing and developed countries and within countries. Countries with intermediate levels of mortality should aim to achieve by the year 2005 a maternal mortality rate below 100 per 100,000 live births and by the year 2015 a maternal mortality rate below 60 per 100,000 live births. All countries must expand the provision of maternal health services in the context of primary health care. These services, based on the concept of informed choice, should include education on safe motherhood, prenatal care that is focused and effective, maternal nutrition programmes, adequate delivery assistance that avoids excessive recourse to caesarean sections and provides for obstetric emergencies; referral services for pregnancy, childbirth and abortion complications; post-natal care and family planning. All births should be assisted by trained persons, preferably nurses and mid-wives, but at least trained birth attendants".

All thirteen Pacific Island countries that responded to the Field Inquiry stated that measures had been taken to reduce maternal morbidity and mortality. Some specific measures reported by PICTs in the Field Enquiry Questionnaire are cited in Table 7. While responses for various countries were not comprehensive, it is well known that many of these measures have been undertaken by most of the countries.

Several initiatives have been undertaken in many countries in the Pacific. Most of the countries have improved prenatal and postnatal care, conducted training of health care providers and conducted IEC/Advocacy campaigns to reduce maternal mortality and morbidity rate. While Samoa and Solomon Islands cited creation of networks of FP/STI clinics, numerous other countries have also expanded these facilities over the past decade. PNG, Samoa and Solomon Islands reported making exerted efforts to improve transportation for emergency obstetric care as well as promoting partnerships with UN agencies/NGOs. Improving the information system as a basis for monitoring maternal morbidity was mentioned by Kiribati and Samoa.

PICTs did not specifically mention access to post-abortion services. In some of the larger PICTs where morbidity from complications of unsafe abortion is not infrequent, the lack of access to post abortion services by vulnerable groups is an area of concern.

In the small island countries, Maternal Mortality Ratios (MMRs) do not provide a valid estimate of maternal health. Despite the efforts to improve

Table 7: Pacific Island Countries' Responses to Specific Measures Taken for Reducing Maternal Morbidity and Mortality

Description of Measure	*Country*
Creation of networks of FP/STI clinics	Samoa, Solomon Islands
Improved prenatal and postnatal services	FSM, Marshall Islands, Palau, PNG, Tonga
Training of health care providers	Cook Islands, Fiji, Kiribati, Palau, PNG, Samoa, Solomon Islands, Tuvalu, Vanuatu
IEC/Advocacy to reduce maternal morbidity	Cook Islands, FSM, Fiji, Marshall Islands, Niue, Palau, Samoa, Solomon Islands, Vanuatu
Improved transportation for emergency obstetric care	PNG, Samoa
Promote partnerships with UN agencies/NGOs on reducing maternal health services	PNG, Samoa, Solomon Islands
Improving data collection and record keeping for monitoring	Kiribati, Samoa

RH services made by many PICTs, the MMRs fluctuate widely. Given the small size of the populations for most PICTs (e.g. Tokelau with 1,500 population or Niue with 1,600) and the relatively few births per annum, maternal deaths occur very infrequently and for several years not at all. When a maternal death does occur in a year, the MMR for that year explodes e.g. in 2002, Tuvalu had an 614 maternal deaths per 100,000 live births and Tokelau had an MMR of 170 maternal deaths per 100,000 live births. On the other hand, in previous years, when there were no deaths, the MMR was 0. In some of the more populous PICTs, MMRs have remained over 100 (PNG, Solomon Islands, FSM). The limitations of the MMR in the Pacific are a matter of concern when trying to monitor and compare progress towards maternal health.

Nine PICTs report that the proportion of deliveries attended by trained/skilled health personnel exceeds 95 per cent. These countries are Fiji, Nauru, Palau, Cook Islands, Niue, Samoa, Tokelau, Tonga and Tuvalu. The other countries report that greater than 85 per cent of deliveries are attended by trained/skilled health attendants. For all countries, with the exception of PNG, these figures represent significant improvements since 1990-1994.

There is no room for complacency when reviewing maternal health services in the Pacific. Many countries are continuing to forge ahead with improvements in availability of basic and comprehensive emergency obstetric care to its population through training of health care personnel, use of nationally accepted, evidence-based protocols and upgrading of health facilities. Improved education/advocacy strategies in the community and strengthened mechanisms for transportation are also being instituted. However, implementing these strategies continue to be formidable challenges in resource-restrained countries where small populations are widely dispersed. The lack of appropriate data and indicators for monitoring maternal health and emergency obstetric care in the Pacific complicates the situation. Unless appropriate monitoring mechanisms are instituted, determining the progress of maternal health in the Pacific will continue to be difficult.

Achieving Reproductive Health Commodities Security

ICPD PoA states that "all countries should take steps to meet the family planning needs of their populations as soon as possible and should in all cases by the year 2015, seek to provide universal access to a full range of safe and reliable family planning methods and to related reproductive health services which are not against the law".

In the Global Survey, countries were asked if governments had taken measures *to achieve reproductive health commodities security*. Of the thirteen Pacific Island countries, nine countries stated that their governments had taken measures to achieve reproductive health commodities security (RHCS). Responses cited for achieving RHCS are included in Table 8.

Table 8: Specific Measures Taken for Achieving Reproductive Health Commodities Security by Pacific Island Countries

Description of Measures	*Countries*
Logistics management systems, procurement plans	FSM, Samoa, Vanuatu
Assistance from international agencies in securing/supplying commodities	Cook Is, FSM, Kiribati, Niue, Palau, PNG, Samoa, Tokelau, Tonga, Tuvalu, Vanuatu
Training of management/administration staff in logistics management	Vanuatu
Government partnerships with NGOs/private and religious sectors for reproductive health provision	Cook Islands, Tuvalu

Of the countries that stated no measures were taken by government to achieve reproductive health commodities security, reasons cited were "government is not currently aware that it is an issue" and "plans are currently underway to undertake measures". Measures discussed included logistics management systems and procurement plans, and training of management/ administration staff in logistics management.

In the Pacific, RH commodities including contraceptives, are supplied by UNFPA to the following PICs: Cook Islands, FSM, Kiribati, Marshall Islands,

Nauru, Niue, Palau, Samoa, Solomon Islands, Tokelau, Tonga, Tuvalu and Vanuatu.

Fiji no longer receives contraceptives from UNFPA as Fiji purchases its own contraceptives. However, other RH commodities are supplied to Fiji. A regional depot, which services Pacific Island Countries, has been established in Fiji. Logistics are managed by UNFPA. Many countries also receive RH Commodities from Family Planning Associations and IPPF. Hence, in the majority of the PICTs, assistance is received from international agencies in securing and supplying RH commodities.

In 2003, a meeting occurred of the Ministers of Health for Cook Islands Islands, Fiji, Niue, Solomon Islands and Vanuatu to endorse a Pacific Plan of Action for RHCS in the Pacific. The Pacific PoA included agreement that each government would demonstrate political leadership to improve RH through ensuring it has in place and implements an up-to-date multi-sectoral policy in RH, integrated into national health policies, strategies and action plans to the fullest extent possible. It was pledged that efforts would be made in the establishment of a regional warehouse facility and in achieving the best value for money for the provision of the full range of RH commodities required in the PICs. Furthermore, commitment was made to ensuring adequate storage facilities and to instituting an efficient, regular and timely distribution and supply system. Training in improving RHCS and Logistics Management Information System (LMIS) was considered essential. In 2004, at the annual meeting of the Commonwealth Ministers of Health on the eve of the World Health Assembly, the support for the Pacific Plan of Action for RHCS was widened to include endorsement from the other PICTs. Political commitment at the highest level has assisted in ensuring RHCS issues are being addressed in all PICTs.

The logistical difficulties imposed by small island populations residing in widely dispersed atolls/islands, as well as expensive and often in-frequent transportation have sometimes resulted in inadequate supplies being available in some centers and overstocking of nearly expired commodities in other centers. In some countries, storage of certain climate-vulnerable commodities at the peripheral clinics remains problematic where temperatures soar, humidity is high and electrical power does not exist.

There is a general need for improvement in quality assurance systems, in particular to monitor quality and viability during storage, transportation and distribution at user outlets. There is deficiency in trained health personnel in RHCS management such as logistics and forecasting throughout the Pacific. In November 2004, the first regional RHCS workshop is planned to improve the capacity of management in procurement, forecasting, monitoring and LMIS. Condom packaging needs to be improved and condoms need to be made accessible in socially acceptable locations.

While there has been substantial progress in the Pacific in RHCS, greater cooperation between partners supplying commodities could facilitate more efficient delivery of RH commodities. Clearly, training in procurement, storage, distribution, projections and LMIS by relevant staff is needed to improve the situation in each PICT if the goals of achieving universal access to a wide range of family planning methods are to be achieved.

Expanding Contraceptive Choice

ICPD PoA states "To meet the needs of the growing number of couples of reproductive age and to close the existing gap in services, family planning and contraceptive supplies will need to expand very rapidly over the next several years".

In the Global Survey, countries were asked if governments had taken measures *to expand contraceptive choice including emergency contraception and female condoms*. All thirteen countries responded in the Field Inquiry questionnaire that some measures had been taken to expand contraceptive choice, including emergency contraception and female condoms. Various measures cited by the countries are included in Table 9.

Table 9: Pacific Island Countries' Responses of Measures Taken for Expanding Contraceptive Choice including Emergency Contraception and Female Condoms

Description of Measure	*Countries*
Training of providers in contraceptive management	Marshall Islands, PNG, Solomon Islands
Availability of female condoms	PNG
Availability of emergency contraception	Cook Islands, Fiji, Marshall Islands, Palau, Tonga

Three Pacific Island countries, namely Marshall Islands, PNG and Solomon Islands, cited training of providers in contraceptive management. Female condoms are available in Papua New Guinea. PNG stated that female condoms are promoted more for protection against HIV/AIDS and STIs than for prevention of pregnancy. No other PICTs reported using female condoms. While five countries cited promoting availability of emergency contraception for patients, it is well known that the other Pacific Island countries are also providing emergency contraception. However, as previously mentioned, emergency contraception is not popular and those most in need of emergency contraception e.g. adolescents and unmarried women, do not have access to it.

None of the countries discussed an increase in number of service delivery points, social marketing campaigns, improvement in logistics of contraceptive availability or subsidized free contraceptives. However, in the Pacific, contraceptives are provided by UNFPA to all countries, except Fiji.

To further expand the contraceptive choice of the female condom, more education is required as the communities in most PICTs are unaware of this method of contraception and thus there is no demand for it. The expansion of access to emergency contraception not only requires education of the community and health care providers but also involves removal of barriers to services for special groups such as adolescent and unmarried women in most PICs. Furthermore, because existing forms of combined oral contraceptives, progestion only pills and copper T 380A can be used for the same purpose, health care providers are less inclined to order specially packed emergency oral contraceptives.

Preventing and Managing Complications of Unsafe Abortion

ICPD PoA states that "governments should take appropriate steps to help women avoid abortion, which in no case should be promoted as a method of family planning, and in all cases provide for the humane treatment and counselling of women who have had recourse to abortion."

In the Global Survey, countries were asked if governments had *taken any measures to prevent and manage complications of unsafe abortion.* Of the thirteen Pacific Island countries, eight countries responded that measures had been taken by governments to prevent and manage complications of unsafe abortion.

Table 10: Pacific Island Countries' Responses of Measures Taken to Prevent and Manage Complications of Unsafe Abortion

Description of Measures	*Countries*
Training of health care providers to provide post-abortion services	Solomon Islands
Provision of post-abortion services	Fiji, Palau, PNG, Samoa, Solomon Islands
Family planning services and contraceptive services available	Fiji, Samoa, Solomon Islands
Others e.g. awareness campaigns	PNG, Tuvalu, Vanuatu

In their responses, Fiji, Palau, PNG, Samoa and Solomon Islands cited their governments' efforts to provide management of complications arising from unsafe abortion by improving the skills of health care providers. There is need for these services to be extended to other PICTs.

Of the countries that did not cite any measure taken, reasons given were that "unsafe abortion is not a problem", "there were restrictive abortion laws" and "abortion was illegal".

In most PICs, the government policy governing abortion is that unless there is a high risk medical condition in the pregnant women where her life is endangered or when rape has occurred, abortion is not permitted.

Data to support the prevalence of unsafe abortion is not available. In most countries, cases of complications of abortions are admitted to the main hospitals; and in some countries deaths due to illegal abortions have occurred with concomitant legal cases against the practitioners pending in court.

It would appear where unmet need for contraception is high and availability of quality family planning services is inaccessible to certain sectors of the population, unsafe abortion is relatively high. The expansion/provision of adequate family planning services to groups at high risk of unwanted pregnancies is vital to reducing unsafe abortions. Furthermore, morbidity and mortality resulting from unsafe abortions can be potentially reduced if adequate post-abortion care is provided.

Reducing and Managing Sexually Transmitted Infections, Including HIV/AIDS:

ICPD PoA states that countries should aim "to prevent, reduce the incidence of, and provide treatment for, sexually transmitted diseases, including HIV/AIDS, and the complications of sexually transmitted diseases such as infertility, with special attention to girls and women. Reproductive health programmes should increase their efforts to prevent, detect and treat sexually transmitted diseases and other reproductive tract infections, especially at the primary health-care level. Information, education and counselling for responsible sexual behaviours and effective prevention of sexually transmitted diseases, including HIV, should become integral components of all reproductive and sexual health services".

In the Global Survey, countries were asked if governments had *taken any measures to reduce and manage sexually transmitted infections (STIs), including HIV/AIDS.* All thirteen Pacific Island countries stated that measures had been undertaken by government to reduce and manage STIs, including HIV/AIDS. Classification by action reported by PICTs is tabulated in Table 11.

Respondents from five countries discussed national plans, programmes, strategies and policies for preventing and managing Sexually Transmitted Infections, with emphasis on HIV/AIDS. Several countries cited improvements in STI prevention and management. PNG and Samoa discussed inter-agency collaboration and partnerships. IEC/Advocacy campaign and educational initiatives have been undertaken in several countries.

Subsequent to the United Nations General Assembly Special Session (UNGASS) on HIV/AIDS in 2001, PICTs were called upon to strengthen their response to HIV/AIDS. Although the overall prevalence of HIV in the majority of Pacific Island Countries and Territories appears low, there is substantial concern as the rates of infections are rapidly increasing in countries where the incidence of Sexually Transmitted Infections (STIs) is very high, teenage pregnancies are numerous and condom usage is low. While over 86 per cent of HIV infections occur in Papua New Guinea, the number of

Table 11: Pacific Island Countries' Response of Measures Taken to Reduce and Manage STIs including HIV/AIDS

Description of Measures	*Countries*
National plans/programmes/strategies	Cook Islands, Fiji, PNG
National policies on prevention/control of STIs	Marshall Islands
National commission/agency/ministry/desk established by government	PNG, Samoa
STI prevention, treatment and management service provision	Marshall Islands, Palau, PNG, Samoa, Tonga, Vanuatu
Partnerships with NGOs, UN and other international organizations	PNG
Intra-governmental agency partnerships for service provision	Samoa
IEC/advocacy campaigns on prevention and treatment	Cook Islands, Niue, PNG, Samoa, Solomon Islands, Vanuatu
Educational initiatives that target vulnerable populations	Kiribati, Samoa, Tuvalu

unreported cases in the Pacific is unknown, as surveillance levels remain low in all countries.

A regional strategic plan 1997-2000 was developed to provide a framework for all stakeholders to address STIs/HIV/AIDS. Numerous initiatives in the Pacific have focused on preventive activities in youth. Examples include the UNFPA sponsored SPC Regional Adolescent Reproductive Health (ARH) Project, peer education programmes, church youth organizations, local NGOs (e.g. Wan Smol Bag Theatre Group in Vanuatu), Pacific Life Stars Programme and Regional Youth Congress on AIDS. Theatre Group training by Wan Smol Bag also was conducted in Kiribati, Solomon Islands, Tonga and Tuvalu.

In Table 12, the current status of national STI/HIV/AIDS laws, policies and strategic plans is summarized for selected PICs. While all countries have National AIDS Committees, it is evident that wide variation exists in the quality of HIV/AIDS/STI Strategic Plans and capacity of countries to respond effectively.

A situation analysis suggests that countries lack the financial and human resources to continue the momentum to implement an effective and sustainable response. While numerous activities have occurred by NGO and the ministries/departments of health, there is a need to coordinate these activities as well as there is a need to improve STI surveillance and monitor and evaluate the impact of these activities in each country. The geographical dispersion of islands and lack of infrastructure on the larger island have added to the difficulty associated with undertaking surveillance. Most PICTs send specimens off-island for confirmation. There remains the need for further capacity building in counselling, education, clinical case management, infection control and STI/HIV/management programmes in PICTs. While a multi-sectoral approach to the development of a regional strategy (current 2004-2008) signifies collaboration and partnership, coordination of activities at the country level could be further strengthened. The persistence of stigma and discrimination as well as cultural barriers to prevention in at risk groups pose formidable challenges to addressing STIs and HIV/AIDS in PICTs.

Table 12: National STI/HIV/AIDS Policies and Strategies in Pacific Island Countries

Countries	*National Laws*	*National Policies*	*National Strategies/Strategic Plans*
Fiji	NACA Bill under review	Interim 2002 document	NSP 2004-6
Solomon Islands		1987 under review	Endorsed in 2003
Vanuatu		Endorsed in 2004	Endorsed in 2004
PNG	National HIV anti-discrimination Law passed (2003). National HIV/AIDS Management and Prevention Act (2003). Other National Laws pending.	Revised in 2004	NSP 2004-8
FSM	National Law pending	Planning phase	Pohnpei Strategic Plan
Kiribati	HIV AIDS Prevention and Management Bill	Updated in 2004	NSP 2004-8
Palau	HIV Law 2003 revised	Updating 1994 policy	2000 SP being updated
Guam	National Law	National Plan/Policy 2003	NSP 2004-8
Cook Islands	Public Health Act, July 2004	National Policy 1993, 2003	NSP 2004-8
Tonga			NSP in planning phase

Involving Beneficiaries of Reproductive Health Services

All thirteen countries stated that governments have taken measures to involve beneficiaries of reproductive health services.

Fiji, Marshall Islands, Palau and Solomon Islands reported consultation with and inclusion of community representatives and NGOs in reproductive health planning and programming. Papua New Guinea (PNG) reported the involvement of community-based organizations in policy and programme developments of RH projects and the creation of community/local action groups. Tuvalu reported public hearings to address reproductive health issues of concern. IEC/advocacy campaigns involving local beneficiaries were reported by PNG and Solomon Islands.

While all thirteen countries responded that measures had been undertaken to involve beneficiaries, specific measures undertaken were less clear in the responses.

None of the countries cited surveys to solicit consumer views, training of community health workers, training of peer educators or peer counseling, although it is well known that the training activities have been undertaken and are ongoing in some Pacific Island countries.

In the Adolescent Reproductive Health programmes in most PICTs, youth involvement in the planning and implementation of both IEC and service provision programmes has been a key feature. Peer education programmes have been initiated in Fiji, Kiribati, Tonga, Solomon Islands and Vanuatu. These activities have included consultations with youth organizations and focus group discussions to determine the needs of adolescents in reproductive health. Research is needed to determine the impact and effectiveness of peer education programmes in these countries.

Major Constraints to Implementing the Reproductive Health

In general, there are major constraints in implementing the reproductive health approach and measures in the Pacific.

Constraints to implementing the Reproductive Health Approach in the Pacific discussed in the Field Inquiry by the countries' respondents, included lack of financial resources and low budget allocations, lack of or poor communication, difficulty in reaching poor and/or rural people, lack or low supply of equipment and supplies, lack of human resources, negative attitudes and cultural constraints. Other constraints discussed by Pacific Island Countries' respondents included influence of religious groups, inappropriate personnel involved in delivery of services, changing socio-cultural environment, lack of involvement of men, poorly trained staff and lack of adequate facilities.

Several respondents discussed ways in which constraints were overcome. While all Pacific Island countries are recipients of aid for reproductive health services, several countries cited the provision of donor assistance as a means of overcoming financial constraints, particularly with regards to supplies, equipment, facilities and human resources. A few countries mentioned that building partnerships with international organisations and other institutes were contributing to capacity building as well as improving reproductive health service provision. To overcome negative attitudes and cultural/religious constraints to enabling environments, several countries discussed IEC/advocacy campaigns that were undertaken. Some countries discussed providing flexible hours for services as a means of overcoming some of the inadequacies related to lack of privacy and inconvenient hours of operation.

Cultural Context

Respondents discussed the socio-cultural conditions, beliefs and practices that both promoted and constrained reproductive rights and reproductive health in their countries. It is interesting to note that most Pacific Island countries perceived culture as both contributing and constraining the promotion of reproductive rights and reproductive health. Four Pacific Island societies stated that culture was only a constraining factor to the promotion of reproductive rights and reproductive health, while two Pacific Island countries cited that culture was only a contributing factor to promoting reproductive right and reproductive health.

Several countries discussed how young people were receptive to information, education and communication campaigns on reproductive rights and reproductive health. The involvement of traditional and religious authorities was discussed as providing an enabling environment for the promotion of reproductive health services because they played a pivotal role in community acceptance and mobilization. Women's groups and the roles women have traditionally held in some Pacific Island societies, e.g. Samoa, were perceived as contributing factors to the promotion of reproductive rights and reproductive health. Women could be perceived as agents promoting positive change towards their empowerment and should contribute to cultural shifts in collective societal beliefs related to reproductive rights. Changes in societal attitudes were facilitating progress in some countries. In the Cook Islands, education of young people and families was contributing to more positive attitudes for promoting reproductive rights and improved decision-making.

In Vanuatu, traditional leaders and religious groups were becoming more accepting of reproductive rights and reproductive health which facilitated wider discussions, more open attitudes and shifts in societal thinking and beliefs. In Kiribati, the cultural practice of fathers and in-laws providing care for pregnant women and mothers was perceived as contributing to greater promotion of reproductive rights and reproductive health through increased awareness and involvement of men in matters related to reproductive health. The cultural environment in which the private sector operated was also perceived as playing an important contributing role in promoting reproductive rights and reproductive health in some Pacific Island countries.

On the other hand, many Pacific Island countries respondents perceived cultural factors as constraining the promotion of reproductive rights and reproductive health. In several Pacific island countries, the lack of gender equality constrained the promotion of reproductive rights and reproductive health. In Solomon Islands, Kiribati, PNG and other countries, where males are generally the main decision-makers and most females are not aware of their rights, promoting a rights-based, gender-equitable approach to decision-making in reproductive health matters remains a challenge. With more information, education and communication as well as advocacy campaigns for gender sensitization, it is hoped that changes in attitudes will occur more widely. In some countries, the strong conservative religious presence has prevented open discussions on sexuality and provision of contraceptive services especially for adolescents. In some outer islands, the older generation with conservative religious beliefs has been unwilling to accept sexual and reproductive rights, especially for adolescents and youth. In their responses, one of the countries cited misunderstanding stemming from cultural beliefs between health care providers and clients with regards family planning as constraining promotion of reproductive rights. Socio-cultural attitudes on reproduction and sexuality have constrained progress in promoting reproductive rights in countries where discussion on sexual matters are forbidden.

Summing Up

It is evident that since 1994, substantial progress has been made in the Pacific, towards improving reproductive health and advancing reproductive rights, which were outlined in the ICPD PoA and endorsed by all PICTs.[8] However, continued advocacy with parliamentarians, senior planners and policy makers, communities and development partners is vital to ensuring sustainable change. Further substantial progress will not be possible unless broader issues such as gender inequality and male involvement in responsible reproductive health decision-making are adequately addressed in certain patriarchal Pacific Island societies. Sustained and coordinated action is needed by governments and its partners to address priority areas of concern in the Pacific: low contraceptive prevalence, high teen fertility rates, rising levels of HIV/STI infections and substantial maternal morbidity/mortality. The need to ensure that quality, comprehensive reproductive health services and IEC are available to the population, and the need to strengthen capacity in the planning, monitoring and evaluation of programmes will continue to present formidable challenges for most PICTs during the post-ICPD+10 era.

20

Integration of Reproductive Health Components

Important Considerations and Selected Initiatives

Conceptual Framework of Reproductive Health

The consensus reached at the International Conference on Population and Development marked a shift in health and development concepts and policies. The fundamental conceptual shift was from emphasizing fertility reduction as a key end in itself and family planning programmes as critical to achieving this, to articulating the more holistic concept of reproductive health rights and fertility regulation as one of many rights linked to improving levels of reproductive health. It was accepted that reproductive health "implies that people are able to have a satisfying and safe sex life and that they have the capability to reproduce and the freedom to decide if, when and how often to do so" (paragraph 7.2).

An underlying value of the concept of reproductive health is that individual choice is paramount and that human development is a process of enlarging people's choices. In addition, if people are equipped and have the means to make rational choices they will usually decide on actions which lead to improved levels of (reproductive) health. Three critical choices for people at all levels of development can be seen to be those which lead to a long and healthy life; to the acquisition of knowledge; and to access to the resources needed for a reasonable quality of life.

The Cairo Conference placed particular emphasis on both the rationale for enhancing people's choices and the probable ways of achieving this in relation to the complex and intimate nature of human behaviour concerned with sexuality and reproduction. The Programme of Action agreed at the Conference defined "reproductive health as a state of complete physical, mental and social well-being and not merely the absence of disease or infirmity, in all matters relating to the reproductive system and to its functions and processes".

The consensus regarding the appropriateness of the concept of reproductive health developed as a result of changing perspectives on development over the past 40 or 50 years. The reasons for these changing perspectives are complex. In the period immediately after the Second World War, the main health concern of international development efforts in developing countries was to reduce overall mortality, particularly among children. By the 1960s, concern had moved to limits to economic growth and excessive population increase. This, together with the expansion in the availability of modern methods of contraception, led to considerable emphasis being given to the reduction of population growth. To a large extent this was driven by the demographic imperative. In many countries, family planning programmes were established as separate vertical structures. Some of these much focused programmes have had notable achievements in terms of contraceptive prevalence and fertility reduction. However, increasingly during the 1980s, concern was expressed about the sustainability of separate family planning (and other vertical) programmes with their own hierarchies, financial arrangements, personnel and structures. Almost at the same time, the spread of the HIV pandemic forced the people to confront sexuality and sexual behaviour in a new way. In addition, there was slow appreciation that maternal mortality had largely been neglected as a continuing serious health problem in developing countries. This resulted in the articulation of maternal health or "safe motherhood" as a basic reproductive health right. While family planning programmes had contributed to reducing the number of times women are exposed to and experience the significant risks of pregnancy, childbirth and the puerperium, different interventions are needed to reduce the potential risks experienced during these crucial stages of reproduction. The evident failure of existing programmes to deal with some of these fundamental issues and rights, and an increasing appreciation of the crucial interrelationship between fertility regulation, reproduction, sexual behaviour and sexually transmitted diseases, led to the realization that they should be considered in a holistic way—reproductive health.

In many ways the Bali Declaration on Population and Sustainable Development adopted in 1992 anticipated the consensus arrived at in Cairo two years later. The Conference recommended that there was a need for countries to give priority to: Strengthening policy development and related processes as well as to expanding and streamlining delivery systems for family planning and MCH within the primary health-care framework, to adopting innovative management and multi-sectoral approaches, and to encouraging wider community and inter-sectoral participation in programme implementation efforts, and in countries where fertility has been reduced to a low or acceptable level, programme strategies should aim to build upon achievements made so far with a view to attaining sustainability (recommendation 17).

Specifically with regard to reproductive health care, it was noted that it "should be improved considerably in the region. Policies and programmes should strive to incorporate the totality of reproductive health care and aim at reducing maternal morbidity and mortality, induced abortion, sterility, childlessness, sexually transmitted diseases (STDs) and spread of human immunodeficiency virus (HIV) and acquired immunodeficiency syndrome (AIDS)" (recommendation 19).

Although in certain respects the concept of reproductive health developed from concern about how family planning programmes were being provided, it goes far beyond this. Reproductive health acknowledges that ultimately it is concerned with choices to improve levels of reproductive health and, for instance, the most persuasive justification of fertility regulation is the improvement of individual health and in particular maternal health. The movement from specific concerns, be they family planning or maternal health or sexually transmitted diseases, to a more coherent concept of reproductive health is basically a recognition that in order to attain reasonable levels of reproductive health, there must be an expansion of choices for people. These choices are not only in terms of contraceptive technologies for regulating fertility, but more fundamentally in terms of the choices people make in their sexual and reproductive lives.

In this regard, reproductive health services are a crucial means through which people can express these choices. In reproductive health terms, these services provide the necessary means for people to manifest choices and control, over whether and when to have children, and the number and timing of their children, but also to have more control over their sexual lives and the ability to avoid and prevent STDs.

The Cairo Programme of Action proposed that reproductive health care in the context of primary health care should/could include:

- family planning counselling, information, education, communication (IEC) and services;
- education and services for prenatal care, safe delivery and post-natal care, especially breastfeeding and infant and women's health care; prevention and appropriate treatment of infertility; abortion care [as decided at the national or local level], including prevention of abortion and the management of the consequences of abortion;
- treatment of reproductive tract infections, sexually transmitted diseases and other reproductive health conditions; and
- information, education and counselling, as appropriate, on human sexuality, reproductive health and responsible parenthood.

  Referral for family planning services and further diagnosis and treatment for complications of pregnancy, delivery and abortion, infertility, reproductive tract infections, breast cancer and cancers of the reproductive system, sexually transmitted diseases, including HIV/AIDS, should always be available, as required (paragraph 7.6).

Rationale for Reproductive Health Programmes

While the rationale for the concept of reproductive health is very persuasive, it is also argued that on practical grounds the integration of components of reproductive health services has considerable benefits in that, as stated in the Programme of Action, "family planning programmes work best when they are part of, or linked to broader reproductive health programmes that address closely related health needs and when women are fully involved in the design, provision, management and evaluation of services" (paragraph 7.13).

The potential synergy and benefits to be achieved from the integration of particularly the core components of reproductive health care have been documented elsewhere in terms of increased utilization and coverage of various components, cost efficiency and unit cost savings to the provider and also frequently the users of services.

With all concepts, their translation into practical effective programmes is often a challenge and, as with the primary health-care approach, where there continue to be tensions between those advocating an integrated or comprehensive approach as against a vertical and selective approach, similar tensions apply to a certain extent within reproductive health care. Certain commentators have cautioned against the danger of insisting that all family planning programmes must include other components of reproductive health, as that might reduce the attention given to adequate provision of contraception. Analogous reservations have been expressed by those concerned with other components, such as maternal health.

The challenges, *however*, are to maintain, and if possible improve, the effectiveness of components of reproductive health care, while achieving synergy and more cost-effective provision of services through the integration of the provision of various components.

Experience in the Integration of Components into Comprehensive Reproductive Health Programmes

Since the Cairo Conference there has been increasing experience in countries of the ESCAP region of initiatives to integrate the components of reproductive health services. In addition, WHO has involved countries in preparing a Regional Reproductive Health Strategy for South-East Asia (WHO, 1996). Many of the issues related to integrating component services into more comprehensive reproductive health care have been concerned with: setting priorities within reproductive health care; consolidating successful components and then extending the scope of reproductive health care; making sure that services are technically adequate and acceptable to clients; and giving priority to under-served groups.

Setting Priorities within Reproductive Health Services

Given the marked differences between countries in terms of the characteristics of their reproductive disease burden, the level of services already being provided, cultural norms and resource availability, the mix of functions included in reproductive health services will and should vary from country to country. In Bangladesh, as part of the Government's Health and Population Strategy (Government of Bangladesh, 1997) an Essential Package of Services (EPS) has been defined covering child health care, communicable disease control, limited curative care (treatment of common conditions) and reproductive health services. This has drawn on the extensive experience in Bangladesh of operational research concerned with identifying the most appropriate way of delivering reproductive health services. It was realized in Bangladesh that the likely costs of delivering all the elements of the EPS would exceed the available resources. For this reason, candidate interventions were prioritized for four levels of care by a task force with membership drawn from both Directorates of the Ministry of Health and Family Welfare, technical staff from several international agencies, NGOs and research institutes. A modified Delphi technique was used to rank various activities for each functional area of reproductive health care and the other candidate components of the EPS using six criteria for prioritization (EPS, 1997):

a) Potential health impact
b) Cost
c) Feasibility of provision
d) Public need/public health importance of the problem
e) Potential for private provision and financing
f) Economic criteria (externalities and economies of scale)

A similar exercise has been carried out in India. A new approach to family planning, one that locates these services within the larger context of reproductive health care, has been adopted. This significant change from principally a "population control" approach to one that is intended to provide a high-quality range of reproductive health services also coincided with the abolition of contraceptive targets for family planning providers by the Government of India. The framework for reproductive health is flexible because in a country with such a diverse and heterogeneous population it is not possible to define one reproductive health package. To allow for these variations, the framework identifies two main types of service package, an essential version and a comprehensive version. The essential reproductive health package could include the following components:

- Prevention and management of unwanted pregnancy
- Services to promote safe motherhood
- Services to promote child survival
- Nutritional services for vulnerable groups
- Prevention and treatment of reproductive tract infections and sexually transmitted diseases

- Reproductive health services for adolescents
- Information, education, and counselling on health, sexuality, and gender
- Establishment of effective referral systems

A comprehensive reproductive health package could include:

a) All the components of the essential package
b) Prevention and treatment of gynaecological problems, including cervical cancer
c) Screening and treatment of breast cancer

In Bangladesh, following the decisions regarding the particular content of reproductive health functions to be included in the Essential Package of Services, further work has been carried out to define the standards and content of care to be provided for each specific category by different level of care. These clinical guidelines are to be made available to the different cadres of health workers providing care.

Although people in Cambodia as yet lack wide access to reproductive health services, the programme strategy of a minimum service package has recently been developed with technical support from WHO and donors; it is innovative, and conforms to the broader principles of reproductive health. China has announced 'its intention to move from an administrative to a service approach, with the provision that "quality service in family planning should be provided to the people of childbearing age, particularly the reproductive health care for women to protect their health" (China, 1995). The Lao People's Democratic Republic has adopted National Birth Spacing Policies which are aimed at reducing maternal and infant mortality and the increasing access to and availability of birth spacing methods and services, and proposes the integration of birth spacing with MCH services.

In the Philippines, the Government, in response to changing needs, has established the Task Force on Reproductive Health and is reviewing how to merge the existing separate service units structurally, including the Family Planning Service, the Maternal and Child Health Services, the Nutrition Services, the STDs/AIDS unit and Dental Health Services, as divisions within a single Bureau of Family Health and with a unified leadership. In Thailand, the Ministry of Public Health announced on World Population Day (1997) a new reproductive health policy, which emphasizes further integration of components of reproductive health into a comprehensive package of services (UNFPA, 1997).

Other countries have also been identifying their priority components of reproductive health for service provision. In Maldives, where the TFR is about 6.4 per woman of reproductive age and the contraceptive prevalence for the country as a whole is around 16 per cent—but with wide variations between atolls from less than 4 per cent to just over 32 per cent and maternal mortality ranges from about 120 in the capital to over 500 per 100,000 live births in the outer atolls—priority is being given to maternal health and family planning.

In Sri Lanka, TFR and maternal mortality are low, at around 2.3 per woman of reproductive age and less than 50 per 100,000 live births, and relatively more emphasis has been placed on other components of reproductive health care, including reproductive tract infections and malignancies. While the information on cause-specific mortality rates for reproductive mortality is limited, there are indications that for women in Sri Lanka aged between 15 and 49 years, about three times as many deaths are due to reproductive tract carcinoma as to maternal causes. Consequently, "*well-women clinics*" are being established principally for the screening of women for early diagnosis of cervical cancer (by downstaging) and for breast neoplasms by palpation. These clinics are also providing, for women who attend for screening, if needed, family planning, and services for the treatment of reproductive tract infections.

Prevention and management of STDs has seldom ranked high in national health priorities, despite the considerable morbidity caused, especially among women and newborn babies. However, in recent years, with the spread of the HIV pandemic, the situation has changed. While most countries now recognize that control of STDs is essential for the achievement of reproductive health, they experience many constraints in addressing these problems, particularly as part of services provided at the primary health care level. The constraints include inadequate data on the local epidemiology of STDs, lack of rapid, reliable and cheap diagnostic tests, and the fact that most primary health care delivery points for reproductive health care are predominantly for married women, which makes it particularly difficult for adolescent, single women and men to use them. Syndromic management of STDs is being accepted as the most effective way of treating people with reproductive tract infections where there is no access to ancillary diagnostic tests, and is being adopted by many countries, for example, Bangladesh, Nepal and most Pacific island countries.

There have been several examples of the integration of STD care into reproductive health services. In Cambodia, it has been agreed to have integrated services for screening and syndromic management of reproductive tract infections and STDs and preventive counselling on HIV/AIDS, with birth spacing, at all functional operational districts. Several countries are either re-establishing antenatal screening of pregnant women for syphilis (e.g. Sri Lanka) or have recently introduced this (e.g. Solomon Islands). In Indonesia, counselling and screening procedures for women wanting IUDs have been extended to cover STDs. In Thailand, strenuous efforts have been made to diagnose and treat those diseases at all opportunities when people use health services, including reproductive health care. This has been associated with dramatic falls in the incidence of such diseases. A whole series of opportunities for integrating STD and reproductive tract infection services into maternal and child health care are being explored in Bangladesh. This has also included the strengthening of STD services for men in urban-based clinics.

Many countries have undertaken surveys to improve understanding of the epidemiology of reproductive tract infections and associated socio-cultural factors, for instance, studies on:

a) the incidence of STDs and their sensitivity to various antibiotics in Indonesia;
b) cultural practices and attitudes to reproductive tract infections (Bangladesh, Cambodia, Indonesia and the Philippines);
c) male condom acceptability (Indonesia and Myanmar); and
d) female condom acceptability (Thailand).

Making Sure that Reproductive Health Services are Technically Adequate and Acceptable to Clients

Important issues in improving reproductive health are attempts to ensure that reproductive health services are accessible and acceptable to those for whom they are intended and that they provide care that is based upon evidence which indicates that it is technically efficacious. These issues are clearly related to the quality of care. Critical inputs into ensuring technical adequacy and good quality of care are the setting of clinical and management standards and preparing guidelines for effective care. These standards are also invaluable in providing a basis for the monitoring of reproductive health service delivery. Several countries have developed standards for the provision of components of reproductive health care. For instance, in Sri Lanka, the Family Health Bureau of the Ministry of Health has published the Handbook on Contraceptive Technology (Family Health Bureau, 1997), which has been distributed to all medical officers and gives comprehensive practical information on major contraceptives. It is intended that this manual will not only be used by general duty medical officers but will also serve as a guide for counselling clients and for training other health workers. A similar exercise has recently been completed in Maldives, where National Guidelines and Minimum Standards for Family Planning Services have been prepared for reproductive health service providers (Department of Public Health, 1998). In Nepal, work is beginning on the preparation of sets of clinical and management guidelines initially for the following components of reproductive health:

a) family planning;
b) maternal care,
c) reproductive tract infections/STDs,
d) complications of abortion,
e) adolescent health, and
f) infertility.

Many countries are increasingly giving attention to the quality of services, and in many instances this also necessitates an examination of how reproductive health service components can be integrated as part of improvement in choice and convenience for clients and providers. For instance, Indonesia has recently developed, with UNFPA support, a project designed to address quality issues exclusively, together with a shift in programme strategies in favour of a more "cafeteria-oriented" approach of providing broader choice. The project also provides for greater cooperation among different agencies involved in reproductive health care, mainly the Ministry of Health and the National Family Planning Coordination Board (BKKBN). UNFPA support to similar projects is being considered for:

a) Mongolia, and
b) the Democratic People's Republic of Korea.

There are many, and an increasing number of, examples where reproductive health service IEC efforts for improving reproductive health are based upon locally relevant socio-cultural information and are being implemented in a coordinated way, directed towards providers and potential clients of reproductive health services. In most countries in Central and South Asia, socio-cultural research has been accepted as a prerequisite to the development of effective IEC strategies for addressing various reproductive health issues. In new UNFPA-assisted sub-programmes, socio-cultural research on such issues as adolescent reproductive health and male participation has been incorporated as a key strategy.

A common problem is poor utilization of the existing data generated through knowledge, attitude and practice (KAP) studies, focus groups and socio-cultural research. This could be attributed partially to the lack of information about the availability of data or poor presentation and packaging of data. For example, a review of IEC projects in Sri Lanka found that several qualitative and quantitative studies on the sexual and reproductive health of adolescent and youth had been conducted in the previous two years. However, very little use of the data was made by the managers of projects dealing with the issues of adolescent reproductive health: the managers were simply not aware of the existence of the studies.

To reorient the polices and programmes to the reproductive health approach, restructuring of the health service delivery system and development and application of a new set of duties and responsibilities for service providers as well as health units is important. This applies equally to IEC programmes in support of reproductive health. With regard to the structure and framework of IEC, there are a variety of models followed in South Asia, which can be grouped into two main categories. In some countries, special units have been established to develop IEC programmes, such as the IEC Centre in the Islamic Republic of Iran, and in some countries IEC functions have become integrated with health education units. In countries such as Bhutan, Maldives and Sri

Lanka, where such functions have become part of heath education units, IEC responds better to substantive reproductive health issues. Where it remains as a separate entity, it often focuses on form rather than content.

Frequently, IEC personnel have media and materials production backgrounds. In most countries in the region, such personnel learn on the job about the substantive issues of reproductive health and have no special training or orientation in this area. For an IEC programme to support substantive issues of reproductive health, it is essential that the personnel receive training in reproductive health. Even after many years of support to the IEC area, there is still a lack of IEC professionals in most countries. There could be a number of reasons for this; there is a general lack of long-term degree programmes in IEC in the region; those IEC officers who attend short-term training in IEC skills leave the government for more profitable jobs with the private sector after a few years of service; and lack of advancement opportunities and career paths for IEC personnel within the health ministry.

The biggest obstacle in reorienting IEC programmes to include the reproductive health approach in many countries of the region is basically that it is felt that the programmes are not "ready"; for instance, although knowledge levels of family planning are almost universal, contraceptive use is low and unmet needs high in countries such as Nepal and Pakistan. In Bangladesh, there is concern that extension of the scope of services will dilute family planning efforts and thus distract the country from reaching sustained high levels of contraceptive use. This situation will continue (i.e. the KAP gap—high knowledge, low practice) unless programmes redefine knowledge as more than awareness-raising and as an increase in functional and effective knowledge, leading to behaviour change and, in the case of service providers, to better quality services.

In Pakistan, with low contraceptive prevalence and a high unmet need for family planning, IEC efforts should still largely be directed towards the immediate issues of family planning. While there have been some attempts at including the other aspects of reproductive health, by and large this has been sporadic and arbitrary.

In Nepal, the new IEC country programme shows willingness to include maternal care, male involvement and adolescent reproductive health issues. Family planning IEC messages are targeted mainly at the unmet need group. The strong linkages of the IEC programme with service delivery and the training of service providers, all of which have strong reproductive health components, mean that the IEC programme essentially supports and complements the reproductive health components of the other two.

Another major obstacle in making the transition to integrated reproductive health care is that much is known about IEC for family planning (in terms of strategy, approaches, concepts, kinds of messages and misconceptions), because a considerable amount of communication research has dealt with these issues, and programmers have had more than 30 years experience dealing with this type of IEC. However, IEC for reproductive health is a fairly recent development; it remains to a large extent uncharted territory; and knowledge and research on IEC reproductive health approaches and methods are at best perfunctory. A major advantage of these long years of experience and the body of knowledge regarding family planning IEC is that programmers and planners can build on this knowledge and experience to develop better and more effective reproductive health based IEC programmes. For example, the concept and practice of good interpersonal communication and counselling as a desirable skill among family planning service providers to promote better quality service for family planning clients are well established and can form a base on which to draw for similar developments with reproductive health services.

Consolidating Successful Components of Reproductive Health Services and Then Extending the Scope of Reproductive Health Care

Sri Lanka has been very successful in providing the major components of reproductive health care, essentially through integrated services provided by the Family Health Bureau of the Ministry of Health. They are now extending the scope of reproductive health care by providing screening services for breast cancer and cancers of the reproductive system through "*well-women's clinics*".

In India, the rural health infrastructure is largely in place but problems with the implementation of services, including reproductive health care, have been well documented. Attempts are continuing to improve reproductive health service provision, partly through the phasing out of the contraceptive target system, improving client choice and establishing a "bottom-up" planning exercise, starting with those developed by each block and followed by district and state plans for reproductive health care (World Bank, 1996). Although the integration of family planning and maternal and child health programmes was decided upon in the mid-1970s, it has only been implemented to a limited extent. Recent efforts have emphasized the integration of services and that reproductive health services be conveniently located and provide as much choice as possible in both integrated and specialized services. Mobile teams have for many years been involved in providing family planning services. More recently the range of care provided by these teams has been extended to include MCH services. While most efforts in India are concentrating on the central concerns of reproductive health care, increasing attention is also beginning to be given to other components of reproductive health, such as the prevention and treatment of infertility.

In Bangladesh, total fertility has fallen impressively, from 5.1 in 1984-1988 to 3.3 in 1994-1996, and contraceptive prevalence for modern methods has increased from 18.4 to 41.5 per cent (Ministry of Health and Family

Welfare, 1997). Over the same time period, the mix of contraceptive use has changed markedly, with a relatively far greater increase in pill use and a relative decline in clinical methods (e.g. an increase in female sterilization and a decrease in male sterilization). In order to consolidate and further expand on the levels of contraceptive prevalence achieved in Bangladesh, and to maintain a reasonable choice of contraceptives, particular efforts are being made to train service providers in clinical methods. Following experiments carried out at the International Centre for Diarrhoeal Disease Research, where family planning services are being provided increasingly at fixed satellite clinics as part of a cluster of MCH and family planning services (International Centre for Diarrhoeal Disease Research, 1996), there is a gradual move away from door-to-door provision of family planning services to integrated services available at static clinics. This takes account of the changes, albeit slow, occurring in the status of women in rural Bangladesh with an increasing acceptance that women can travel short distances from their homes for health care.

Giving Priority to Under-served Groups

As the components of reproductive health care are increasingly integrated into packages of services, it is important that this should occur for groups of populations who are deprived and already under-served. There are several examples where this is happening. In Bangladesh and Sri Lanka for instance, with the rapidly expanding garment industry, which predominantly employs young female workers, services are being established, principally by NGOs, for the provision of limited reproductive health care.

Urbanization is a particular challenge for the provision of integrated reproductive health care. In 1996, about 38 per cent of people in developing countries lived in urban areas; however, the growth rate during the period 1990-1995 in less developed regions was 3.4 per cent, considerably more than the overall growth rate (United Nations, 1998). Most of this growth was due to migration from rural areas; however, particularly among the poorest groups living in urban slums, fertility rates are higher than for people living in rural areas. In addition, their other reproductive health needs are also greater and frequently they have severe problems of accessing existing services. In Bangladesh, the Asian Development Bank and UNFPA are working with the Government and municipal authorities in the four largest cities in the country to establish reproductive health clinics for people living in slums to provide the Essential Package of Reproductive Health Services.

Critical Issues for the Integration of Reproductive Health Components

For the successful integration of components into a locally coherent reproductive health care service, there are certain critical issues which can help facilitate or alternatively hinder integration, among these being management arrangements, financial aspects, appropriate training of reproductive health care providers and logistic systems. In addition, the policy environment is important with regard to awareness of gender issues and a willingness to accept innovation in the delivery of reproductive health services.

Management Arrangements to Facilitate the Integration of Reproductive Health Services

Significant recommendations on how government policies and programmes can be designed and implemented were made in the Programme of Action of the International Conference on Population and Development (chapter 12). This emphasizes the need to involve intended beneficiaries in the design and implementation of population policies, programmes and projects. The role of NGOs and the private sector in this process was highlighted in the Programme of Action. This in turn requires the building of capacity for such participation and the development of commitment at a senior level to encourage and support the process. It has been recognized that the lack of adequate management skills critically reduces the ability for strategic planning, weakens programme execution, lessens the quality of services and thus diminishes the usefulness of programmes to their beneficiaries. Two common developments that have significant implications for institutional and management arrangements in countries of Central and South Asia are integration and decentralization. More and more governments are recognizing the importance of these two principles and this trend significantly increases the requirement for trained staff to meet new and expanded responsibilities at the lower administrative levels. It also means that institutions at higher administrative levels need to develop skills in policy analysis, evaluation and strategic planning (paragraph 13.7). The following actions have been recommended in this context:

- *Formulate and implement* training programmes, particularly at decision-making and managerial levels, incorporating user and gender perspectives.
- *Ensure* efficient placement of trained personnel, giving particular attention to continuity and retention of managerial and technical personnel.
- *Continuously upgrade* the management skills of service delivery personnel.
- *Promote* the sharing of experience of population programme management in order to build national capacity and, to facilitate this, develop and maintain databases of national institutions and experts.
- *Ensure* the involvement of programme beneficiaries at all levels, in particular at rural levels, for better overall programme management.
- *Develop* and implement a client-centred management information system for reproductive health, including family planning.

These recommendations of the Cairo Conference have significant implications for the institutional and management arrangements required to meet its goals. Experience in the region shows that countries are at different stages in the continuum from vertical family planning services to more comprehensive reproductive health care services. In addition, UNFPA, by applying the programme approach, has encouraged better understanding of the inter-linkages between different reproductive health components, especially maternal care, STDs/reproductive tract infections and family planning, as well as the integration of supporting activities such as IEC, training, research and logistics. The development of the programme approach has been a catalyst to the integration of reproductive health service components in, for instance,

a) Bangladesh,
b) the Democratic People's Republic of Korea,
c) the Lao People's Democratic Republic,
d) Maldives,
e) Mongolia, and
f) Viet Nam.

Integration

There are several reasons for which integration with other elements is useful in the delivery of family planning services. For example, the populations involved in family planning and the prevention and treatment of reproductive tract infections are broadly the same. The methods of counselling and management are similar, and maternal care efforts give family planning a more caring connotation. Moreover, there are several advantages of integration, such as cost-efficiency from the perspective of both—provider and user, an expanded knowledge and skill base of health care providers and enhanced teamwork of service providers. However, there is also a need to recognize problem areas, such as increased workload, inadequacy of existing primary health care facilities to provide a full range of services, and inadequate referral care and client-oriented recording systems. Recognition of these problems is an essential step towards functional integration of reproductive health care services, with an incremental approach. Several countries have begun to take the necessary steps to formally integrate family planning services with other reproductive health care. In Bangladesh, the Ministry of Health and Family Welfare has two service directorates, Health Services and Family Planning, each headed by a Director-General with a hierarchy of several directors, deputy directors and assistant directors. Consideration is being given to a restructured and reorganized arrangement with full management integration at all levels. In Pakistan, a separate ministry, the Ministry of Population Welfare, is responsible for family planning services, while the Ministry of Health is responsible for most other components of reproductive health care. Here, while full integration is unlikely in the near future, consideration is being given to functional integration at the service delivery level.

Other countries, such as China and Viet Nam, have made slow progress in integrating reproductive health service at the central level, principally because of the strong and well-established vertical structures. However, programme managers in these countries say that they are working towards functional integration at the grass-roots level. Malaysia, the Philippines, Sri Lanka and Thailand, with responsibility for family planning within the ministries of health, have been successful in promoting family planning through an integrated approach.

Decentralization

The second significant management issue is decentralization, the transfer of responsibility and authority from the central level to lower levels. This is usually a political decision, requiring legal modifications of power-sharing arrangements, resource mobilization practices and flow of funds. Decentralizing the management of public health programmes should promote much greater community participation and forge cooperation with local NGOs and private health-care providers. At the same time, it must be recognized that not all management functions should be decentralized. Policy formulation, including the setting of goals and strategies, interfacing with external donor agencies, most large-scale procurement, and quality control, are some examples of top-level functions for which there is often no justification to decentralize. There are examples in the region of top levels not being willing to give up certain functions which should be carried out at lower levels because this is perceived as a loss of power. However, there are other examples showing considerable decentralization of decision-making in health services, for instance, in the Philippines and Sri Lanka.

An essential precondition for successful decentralization is that staff at both levels must adapt to their new roles and develop new skills. It should also be remembered that decentralization is not an end in itself—it is only a means to an end. Often insufficient attention is given to building the capacity of the central level for evolving into a new role, and the capacity of the lower levels to assume new responsibilities. In a study of decentralization experiences, the Management Sciences for Health recommends that central-level staff should be developed to act as both technical programme specialists and general management advisers to the lower-level managers. As technical programme specialists, they carry the main responsibility for strategic management, which includes both strategic decision-making and the development of programme standards and organizational guidelines. Difficulties arise during the transition when such central-level staff are expected to carry out their old work responsibilities while simultaneously assuming their new roles.

Human Resources for the Development of Integrated Reproductive Health Care

The major challenges in human resources development in the countries of

Central and South Asia to achieve the goals of the Programme of Action of the Conference is to focus on building capacity at two levels—the institutional level and the individual level. At the institutional level, this has been directed to addressing management and performance issues of policies, standards, programmes, institutes and centres. Gender issues are beginning to be mainstreamed at the institutional level. At the individual level, accountability and quality have to be the responsibility of individual practitioners, and human resources development has to assist in dynamic and creative ways to enhance and reward these capacities.

Of all the changes in human resources development to achieve the provision of integrated reproductive health services, the need for improved training has attracted the greatest response. Innovative educational programmes with more relevant curricula have often had a startling and positive effect on the effectiveness of training in the short term, for instance in the Islamic Republic of Iran and Nepal. Less is known, however, about the cost-effectiveness of training, and the longer-term effect of training on work performance. Training, however, continues to be driven by supply-side interests, and to be inefficient. It is often managed to meet the convenience and capacity of the suppliers of training—ministries, donors, and institutes—rather than the demands and/or needs of trainees or the consumer side of human resources.

In order to attain integrated reproductive health care, substantial and continuing investments are required in the development of human resources. The public sector frequently compartmentalizes the management of human resources into three distinct areas, often dealt with separately: planning, management and production. This separation has created huge inefficiency and reduced the returns on human capital investment.

Human resources planning has traditionally, and especially in the health sector, been about calculating numerical personnel requirements by occupational category and location. There is evidence that most planning has been disjointed and verticalized with little appreciation of the effective mix of categories, or the impact of personnel surplus or deficit at particular locations. Human resources planning is usually driven solely by supply-side mechanisms, and with strong supply forecasting. However, despite long-standing patterns of chronic shortages in rural areas and relative oversupply in urban areas, supply forecasting has been unable to solve these inequalities in distribution. There is also little appreciation of the dynamics of demand, how supply is affected by changes in other sectors such as education, or the degree of flexibility in modelling that might be possible. Productivity and cost analyses are rarely carried out, and it has proved difficult to identify the nature or periodicity of shortages accurately. Career path analyses, which would permit better long-term forecasting, are seldom undertaken. As social development parameters change, most forecasts in the health sector do not take into account upward or horizontal mobility of cadres, average length in service and the impact of marriage, births and education patterns on career paths. Wastage is probably high and/or endemic in most countries, and could be reduced by better planning.

Management of skilled and semi-skilled personnel is also part of the human resources dilemma. The problem of wastage of human resources can be tackled through introducing more comprehensive health services, and less verticality of programmes, which, in turn, is intended to introduce higher productivity and greater efficiency in services with fewer resources. If these improvements are to be achieved, the management of human resources has to be drastically improved. Studies in the region reveal consistently: poorly defined functional roles and responsibilities; isolation of staff in rural areas; lack of incentives to maintain acceptable standards; absence of housing, transport and other infrastructure to carry out functions; inadequate policies; irregular salaries; and unrealistic expectations coupled with region-wide low status of women. Generally speaking, the further from the centre, the worse the working conditions and the weaker the management. Where decentralization policies have been adopted, the operational modalities usually remain concentrated in the centre, reducing effectiveness and creating a huge amount of system inertia. Despite severe under-performance of the service delivery systems at the periphery, savings are sought by reducing supervision and supervisors.

Logistics and Management Information Systems for Integrated Reproductive Health Services

Reproductive Health Logistic

The Programme of Action noted that reproductive health care programmes must make significant efforts to improve the quality of care. Among other measures, programmes should make services safer, affordable, more convenient and accessible for clients and ensure, through strengthened logistical systems, a sufficient and continuous supply of essential, high-quality contraceptives (paragraph 7.23).

Logistical support to reproductive health (including family planning) programmes must recognize, plan and account for a complete "basket of commodities", and not just a handful of contraceptives. This involves significant investments of money and effort in the following:

- Building storage capacity;
- Integrating existing vertically structured and managed logistical operations;
- Creating logistics-specific positions to staff intermediate storage depots;
- Training of logistics personnel and field workers in appropriate shelf-lives, storage conditions and handling practices for a variety of heat, humidity and light-sensitive materials; and

- Rationalizing (making more efficient and less costly) the mechanisms for the transport and distribution of commodities from higher-storage levels to service delivery points within the reach of those in need.

A recent description of some of the problems associated with logistics systems in one country (India) illustrates the situation seen in many other countries. In terms of logistics management, the key problem is that there are several individuals charged with the responsibility for handling the State and district logistical operations. Several key programme managers have partial responsibilities for materials management for their respective programmes, but they are neither able to direct resources to improving the system as a whole nor to devote substantial amounts of time to the development of a comprehensive system. They are burdened with the tasks of normal programme administration and often saddled with many other administrative responsibilities and special assignments. This lack of focus is reflected in the assignment of clerical staff to handle materials, most of whom have neither had the training for handling them nor developed an appreciation of the value of the items for which they are charged with caring. Junior gazetted officers, who supervise these clerks, also fail to show significant appreciation of the situation in which materials of considerable value are stored and handled. Hence, spoilage and damage attributed to poor storage conditions and mishandling are common.

Particularly noticeable is the perennial lack of adequate investment in the development of a physical infrastructure capable of storing and handling materials and equipment associated with the family welfare programme. A similar lack of investment is seen in the training of staff who must handle this materials base. The result of this investment shortfall is large and widespread system losses owing to over-supply, poor materials management and handling practices, lack of accountability and wasted opportunity costs owing to lack of drugs, medicines, contraceptives and equipment, when clients and patients arrive at service delivery points which are out of stock (UNFPA, 1997).

Reproductive Health Management Information Systems

Reproductive health management information systems should facilitate the process of transmitting, compiling, analyzing and presenting data; unfortunately, however this process is so protracted that the date are often obsolete by the time a feedback report is prepared, and decisions are consequently made without any valid information input. Furthermore, in strong vertical programmes the transmission of data does not follow hierarchical lines of communication, with the result that reports often fail to reach line managers, particularly at the district level.

Data recorded and reported at a service facility should be relevant to the management of patients and health units. A health information system should provide information support for decision-making at all levels of health services, and should therefore fit into the overall management structure of the health service system. Each level has specific functions, including decision-making, which lead to improved health in the population. They relate to the management of:

a) patients/clients,
b) health units, and
c) the system.

The first two are directly related to the delivery of health care to the population, while the third provides coordination and management support at the service delivery levels. The decisions that have to be made in the first two categories are operational, whereas those concerning the system have to do with strategic planning or management control.

Restructuring of a health information system to facilitate reproductive health services rarely needs to involve a total overhaul of the system in a particular country or region. The least functional aspects of the system should be focused on, or restructuring should be planned in connection with continuing reforms of the health system. The restructuring process can be broken down into steps dealing with the development of the information-generating process and steps related to the establishment of the management structure for the generation and use of information.

It is generally observed that there are two critical areas in the development of functional reproductive health information systems, which suffer from either too much input or too little consideration:

a) identifying information needs and indicators and users of these; and
b) ensuring that information is used at appropriate levels to improve patient/client care and the management of the system.

Financing Reproductive Health Services

In service delivery, many developing countries are now moving from a narrow "family planning" approach aimed at slowing population growth to the "reproductive health" approach recommended in the Programme of Action. This approach puts clients' needs first and addresses a broader range of reproductive health and rights issues, including avoidance of unwanted fertility, maternal care, and prevention and management of reproductive tract infections. These efforts are taking place under very diverse conditions and, often, existing vertical institutional arrangements. Common concerns across governments are the importance of securing financial efficiency and sustainability, as well as an equitable allocation of scarce resources across priority programmes.

In South Asia, in the context of a limited and rudimentary revenue base and rising demand for services, adopting the reproductive health approach needs to be affordable in order to be successful, and governments have to select the most cost-effective strategies. However, to secure cost-effectiveness and affordability, managers and decision makers need to know what it will cost to introduce reproductive health services, including family planning services, at different levels, and how these should be financed. In other words, in order to design and implement a strategy at the primary level, it is necessary to know what is currently being spent on reproductive health and related services, on other health services, and who pays for them (public and private financing, including out-of-pocket payments).

The Cost of Integration—Is Reproductive Health Affordable?

Low-income countries are unlikely to have the resources to implement immediately the complete range of reproductive health care all at one time. Instead, some countries have introduced selective components of reproductive health services at the functional level along with existing family planning services. Research indicates that that this approach can be affordable.

A recent study has examined the comparative financial cost data of adding and changing services to include reproductive health in a public sector family planning programme. The main findings were that incremental reproductive services added little to total costs because the bulk of the expenditure had already been incurred for staff and facilities which formed the majority of recurrent costs; there were considerable cost savings from combining services, for instance, where more than one service was provided at the same visit, such as an IUD check combined with a Papanicolaou smear and reproductive tract infection screening, and from the use of specially trained nurse-midwives instead of doctors; and where there was underutilization, the total costs were allocated over a smaller number of outputs, and hence the cost of adding reproductive health services was low.

Experience from Matlab in Bangladesh has shown how an integrated and horizontal health and family planning service delivery programme with relatively high worker-to-client ratios can outperform the vertical, less integrated government programme with low worker-to-client ratios. Although, in the aggregate, the Matlab project is more expensive than the Government's programme, it is also more effective, generating sufficiently high outputs to offset the extra costs of the intensified delivery system.

Research using facility-based information suggests a number of potential cost/time savings from changing current practices and procedures for the present government family planning programme in Bangladesh. Such changes would not only improve the existing programme but also facilitate the provision of reproductive health services. The Government of Bangladesh is currently in the process of designing an Essential Package of Services as part of the Fifth Health and Population Project. The preliminary results suggest that the integration of family planning, maternal and child health care, management of reproductive tract infections/STDs, and adolescent health, is affordable.

In India, the Government has been progressively shifting its Family Welfare Programme from a focus predominantly on family planning to broader efforts to improve maternal and child health. The *"essential reproductive and child health package"* comprises a number of components, but services are often limited owing to lack of resources, inadequate training, inefficiency and poor quality. For these reasons, considerable attention is now being devoted to the identification of low-cost management and organizational interventions to improve the situation.

Therefore, while there appears to be plenty of scope for the integration of reproductive health into existing programmes, in part because additional financial resources can be mobilized through increased efficiency of programmes, strategies need to be identified for alternative ways of generating sustainable funding.

Options for Financing Reproductive Health Services

Reproductive health and family planning services have traditionally been provided by the public sector, often at relatively high unit costs. If these services are to be extended in scope and coverage, the role and different modes of private sector participation need to be examined.

The Role of the Public Sector

Governments have often engaged in many health-care activities rather than focusing on areas in which they have a comparative advantage, such as financing public goods delivery (e.g. quality control and regulation of contraceptives), or areas with large positive "externalities" (e.g. treatment of STDs). Another area where the market tends to fail and the government has an advantage is in situations when individuals cannot judge the value of a service, at least not without incurring large costs. Examples of such cases are emergency care for obstetric complications and care for complications of abortion. In these situations, the government has a role in accrediting providers or facilities and fostering quality assurance. In addition, steps to ensure equity in service delivery call for government intervention. People with low or no income have the least capacity to pay for health services and suffer the largest burden of diseases, for example maternal mortality and reproductive tract infections. Notwithstanding the problems of discriminating between rich and poor, public subsidies are needed to secure a minimum level of equity.

Mixed Modes of Financing and Delivery

Even if services are to be financed by the government, they need not be provided by it. Instead, combinations of public and private modes of finance and service delivery may be viable. Similarly, private sources can be used to finance public or private provision. In some developing countries, however, the private sector might be so rudimentary that contracting out would not be an option. This is often the case in remote, rural areas where, increasingly, community-based organizations are providing care instead.

NGOs financed from public or private sources play an important role in the delivery of reproductive health services in some developing countries; however, they are often highly dependent on donor funding. NGOs can be more efficient and provide services with greater consumer satisfaction than do public providers. They may be more innovative, testing out new services and delivery modes that are later adopted by other providers. For example, the Bangladesh Women's Health Coalition successfully developed menstrual regulation techniques (Kay, Germain and Bangser, 1991). Furthermore, its clinics have shown that integrated women's reproductive health services, with attention given to quality, can increase the effective use of services at low cost in comparison with government family planning clinics.

In certain circumstances, governments could decide to subsidize NGOs to deliver reproductive health services to low-income segments, complementary to the government programme, as NGOs might be better able to contact women in under-served areas.

- *Private Sector Financing*: The private sector is diverse and offers a number of options for raising revenue, such as by user fees, private providers, community-based and employment-based programmes and insurance schemes.
- *User Fees*: As a means to recover costs, both the public sector and NGOs could charge clients for the services provided, either by service or as a flat rate per visit, with the purpose of recovering the full cost or part of the cost of service delivery. Whether the introduction of user fees is likely to discourage use is a major concern and depends on the prevailing elasticity of demand in specific geographical areas and of different user groups and experience varies. It is important that programme managers determine whether they are willing to accept declines in use, and if so, how much of a decline is acceptable in order to raise revenues. Furthermore, when user fees are charged in association with incremental improvements in quality, clients are likely to respond more positively. There are often trade-offs between equity, quality and user fees. Finally, any cost-recovery scheme should be transparent and well-managed in order to be credible to user groups.
- *Fee-for-Service Provider*: Fee-for-service providers include private medical practitioners, nurses and midwives who charge their clients for services rendered, and have several potential advantages over the establishment of public clinics and NGOs. First, most medical providers already have a presence in the community and an established client base. Second, private providers may offer more privacy and convenience (less waiting time, more flexible hours) than many clinics.

The competition is biased, insofar as most public clinics offer subsidized services, while private providers do not. In Indonesia, the KB Mandiri campaign used private midwives to provide contraception and increased use significantly.

- *Community-based Programmes*: In most countries of the region, a broad range of community institutions, self-help groups, mothers' groups, youth clubs, traditional birth attendants, volunteers and field workers are involved in the delivery of reproductive health and family planning services. There is clearly scope for more involvement of similar groups, for instance, village grocery shops and tea stalls could be used in the distribution and possibly marketing of contraceptives and information material. The Nepal Red Cross Society, for example, has been training local volunteers since 1989 to resupply pill and condom acceptors, charging the same for the contraceptives as the government provider.
- *Employment-based Programmes*: Another vehicle for private sector funding for reproductive health and family planning is employer involvement in the provision of services for employees. Companies can provide services themselves or contract other organizations, often NGOs, to supply them. For the companies involved, provision of this type of service entails a trade-off between the financial costs and the potential benefits, such as reduced cash outlays for maternity leave, medical care, training costs and labour turnover; however, the net results are likely to be positive. In general, those companies with generous benefit packages, workers with initially low contraceptive use and health status, and a large workforce, have great incentives for running successful family planning and maternal and child health programmes; a successful example can be found in the Philippines.
- *Health Insurance Schemes*: Group "*private third party payment*" systems, sometimes involving a health maintenance organization, can result in benefits by covering reproductive health care and family planning similar to those of employment-based programmes: savings generated through reduced outlays, for instance, for maternity care and the management of reproductive tract infections/STDs. The amount of savings depends on the unit costs of providing health care to pregnant women and dependants, and the number of pregnancies prevented. In order to hold down costs, insurance companies and health maintenance organizations may contract low-cost providers, such as NGOs, and local community-based organizations. Several projects have explored the place of health maintenance organizations in the financing of reproductive health and family planning care. Through the Enterprise Project, 1985-1991, feasibility studies established or expanded existing health maintenance organizations in India, Indonesia and the

Philippines. These were shown to be feasible and cost-effective in the long run. Another example of risk-sharing in health care is the Kasturba Hospital in rural Sevagram in India, where the hospital provides basic low-cost health-care services, including outreach, against regular premium payments from *'sorghum'* funds in the member villages. The hospital thus serves as a health maintenance organization in a remote, rural area.

Gender Issues and Integration of Reproductive Health Care Components

The Fourth Asian and Pacific Population Conference, held in Bali in 1992, recognized that a woman's health was closely related to her status, and high rates of maternal mortality and morbidity were common where women were socially, economically and politically disadvantaged. The Bali Declaration included in its issues and recommendations the need to improve women's status as reflected in her legal rights, education, health, employment, position in the household and decision-making, as essential for the success of population programmes and for sustainable development. This was reaffirmed by the Programme of Action of the International Conference on Population and Development held at Cairo in 1994.

These conferences also emphasized the need for a holistic and gender-sensitive approach to health care, underscoring the need to address reproductive health rather than just family planning and maternal and child health. The quality of care was stressed, as also was male involvement. In South Asia, with a patriarchal system and strong son preference, discrimination against the female begins even before birth. The sex ratio is adverse for females in most countries in the region, and under-five child mortality is higher for girls. There is discrimination against girls in terms of nutrition, and access to health care. Later, their health status is compromised by early marriage and frequent childbearing because of lack of reproductive rights or choice.

Male involvement and responsibility need to be enhanced in issues related to reproduction (not just increased condom use) and on decisions concerning health and family welfare, including child-rearing. This also includes the need to socialize adolescents and youth to achieve more equitable gender relations and roles in the longer run.

Gender dynamics within the health system need to be developed to foster both greater responsiveness to the gender needs of clients through training and more equitable participation of women service providers and managers at all levels.

Some significant initiatives have been taken since the Bali and Cairo conferences to implement more gender-sensitive reproductive health programmes by countries in the region:

- Women's health is no longer viewed as a contraceptive and maternity issue and most countries have expanded their programmes to include the reproductive health perspective and provide more holistic services. India has abolished targets in family planning and thus men and women are no longer viewed as mere demographic targets. Family planning is promoted more in the context of improving the health of adults and that of their children.
- In Bangladesh, the National Institute of Population Research and Training has institutionalized gender training and incorporated relevant gender issues in the basic curricula of several categories of health staff. In India, the Government, with the technical assistance of the Institute of Development Studies, Sussex, United Kingdom, has developed a specific module on gender and health for extensive use in training conducted in the states, and at national training institutes for various categories of staff, including the civil service.
- In the Philippines, the Commission on Population has drafted a Gender-responsive Policy Framework with Reproductive Health Perspectives (Philippines, 1996). In addition, a series of research studies have been undertaken on "women-centred participatory research and development for women's health", as a woman's consortium project, with UNFPA support. The findings have important implications for improving gender sensitivity in reproductive health services in the Philippines.
- Bangladesh and Nepal have been particularly successful in the organization of outreach and satellite clinics and collaboration with NGOs and family planning associations, which have vastly improved access to services for women whose mobility is restricted owing to socio-cultural norms, thus affecting their health-seeking behaviour.
- There have been special efforts to recruit more female health workers in, for instance, Nepal and Pakistan, where there was a deficiency in this regard.
- Increasingly, male involvement and responsibility are being stressed by service providers and in IEC, and there is a growing demand for the training of doctors in no-scalpel vasectomies. Indonesia has developed plans to extend its counselling programmes to include training materials on male participation. The Philippines has established a reproductive health centre for men, and is experimenting with innovative ways for male involvement. China is becoming more sensitive to gender issues and, for instance, in a minor aspect of male involvement, is promoting male sterilization. Further examples are a regional conference held in Azerbaijan on male participation and the preparation of training modules on this subject in Sri Lanka.

Open discussions are frequently held now on issues that adversely affect women's health, including abortion and violence, and strategies are being formulated on how to best deal with these and related issues.

A significant number of NGOs in the region are incorporating reproductive health in their existing activities as well as reproductive health and sex education for adolescents. Notable examples are found in Sri Lanka (Sarvodaya and Mahila Samiti), Maldives (Island Women's Committees) and Nepal (Mothers' Club, Sristi-CEDPA and RUWDUC).

Conclusion: Programme Needs to Achieve the Integration of Reproductive Health Components

As anticipated in the Bali Declaration in 1992 and in the Programme of Action of the International Conference on Population and Development in 1994, the attainment of integrated reproductive health services as an important contribution to achieving improved reproductive health is a complex process. However, in the years since these two meetings considerable experience has been accumulating regarding how this might be achieved. It is clearly important that an environment conducive to the aims of reproductive health should apply within countries, and a critical aspect of this is appreciation of gender issues in relation to sustainable development.

More narrowly, with regard to the integration of components of reproductive health services, management and administrative issues related to integration, decentralization and logistic support for an integrated reproductive health service, appropriate development of human resources and relevant management information systems are crucial. From a technical service delivery viewpoint it is important that clear and explicit priorities be determined for the particular components of reproductive health care and that these should include critical assessments not only of the cost-effectiveness of specific interventions, but of the resources needed to provide packages of reproductive health care and how these resources will be generated and managed.

It continues to be important that experience with the implementation of integrated reproductive health care be monitored and evaluated in order that successes can be documented and replicated more widely.

21

Reproductive Health in Policy and Practice

Case Studies from Brazil, India, Morocco, and Uganda

At the International Conference on Population and Development (ICPD) held in Cairo in 1994, representatives of 180 countries reached a new consensus about how world population issues should be approached. They agreed that population policies should address social development beyond family planning, especially the advancement of women, and that family planning should be provided in the context of comprehensive reproductive health care. Such care includes:

a) family planning;
b) safe pregnancy and delivery services;
c) prevention and treatment of sexually transmitted infections (STIs); and
d) information and counseling on sexuality; and other women's health services.

Earlier UN conferences had looked at population from a broad, societal point of view, emphasizing problems such as rapid population growth and the slow pace of economic development in southern countries. Many governments supported family planning programmes as a means to address these issues. By the time of the Cairo conference, there was growing concern that some policies and programmes placed too much of an emphasis on reducing fertility and population growth and focused too narrowly on a single intervention: family planning programmes. Critics maintained that these programmes were insufficiently concerned with improving the lives of individuals, especially women. The heart of the Cairo agenda is simple: Responding to the needs of individuals will help solve the aggregate problem of rapid population growth. Addressing a broad array of individual needs, however, is complicated in practice. The Cairo Programme of Action contains a few hundred recommendations in the areas of health, development, and social welfare. Since the Cairo conference, governments and NGOs have faced the challenge of how to implement the new agenda on the ground. And few models exist in the developing world for providing comprehensive and complex services in resource-poor settings.

Nevertheless, in some countries, attempts have been made to integrate family planning with other services, to eliminate contraceptive "targets" as a means of measuring staff performance, to develop new reproductive health strategies, and to revise laws affecting women's status and rights. In an effort to capture some of these experiences, the Population Reference Bureau (PRB) coordinated a project to conduct case studies in four countries:

a) Brazil,
b) India,
c) Morocco, and
d) Uganda.

The Broader Context

Major changes are taking place in much of the developing world that affect the context in which international population and health policies are conceived and implemented. Among the most important changes are: greater openness in political decision-making; decentralization of authority from national to local governments; the increasing political importance of women's issues; and institutional and financial reforms in the health sector.

The Policy-making Process

Brazil, Morocco, India, and Uganda all demonstrate increased openness in political decision-making, decentralization of authority from national to local governments, and growth in the importance of NGOs, also known as "civil society." In some ways, these changes complicate the decision-making process, but they make it more likely that citizens will affect and accept the decisions that are made and press for their implementation.

In Brazil, the case study authors note that "*Since the 1980s, democratization has definitely lengthened the policy decision-making process. But it has also given voice to the advocacy community and allowed for debate of the reproductive health and rights agenda. The adoption of this agenda by other actors and voices would not have occurred without open political debate about its meanings*".

Similarly, the devolution of authority from central to local or regional governments entails both challenges and opportunities. Since the community participates more directly in setting priorities, developing programmes, and allocating resources, decentralization should result in programmes and policies that are more responsive to local needs. But responsibilities may be transferred before local governments have the capacity to manage them, and local communities may be slow to perceive or act on national-level priorities, for example, reducing the spread of HIV infections. As a result, progress on national objectives is bound to be uneven across states and localities. Still, the process of decentralization is unlikely to be reversed in the foreseeable future, and it poses an interesting challenge to UN conference organizers. National representatives engage in conference discussions and sign on to international agreements, yet local authorities are increasingly responsible for implementing these agreements. They may have quite different priorities.

Recently, NGOs have grown in number and influence in the policymaking process. In Morocco, 76 NGOs (one-third established since 1994) now work on issues related to women and development. In other countries, NGOs are credited with influencing the latest generation of national policies. Partnerships that broaden the base of support for new policies and programmes are also increasing—for example, collaboration between government and NGOs and cooperation within the NGO sector among academics, advocates, and service organizations. And there is no question that national and international policy meetings have become livelier and more diverse in the 1990s with the growing presence of NGOs.

The Political Importance of Women

Thanks largely to the activities of women's rights advocates, the situation of women has moved to the forefront of both national and international policy debates. Since the Cairo and Beijing conferences, there is greater discussion of gender issues, or the differences in men and women's socially prescribed roles. Governments and donor agencies increasingly acknowledge the inferior legal, social, and economic positions of women and their detrimental effects on national development. As a result, many new policies and programmes attempt to reduce gender inequalities.

There are signs of real change in the status of women—at least on paper. Uganda's new Constitution guarantees the political participation of women by reserving 30 percent of all electoral seats for them. The government has also adopted several other new policies: The National Gender Policy aims to take into account gender in all aspects of development; the Land Act provides a new mechanism for women to own land; and the Universal Primary Education policy reserves one-half of all school enrollments for girls. Similarly, recent legislation in India reserves one-third of the seats on local governing bodies for women, and Brazil has established a quota reserving 30 percent of seats for women on national and local parliamentary bodies. It will take time, however, for communities to adapt to these changes, and a number of social barriers stand in the way of their effective implementation.

Reforms in the Health Sector

Equally dramatic changes are taking place in the organization and financing of national health systems. Reform is often a condition of receiving funds from international financial institutions, such as the World Bank, and is also prompted by the increased need for economic austerity. As in the case of political decentralization, health sector reform may assist or detract from progress in meeting reproductive health goals.

On the positive side, reforms often aim to channel public subsidies toward the neediest citizens and emphasize the provision of low-cost primary health care services over expensive, high-tech interventions. Also, in most settings, health reform requires managers to consider more integrated approaches to service delivery than in the past. Such reforms are generally consistent with the Cairo agenda. On the other hand, in striving to allocate overall health resources more effectively, planners weigh the various components of reproductive health care (family planning, prevention of sexually transmitted diseases, and maternity care) against a host of other health needs (combating malaria, tuberculosis and childhood diseases, and dealing with problems related to smoking, drug abuse, and injuries). Some elements of reproductive health may receive priority attention in government budgets if needs appear urgent and affect a large proportion of the population; other elements may not. Those who hope to influence resource allocation for reproductive health need to understand and participate in debates on health financing, including priority setting.

Box 1: The Women's Movement in Morocco

Despite a constitutional guarantee of equal political and legal rights, Moroccan women suffer great disadvantages. They are much more likely than men to be illiterate (90 percent versus 60 percent in rural areas and 50 percent versus 25 percent in urban areas); far less likely to participate in the labor force (one-third of women versus 80 percent of men); and have fewer rights than men in relation to marriage, divorce, and inheritance. These disadvantages are codified in the personal status laws and reinforced by social custom.

Recently, important legal and policy changes have taken place. The government established a special ministry to deal with issues related to childhood and the family. NGOs focusing on women's issues and advancement, including micro-credit schemes for poor women, have proliferated. The personal status laws have been revised, and steps have been taken to try to combat illiteracy and reduce domestic violence. The changes in the personal status laws mandate that marriage may be concluded only with the wife's full consent, that polygamy may be practiced only with the knowledge of the first and subsequent wives, and create legal restrictions on the husband's right to unilaterally divorce his wife. Advocates for women criticize these reforms on the grounds they do not go far enough, and it is likely that the changes have not yet affected women's daily lives, especially in rural and isolated areas.

Policies in Support of Reproductive Health

While they are but one element in programme implementation, national policies provide important impetus and guidance to local initiatives. The case studies analyze the evolution of national reproductive health policies over the last five years. In all four countries, governments have drafted and debated an impressive array of new legislation and strategy documents.

The Indian case study provides the most dramatic example of a major national policy shift—the removal of centrally mandated targets from the national family planning programme. Several factors contributed to this change. The government recognized that India's family planning programme had stalled in terms of lowering the birth rate. The focus on sterilization ignored the birth-spacing needs of younger women, and the target system contributed to false reporting of contraceptive use. At the same time, women's groups and NGOs were increasingly voicing concerns about the poor quality of services and their heavy reliance on sterilization as the main method of contraception. The international donor community also strongly supported a rethinking of the government's policy. Soon after the Cairo conference, health officials in India experimented with the removal of method-specific targets and, in 1996, the government abolished the use of nationally prescribed targets for acceptors of different family planning methods throughout the country.

In Brazil, a flurry of policy debates preceded and followed the Cairo conference, the most heated of which concerned abortion. In Morocco, changes in policies affecting women's status have marked the most significant departures from the past. In Uganda, in addition to the changes noted on the preceding page, new population and adolescent policies have been drafted since 1994.

Brazil and India offer insights into the time and process necessary for policies to be diffused and adopted throughout an entire country. In Brazil, it has taken over 10 years for health reform to move from the level of national policy to real change on the ground. Key ingredients of progress observed after 1995 have been the persistence of the advocacy community and the strengthening of local health systems. In India, where national policy changes were debated very little before they were decreed, evidence from communities indicates that it may be some time before the changes are widely understood and adopted in practice. Local health care providers are just beginning to understand what the policy changes mean and how new procedures might work. The contrast between Brazil and India suggests that wider policy debate leads to wider acceptance of policy changes.

Not surprisingly, case study interviews reveal that a relatively small number of government officials and NGO representatives are fully conversant with the Cairo recommendations. In general, the responsibility for implementing reproductive health programmes has been primarily with health officials whose mandate has expanded from maternal and child health programmes, including family planning, to include reproductive health more broadly. Other ministries, such as those concerned with population, women's affairs, or youth, have contributed to policy development. But they have generally been in weaker positions than the ministries of health to initiate and define new policies.

The Cairo Programme of Action has provided policymakers at all levels with language and concepts to help them promote the new reproductive health agenda. In Ceará, Brazil, the director of the women's health programme observed: "*We have constantly used Cairo language in our dialogues with health managers, health agencies, and health professionals. Cairo language has been a critical political instrument*". Cairo has also produced greater high-level political awareness of and support for reproductive health; a donor community willing to support new initiatives; and increased national debate and NGO activity. Where health ministries have taken advantage of these opportunities, concrete changes can be seen.

Box 2: The Abortion Debate in Brazil

In Brazil, the adoption of the Cairo agenda did not represent a major policy shift, as the country had adopted a comprehensive reproductive health programme a decade earlier. The conference served, however, to amplify the Brazilian debate on abortion and expand access to abortion services. The Programme of Action called for the provision of safe abortion services where legal and for compassionate care for the complications arising from unsafe abortion, whether legal or not.

Reproductive health and rights advocates in Brazil had worked since 1985 to ensure access to abortion services in the two cases permitted by law: when a woman's health was at risk or she had been raped. Doctors were reluctant to provide the procedures, both because of a lack of information about the legal provisions and because of their own personal convictions. In the early 1990s, a legislative provision was submitted to the Brazilian Congress, calling on the public health system to make abortion universally available in these narrowly defined, but legal, circumstances. In 1995, in the aftermath of the Cairo and Beijing conferences, a new "right-to-life" provision was presented to Congress. A special committee debated and rejected the provision, sparking a heated public debate on abortion. In 1997, a congressional committee approved access to legal abortion, prompting both conservative reactions and a national mail-in campaign to lawmakers on the part of reproductive rights advocates. *On the one hand*, the debate has led to harsh confrontations between reproductive rights advocates and conservative religious coalitions. On the other hand, open debate has increased understanding among health managers and professionals of the need for and meaning of legal abortion services. As one health manager in Recife said, "We have used the [Cairo] argument: abortion is a public health problem, when it is legal it must be safe, and incomplete abortion must be subject to adequate and compassionate care." Since 1994, the public health system has expanded support for legal abortion services from two to 12 locations and has made improvements in the quality of post-abortion care.

Improvements in Reproductive Health Services

The Cairo Programme of Action defined reproductive health in a comprehensive fashion for the first time in an international policy document. The definition states that "reproductive health is a state of complete physical, mental, and social well-being and not merely the absence of disease or infirmity...."

It goes on to state that reproductive health care should enhance individual rights, including "the right to decide freely and responsibly" the number and spacing of one's children, and the right to a "satisfying and safe sex life."

Operationally, reproductive health care encompasses many elements, including family planning information and services, prenatal care, safe delivery and postnatal care, prevention and treatment of infertility, abortion (where not against the law), care for complications of unsafe abortion, prevention and treatment of STIs, including HIV/AIDS, elimination of harmful practices such as female genital mutilation, and other women's health services such as diagnosis and treatment for breast and cervical cancers. The Programme of Action calls on all countries to provide these services through the primary health care system by 2015.

An agenda of such ambitious proportions cannot be implemented overnight, especially in poor countries. All the case study countries have made significant strides toward the Cairo goals, but none has been able to address all of its elements. "We could not take Cairo wholesale, even if we wanted to," said a programme manager in Uganda, "until the systems are ready and people are in place to handle the workload." The comprehensive definition has been used mainly in developing national strategy documents; at the operational level, each country has tackled those elements where improvements seem most feasible.

Pre-Cairo Efforts Boosted

The Cairo conference revitalized efforts that were already under way to improve the quality of family planning services. These efforts include: offering clients a greater choice of contraceptive methods; improving the ability of practitioners to provide information and counseling; and reaching underserved groups, such as adolescents and men. As noted in Box 4, the most radical change in service delivery has occurred in India, where the government has abolished centrally determined programme targets.

Important changes have occurred in the area of contraceptive choice. In India, recent service statistics and interviews with providers reveal that the longstanding reliance on sterilization is beginning to change. Women are now more aware of reversible methods of contraception and are beginning to ask for them. In Brazil, primary health programmes are providing more reversible methods to underserved populations, and sterilization procedures may decline now that the government has placed ceilings on the numbers of Caesarean sections that can be performed in public hospitals. (Women often seek the two procedures at once.) In Morocco, where the family planning programme had provided mainly oral contraceptives, interviews with women reveal an increased awareness of other methods, such as intrauterine devices and hormonal injections.

In terms of the broad array of services included under the rubric of reproductive health, attempts were being made before Cairo to increase access to services to prevent the spread of STIs and to ensure "safe motherhood," including care for obstetric emergencies. Safe motherhood initiatives have existed for some time but have received relatively little funding or high-level attention. The following efforts reflect renewed commitments to improving maternal health:

- In Uganda, public education has increased awareness among midwives, traditional birth attendants, health practitioners, and community leaders of the importance of safe pregnancy and delivery. New systems of supervision and referral are being tested to speed transport of women to hospitals when they need emergency care.
- The Moroccan health ministry has added nutritional supplements in iron and iodine to address the high incidence of anemia among pregnant women. It has also strengthened infrastructure and training at hospitals that deal with obstetric emergencies. Both prenatal and delivery services in Brazil have improved; between 1995-97 alone, prenatal consultations in the country rose by 51 percent.

Post-ICPD Programme Initiatives

As interest in reproductive health grew in the aftermath of the Cairo conference, governments and NGOs developed a number of new programme initiatives. Some were made possible by new funding from donors; others emerged within existing health budgets. Many initiatives are too new to be evaluated, but their existence deserves mention:

- In 1995, the Moroccan government developed a national policy and programme to address STIs/HIV. The programme includes free anonymous screening and collaboration with NGOs in service provision.
- In Brazil, the public health system is now supporting legal abortion services in 12 locations and strengthening services that provide post-abortion care. Linkages have been built between the reproductive health and HIV/AIDS prevention programmes. In 1996, a pilot cervical cancer screening project began in five state capitals, and in 1998, a national cervical cancer prevention programme was launched.
- In Uganda, special outreach programmes for young people are operating in most districts in the country, encouraging safer sex and

responsible parenthood. A new programme to replace the practice of female genital mutilation with safer, alternative rituals has shown some early success.

- Along with abolishing targets, the Indian government has instituted a new programme, the "reproductive and child health" initiative.

Areas Still to be Addressed

Some of the areas that have received the least attention appear to be those that health planners consider unaffordable (e.g., treatment of AIDS, cancers, or infertility), or those that are deemed controversial or socially unacceptable (e.g., addressing unsafe abortion or providing services to adolescents). In Brazil, the wealthiest country in our study, most elements of reproductive health have been introduced or tested at some level of the public health system. But case-study authors note that programme components need stronger linkages, and greater efforts are needed to ensure the quality of care in the private sector, which serves nearly one-third of women.

On socially controversial issues, even where little progress has been made in terms of programmes and services, there are signs that public discussions are now taking place. For example, violence against women, rape, and male responsibility in the family are increasingly discussed in public meetings, and some pilot projects have begun to address them. In Brazil, the expansion of abortion services in the case of rape is taking place under the framework of gender-violence prevention. But in general, it will take time before these new initiatives will be fully integrated in large-scale programmes.

Addressing Adolescent Needs

Adolescents deserve special mention both because of their large and growing numbers and because they are often sexually active and are therefore exposed to the risks of unwanted pregnancies, unsafe abortions, and STIs. Unfortunately, public health systems in most countries have neglected their needs.

In Uganda, where the rate of pregnancy among adolescents is one of the highest in Africa, UN agencies, NGOs, and private foundations have supported small, community-based programmes to provide reproductive health information and services to teens in many parts of the country. The Ugandan government now has a draft adolescent health policy to provide guidance to health care providers and to incorporate adolescent programmes into mainstream health services and other relevant programmes. In general, however, adolescents do not seek care or will not use the same services as adults. Or health providers may be too overworked to reach out to young people and may not approve of their behaviour. In Morocco, the government does not officially support reproductive health services for teens because of religious prohibitions on premarital sex, but some NGOs have developed special activities oriented toward adolescent needs.

In Brazil, a national adolescent health policy was established in 1988. Although its implementation has been uneven across the country, some best practices can be found. In Ceará, the women's health and adolescent programmes are working closely together, and in Recife and Cabo, all family health programmes have specific activities for teenagers. There is evidence that when comprehensive care is offered—including pregnancy care, postnatal care, and access to a range of contraceptive methods—the teens develop a strong attachment with the service. As one nurse reported, "They hear everything, they follow what we say, they become like daughters".

Service Integration

The Programme of Action calls for better linkages among all reproductive health services to address individual health needs in a more holistic fashion. Service integration is not entirely new in any of the countries studied; most had previously combined family planning and maternal and child health programmes in the public health system. Nevertheless, there are signs that service integration is increasing, and this integration has taken different forms.

In Uganda, health centers now provide, on a daily basis, family planning, prenatal and postnatal care, STI/HIV counseling, nutrition education, and childhood immunizations. Previously, specialized providers had offered different services only on designated days. Clinic nurses see this integration as a "mixed blessing." On the one hand, their workload has increased without a comparable increase in pay. On the other hand, they report that integration saves time for both providers and clients, and the increased responsibilities have enhanced the status of providers. Interestingly, the case study notes that integration has proceeded more rapidly in health centers than in hospitals, though the latter provide a wider range of services. Reports in Uganda also show that more clients are using the family planning and STI treatment services—both previously stigmatized in some communities—now that they are part of a broader package.

In Brazil, the women's health programme (Programa de Assistencia Integral a Saude da Mulher, or PAISM), designed over a decade ago but not implemented, is now integrated in the public health system as part of a larger strategy of basic health care. Originally designed to meet a range of reproductive health needs, it operated until 1996 in relative isolation from the national health system. Through the process of health reform and decentralization, the programme's concepts have begun to be incorporated into basic health services at the municipal level. In different ways, the Uganda and Brazil cases show that innovations may advance more quickly and effectively at lower levels of the health system.

Box 3: Combating STIs and HIV in Uganda

The HIV/AIDS epidemic in Uganda has posed a major challenge to social and economic development and prompted an unprecedented government response. It is estimated that 1.5 million Ugandans are infected with HIV (out of a total population of 21 million) and that one million children have been orphaned by AIDS deaths. The age group most affected by AIDS (ages 15 to 50) occupies a critical position in family support systems, the labor force, and leadership in society.

The government recognized early the devastating impact that AIDS would have on development, and the key role of STIs in fueling its spread. With financial support from major donors, it instituted a multi-sectoral strategy, beginning in the late 1980s, involving the Ministries of Health, Labor, Gender, Defense, Education, Information, and Agriculture. Programmes include public information campaigns, research, voluntary testing and counseling, safe blood for transfusions, school health programmes, home-based care of people living with AIDS, and a nationwide campaign to treat STIs. The STI/HIV control programme is supported by the World Bank and emphasizes outreach to underserved groups, especially young people, and involvement of parents and local communities.

The Uganda AIDS Commission, which coordinates policies and programmes throughout the country, includes parliamentarians, government officials, and religious leaders. The case study authors note that, "The deliberate government openness to the STI/HIV problem has facilitated collaborative research in HIV/AIDS care and control from which the international community stands to benefit."

These efforts are seeing results. Almost the entire adult population is now aware of the dangers of HIV and, in some parts of the country, rates of infection among women seeking prenatal care have decreased by one-third or more. Moreover, the STI/HIV campaign has led to greater openness in dealing with sexual health problems and has increased the commitment of the government to providing reproductive health services to every segment of the population.

Women's Perceptions of Services

As well as documenting service improvements, each case study tried to find out whether women thought the services were meeting more of their needs. The researchers received mixed responses:

- There are small signs that improvements are benefiting women, as noted in the examples above. In Uganda, the integration of reproductive health services in local health centers has made life easier for some women: One pregnant woman said, "These days it is much better coming here because they treat for everything daily … it saves money." In India, providers and clients noted that the reduced pressure to achieve family planning targets meant more time to discuss family health matters. In Brazil, innovative approaches to post-abortion care have been a breakthrough in terms of responding to women's health and emotional needs.

- On the other hand, the studies contain many examples of women's complaints about the inadequate treatment or lack of information they receive in health facilities. Research on client satisfaction in Morocco revealed a number of communication problems between providers and clients. Some of these problems stemmed from the hierarchical (superior) attitudes of providers, and from a lack of female practitioners. Women's criticisms revealed two major areas of frustration:
    - "Why don't they explain the details of contraceptive methods to us?" and
    - "Why are we only offered family planning and not other care?"
- It would be hard to exaggerate the importance of improving client-provider relations along with improvements in other aspects of services. As programmes develop, complaints about services may actually increase, as women become more educated about what they want and need from the health system. Women's complaints and requests may then become the main impetus for addressing weaknesses in services.

Box 4: The Target-Free Approach in Two States in India

In Tamil Nadu and Rajasthan, family planning targets are no longer handed down from the central government but are determined locally with the help of an eligible couples register. A new community-assessment manual helps grassroots workers identify couples' needs for family planning by segmenting them in terms of how many surviving children they have and whether they currently use contraception. An auxiliary nurse-midwife in Tamil Nadu explained that "When we enumerate the eligible couples in our population, we ask a question about the number of living children and, on the basis of that, we advise women with one child to use a temporary method and those who have more children to undergo sterilization."

Different states and communities determine the family planning workload differently, but they do translate the workload into targets and expect the workers to achieve them. The needs of the clients and the opinion of the health worker are still secondary to the process. Nevertheless, both clients and health workers report some satisfaction with the new approach. Clients report that, "The health worker is not pushing contraceptives alone." Workers report that targets are now more realistic and that they are not scolded for not meeting them, as they had been in the past. In particular, some workers feel that the former family planning targets did not allow them to concentrate on other maternal and child health services. "Now the pressure is off and we are able to inquire about women's health, their children's health. We are also better accepted in the community. People do not identify us only as family planning workers but consult us about ailments of all family members."

In Tamil Nadu, training in the new reproductive and child health approach has been initiated and includes previously neglected topics such as quality of care, informed choice, and assessment of community needs. Rajasthan has only just begun retraining health workers. Community-level planning has not developed in either state to the extent the central government envisioned, and it is too early to tell how well the new concepts will take hold, especially in a country as large and diverse as India. Nevertheless, government officials in these two states are making attempts to redress some of the limitations of the old approach.

Factors that Help or Hinder Change

The case studies identify a number of factors that have facilitated changes in policies and programmes related to reproductive health. Many of these factors relate to changes in the social, political, and economic context in which programmes operate, such as health reform, NGO advocacy efforts, and high-level political commitment.

In Brazil, health reforms have paved the way for improved reproductive health services by establishing a universal health care system that emphasizes decentralized decision-making, equity and access, and primary health care. Moreover, Brazilian advocates persevered for years in keeping reproductive health and rights on the national agenda, despite short-term setbacks. In Morocco, a growing civil society—in particular, groups dedicated to advancing the status of women and addressing HIV/AIDS—has helped to advance the reproductive health agenda.

High-level national leadership and support from international donors have also played an important role-for example, the forthrightness of the Ugandan government in addressing the HIV/AIDS crisis and the recognition of the Indian government that radical change was needed in its family planning programme. Moreover, no progress would be possible without an openness to change on the part of managers and front-line workers in the health system—many of whom have shown a willingness to consider new ideas and approaches and a commitment to improving the services offered to clients.

The studies also describe fundamental barriers to improving reproductive health, which affect some countries more than others:

- Bureaucratic divisions and poor communication within health ministries (e.g., between departments concerned with family planning and STIs) and among different government ministries (e.g., health and women's affairs) impede the implementation of holistic approaches to improving health and reducing gender inequalities.
- Health provider attitudes are slow to change. Many public sector employees are underpaid and overworked; some are said to show little concern for the needs of the clients that they serve. In some places,

institutional cultures have never placed a high value on individual or "consumer" rights.

- Health ministries, medical schools, and training programmes tend to emphasize the technical aspects of reproductive health and give inadequate attention to the social context in which health decisions are made (for example, the inability of women to seek urgent medical help in their husband's absence, or to negotiate condom use to protect themselves from STIs).
- Governments are often reluctant to confront controversial issues such as abortion, adolescent sexuality, or STI/HIV prevention, because of opposition from traditional or conservative groups.
- In many countries and regions within countries, infrastructure and human resources are extremely weak. Remote and poorly educated communities often have little accurate information about reproductive health problems and the means to address them.
- Every service improvement and new programme initiative requires training or retraining health personnel. Upgrading the skills of thousands of health personnel is a mammoth undertaking that will take much time.

The progress that has been made seems all the more remarkable, given such barriers. A final barrier is the inadequacy of financial resources and the misuse of existing funds, both of which prevent many improvements from taking place.

Resources for Reproductive Health

The case studies examine trends in reproductive health expenditures over the past few years, including allocation among programme areas and attempts to target particular groups. The analysis sheds light on the priorities and roles of government, the private sector (NGOs, commercial organizations, and consumers), and international donors.

Levels and Trends in Overall Funding

The Cairo Programme of Action called for a major increase in worldwide spending for reproductive health programmes, from around US$5 billion in the early 1990s to US$17 billion by the year 2000. These totals include spending from all sources (government, consumers, and donors). The large increase was needed for several reasons: to improve the quality of existing programmes, to add new programmes (e.g., treatment of STIs), to meet increased demand for services, and to accommodate the growing number of people of reproductive age.

The case studies document some increases in government and donor funding, but not of the magnitude envisioned in Cairo. The studies reveal less about private spending, leaving us with an incomplete picture of resource flows. While government expenditures are usually published annually, health spending by private individuals is only measured periodically in surveys. Moreover, it is difficult to obtain detailed data on either public or private expenditures—for example, breakdowns that would distinguish family planning from other reproductive health services.

Information on total health spending provides some parameters within which to consider possibilities for reproductive health improvements. Annual per capita health spending varies widely, from a low of US$12 in India and Uganda to US$320 in Brazil. The differences are striking and must be kept in mind when reviewing progress to date. In Uganda, reproductive health care consumes about 60 percent of the government's primary health care budget. But one or two dollars per person buys little modern health care, even accounting for the fact that salaries are low.

With regard to funding trends, the Brazilian government has approved budget increases for the health sector each year since 1995 and set aside fairly substantial funds for service improvements in 1997, even during a period of economic austerity and health sector reform. In India and Morocco, there has been consistent growth in the government's health budget, but after accounting for inflation and population growth, per capita increases have been minimal or nil. In Uganda, the government has had trouble fully funding its budgetary commitments in the health sector because of weak tax collections.

International donors have committed funds for new reproductive health initiatives in Uganda, India, and Morocco. In India, the World Bank is supporting the new Reproductive and Child Health approach, and in Morocco and Uganda, bilateral and multilateral donors have underwritten much of the upgrading of infrastructure, personnel training, and pilot projects. In all cases, the governments are expected to finance staff salaries and most operating costs.

Investment Trade-Offs

While more resources are needed, the case studies provide evidence that existing funds could be used more effectively. As noted in the Brazil study, "Local level managers often say that limited financial resources are not the major obstacle to improving reproductive health services. In their evaluation, the commitment of managers, the training and attitude of health professionals, and the '*curative biases*' of the system are more relevant at this stage". A number of imbalances in the allocation of resources appear in one or more of the country studies:

- Some public health systems have devoted more resources to relatively costly curative care in hospitals than to cost-effective preventive services in local health centers. The result is that a few people receive expensive treatments, while a great many have little or no access to health care at all.

- Relatively well-off urban dwellers often consume disproportionate shares of public health resources because they live close to facilities and are more likely to seek care. The poor and those living in remote and rural areas have least access and are therefore least likely to benefit from public health subsidies.
- Investments in infrastructure (clinics and equipment) have not always been matched by equivalent investments in personnel and training. Facilities may then be unable to operate or may operate with staff lacking the necessary motivation and skills.
- Some health systems require doctors—whose services are scarce and expensive—to provide contraceptives and other reproductive health services that could safely be provided by nurses or paramedics.

While some imbalances stem from habits or rigidities in the system, others stem from different judgments about priorities, efficiency, and equity. Greater public debate, decentralization of health authority, and public scrutiny of funding decisions may help ensure adequate discussion of these issues, identify obvious instances of waste, and promote more effective use of resources.

22

Components of Reproductive Health Programmes

Reproductive Health and Rights

In September 1994 in Cairo, 184 governments endorsed a historic plan to achieve a balance between the world's people and its resources. For the first time, an international agreement on population made the reproductive health and rights of women central. The International Conference on Population and Development agreed that universal access to reproductive health care should be achieved by the year 2015. The challenge before policy-makers, programme managers and advocates is to persuade governments, energize donors, and enable women's groups and other non-governmental organizations to ensure that the agreements made in Cairo are fully implemented.

What is Reproductive Health Care?

Reproductive health care seeks to meet the health needs of women and men associated with sexuality and child bearing. Programme goals and the constellation of services encompass, and go beyond conventional family planning, and maternal-child-health care.

Components of Reproductive Health Care Include:

- Counseling about sexuality, pregnancy, contraception, abortion, infertility, infection, and disease;
- Education on sexuality and gender relations;
- Prevention, screening and treatment of reproductive tract infections, sexually transmitted diseases (STDs), including HIV/AIDS, and gynecological problems;
- Fully informed, voluntary choice among a range of contraceptive methods;
- Prevention and treatment of infertility;

- Safe abortion services;
- Prenatal care, supervised delivery, and post-partum care; and
- Health services for infants and children.

Quality of Care is a Priority, and is Ensured by:

- Maintaining high standards of technical competence;
- Treating clients with respect and compassion;
- Designing service delivery to meet clients' needs; and
- Providing follow-up care.

The International Conference on Population and Development estimated that $17 billion each year will be needed by the year 2000 to provide universal access to reproductive health services in resource-poor countries.

What are Reproductive Rights?

Reproductive rights embrace existing human rights. Reproductive rights include:

- The right of all couples and individuals to decide freely and responsibly the number, spacing and timing of their children, and to have the information and means to do so;
- The right to attain the highest standard of sexual and reproductive health, and the right to services and information that make this possible;
- The right to make decisions concerning reproduction free of discrimination, coercion, and violence.

How Can Reproductive Health Become a Reality?

- *By modifying existing family planning and health programmes to*:
    - Expand services to address women's multiple reproductive and sexual health needs;
    - Intensify staff supervision and training, and use systems that reward good quality care, not simply numbers of clients served;
    - Design services to protect women's rights and foster their empowerment;
    - Provide information and services to women who are older or younger than reproductive age, regardless of marital status;
    - Encourage and support men to take their share of responsibility for sexual and reproductive behaviour, prenatal, maternal and child health, child rearing, STD and HIV/AIDS infection, and violence; and
    - Invest in research to fill critical gaps in technology and services including
- *By Respecting Certain Principles*:
    - Programmes and services must be designed to suit particular

circumstances, and ensure that these services are accessible and affordable to all women;
  - Programme design and implementation must involve women at all stages; and
  - Programmes should support both women and men to share responsibility for their sexual behaviour, their fertility, and the heath and well-being of their partners and children.
- *By Making Better Use of Resources*:
  - It is not necessary to wait for new money, new data or additional staff;
  - Existing resources can be used more imaginatively and efficiently;
  - Services can be integrated and connected instead of separate; and
  - Budget priorities can be reordered.

How Can Reproductive Rights Be Ensured?

- Governments, donors and the community must take concerted actions to guarantee that all couples and individuals who want reproductive and sexual health services get them;
- Laws and policies must be established and enforced to prevent discrimination, coercion and violence associated with sexuality and reproduction;
- Women and men must work together to know their rights, hold their governments accountable for protecting these rights, and build support for these rights through public education and advocacy.

These concepts of reproductive health and rights are derived from the work of international women's health advocates worldwide.

Sexual Health

Overview

Sexual health means having a responsible, satisfying, and safe sex life. Achieving sexual health requires a positive approach to human sexuality and mutual respect between partners. By recognizing sexual health—and sexual rights—health and education systems can help prevent and treat the consequences of sexual violence, coercion and discrimination, and ensure that healthy human sexuality is experienced by all people and is accepted as part of their overall well-being. An expert group to the World Health Organization has described sexual health as "the integration of the somatic, emotional, intellectual, and social aspects of sexual well-being in ways that are positively enriching and that enhance personality, communication and love" (1976).

What is Sexual Health?

The basic elements of sexual health include:

- A sexual life free from disease, injury, violence, disability, unnecessary pain, or risk of death.
- A sexual life free from fear shame, guilt, and false beliefs about sexuality.
- The capacity to experience and control one's own sexuality and reproduction.

Ensuring sexual health requires:

- Respect for each individual's right to bodily integrity—the right to control one's own body.
- Support for all the emotional and social dimensions of sexuality that enhance well-being and personal relationships.
- Equal balance of power in sexual relations.
- Access to safe, good quality, and affordable sexual and reproductive health information and services.

Assuring Sexual Health

Sexual health for women and men is assured by policies and programmes that empower women and encourage men to take responsibility for their own sexual behaviour. The Programme of Action adopted by 184 countries at the International Conference on Population and Development (ICPD) in Cairo in 1994 informs debate on how to better define and understand sexual health, as well as the steps necessary to achieve sexual health for women and men everywhere, including:

- *Achieve Equality in Sexual Relations*: Sexuality and gender relations lie at the heart of reproductive and sexual health, yet most health and education programmes and policies still reinforce different standards for men and women, as well as male dominance. The ICPD Programme of Action states:

  > Equal relations between men and women in matters of sexual relations and reproduction, including full respect for the physical integrity of the human body, require mutual respect and willingness to accept responsibility for the consequences of sexual behaviour. Responsible sexual behaviour, sensitivity and equity in gender relations, particularly when instilled during the formative years, enhance and promote respectful and harmonious partnerships between men and women. (para. 7.34)
- *End Violence against Women*: Every woman has the right to be free from violence in both the public and private spheres. When this right is infringed, women cannot freely enjoy their basic human rights. The

Vienna Declaration and Programme of Action adopted at the World Conference on Human Rights in 1993 recognizes the:

... importance of working towards the elimination of violence against women in public and private life, the elimination of all forms of sexual harassment, exploitation and trafficking in women, the elimination of gender-bias in the administration of justice and the eradication of any conflicts which may arise between the rights of women and the harmful effects of certain traditional and customary practices, cultural prejudices and religious extremism. (para. II. 38)

- *Change Male Roles*: Many men do not take responsibility for their own sexual behaviour, their fertility, the transmission of STDs, and the well-being of their sexual partners and the children they father. The ICPD Programme of Action states:

  Special efforts should be made to emphasize men's shared responsibility and promote their active involvement in responsible parenthood, sexual and reproductive behaviour, including family planning; prenatal, maternal and child health; prevention of sexually transmitted diseases, including HIV; prevention of unwanted and high-risk pregnancies; shared control and contribution to family income, children's education, health and nutrition; and recognition and promotion of the equal value of children of both sexes. (para. 4.27)

- **Ensure that health and education systems deal with sexuality and gender relations:** Parents and communities need to invest in health and education systems that place a value on creating supportive environments for the exploration of gender relations and sexuality, and that recognize sexuality as good and sexual health as central to overall well-being. The ICPD Programme of Action says that:

  Recognizing the rights, duties and responsibilities of parents and other persons legally responsible for adolescents to provide, in a manner consistent with the evolving capacities of the adolescent, appropriate direction and guidance in sexual and reproductive matters, countries must ensure that the programmes and attitudes of health care providers do not restrict the access of adolescents to appropriate services and the information they need, including on sexually transmitted diseases and sexual abuse. (para 7.45)

Sexual Rights

Overview

Definition and recognition of sexual rights are necessary to prevent sexual violence, coercion and discrimination across the world. Health, education and legal systems can promote sexual rights for all the world's women and men.

What Are Sexual Rights?

Sexual rights embrace basic human rights and include:

- Full respect for the physical integrity of the human body.
- The right to the highest standard of sexual and reproductive health.
- The right to necessary information and services, with full respect for confidentiality.
- The right to make decisions concerning sexuality and reproduction free of discrimination, coercion and violence.

Why is Recognition of Sexual Rights Important?

Recognizing sexual rights will help ensure that women and girls are not subject to:

- Unwanted sexual relations, including unwanted pregnancy and child-bearing;
- Physical, sexual and psychological violence in the community or work place, including sexual abuse, sexual harassment and intimidation, and rape;
- Coercive or unsafe contraceptive services and coercive or unsafe abortion;
- Physical, sexual and psychological violence in the home, including marital rape, battering, imprisonment, and incest;
- Unwanted medical interventions or bodily mutilations, including female genital mutilation;
- Discrimination and violence on the basis of sexual orientation;
- Transmission of STDs and HIV/AIDS; and
- Systematic rape as a weapon of war.

The Basis of Sexual Rights

Sexual rights embrace certain human rights that are already recognized in national laws and international human rights documents:

- Everyone has the right to liberty and security of person. (International Covenant on Civil and Political Rights, article 26.)
- All persons are equal before the law and are entitled without any discrimination to the equal protection of the law. (ICCPR, article 26.)
- No one shall be subject to torture, or to cruel, inhuman or degrading treatment or punishment. (Universal Declaration of Human Rights, article 5, ICCPR, article 7.)

The international community has also said:

- *Cairo 1994*: Countries should act to empower women and should take steps to eliminate inequalities between men and women as soon as possible by... eliminating all practices that discriminate against women; assisting women to establish and realize their rights, including those that relate to reproductive and sexual health. (International Conference on Population and Development, para. 4.4c.)

- *Nairobi 1985*: The ability of women to control their own fertility forms an important basis for the enjoyment of other rights. (Nairobi Forward-Looking Strategies, para. 156.)
- *Mexico City 1975*: The human body, whether that of woman or man, is inviolable and respect for it is a fundamental element of human dignity and freedom. (World Conference of the International Women's Year, article 11.)

Cairo and Beijing

Cairo, 1994

At the International Conference on Population and Development (ICPD), 184 governments reached an unprecedented agreement on a new 20-year Programme of Action to achieve a balance between the world's people and its resources. Previous international agreements set demographic targets for limiting the world's population, and focused on contraceptive services to achieve them. In Cairo, the international community recognized the relationships between consumption and production patterns, economic development, population growth and structure, and environmental degradation. They emphasized the importance of women's sexual and reproductive health and rights over numerical population goals.

The Programme of Action called for reforms in the global economy to place greater emphasis on social development and to support the most vulnerable members of society, including the poor, and especially women, who represent the majority of the world's poor. For the first time, the reproductive rights of women were central to an international agreement on population. This transformation of the meaning of "population" was due in large part to the influence exerted by non-governmental organizations (NGOs), especially women's groups from all over the world.

Beijing, 1995

In Beijing at the United Nations Fourth World Conference on Women, governments reaffirmed and moved beyond what they had agreed on at Cairo. The conference was an acknowledgment that women's issues are the world's issues. The final document, the Platform for Action, reaffirmed the human rights of women and the critical importance of reproductive and sexual health and rights to women's empowerment and to the development of Southern countries.

In Beijing, women served as delegates because they were professionals, experts, elected officials, activists and leaders of women's organizations. From these women, and their diverse perspectives, the overall messages of the conference emerged:

- Equality between men and women is not up for debate: it is desired, essential and will be achieved.
- Coercion, discrimination and violence must be eradicated from the lives of women wherever they occur—in economics, politics, health care and within communities and families.
- The Cairo vision of population—placing the health and well-being of women and their families before demographic goals—is truly global policy.
- Women's rights are human rights.

23

The World After the Beijing and Cairo Conferences

In Beijing at the United Nations Fourth World Conference on Women, governments reaffirmed and moved beyond what they had agreed at recent global conferences on the environment (Rio 1992), human rights (Vienna 1993), population and development (Cairo 1994) and social development (Copenhagen 1995). Indeed, this series of conferences made the achievements in Beijing possible.

The Beijing Conference was a turning point in the world's understanding; an acknowledgment that women's issues are the world's issues, and vice versa. It provided a clear indication of global priorities for the next century, and of women's centrality to them. The Conference's final document, the Platform for Action, demonstrates that the agreements reached in Cairo at the International Conference on Population and Development (ICPD) is accepted global policy. And for the second time in 12 months, countries of the world reaffirmed the human rights of women and the critical importance of reproductive and sexual health and rights to women's empowerment and to development.

Beijing marked the first time a United Nations women's conference had as its central focus the human rights of women-economic, social, cultural, civil and political. Beijing also represents the coming of age of the international women's movement, with women playing key roles in the inter-governmental negotiations as delegates, advisors, and advocates. Since the 1985 UN World Conference on Women in Nairobi, women around the world have mobilized in their communities, countries and internationally to gain access, successfully, to the arenas where policies are made and implemented.

Billed as a conference on equality, peace, and development, the Beijing meeting, at its core, was about eliminating coercion, discrimination, and violence in the public and private lives of women. Governments urged that:

economic and employment policies recognize women's unpaid contributions to the economy, eliminate differentials in pay between men and women for equal work; and women be guaranteed equal access to public office, education, basic health care, and all other aspects of public and private life. In addition, they called for elimination of violence in the home and in public, where rape is not only a crime against the individual, but is still used as a weapon of war. Finally, the governments represented in Beijing reaffirmed what they had agreed in Vienna in 1993, that international human rights laws and standards must not be diluted by religious practices, or tradition when applied to women.

The conference opened with 35 percent of its Platform in "square brackets" because governments could not agree to terms. [Square brackets are placed around language that has not been accepted by consensus, pending further negotiation or, ultimately, reservation by a delegation at the end of the conference. All brackets must be removed by the conference's end; reservations are the means for countries to state on the record that they do not agree with particular sections or words of the final agreement.] Yet, by its final session, the conference had, as Norwegian Prime Minister Gro Harlem Brundtland said in her closing speech, "unbracket[ed] the lives of girls and women." When the negotiations ended, just before dawn on the morning of September 15, governments had agreed to the strongest international document ever detailing the reality of women's lives and which called for sustained and precise action.

A Global Shift

The Fourth World Conference on Women was the culmination of a series of global conferences that caused a re-examination and reshaping of governments' understanding of the role of the international community, as well as the global understanding of development. The agreements reached at the Earth Summit in 1992 and the World Conference on Human Rights in 1993 created momentum for the breakthrough agreements reached at the International Conference on Population and Development (ICPD) in Cairo. There, 184 governments reached an unprecedented consensus on a twenty-year Programme of Action to balance the world's peoples with its resources. The Programme puts women's equality, empowerment, reproductive rights, and sexual health at the center of population and development policies.

Previous international agreements on population have set demographic targets for limiting population growth and have focused on contraceptive services as the method to achieve these goals. By contrast, in Cairo the international community recognized the interrelationships between consumption and production patterns, economic development, population growth and structure, and environmental degradation. Also in Cairo, the understanding of the term "population" was broadened significantly, in large part due to the influence of non-governmental organizations (NGOs), especially women's groups from all over the world.

Impact of the Women's Movement and Southern Leadership

The outcome of the ICPD provoked some conservative delegations to threaten to use the Beijing conference to turn back agreements women had achieved in Cairo. Most of the opposition came from delegations that had not fully accepted the Cairo accord, specifically its provisions on reproductive health and reproductive rights. Such groups included the Holy See, conservative Islamic countries, and several states in Latin America. Despite this challenge, governments of the world were able to achieve a consensus on a Platform for Action that included verbatim language from Cairo (including reproductive and sexual health and reproductive rights), as well as language that extends and operationalizes the Cairo Programme of Action in key areas.

As in Cairo, much of the progress achieved in Beijing was due to the capacity, skill, and tenacity of women's NGOs from all over the world, who worked at regional conferences, preparatory meetings and at the Beijing conference itself to move government delegations towards consensus. Rooted in the experience of domestic campaigns over the last 20 years, the series of international women's conferences (Mexico City, 1975; Copenhagen, 1980; Nairobi, 1985), and the force of women's organizations at the recent global conferences, women had refined an inside-outside lobbying strategy. They gave priority to ensuring that feminists were made members of government delegations, worked with delegations at preparatory meetings, and had crafted specific language for negotiation. Many of the over 7,000 women from NGOs who were accredited to the conference worked as a pressure group, and interpreted the complexity of issues and negotiations to the international media.

Contrary to assertions in the press and by opposition delegations, the bulk of the progress came not from Northern radical feminists, but from women of the South. It was clear, the political fulcrum had shifted from Northern to Southern countries, and from men to women. Consensus on sexual rights, abortion, adolescent access to services, the right to inheritance and succession, and most other issues covered by the Platform for Action were forged primarily by delegates who were neither white, nor liberal, nor necessarily feminist. What really happened is that governments of the world, represented by women delegates, stepped forward to acknowledge the realities of women's lives. Delegates wanted to leave Beijing with a document that reflected those realities and that committed the world's governments to take concrete and effective action to end coercion, discrimination, and violence against women of all forms.

Central to this process was the leadership of Africa which had been given focus and energy by the moral authority of South Africa; the courage of many

Latin American countries in breaking free of the influence of the Vatican hierarchy, and the steadfastness of the Caribbean. These countries placed women in key positions in their delegations who were not swayed from progressive language on human rights, sexuality, and inheritance, among other contentious issues.

The Preparatory Process

The Conference in Beijing was prefaced by a preparatory process that gained momentum over a two year period. Part of the planning for Beijing took place in the context of the ongoing review of implementation of the recommendations of the last women's conference in Nairobi. Unlike other world conferences held in the 1990s, the focus of preparations for Beijing was at the regional level. Five regional conferences were held, in Indonesia, Argentina, Austria, Senegal, and Jordan, focusing on the specific priorities in each region. This process helped Africa, Latin America and the Caribbean, in particular, to work as strong regional groups in Beijing.

In March, 1995, at the annual session of the United Nations Commission on the Status of Women, the draft Platform for Action, compiled by the Conference Secretariat from the five regional conferences, was negotiated for the first time. With only this one chance to negotiate a document never seen in its entirety, the deliberations were tense. This mood was exacerbated by what were widely understood to be deliberate "blocking" tactics by delegations opposed to a constructive agreement on women's equality. Furthermore, many delegations were ill-prepared to negotiate and the Conference Secretariat was afraid of potential controversy. As a result, the draft Platform for Action emerged from the four week preparatory committee process with more than a third of its text unresolved. Among the concepts bracketed were "gender" and the "human rights of women."

Over the summer, a contact group convened to resolve the use of the word "gender" and informal negotiations were held in early August to remove some of the more redundant brackets. Apparently unsettled by the chaos of the preparatory process during the Commission on the Status of Women, diplomats in August tried to bring some order to negotiations, both in terms of process and tone. They were successful.

Indications of a Tide Turned

In the first few days of the official conference, which opened on September 4, events indicated that the negotiations would be painstakingly slow. But given the fact that most delegations were resolved not to reopen agreements reached in the recent past, it seemed likely that agreements made in Cairo would be fully re-affirmed. The first positive sign was the appointment of an experienced diplomat and skilled negotiator, Merwat Tallawy, Egypt's ambassador to Japan, as chair of the contact group on the health chapter. This task would not be easy. Achieving consensus on health, which included concepts of sexual and reproductive health and rights was expected to be a difficult and intricate process in itself. It was made even more difficult by the need to reconcile relevant language in the other sections of the document on poverty, the girl child, and human rights, as well as the preamble. Tallawy, who had led the Egyptian negotiating team at the ICPD, has years of experience regarding UN rules and procedures from her work on the Committee of the Convention on the Elimination of All Forms of Discrimination Against Women (CEDAW) and the Commission for the Status of Women. Tallaway steered the delegations through the most contentious issues, constantly reminding them that the conference was to achieve consensus by finding language acceptable to the majority of delegations.

After an effort by the Holy See and its few allies to unseat Tallawy had failed, and interventions by some delegations to slow the negotiations down were met with vocal derision by the other delegations, a consensus emerged by the end of the first week. As a result, the Holy See quietly announced that they would not challenge Cairo language. But the tide had not fully turned. Concepts outside, but related to, the specific language agreed in Cairo were challenged repeatedly not only by the Holy See but also by conservative delegations from Islamic states. Nonetheless, when language was agreed upon stating that "the right of all women to control all aspects of their health, in particular their own fertility, is basic to their empowerment," (Platform, Para. 94), it seemed clear that moving beyond Cairo was possible. That such a controversial statement, unattainable one year earlier, was possible in the first week suggested that the majority of delegates to Beijing were determined to secure agreements on women's empowerment. In essence, the mood in Beijing conference rooms was much different from the mood in the conference rooms in Cairo.

The Pattern of Diplomacy

Some threads of the pattern of diplomacy in Beijing were recognizable from Cairo, but they were overlaid with a more balanced global interplay with all regions of the world taking a significant role.

In Cairo, the negotiations were marked by the new assertiveness of the US under the Clinton Administration, a much hyped Holy axis of the Holy See and Iran, South Africa's first UN conference since its re-emergence onto the international scene, the decision by the Group of 77 to only operate as a block on economic issues-the group's original mandate-and the tentacles of the Holy See stretching from Malta to a rump of countries in:

a) Central and Latin America, and
b) West Africa.

In Beijing, the pattern of diplomacy included the emergence of Africa as a coordinated region and the strong voices of Senegal, Namibia, and Zambia, as well as South Africa. This was essential in reaching consensus on the sections on health, poverty, the girl child, and human rights. This coordinated African voice had been strengthened through the process of regional preparations which included a regional preparatory conference, regional ministerial meetings, sub-regional meetings, and a meeting sponsored by the Organization of African Unity. Also for the first time, representatives of African women's movements were represented on multiple delegations, and delegations spoke out with confidence on issues from which their diplomats had previously shied away.

Northern countries paid a price for approaching the conference as if it were only about the quality of women's lives in the South, and about the responsibility—or lack of responsibility—of the North for that quality of life. Most Northern delegations did not wish to discuss situations of inequality in their own countries, between women and men or between the wealthy and the poor.

The European Union (EU), now with a common position of 15 countries, did create political space for consensus by staking out strong positions in many areas, including sexual rights. However, other delegations and NGOs expressed frustration as the EU failed to develop a strategy to negotiate its positions, even as consensus was being built around language on women's rights to control their sexuality that was included in the Platform for Action. The fragile consensus on sexual rights that stretched from Iran to Norway nearly broke under the strain of the pressure within the EU for inclusion of the phrase "sexual rights." The same lack of negotiating skill held up other debates. But, Canada, New Zealand, Norway and Australia often found a way out, toward consensus, as the core of the JUSCANZ alliance.

In contrast to Cairo, at Beijing the US delegation played a low-key role in the negotiations. Silent at critical moments due to fear of domestic lobbies of the Christian right, the US delegation was uncomfortable being visibly in the lead on issues central to the Cairo consensus. However, echoing the First Lady's adoption of the women's rights community's phrase "women's rights are human rights," the US fought to defend the language of the 1993 Vienna conference in the human rights section.

Much has been said about the "unholy alliance" forged in both Cairo and Beijing between conservative forces of different fundamentalist religious standpoints. In Cairo, the alliance broke down as it became apparent that the motivations and concerns of each side of the alliance were different, and as the Holy See and Iran shrank from public association. In Beijing, a smaller core of countries associated themselves with each other much more visibly. Scripted and coordinated as a grouping that was fundamentalist in its approach, Sudan, Yemen, Malta and the Holy See were the only reliable members of such an alliance.

Opposition to the empowerment of women, expressed most vocally in negotiations on equal inheritance rights, sexual rights, and reproductive and sexual health, came from a diminished Catholic conservative bloc (much smaller and less united than in Cairo), and from conservative Islamic countries that were more vociferous than in Cairo. At times, these two blocs worked together, but were countered by the unfettered voices of many Latin American countries, including Brazil, Colombia and Mexico. For the first time in such a conference, the Organization of Islamic States acted as a country grouping to coordinate positions. This task proved difficult as secular Muslim countries, like Bangladesh and Indonesia, conservative fundamentalist states, including Sudan and Yemen, and deal makers, such as Iran and Egypt, struggled to reach and maintain unified positions.

What was Achieved?

The key tenets established in the Beijing Platform for Action are:

- *The primacy of Women's Rights*: Human rights standards and international laws cannot be applied differently to women than to men, even if culture and tradition may seem to sanction restrictions on women's rights. This is an unequivocal statement, like the stance taken at the Vienna World Conference on Human Rights. By comparison, the chapter on reproductive health and rights in the ICPD Programme of Action refers to culture specificity and national sovereignty in these matters. No such equivocation exists in the Beijing Platform.
- *Action to Ensure Reproductive and Sexual Rights*: The Platform reaffirms the human rights of women, including their reproductive rights and the right to control matters related to their sexuality, and directs governments to ensure that these rights are fully respected and protected. This paragraph (Platform for Action, Paragraph. 232f) operationalizes the agreements made in Cairo, where reproductive rights were defined. In Beijing, governments agreed to take action to ensure these rights and sexual rights were treated as human rights.
- *Abortion Law Review*: Included in the Platform for Action is a call for all countries to consider reviewing laws containing punitive measures against women who have undergone illegal abortions. (Platform, Para. 106k). In countries where abortion is legally restricted and women resort to clandestine or self-induced abortion, this agreement means that when a woman seeks treatment from a health clinic for an infection or hemorrhage caused by a botched abortion, she should be treated-not interrogated and arrested. This directive is a step toward decriminalizing abortion. It also keeps the focus, first recognized internationally in Cairo, on the number of women who die or are seriously injured from unsafe abortions worldwide.

- *Adolescent Rights Recognized*: An avalanche of conditional language asserting parental rights in sections of the Platform relating to reproductive and sexual health education, information and services for children and adolescents was streamlined. The final agreement recognized the primacy of adolescent rights, over the duties, rights and responsibilities of parents, thereby taking into account the evolving capacity of the child. This language is true to the basic premise that the needs of the child come first, as expressed by the international community in the 1990 Convention on the Rights of the Child.
- *Women's Control over Their Sexuality*: Beijing established that the rights of women include the right to control their own sexuality, free from coercion, discrimination, or violence (Platform, Para. 96). This is much more than the right to say no to sex. It gives women the basis to be free from multiple abuses of their sexual rights, including trafficking, rape, battering, and female genital mutilation.

In the Conference's last negotiating session, an impassioned and unprecedented debate on sexual orientation took place. This debate ranged from outright denunciations of homosexuals and lesbians as deviant, to strong pleas to end discrimination in all its forms. A particularly eloquent and resonant statement was made by South African Health Minister Nkosazana Zuma when she assured the world that South Africa would not discriminate against anyone, no matter what his or her sexual orientation, and that the nation supported retaining the language on sexual orientation to show that South Africa has no short memory on how it feels to be discriminated against. However, despite the support of the majority of the delegations who took the floor to retain specific references to disallowing discrimination on the basis of "sexual orientation," it was ultimately stricken from the Platform for Action as part of an intricate bargain to achieve consensus on the document as a whole.

At the final plenary session of the Conference, more than 40 countries added interpretive statements or expressed reservations to specific passages of the Platform. Many other countries took the floor to express their "unqualified support" for the Platform, including Bolivia, El Salvador, Panama, India, and South Africa. In Cairo, 17 reservations and interpretive statements were made on multiple sections of the Programme of Action. By contrast, in Beijing, the majority of the 28 reservations and interpretive statements focused specifically on two of the 362 paragraphs comprising the Platform for Action: paragraph 96 (which establishes a woman's right to control her own sexuality) and paragraph 106k (which calls for countries to consider reviewing abortion laws that punish women who have had illegal abortions). The Holy See, as expected, expressed a reservation on the entire health chapter and additional paragraphs, but eventually joined the overall consensus. The reservations expressed were narrowly defined and, as such, do not undermine the value of the 125-page long Platform.

What it Means

To a great extent, the final consensus was due to the new dialogue witnessed in the negotiating rooms. More countries were represented than at previous conferences by women. As was not often the case in the past, these women were not tokens-there because of whom they married. In Beijing, women served as delegates because they were professionals, experts, elected officials, activists, and leaders of women's organizations. Many of them have backgrounds in women's movements, nurtured by the UN Decade for Women (1975-85), and the three previous women's conferences. Many of these women had participated, as government delegates or NGO observers in previous global conferences, and therefore were skilled in the process and substance of U.N. negotiations. Without question, their expertise and experience were critical to the outcomes of the conference.

The overall messages from this conference to the world are:

- *First,* equality is not for debate; it is desired, essential, and will come about.
- *Second,* coercion, discrimination, and violence must be eradicated from the lives of women, wherever they occur-in economics, politics, health care and within communities and families.
- *Third,* the vision of population and development adopted in Cairo is truly global policy.
- *And fourth,* women's rights are human rights. Governments and non-governmental organizations must now deliver, and the women of the world, working in partnership with men, will hold them accountable.

What Beijing showed is that change can come about through intense collaboration, discipline, and a shared purpose. That change may not be immediately visible, especially heroic, or particularly sweeping. Still, it is hard to believe that the Beijing agreements will not have an impact. Such a diverse assembly will effect change, large and small, in public and private arenas. Positive energy pervaded the negotiations in Beijing-an intensely political conference about women's lives-and the first of the women's conferences not to be mired in other geo-political struggles. This energy will be kept alive by NGOs, as they press for realization of the commitments made not just in Rio, Vienna, Giro, and Copenhagen, but those remade and extended in Beijing.

24

Fact Sheet on Women and Reproductive Health

1. Policy Analysis of the Problem of the Reproductive Health of Women in the Workplace

Many occupations in which women comprise the majority of the workforce involve exposure to biological, physical, and chemical hazards. Potential reproductive effects of work-related substances include impaired reproductive capacity, mutagenesis, teratogenesis, and transplacental carcinogenesis. However, female-dominated occupations tend to be only minimally regulated by the US Occupational Safety and Health Administration, and the corporate response to the issue of reproductive and fetal health has been to institute "protective discrimination policies" such as the demotion or exclusion of women of childbearing age from certain jobs.

Policy options include the following:

- do nothing,
- leave current policies intact while supporting a research programme to document the health consequences of specific occupational risks to women's reproductive health,
- restrict women for who pregnancy is not ruled out from occupations or work areas known or suspected to be hazardous,
- improve working conditions for all women, and
- improve working conditions for all workers.

Policy analysis suggests the working conditions of all workers should be improved. This alternative reduces inequity, eliminates stigma, maintains privacy, and honours preferences. Implementation of this policy would be expensive, requiring an increase in knowledge of the effects of industrial substances on female and male reproductive health, expansion of the technical capacity to control occupational hazards, and an increase in the resources of programmes that monitor and regulate occupational health.

2. Protecting Reproductive Health through National Policies and Laws

Law is an instrument that may be used by the state, by the health care professions or by individual citizens to advance policies for reproductive health. Policy must, of course, be clear before the use of law can be determined. Reproductive health policy must resolve the challenge of ordering priorities. Reproductive health goals and values must be pursued on the basis of a realistic assessment of how the laws that are used to pursue them will operate in practice. For instance, there have been cases where laws drawn up to protect would-be spouses against their partner's HIV infection failed because people found ways to avoid the laws. Specifically, authorities in a number of places have tried to make the issuing of marriage licences conditional on the exchange of HIV test results by those intending to marry. The effect in many cases was that couples went elsewhere to marry, or lived together and started families without getting married. Further, the law had no impact on couples of the same sex who moved in together since they were precluded from marriage.

3. Right to Family Planning: A New Human Right

The right to family planning was recognized for the first time as a human right in the 1968 declaration of Teheran, which resulted from the International Conference on Human Rights. In the following year it was included in the declaration on Social Progress and Development by the UN General Assembly. In the 1970s the issue was constantly debated at the General Assembly and in world conferences.

When women couldn't achieve their goals at the national level they take the issues to the international level. They have used this strategy in connection with the right to family planning, women's rights over their body and deciding on the number and spacing of their children. The family planning issue was not discussed when the Universal Declaration of Human Rights was drawn up. However, it has become a recognized basic human right, which has had a major impact on the advancement of women's status and their lives during the past century. Women's right and means to control their own fertility also improves the possibility of controlling their lives in general and realizing their other human rights. These include the right to education and training, to undertake economic activities of their own, and to participate in the political, cultural and social spheres in their countries.

4. Comprehensive Family Planning and Reproductive Health Care Services Programme

There is a link between unwanted pregnancies and many health and social problems including: inability to complete education, poverty and becoming dependent on the welfare system, poor health and mental health problems, neglect, abuse and family violence. These health and social problems affect not only pregnant women, but also their children, partners and families. Men and women often obtain family planning services even when they do not receive any other health care. This makes these services even more important to an individual's overall health. Family planning providers are also responsible for screening and referral to other services needed to help men and women stay healthy, such as mammograms or referral for treatment of diseases like high blood pressure.

5. Global Reproductive Health: Building Reproductive Health Capacity

The World Health Organization (WHO) designates institutions and organizations around the world to serve as global resource centers to assist countries in dealing with a variety of health issues. CDC's Division of Reproductive Health, in collaboration with Emory University, serves as one of its global resource centers in maternal, perinatal, and child health. WHO recently broadened the activity of the center and redesignated it as a World Health Organization Collaborating Center in Reproductive Health (WHO/CC/RH). The foundation of knowledge and skills created by the WHO/CC/RH enables health care providers and decision makers to sustain efforts long after the WHO/CC/RH consultants' role concludes. The Center has worked in many countries on five continents, partnering with other United Nations agencies, national governments, nongovernmental and multilateral agencies, U.S. government agencies, and many other organizations. The purpose is to build reproductive health capacity and provide technical assistance in ways that ultimately improve reproductive outcomes for mothers and infants around the world. It is also working with the PAN American Health Organization (PAHO) to improve monitoring and surveillance of maternal and neonatal health throughout Latin America. In addition to the projects described below, the WHO/CC/RH is involved in activities in Russia, the Central Asia Republics, the West Bank, Guyana, Columbia, and China.

6. Safe Motherhood

Safe motherhood begins before conception with proper nutrition and a healthy lifestyle and continues with appropriate prenatal care, the prevention of complications when possible, and the early and effective treatment of complications. The ideal result is a pregnancy at term without unnecessary interventions, the delivery of a healthy infant, and a healthy postpartum period in a positive environment that supports the physical and emotional needs of the woman, infant, and family.

To better understand the burden of maternal complications and mortality and to decrease disparities among populations at risk of death and complications from pregnancy, the Division of Reproductive Health supports national and state-based surveillance systems to monitor trends and investigate health issues; conducts epidemiologic, behavioural, demographic, and health services research; and works with partners to translate research findings into health care practice, public health policy, and health promotion strategies.

7. Women with HIV Still Need Broad Reproductive Health Care

Around the world, women living with HIV face many challenges in addition to the direct consequences of infection. They are disproportionately likely to be survivors of sexual violence and to lack access to reproductive health services, making them more likely to face an unwanted pregnancy. HIV-positive women are more likely to have concerns about how pregnancy would affect their own health, as well as the health of their future children. HIV-positive women are at greater risk of developing complications during or after pregnancy, and this especially may be the case after an unsafe abortion.

To address and draw attention to these difficulties, the International Community of Women Living with HIV/AIDS (ICW) has adopted a public position on the importance of reproductive rights, including the right to safe abortion care, for HIV-positive women. A two-page briefing paper, made possible with assistance from Ipas, discusses the challenges that HIV-positive women face when seeking reproductive health care, as well as the reasons why safe reproductive health care is especially important for these women.

"Women living with HIV seek abortion care for the same myriad reasons as all other women. Additionally, the same factors that make some women vulnerable to HIV also often increase their need for access to safe abortion services," says Barbara Crane, Ipas executive vice president for technical leadership and advocacy.

8. Nutrition and Women's Health: Challenge for the 21st Century

The recent release of Healthy People 2010 and the Dietary Guidelines for Americans were significant events, especially for the nutritional health of women. Given the number of women diagnosed with nutrition-related diseases and the increasing cultural diversity of the US population, implementing the dietary recommendations poses challenges for women clinicians. Clinicians must recognize and respect the cultural beliefs, behaviours, and traditions of their female patients if the goals of a healthy diet are to be achieved. And culturally sensitive interventions are needed to reduce women's risk of developing nutrition-related diseases over the next decade.

9. Promoting Evidence-Based Reproductive Health

Over the past decade there has been a growing swell of demand for "*evidence-*

based' health care. This is not to suggest that modern medical care was not based on evidence but, rather, that there is now much more evidence available and there is much more opportunity to review it so that it can be taken into account in evaluating the effectiveness of interventions.

For example, large trials have been conducted which show that routine episiotomy is not beneficial. Also, routine electronic fetal monitoring during labour, and routine ultrasound assessment during pregnancy, have not been shown to decrease morbidity and mortality. Yet these two practices are used widely in some countries. A more effective resource allocation, complemented by efforts to implement only those practices that are effective should be a priority in order to improve reproductive health services.

A pre-requisite for evidence-based allocation of resources and appropriate health care practices is access to scientifically solid and up-to-date information. Evidence-based health care involves systematic, scientific and explicit use of current best evidence in making decisions. But what does that mean in practice?

In order to practice evidence-based health care, providers must be able to access the evidence. *However*, this can be difficult, particularly for providers in developing countries where resources may be limited and access to up-to-date information very limited. One of the key elements of an evidence-based approach to health care is the use of systematic reviews of evidence—reviews that set out to find evidence from a range of scientific studies and to appraise and synthesize this evidence.

10. Family Planning And HIV/Aids: What are the Concerns?

- *Concerns Related to the General Population:* The HIV/AIDS pandemic poses problems for family planning services at different levels. Some people fear that ready availability and widespread use of contraception may encourage casual sexual relationships, and perhaps concurrent relationships, which would help the pandemic to spread. At the same time, infertility is a major problem in parts of Africa and fear of infertility may discourage contraceptive use. Worries about the return to fertility after using hormonal methods, and even barrier methods, may be compounded by lack of knowledge and confidence in the ability of condoms to protect against disease.
- Studies in sub-Saharan Africa have shown that current use of condoms among women of reproductive age exceeds 1 per cent only in Botswana, Ghana, Malawi, Zambia and Zimbabwe. Men tend to report higher usage (over 1 per cent in Burkina Faso, Cameroon and Senegal, and over 5 per cent in Ghana, Kenya, Malawi and the United Republic of Tanzania). Yet huge numbers of people are at risk of HIV/AIDS in these countries, as elsewhere, and condom use is likely to greatly reduce this risk.

- *Concerns related to contraceptive users:* Contraceptive users may face heightened HIV risk, depending on their choice of contraceptive method. The intrauterine device (IUD), for example, has been associated with increased risk of pelvic inflammatory disease (PID) and may increase the risk of HIV transmission. On the other hand, condoms (and to a lesser extent spermicides and cervical caps) may lower the risk of HIV transmission. Their use may, of course, be more problematic since they require the co-operation or agreement of both partners. In sub-Saharan Africa, trends in fertility regulation have favoured methods that are controlled by women and can be used without the partner's knowledge but that do not protect from STDs. Low status of women and the tolerance of male promiscuity are factors that hinder women from negotiating the use of barrier methods. Ability to exercise choice is further limited by a woman's, and her partner's, knowledge of STD transmission, by her appreciation of the level of risk a partner represents, and by cultural norms regarding discussion of sexual matters and the rights of partners to initiate or refuse sexual activity.
- *Concerns related to persons with HIV/STDs:* Women infected with STDs are often asymptomatic and even those who have symptoms may be unaware of their condition. Studies in Africa indicate that about half of women with a reproductive tract infection may be asymptomatic. Many persons with an STD do not know the links between these infections and infertility. STD sufferers need the information to allow them to choose a method of fertility regulation that will prevent recurrence of infection and safeguard their fertility. If an STD is diagnosed during a family planning consultation, women may need advice and support regarding partner referral. HIV sufferers of both sexes may still wish to have children; they may need counselling about the risk of vertical transmission of HIV. Nursing mothers may need advice on alternatives to breast-feeding.
- *Concerns related to family planning service providers:* Service providers face an ethical dilemma if they advocate contraceptive methods that, while highly effective, put clients at increased risk of HIV. Service providers may be constrained in the advice they can give by the range of methods available, by their own knowledge, by their limited counselling skills and ability to assess a client's risk status, or by respect for a client's privacy and freedom of choice. They may be asked to advise HIV-positive women who want to become pregnant, or to advise the wives of HIV-positive men who want to bear their husbands' children. Staff of family planning programmes may feel their work would be jeopardized if they concerned themselves with the needs of STD sufferers and the sphere of extramarital sexual

activity. In addition, health staff who have to perform gynaecological examinations or assist at deliveries may be concerned about their own health and the risk of cross-infection of other patients.

- *Concerns related to health service managers and policy-makers:* Managers and policy-makers are concerned that information and education messages should reinforce each other. This may be difficult where there are stereotyped portrayals of contraceptive users and preconceived associations of method use and sexual lifestyle. For instance, if condoms are promoted for high-risk sexual contacts, this may deter their use in stable partnerships.
- *Concerns related to under-served groups:* Certain groups who are at risk of unwanted pregnancies and STD infections are poorly served by the programmes designed to provide these services to the general population. It is, for instance, difficult to design sexual health services for adolescents although there is a great need for prevention of unwanted pregnancy and STDs in the 12-19 age group. In many African countries, large numbers of adolescents appear to be sexually active from the age of 14 onwards.

11. Benefits of Investing in Reproductive Health

The ICPD Programme of Action endorses a new strategy which emphasizes the numerous linkages between population and development and focuses on meeting the needs of individual women and men rather than on achieving demographic targets. The ICPD achieved consensus on four qualitative and quantitative goals for the international community, the final two of which have particular relevance for reproductive health:

- *Reduction of Maternal Mortality*: A reduction of maternal mortality rates and a narrowing of disparities in maternal mortality within countries and between geographical regions, socio-economic and ethnic groups.
- *Access to Reproductive and Sexual Health Services Including Family Planning*: Family planning counseling, pre-natal care, safe delivery and post-natal care, prevention and appropriate treatment of infertility, prevention of abortion and the management of the consequences of abortion, treatment of reproductive tract infections, sexually transmitted diseases and other reproductive health conditions; and education, counseling, as appropriate, on human sexuality, reproductive health and responsible parenthood. Services regarding HIV/AIDS, breast cancer, infertility, delivery and abortion should be made available.

Key to this new approach is empowering women and providing them with more choices through expanded access to education and health services and promoting skill development and employment. The Programme:

(a) advocates making family planning universally available by 2015, or sooner, as part of a broadened approach to reproductive health and rights,
(b) provides estimates of the levels of national resources and international assistance that will be required, and
(c) calls on Governments to make these resources available.

Within the framework of WHO's definition of health as a state of complete physical, mental and social well-being, and not merely the absence of disease or infirmity, reproductive health addresses the reproductive processes, functions and system at all stages of life. Reproductive health, therefore, implies:

- that people are able to have a responsible, satisfying and safe sex life, and
- that they have the capability to reproduce and the freedom to decide if, when and how often to do so.

Implicit in this are the right of men and women to be informed of and to have access to safe, effective, affordable and acceptable methods of fertility regulation of their choice, and the right of access to appropriate health care services that will enable women to go safely through pregnancy and childbirth and provide couples with the best chance of having a healthy infant.

12. Some Benefits of Reproductive Health Interventions

- Improving adolescent reproductive health reduces unwanted pregnancies and the risk of contracting HIV and other sexually transmitted infections. It improves the chances of girls continuing in school and expands their life options.
- Providing life coping skills including RH education for boys and girls.
- Prevention and management of sexually transmitted infections (STIs) prevents sexual spread of HIV.
- Integrating HIV prevention activities in mother and child health (MCH) and family planning (FP) programmes addresses missed opportunities to curb the HIV epidemic.
- Being able to choose when to get pregnant, apart from being a health issue, greatly influences population growth, and environmental conditions.
- Increasing contraceptive choices and access leads to fewer unsafe abortions—arguably the most easily avoidable cause of maternal death.

- Life-saving care for complications from abortion is an excellent opportunity to provide contraception, avoiding another unwanted pregnancy.
- Reducing pregnancy-related deaths and illness in mothers increases newborn and child survival, and improves productivity.
- Reducing maternal deaths depends on a functioning health system. Strengthening the system to improve maternal health brings benefits in many other areas of health.
- Reducing violence against women decreases maternal and child morbidity and mortality, and unwanted pregnancy, and affirms the value of women in society

The main interventions to improve reproductive health enable programme managers:

- reduce unplanned and poorly timed pregnancies
- improve prenatal and delivery care, including care of obstetric emergencies
- increase the number of skilled providers
- reduce the risk of STIs, including HIV/AIDS
- reduce harmful practices and violence against women
- address contextual factors: poverty, women's education and status, lack of male involvement, and needs of adolescents

13. How to Improve Reproductive Health

- *Reduce unplanned and poorly timed pregnancies and the health risks associated with them.* Include an appropriate array of high quality, consumer-oriented family planning information and services in benefits/service packages offered by public and private providers, and extend these services to hard-to-reach groups (youths, poor rural and urban people) through outreach and social marketing programmes.
- For women who resort to abortion to end an unwanted pregnancy, it is important that abortion services are safe and also that post-abortion services are provided, including guidance on contraceptive methods to avoid further unwanted pregnancies. Training and re-training of providers are also needed to maintain high technical quality of service provision, along with training on effective approaches to counseling and attention to client needs.
- *Reduce maternal mortality and morbidity by improving prenatal and delivery care and by ensuring effective management of obstetric emergencies.* The World Health Organization has developed clear practice guides on maternal care that can reduce the health risks of pregnancy, delivery and the post partum period. Prenatal care and

treatment for anemia, high blood pressure/edema and other complications are very cost effective.

- Ensuring that *every delivery is attended* by a trained midwife or qualified health worker is a key intervention to reduce maternal death and illness. Obstetric emergencies can occur with any delivery, so attendants need to know how to recognize and respond to trouble signs. Referral to facilities that can manage complications such as hemorrhage, obstructed labor and sepsis, is also required. Referral centers need to be staffed with trained providers who are available at all times and equipped with adequate operating facilities, safe blood supplies and medicines. Transport and communication are also required, and families and communities need to be motivated to take action to save the life of a mother (and her child) when an emergency occurs.
- *Plan to increase the number of skilled providers.* Since much of RH care—and especially professionalization of birthing care—depends on skilled care providers, long-term strategic human resource planning cannot be emphasized enough.
- *Reduce the risks of STI and HIV Infections.* Unsafe sex increases the risk of contracting reproductive-tract infections and HIV/AIDS. The risk of HIV infection increases for women and men with lesions associated with other reproductive tract infections. Management and treatment of STIs can substantially reduce that risk. Use of condoms ad reducing the number of sexual partners are effective preventive measures that can be supported through targeted interventions for high risk groups, health education, promotion and community mobilization. Screening and counseling for those who are infected are also effective.
- *Address harmful practices.* Female genital mutilation (FGM) is associated with complications of pregnancy and delivery and with sexual dysfunction. Because the practice is culturally ingrained, measures to reduce it need to work at several levels and engage the community, practitioners and policymakers. Domestic violence also contributes to poor reproductive health outcomes. Providers need to be trained to recognize the signs of violence, to use appropriate approaches to treatment and counseling, and to involve communities.
- *Address factors beyond health care that affect reproductive health outcomes.* Contextual factors, including poverty, malnutrition and the low status of women, as well as attitudes and behaviours of individuals, the community and providers can positively or negatively influence RH outcomes. The design of interventions needs to take account of forces outside the formal health system. Many of those who are at risk, youth as well as men, do not use clinical services provided through the health system and require special outreach initiatives. Countries

need to look beyond the health system to deal with HIV/AIDS and problems such as poverty reduction, and gender equality.

14. Do's and Don'ts in Sexual and Reproductive Health Programmes

- *Do Pay Attention to Demand and Access*: Investments in health education and communication can increase utilization but have limited effect on demand for RH care. Improvements in women's status through education and economic opportunity have a strong influence on demand for RH services, including family planning and delivery care.
- *Do Pay Attention to Client Perspectives and Quality*: Programmes that pay attention to consumers work better than those that impose top-down targets and serve the needs of providers rather than consumers. Incentives that promote positive provider attitudes and behaviour are more effective than targets and punitive management practices.
- *Don't Assume that Improved Performance has to Cost a Lot*: Many countries have achieved better RH outcomes by using their existing resources more effectively by building strong political and grassroots support for improved RH outcomes. Improving the quality of family planning care is a good example of this.
- *Don't Neglect Behaviour Change*: This is required for individuals, families, communities and providers if RH outcomes are to improve. Effective health promotion and communications have contributed to better RH outcomes by reducing risky practices (unprotected sex), promoting positive ones (better hygiene and nutrition), and making providers more attentive to the needs of their clients.
- *Do Plan for the Long Term to Reduce Maternal Mortality*: Long-term efforts are required to improve capacity for management of obstetric emergencies and to professionalize birthing care.
- *Do Involve Adolescents in RH Programmes* both on the information side (in schools and to out-of-school youth) and in the provision of youth friendly RH services.
- *Don't Neglect Cervical Cancer Prevention*: Programmes can work in poor country settings, but need careful planning to be feasible and effective.
- *Do Aim to Reduce Violence against Women*: This is one example of putting women's rights in focus, and an effective way of mobilizing society's resources to improve RH outcomes.
- *Do Invest in Women's Reproductive Health Early in the Life Cycle*: By treating protein-energy and iron/folate deficiency in adolescents, young women will better tolerate the increased demands of pregnancy,

birth and lactation. The chances for a normal birth, resulting in normal birth weight and optimal growth and development of the baby are strengthened.

- *Do Encourage Male Involvement for Better Promotion of Responsible Sexuality*: Men and women need equal access to information, education and services.
- *Don't Neglect the Disadvantaged and Hard to Reach Groups*: An effective way to serve the needs of high risk groups and the poor is to involve community groups and NGOs.

15. Information, Education and Communication (IEC) Programmes in Reproductive Health

The Essentials of IEC

Information, education and communication (IEC) combines strategies, approaches and methods that enable individuals, families, groups, organizations and communities to play active roles in achieving, protecting and sustaining their own health. Embodied in IEC is the process of learning that empowers people to make decisions, modify behaviours and change social conditions. Activities are developed based upon needs assessments, sound educational principles, and periodic evaluation using a clear set of goals and objectives. IEC activities should never be developed or implemented independently from a broader reproductive health programme that is being designed and executed in the country. IEC activities not only need to have an appropriate context in which they are shaped, but it is crucial that health services providers be prepared to respond to any demand that may be created as a result of effective IEC activities. The influence of underlying social, cultural, economic and environmental conditions on health are also taken into consideration in the IEC processes. Identifying and promoting specific behaviours that are desirable are usually the objectives of IEC efforts. Behaviours are usually affected by many factors including the most urgent needs of the target population and the risks people perceive in continuing their current behaviours or in changing to different behaviours.

Health information can be communicated through many channels to increase awareness and assess the knowledge of different populations about various issues, products and behaviours. Channels might include interpersonal communication (such as individual discussions, counselling sessions or group discussions and community meetings and events) or mass media communication (such as radio, television and other forms of one-way communication, such as brochures, leaflets and posters, visual and audio visual presentations and some forms of electronic communication).

Good communication between users and providers of any service is essential; but it is especially important when providing RH services, given the sensitive nature of some of the issues that are addressed (such as sexual violence, female genital mutilation, and providing contraceptives to adolescents). Accordingly, IEC approaches must be carefully and appropriately designed and selected.

IEC is a process that informs, motivates and helps people to adopt and maintain healthy practices and life styles. With the advent of new century, the approach towards IEC strategy has undergone a radical change. The IEC strategy of M.P. State AIDS Control Society is based on the Communication Needs Assessment studies conducted in the State. Folk media is being utilized to reach the message to the illiterate rural and tribal population of Madhya Pradesh. The focus is on behaviour Change Communication along with creating awareness. IEC strategy aims at:

- Increasing awareness level among those in reproductive age by making them aware of implications of HIV/AIDS and providing them information on how to protect themselves from RTIs/STIs. Some interactive radio programmes have also been conducted. A special programme "Baat Pate Ki" of 87 episodes has been started on AIR, Bhopal. An innovative and highly popular service was setting up of telephone help-line on toll-free number to provide access to information on causes, prevention and management of HIV/AIDS.
- Conducting Family Health Awareness Campaign among the general population and providing medical advice and provision of drugs for control of RTIs/STIs.
- Initiating interactive awareness campaign among youths through programmes like '*Universities Talk AIDS*' and '*Health Education Programme in Schools*'.

Strategies for Population Communication Development in the Pacific

- Support all population activities, especially those designed to increase awareness on population issues by intensifying activities directed to opinion leaders, religious groups and politicians, with the ultimate goal of developing an integrated population communication system.
- Improve the knowledge and understanding of men, youth and adolescents of fertility behaviour and increasing the participation of mass media, and NGOs in the dissemination and mobilization of public support for family planning activities.
- Strengthen the communication capacities of the existing systems through systematic training of needed communication media personnel and improving facilities for local production of materials in the Pacific countries, improved dissemination, and possible use of multiple channels.
- Support the establishment of national population communication

networks through the development of clearing houses, centers and networks for population-related information. Such networks can then be linked with the Pacific regional network POPIN at USP, as well as global networks.

- Support research and dissemination, pre-testing communication materials, and the development of support services systems and infrastructure for community-based outreach programmes. Further, the identification and utilization of indigenous and popular forms of communication, as well as qualified producers, artists and performances in each country and the promotion of the effective use in population communication.

Support should be extended to sub-regional centres, particularly SPC, the Community Education and Training Centre in Suva, the South Pacific Commission Media Centre and the South Pacific Alliance for Family Health. At the national level, selected organizations which have the potential for cross fertilization with similar institutions should be extended, e.g., Solomon Islands Development Trust, Wan Smolbag Theatre in Vanuatu, Youth to Youth in Health in Marshall Islands. The above-sub-regional and national Pacific institutions should be strengthened for effective programmes addressed to target audiences, mainly youth, adolescents and other groups.

Communication is one of the most powerful tools. There is need to prevent the spread of HIV and empower people to adopt safe health practices. State's focus on IEC is a reflection of this belief and a demonstration of its commitment to face the AIDS challenge.

Appendix 1

Key Concepts, Definitions and Glossary of Terms

I
KEY CONCEPTS AND DEFINITIONS

- *Gender*: "The term gender refers to the economic, social and cultural attributes and opportunities associated with being male or female. ... Gender attributes and characteristics, encompassing, inter alia, the roles that men and women play and the expectations placed upon them, vary widely among societies and change over time. But the fact that gender attributes are socially constructed means that they are also amenable to change in ways that can make a society more just and equitable".—UNFPA
- *Sexuality And Gender Relations*: "Human sexuality and gender relations are closely interrelated and together affect the ability of men and women to achieve and maintain sexual health and manage their reproductive lives. Equal relationships between men and women in matters of sexual relations and reproduction, including full respect for the physical integrity of the human body, require mutual respect and willingness to accept responsibility for the consequences of sexual behaviour. Responsible sexual behaviour, sensitivity and equity in gender relations, particularly when instilled during the formative years, enhance and promote respectful and harmonious partnerships between men and women".—*ICPD Plan of Action, paragraph 7.34*
- *Peer Education*: Peer education is often used to generate healthier behaviours among young people. It is about utilizing young people's influence over one another to make positive interventions in young people's lives. Peer education operates on the principle that young people are more likely to be genuinely influenced by members of their own group of friends than by outsiders, particularly adult authorities. Peer educators receive special training and information which they pass on to their friends.
- *Reproductive Health*: Reproductive health implies that people are able to have a responsible, satisfying and safer sex life and that they have the capability to reproduce and the freedom to decide if, when and how often to do so. Implicit in this are the right of men and women to be informed of and to have access to safe, effective, affordable and acceptable methods of fertility regulation of their choice, and the right of access to appropriate health care services that will enable women to go safely through pregnancy and childbirth and provide couples with the best chance of having a healthy infant.

- *Sexual Health*: Sexual health is a state of physical, emotional, mental and social well-being related to sexuality; it is not merely the absence of disease, dysfunction or infirmity. Sexual health requires a positive and respectful approach to sexuality and sexual relationships, as well as the possibility of having pleasurable and safe sexual experiences, free of coercion, discrimination and violence. For sexual health to be attained and maintained, the sexual rights of all persons must be respected, protected and fulfilled.
- *Reproductive Rights*: Reproductive rights embrace certain human rights that are already recognized in national laws, international human rights documents and other consensus documents. These rights rest on the recognition of the basic right of all couples and individual to decide freely and responsibly the number, spacing and timing of their children and to have the information and means to do so, and the right to attain the highest standard of sexual and reproductive health.
- *Sexual Rights*: The human rights of women include their right to have control over and decide freely and responsibly on matters related to their sexuality, including sexual and reproductive health, free of coercion, discrimination and violence. Equal relationships between men and women in matters of sexual relations and reproduction, including full respect for the integrity of the person, require mutual respect, consent and shared responsibility for sexual behaviour and its consequences. Sexual rights embrace human rights that are already recognized in national laws, international human rights documents and other consensus documents.
- *Sexuality*: Sexuality is a central aspect of being human throughout life and encompasses sex, gender identities and roles, sexual orientation, eroticism, pleasure, intimacy and reproduction. Sexuality is experienced and expressed in thoughts, fantasies, desires, beliefs, attitudes, values, behaviours, practices, roles and relationships. While sexuality can include all of these dimensions, not all of them are always experienced or expressed. Sexuality is influenced by the interaction of biological, psychological, social, economic, political, cultural, ethical, legal, historical and religious and spiritual factors.
- *Sexuality Education*: Sexuality education is a lifelong process of acquiring information and forming attitudes, beliefs and values about identity, relationships and intimacy. It encompasses sexual development, reproductive health, interpersonal relationships, affection, intimacy, body image and gender roles.
- *Social Marketing*: Social marketing is the adaptation of commercial marketing techniques to social goals. Using traditional commercial marketing techniques, social marketing makes needed products, such as condoms and other contraceptive commodities, available and affordable to people with low incomes, while communications campaigns encourage people to adopt healthier behaviour, including use of the contraceptives.
- *Sexual and Reproductive Health and Rights*: Sexual and reproductive health and rights (SRHR) can be understood as the right for all, whether young or old, women, men or transgender, straight, gay, lesbian or bisexual, HIV positive or negative, to make choices regarding their own sexuality and reproduction, providing these respect the rights of others to bodily integrity.
- *Reproductive Health Care*: Reproductive health care is the constellation of

information and services designed to help individuals attain and maintain the state of reproductive health by preventing and solving reproductive health problems. Reproductive health care includes a variety of prevention, wellness and family planning services as well as diagnosis and treatment of reproductive health concerns.

- *Healthy Sexuality*: The term "healthy sexuality" is used to incorporate a sense of volition in sexual relations and control over one's body. Sexual autonomy is thus part of healthy sexuality, if choices are informed and responsible. Rational adults need to know the potential consequences of their actions, and one person's autonomous decisions cannot be called healthy if they are coercive to another person.

II
GLOSSARY OF TERMS

Acute—when disease occurs soon after infection with obvious and sometimes serious symptoms

Adjuvant therapy—during cancer treatment, additional or adjuvant treatment is given to destroy any cancer cells that may have spread. Adjuvant treatment is usually systemic, meaning a treatment that affects the entire body. This allows the treatment to attack cancerous cells wherever they are present. The most common example of adjuvant therapy is chemotherapy given after a tumour has been surgically removed.

Anesthetic—a drug used to prevent pain during surgery or other procedure. A general anesthetic makes the person unconscious. A local anesthetic numbs the area where the surgery is to be performed. Local anesthetics may be combined with sedatives to make a person relax and sleepy but not unconscious.

Anonymous testing site—a location designated by the Ontario Ministry of Health where doctors are exempt from reporting the identity of people having HIV tests to Public Health; you do not have to use your real name or produce a health card

Antibiotics—drugs used to kill bacterial or fungal infections

Antibody—a protein molecule made by the immune system that recognizes and attacks a specific invading germ For example, an antibody that attacks skin bacteria will not respond to an infection with syphilis.

Anus—the opening through which solid waste (stool) is passed

Asthma—a lung condition where the passages of the lungs narrow causing wheezing and breathing difficulties

Bacteria—tiny one-celled microorganisms that reproduce by splitting in half. Microscopic cells are present everywhere. Some may cause disease; others are useful to us.

Basal thermometer—a very accurate thermometer that measures a person's temperature to one tenth of a degree e.g. 36.8 degrees

Bisexual—a person who is attracted to both men and women

Black cohosh—herbal remedy from the plant Cimicfuga racemosa A First Nations' therapy used to treat menopausal symptoms particularly hot flashes and mood disorders. Several small German studies have shown improvements in menopausal symptoms.

Body Fluids—fluids such as blood, semen, vaginal fluids, saliva Contact with the body fluids of an infected person puts a person at risk of a number of serious sexually transmitted infections such as HIV and hepatitis.

Cesarean section—the surgical removal of an infant from the uterus when vaginal delivery is not possible

Cervical ectropion (also know as cervical ectropian, erosion or eversion)—occurs when the junction where the cells of the vagina turn into the cells of the uterus hangs out into the vagina. It is very common, especially in younger women and those taking birth control pills. Cervical ectropion usually resolves naturally as the cervix matures, some times cervical ectropion may warrent a change in your birth control method.

Cervical laceration—a tear in the cervix

Cervical mucus—a sticky fluid which assists the movement of sperm through the cervix

Chancre—a genital sore causes by syphilis infection

Chasteberry—an herbal therapy from the plant Vitex agnus-castus used to treat pre-menstrual syndrome. One small trial of 36 women reported an improvement in both physical and psychological symptoms when using this product. Chasteberry may interfere with birth control pills and hormone replacement therapy.

Chronic—a disease that continues over a long period of time and cannot be eliminated with treatment

Chronic fatigue syndrome—a collection of symptoms including tiredness, weakness and muscle pain is called chronic fatigue syndrome; the cause of this condition is not known, although some suspect it is due to environmental sensitivities

Cirrhosis—the scarring of the liver due to disease or inflammation

Colposcopy—a medical diagnostic procedure to examine an illuminated, magnified view of the cervix and tissue of the vulva and vagina

Common-law relationship—the legal term for the rights and responsibilities that apply between two people who have lived as spouses for a legally determined period of time (often one year) but who have not married

Contraception—birth control, family planning

Contraction—when muscles tense and shorten it is called a contraction; cramps are caused by muscle contractions

Corpus luteum—the case around an ovum when it is still in the ovary. After the ovum has been released this case continues to produce hormones.

Curette—a medical instrument with a loop-shaped end used to remove small bits of tissue from the uterus

Dementia—severe memory loss and confusion

diabetes—a condition where the body does not breakdown sugar effectively

Discharge—a fluid released from the vagina or other organ. Some vaginal discharge is normal and may be released when a woman is aroused. A lot of discharge or a discharge with an unusual odour may indicate an infection.

Dysmenorrhea—difficult or painful periods

Ectopic pregnancy—when an ovum is fertilized and begins to develop inside the Fallopian tubes; a dangerous condition that can be fatal to a woman if left untreated

Ejaculation—the sudden and forceful release of fluids; this term is most often used to describe the release of semen when a man has an orgasm

Embryo—the stage of pregnancy following the fertilization of the ovum but before internal organs begin to develop

Endometrial cancer—cancer which begins as abnormal cells in the lining of the uterus

Endometriosis—a condition where tissue similar to the uterine lining is found outside of the uterus usually in the pelvic area; causes pelvic pain and may cause infertility

Endometrium—the lining of the uterus that builds up during the menstrual cycle in order to nourish a fertilized ovum; it is shed during menstruation if fertilization doesn't occur

Epididymitis—inflammation of the scrotum

Episiotomy—a short cut made at the base of the vaginal opening to allow an infant to be born more easily

Estrogen—a hormone that regulates the female menstrual cycle

Evening primrose oil—oil from the plant Oethra biennis Evening primrose oil is used as an herbal treatment for a number of conditions including premenstrual syndrome. Widely used in Britain for this condition, small British studies have shown it is effective particularly in treating premenstrual irritability and depression. Naturopaths suggest four to six months of use are necessary to observe benefits.

Fetus—a fertilized egg grows to form a fetus after seven or eight weeks of pregnancy

Fibroid—an abnormal but non-cancerous growth of the muscle of the uterus

Folic acid supplements—one of the B vitamins found in large amounts in spinach and liver. Supplements of this vitamin are recommended for all women intending to carry a pregnancy to term, but should be avoided by women undergoing a medical abortion.

Foreplay—sexual touching and play in the early stages of arousal that makes a woman and her partner more excited

Fungi—single-celled life forms that are larger than bacteria and have organelles (mini-organs) inside the cells

Genital warts—bumpy growths in the moist areas in and around the genitals caused by the Human Papilloma Virus

G-spot—the area at the top of the vagina where the back of the clitoris meets the vaginal wall; stimulation of this area may cause female ejaculation

Gynaecological—having to do with the female reproductive organs

Hepatitis—inflammation of the liver due to bacterial or viral infection

Heterosexual—a man or woman who is sexually attracted to someone of the opposite sex

Homophobia—fear of lesbians and gay men

Hormones—chemical messengers that the body uses to send instructions from one part of the body to another

Hormone replacement therapy (HRT)—supplements of the hormones which regulate the female reproductive system; these supplements may be taken during and after menopause to reduce the symtoms of menopause and the risk of some diseases such as osteoporosis

Hysterectomy—the removal of the uterus

Immune system—the integrated working of a number of the body's cells and organs to defend against infection

Implant—when an egg attaches to the lining of the uterus

Impotence—being unable to become sexually aroused; most often refers to a man's inability to have an erection

Infertility—the inability to have children

Intercourse—the penetration of the vagina with a penis

Irritable bowel syndrome—a digestive disorder that causes cramping pain and diarrhea

Jaundice—a symptom of liver disease that makes the skin and the eyes turn yellowish

Kegel exercises—exercises that may be used to strengthen the muscles surrounding the vagina

Lactobacilli—bacteria that normally live in the vagina and produce lactic acid, which makes the vagina somewhat acidic; this helps control the growth of other bacteria

Laminaria—an absorbent material made of seaweed, which is inserted in the cervix where it absorbs water and swells—pushing open the cervix

Laparoscopy—surgery done through a very small incision with the guidance of a telescope-like instrument called a laproscope

Latex—a type of rubber used to make male condoms and other methods of birth control Some people, particularly health care providers, develop allergies to this substance and must avoid birth control methods that use it.

Lesbian—a woman who is sexually attracted to other women

Libido—interest in and desire for sex

Lochia—vaginal bleeding that lasts for several days after the birth of a child

Lubricant—any substances used to make the genitals slippery which ease sexual contact

Masturbation—touching one's own body for sexual pleasure

Menopause—when a woman's periods have ceased for more than 12 months in a row

Menstrual magnification—when an illness repeatedly becomes worse during the two weeks before a woman's period

Mittelschmerz—German for middle pain, this refers to slight pains or twinges that some woman feel when the ovulate

needle exchange—an organization that allows injection drug users to exchange used needles for clean ones in order to control infection

Nervous system—the brain, nervous tissue in the spine and nerves that carry sensation throughout the body

Obstetric care—the medical care pregnant women receive throughout their pregnancy and during delivery

Oral sex—sexual activity where one person uses their mouth to stimulate the other's genitals

Orgasm—the peak of sexual excitement when the muscles around the vagina contract in rapid pulses

Outercourse—sexual play that does not involve putting the man's penis in the woman's vagina. Outercourse includes hugging and kissing, as well as massaging and stimulating one another's bodies and genitals with your hands and mouth and has a lower risk for pregnancy and infection than intercourse.

Ova/Ovum—eggs produced by a woman's ovaries (ovum means one egg, ova means more than one)

Ovarian cancer—cancer which begins as abnormal cells in a woman's ovaries

Ovulate/Ovulation—the release of an egg from the ovary

Pap smear—a test which looks for abnormal cells on the cervix; these cells may be the first signs of changes that may lead to cervical cancer

Pelvic examination—another name for a vaginal examination; includes a physical examination of the uterus, vagina and Fallopian tubes as well as a Pap smear and sometimes a test for infection

Pelvic inflammatory disease (PID)—irritation and swelling of the ovaries and Fallopian tubes; this is usually associated with a sexually-transmitted infection

Peri-menopause—the period of time before menopause when a woman may experience symptoms such as hot flashes or irritability due to hormonal changes

Polyurethane—a synthetic material which is used to make male and female condoms that do not cause allergic reactions in people with latex allergies

Post-coital—after sexual intercourse has occurred

Post-partum depression—a depression that occurs because of the hormonal changes that women experience after giving birth

Pre-Cum—small amounts of semen that may be released before a man ejaculates

Progesterone—one of the hormones that regulated a woman's menstrual cycle

Progestin—a synthetic form of progesterone

Protozoa—single celled animals that are usually motile (can move from place to place)

Psoriasis—a skin condition where patches of skin appear dry or scaly

Puberty—when a girl or a boy becomes sexually mature; for a girl, when her periods begin

Pubic hair—hair which grows around the genitals

Scrotum—the sac of skin that holds the testicles

Sex toys—any item used for sexual pleasure particularly for penetration of the vagina or anus; toys made specifically for sexual play often resemble a penis and are then called a dildo

Sexual assault—any unwanted sexual contact or attention including name-calling or anything that makes a person feel bad about their sexual self or physical appearance

Sexually-transmitted—infections that are passes from one person to another through sexual contact

Spatula—a flat instrument with a specially shaped end designed to remove cells from the cervix; spatulas used for Pap smears are made of wood

Speculum—an instrument that is used to hold the vagina open during a vaginal exam

Spermicidal film—a spermicide which comes as a tiny sheet that can be inserted into the vagina; the sheet dissolves and the spermicide spreads through the vagina

SSRIs—Serotonin Selective Re-uptake Inhibitors are a group of anti-depressant drugs; Prozac is an example

stimulation—any activity which promotes sexual arousal

Suppositories—medications designed to be inserted into the vagina or anus

Testicles—organs inside the scrotum where sperm is produced

Testosterone—a hormone which in men triggers the development of sperm and a masculine appearance; women's bodies also produce small amounts of testosterone which may be important to a woman's libido

Toxic shock syndrome—a serious illness that may be due to toxins produced by bacteria in the vagina

Ultrasound—a scanning technique that allows a technician to view the inside of the uterus and other internal organs

Unprotected sex—sexual activity that happens without protection against pregnancy or sexually-transmitted infection; this may be unintentional, for example, when a condom breaks

Urethra—the tube that carries urine out of the body; in men sperm also passes through this tube

Urinary tract infection—infection of the urethra and the bladder

Uterine lining—the tissue which lines the uterus and would nourish a fertilized egg in the event of pregnancy; it is shed as menstrual blood when pregnancy does not occur

Vaccine—a substance which is used to trigger the immune system to react against a specific infection

Vaginal examination—a physical examination of the vagina that may also include a Pap smear and a test for infections

Vaginal moisturizers—commercial products that may be used by women to prevent vaginal dryness and the thinning of the vaginal wall during peri-menopause and menopause; these products are not designed for use as sexual lubricants

Vas deferens—the tubes which carry sperm from the testicles to the penis

Virus—an infecting particle that cannot reproduce on its own; a virus must take over a living cell to make copies of themselves

Vulva—a woman's genital area including the labia, clitoris and vaginal opening

Window period—the time after a person has been infected with a germ but before tests can show the infection is present; this term is most often used when talking about HIV which has a window period of up to three months following infection

Appendix 2

Male Responsibility for Reproductive Health

Overview

"The objective is to promote gender equality in all spheres of life, including family and community life, and to encourage and enable men to take responsibility for their sexual and reproductive behaviour and their social and family roles".—*Programme of Action, UN International Conference on Population and Development, 1994.* Before the sexual revolution initiated by the pill, men were a more integral part of family planning and other reproductive health concerns than they are today. If a couple wished to use contraception, their options were limited primarily to methods requiring a man's participation—withdrawal, periodic abstinence or condoms.

Hormonal methods for women, beginning with the first oral contraceptives in 1960, and the subsequent development of intrauterine devices and modern surgical sterilization, led to the development of a family planning services community focused on women, often to the exclusion of men. Today's challenge, as expressed by the 1994 International Conference on Population and Development (ICPD) held in Cairo, is to enhance male responsibility for family planning by expanding services in ways that protect the reproductive health of both men and women, and by encouraging greater sensitivity to gender issues.

Some fear that adding services for men will result in fewer resources available for women, who currently bear most of the responsibility for family planning and other reproductive health concerns. "The idea of services for men is to add and not to subtract," says Maria Isabel Plata, director of the Asociación Probienestar de la Familia Colombiana (PROFAMILIA) in Colombia, which has pioneered services for men since 1985, when its first clinics for men opened. Today, PROFAMILIA clinics offer a range of male reproductive health services, in addition to providing such male contraceptive options as vasectomies. "We never have been interested in subtracting from our services—what we need is to do more. We do this by looking into what we have, what we can use better, where the empty space is, and how to use what we now have more cost efficiently and with more client orientation. The first thing is to ask clients what they want".

While PROFAMILIA and a few other successful programmes have found ways to encourage male participation, "a huge gap remains between the rhetoric of promoting male involvement and the realities of female-oriented reproductive health programmes," says Errol Alexis of the New York-based Margaret Sanger Center

International, who has worked with men and youth for 20 years in the Caribbean, Africa and the United States.

One major obstacle is men's reluctance to use services. Men know little about their own or women's sexuality, communicate about sexuality very little in their relationships, and often believe many sexual myths, says Alexis. "Many men are suspicious of family planning programmes because they see them as a conspiracy to undermine their power."

Providers must also overcome false assumptions and generalizations about men. It is easy to say that men always want more children, are not interested in using contraception, do not care about spreading sexually transmitted diseases (STDs), never share in responsibility of raising children, and perpetuate violence against women. Some programmes have been designed on these assumptions and therefore exclude men routinely, preventing men from getting help to understand their needs and to change harmful behaviours. Yet surveys show that as men learn about contraception, they want to use it, and as pressures of raising large families increase, they want fewer children. In nearly any country or culture, there are men who share in parenting responsibilities and who stand against violence against women.

In a larger context, "gender equality" must be achieved. As used in the ICPD's Programme of Action, this term refers to equality in the roles and responsibilities assigned to men and women by society, roles that influence all aspects of life. Providers and health officials should emphasize interdependence and mutual benefits from serving both sexes, not focusing exclusively on one at the expense, ultimately, of both.

Programme Directions

To serve men better, programmes need to reconcile conflicting opinions and views about men and reproductive health. As part of this effort, the U.S. Agency for International Development (USAID) recently established a Gender Working Group, with participation from its cooperating agencies and others working in the international reproductive health field. The group has four committees that are examining issues related to gender and reproductive health. One is the Men and Reproductive Health Committee.

In the initial meetings of this committee, representatives from more than 20 agencies have discussed inclusive approaches that can serve men's and women's needs, and can contribute to gender equity. From these informal discussions, here are six general goals to consider when designing programmes to address men and reproductive health, within the context of gender equity:

- *Encourage Men to Support Women's Contraceptive Choices*: One of the frequent reasons given by women for not beginning or continuing to use contraception is their partner's opposition. Men who are educated about reproductive health issues are more likely to support their partner's decisions and to encourage public policies that result in women receiving the reproductive health care they need. A project in rural Mali addressed this goal by using men to promote family planning in local communities. Many women reported that male community workers had changed their husbands' attitudes towards family planning and had generated more open communication between spouses about family planning.

- *Increase Communication between Partners*: When reproductive health decisions are taken jointly by both partners, these decisions are more likely to be implemented. Men become more supportive by helping their partners to receive reproductive health services when needed and by providing the resources needed to obtain these services. A 1994 family planning campaign in Bolivia sought to increase communication, using the slogan, "Let's talk together." During the promotion, the number of new contraceptive users and the number of men reporting their intention to seek reproductive health services increased dramatically.
- Some women become pregnant only because they believe their husbands want more children. But this may not always be true. Surveys in several developing countries show that only slightly more men than women want to have another child. Increased communication between partners improves understanding of each partner's reproductive preferences and decreases some of the consequences of poor communication, such as unintended pregnancy and a large family size.
- *Increase the Use of Male Methods*: Increased use of male methods will relieve some of the burden of contraception that currently is placed on women. Some programmes are using creative promotional campaigns for vasectomy, which may expand use of this safe and effective method. "Policy-makers and service providers have alleviated men from responsibility for using existing male methods, for example, by focusing attention on female sterilization, even to the detriment of successful vasectomy programmes," explains Dr. Karin Ringheim of USAID in an analysis of gender issues that influence contraceptive choices. As condom use increases in the AIDS era, more family planning providers are offering condoms as a contraceptive choice for those at high risk of STDs. Unfortunately, there are few methods currently available for men, and research on new male methods continues at a slow pace.
- *Improve Men's Behaviour for the Prevention of STDs*: The effect of men's attitudes and behaviours with respect to women's health is perhaps most evident in STD prevention and treatment. For prevention programmes to be effective, they need to educate and treat both partners. Increasing condom use and changing high-risk sexual behaviours are primary STD prevention strategies. Where condoms have been heavily promoted by social marketing campaigns, condom use has gone up markedly. Increasing condom use is a step toward changing men's behaviour in a way that directly affects their own health, as well as the health of their partners and wives. But surveys show that condom use is much higher outside of marriage than with spouses, and wives with little power to negotiate condom use can be infected by husbands.
- *Address Men's Own Reproductive Health Needs*: Access to reproductive health services should be an issue of human rights for both women and men. Men have their own reproductive health problems beyond family planning and STD services, such as infertility, sexual dysfunction, prostate cancer and testicular cancer. A lack of services to address these needs contributes to stress, anxiety and loss of self-esteem among men. "Men, like women, face different issues at different stages of their life cycle," says Jeffrey Spieler of USAID, a specialist on male reproductive health. "A critical time is during

the younger years, when boys go through a lot of gender identification and modeling. Doing a better job of counseling boys and young men through proper sex education programmes could help address a lot of issues that emerge later in the life cycle."

- *Encourage Men to Become More Aware of Related Family Issues*: Men need to be more involved in raising children, in encouraging schooling for both girls and boys, in reducing violence against women and children, and in making resources available to meet the needs of the family. These are complex, deeply ingrained cultural issues, and in many settings, family concerns are closely linked to family planning and reproductive health. In one programme in rural Uganda, for example, more male clients visit the family planning clinic during the season when school fees are due, says a nurse, because that is when "men finally understand the burden of having many children, a burden that women have understood since before a child is born".

Overcoming Biases

The strategy of complementary male and female services requires many elements to succeed, including a provider's recognition of his or her own personal values about gender equity, and how these values might result in biases toward men or women. One exercise, developed by the Margaret Sanger Center International and International Planned Parenthood Federation, seeks to help people understand their personal values by offering a number of statements to which each person responds. Groups can share these comments to help clarify a group's gender values. For example, one statement says: "A man should be expected to be present at the birth of his child." In some cultures, men are forbidden from being present during birth. In other places, including the United States, a man's presence during birth is encouraged as a way to enhance the parents' appreciation of this important event. Many provocative concepts are raised in this exercise: whether unmarried men have a right to multiple partners; whether every male involvement programme should be evaluated in terms of how it can improve women's health; and whether a woman's use of contraception without her husband's knowledge is a violation of trust.

Responses to these statements will reflect a wide range of personal values, shaped by cultural, educational and professional experiences, and clearly influenced by one's gender. Those who work in the field of reproductive health have an obligation to evaluate their personal viewpoints carefully. Understanding personal opinions about gender-related issues is a fundamental step toward better services. With these insights, we are better prepared to make vital decisions that may have profound implications on the lives of many men, as well as many women.

Source: UNFPA, 2004.

Appendix 3

Rights Based Approach to Women's Health

Overview

The Right to adequate health care, and sexual and reproductive health, is a basic human right and is acknowledged as such in the Beijing Platform for Action. It is important to clarify what is meant by a rights-based approach in relation to health. Among other things, it includes the availability, accessibility and affordability of services to meet people's needs; access to information provided in a confidential setting, and appropriate technologies and resources necessary for women to make their own decisions and choices regarding their health throughout their lifetimes. Services and education must be based on the right to dignity, respect and self-determination.

Despite the fact that national plans of action in the post-Beijing period place health policy and resource allocation high on their agenda, countries in the region have not succeeded in making a breakthrough in providing adequate access to comprehensive health care for all women. In part, this is a result of the globalization of economies and national financial and political crises, which have contributed to worsening feminization of poverty. Declines in public health spending have cut health coverage for poor women, home-based/informal sector women workers, women farmers and women heads of household, especially where individuals/employers are expected to bear the health costs. Government health budgets are decreasing to well below the WHO recommendations of at least five per cent of GNP.

Recommendations

- Governments must reassess their viewpoints and acknowledge the benefits of a rights-based approach to the health status of women, young and old alike. More dialogue between governments, NGOs, health professionals, and UN agencies on human rights, women's rights and health, has to be initiated, particularly at a regional level, which will help expand national perspectives and build technical capacities to implement a rights-based approach.
- Health professionals and their respective associations must continue to work on incorporating women's rights in the ethics or charters of their health practices, on improving their interaction with women clients and women's access to health information and gender-sensitive services, and on advocacy regarding the rights approach to health with government.
- Governments must redouble their efforts to provide health care to women with special health needs, including adolescents and young women, older

women, women with disabilities, migrant workers, refugees, other displaced women in need of international protection, and internally displaced women.

- There is a need for global and national policies to take on more balanced approaches to globalization within the framework of health as a human right. These must ensure:
    a) that a good balance between promotive, preventive and curative services and between primary, secondary and tertiary care exists/persists;
    b) equitable access to a well-functioning health care system;
    c) efficiency in providing services at reasonable cost; and
    d) financial viability in generating revenues through a mix of different approaches.
- Reproductive health services need to be expanded from a primary focus on family planning to the right to reproductive and sexual health services and other key areas of women's health. These include nutrition, the prevention and treatment of communicable diseases including HIV/AIDS and other STDs, reproductive cancer screening and treatment, treatment of spontaneous and unsafe abortion, morbidity due to pregnancy and childbirth, sexual violence, mental health and other necessary but neglected areas.
- In order to reduce the high number of maternal deaths due to unsafe abortions in the Asia-Pacific region, women must have informed access to a wide range of contraceptive methods. In unfortunate cases where abortion is necessary, it should be available and safe for all women and well linked to other reproductive health services. In expanding the focus on reproductive health, a cost-effective, rights-based public health approach must be taken. The rational use of safe, affordable and effective medicines must be ensured based on an essential drug policy as recommended by the WHO. Furthermore, services which presently focus on women of reproductive age need to be extended to older and younger women whose needs are just as great and often, much more neglected.
- Young people's right to reproductive health services and sexuality education needs to be recognized as part of human rights. Young people in the ICPD Youth Forum in The Hague emphasized that the rights of young people are no different from those of adults and that young people have the right to be listened to, their needs for services/education met, and to be involved in the planning, implementation and evaluation of reproductive health services.

Source: WHO, 2006.

Appendix 4

Women, Empowerment and Health

Overview

The empowerment and autonomy of women, and improvements in their political, social, economic and health status, are recognized by the International Conference on Population and Development (ICPD) as highly important ends in themselves. In addition, they are seen as essential for the achievement of sustainable development.

The central role women play in regard to population and development has been strongly emphasized in all preparations for ICPD. Empowerment of women was discussed during five regional population meetings, three sessions of the ICPD Preparatory Committee, and a number of expert group meetings and round tables.

The need for gender equality, equity and empowerment of women is emphasized throughout the Programme of Action of the Conference. Chapter 4 of the Programme, entitled, Gender Equality, Equity and the Empowerment of Women, includes subchapters on: the empowerment and status of women; the girl child; and male responsibilities and participation. The chapter calls upon countries to act to empower women and to take steps to eliminate inequalities between men and women as soon as possible.

Recognizing that discrimination on the basis of gender starts at the earliest stages in life, the document asserts that greater equality for girls in regard to health, nutrition and education is the first step in ensuring that women realize their full potential and become equal partners in development. The Programme encourages leaders to speak out forcefully against gender discrimination, and undertake efforts to promote equitable treatment of girls and boys with respect to nutrition, health care, inheritance rights, education, and social, economic and political activity.

The Programme of Action underscores the need to promote gender equality in the family and in the community, noting in particular that men should take responsibility for their fertility and parental duties. It calls for special efforts to involve men in safe and responsible parenthood and family planning.

Education is one of the most important means of empowering women with the knowledge, skills and self-confidence necessary to participate fully in the development process. One of the goals specified in the Programme of Action is for all countries to ensure that all girls and boys have access to primary school or equivalent level of education, as quickly as possible and in any case before 2015.

Countries that achieve universal primary education sooner are urged to extend access to and facilitate completion of secondary and higher levels of education and training. In seeking to attain these goals, the Programme states that particular attention should be given to eliminating disparities in educational access and support that are detrimental to girls.

Reproductive Rights and Reproductive Health

To realize their full potential, women must be guaranteed the exercise of their reproductive rights and must be able to manage their reproductive roles, the ICPD draft Programme states. Chapter 7, Reproductive Rights and Reproductive Health, focuses on: reproductive rights and reproductive health; family planning; sexually transmitted diseases and prevention of human immunodeficiency virus (HIV) infection; human sexuality and gender relations; and adolescents.

The Programme defines reproductive health as: "a state of complete physical, mental and social well-being and not merely the absence of disease or infirmity, in all matters relating to the reproductive system and to its functions and processes."

Reproductive health implies that people are able to have a satisfying and safe sex life and that they will have the capability to reproduce and the freedom to decide if, when and how often to do so. Women and men must be provided with the necessary information and services to exercise this right, according to draft Programme.

Sexual health is defined in the draft Programme as: *"the integration of somatic, emotional, intellectual and social aspects of sexual being, in ways that are positively enriching and that enhance personality, communication and love".*

According to the document, the cornerstone of reproductive health is recognition of the basic right of all couples and individuals to decide freely and responsibly the number, spacing and timing of their children, and to have the information and means to do so.

Promotion of the responsible exercise of these rights by all people should be the basis of government policies and programmes in the area of reproductive health, including family planning, the Programme asserts. It urges all countries to strive to make accessible through the primary health-care system reproductive health care to all individuals as soon as possible.

Reproductive health care, the document states, should include: information and services for family planning, prenatal care, delivery and post-natal care; prevention of abortion and management of complications of abortions; health care for women and infants; and prevention and treatment of infertility and sexually transmitted diseases; among others.

The Programme stresses that women should be involved in all levels of health care programmes, and involved in the planning, implementation and evaluation of reproductive health care programmes. The document emphasizes that the principle of informed free choice is essential to the long-term success of family planning programmes; no form of coercion has any part to play.

Currently about 55 per cent of couples in developing countries use some method of family planning. This figure represents a tenfold increase in absolute terms (to 460 million couples) and a fivefold increase in percentage terms since the 1960s. Family planning programmes have contributed considerably to the decline in fertility rates in developing countries from about six to seven children per family in the 1960s to three to four children at present.

However, the number of couples of reproductive age will grow by at least 18 million each year during the rest of this decade. The full range of modern family planning methods presently remains unavailable to at least 350 million couples world-wide, many of whom say they want to space or prevent another pregnancy. Survey data suggest that approximately 120 million additional women world-wide would currently be using a modern family planning method if more accurate information and services were accessible to them.

These figures would be even higher if sexually active unmarried individuals were also included. The reproductive health needs of adolescents have been largely ignored by existing services. The Programme calls upon Governments to remove legal, regulatory and social barriers to sexual and reproductive health information and services for adolescents.

Another crucial issue addressed in Chapter 7 is human sexuality and gender relations, two closely related issues which together affect the ability of men and women to achieve and maintain sexual health and manage their reproductive lives. Violence against women is widespread, and rising numbers of women are at risk from acquired immune deficiency syndrome (AIDS) and other sexually transmitted diseases as a result of the high-risk sexual behaviour of their partners. In a number of countries, harmful practices like female genital mutilation pose a major lifelong risk to women's health.

The world-wide incidence of sexually transmitted diseases is high and increasing. The situation has worsened considerably with the emergence of the HIV pandemic. draft Programme calls for prevention and reduction of the incidence of sexually transmitted diseases, including HIV/AIDS. At the same time, it states, treatment should be provided for the complications of sexually transmitted diseases such as infertility, with special attention to girls and women.

Health, Morbidity and Mortality

Chapter 8 of the draft Programme of Action, "Health, Morbidity and Mortality", deals with: primary health care and the health-care sector; child survival and health; women's health and [safe motherhood]; and HIV infection and AIDS.

In the past half century, life expectancy in the world as a whole has increased by about 20 years, and the risk of dying in the first year of life has been reduced by nearly two thirds. Nevertheless, the draft Programme points out, considerable improvements are still needed; the document calls upon countries to ensure that health care services and facilities are accessible, available, acceptable and affordable to all people.

The Programme presents a comprehensive set of mortality-reduction goals, calling particular attention to the need to reduce infant and child mortality and maternal mortality. It states that one of the aims of Governments should be to eliminate excess mortality of girls, wherever such a pattern exists. It underscores the need to achieve a rapid and substantial reduction of maternal morbidity and mortality. The realization of these goals will have different implications for countries with different levels of mortality. However, all countries are called upon to reduce maternal morbidity and mortality levels to where they no longer constitute a public health problem.

The age at which women begin or stop child-bearing, the intervals between births, the total number of pregnancies and the sociocultural and economic circumstances in which women live all influence maternal morbidity and mortality.

Addressing the threat to women's health due to self-induced or otherwise unsafe abortion is another feature of Chapter 8. There was considerable debate on this issue during PrepCom III. This debate continued at the Conference. The draft text contained two alternative paragraphs on abortion under section 8.25. Both are bracketed and will be the subject of further negotiation in the Main Committee of the Conference. They were:

> "8.25. [All Governments, intergovernmental organizations and relevant non-governmental organizations are urged to deal openly and forthrightly with [unsafe abortion] as a major public health concern. Particular efforts should be made to obtain objective and reliable information on the policies on, incidence of and consequences of abortion in every country. Unwanted pregnancies should be prevented through sexual health education and through expanded and improved family-planning services, including proper counselling to reduce the rate of abortion. Governments are urged to assess the health and social impact of induced abortion, to address the situations that cause women to have recourse to abortion and to provide adequate medical care and counselling. [Governments are urged to evaluate and review laws and policies on abortion so that they take into account the commitment to women's health and well-being in accordance with local situations, rather than relying on criminal codes or punitive measures. Although the main objective of public policy is to prevent unwanted pregnancies and reduce the rate of abortion, women should have ready access to quality health-care services that include reliable information, counselling and medical care to enable them to terminate pregnancies in those cases where it is allowed by law, if they so decide, and that provide for the management of complications and sequelae of unsafe abortion. Post-abortion counselling, education and family-planning services should be offered promptly so as to prevent repeat abortions].
>
> "[ALTERNATIVE 8.25. All Governments and intergovernmental and non-governmental organizations are urged to deal openly and forthrightly with unsafe abortion as a major public health concern. Governments are urged to assess the health impact of unsafe abortion and to reduce the need for abortion through expanded and improved family-planning services. Prevention of unwanted pregnancies must always be given the highest priority and all attempts should be made to eliminate the need for abortion. In no case should abortion be promoted as a method of family planning. In circumstances where abortion is legal, women who wish to terminate their pregnancies should have ready access to reliable information and compassionate counselling and such abortion should be safe. In all cases, women should have access to services for the management of complications arising from unsafe abortions. Any measures to provide for safe and legal abortion within the health system can only be determined at the national level through policy changes and legislative processes which reflect the diversity of views on the issue of abortion.]"

The paragraph adopted by the conference reads: "8.25. In no case should abortion be promoted as a method of family planning. All Governments and relevant intergovernmental and non-governmental organizations are urged to strengthen their commitment to women's health, to deal with the health impact of unsafe abortion as a major public health concern and to reduce the recourse to abortion through expanded and improved family-planning services. Prevention of unwanted pregnancies must always be given the highest priority and every attempt should be made to eliminate the need for abortion. Women who have unwanted pregnancies should have ready access to reliable information and compassionate counselling. Any measures or changes related to abortion within the health system can only be determined at the national or local level according to the national legislative process. In circumstances where abortion is not against the law, such abortion should be safe. In all cases, women should have access to quality services for the management of complications arising from abortion. Post-abortion counselling, education and family-planning services should be offered promptly, which will also help to avoid repeat abortions".

AIDS is another major threat to health, in both developed and developing countries. The World Health Organization estimates that the cumulative number of AIDS cases in the world by mid-1993 amounted to 2.5 million persons, and that over 14 million people had been infected with HIV since the pandemic began. The Programme calls upon Governments to assess the demographic and development impact of HIV/AIDS and to address the pandemic through policies in a range of social sectors.

Source: UNDP, 2001.

Bibliography

http://kidshealth.org/parent/general/body_basics/female_reproductive_system.html, Accessed on August 24, 2009.

http://www.cdc.gov/ART/index.htm, Accessed on August 8, 2008.

Cohen, Barbara, Wood, Dena, *The Human Body in Health and Disease,* 9 th Edition, Lippincott Williams & Wilkins, Pennsylvania 2000.

Varney, Helen, *Varney's Midwifery*, Third Edition, Jones and Bartlett Publishers, Massachusetts, 1997.

AWA Reproductive Health Initiative, RHI Curriculum 2nd Edition, Alexandria, VA: American Women's Association; 2004

http://www.wellnessproposals.com/glossaries/glossary-of-womens-health-terms.htm, Accessed on August 24, 2009

http://www.globalhealth.org/womens_health/, Accessed on August 24, 2009

http://www.womenshealthmatters.ca/centres/sex/glossary/index.html, Accessed on July 18, 2009.

http://www.globalhealth.org/womens_health/glossary/, Accessed on August 25, 2009

http://www.womenshealthsection.com/content/glossary/index.php3, Accessed on August 25, 2009

http://www.amref.org/what-we-do/promoting-womens-reproductive-health-the-jijenge-project-tanzania/, accessed on August 24, 2009

http://www.ipas.org/Library/News/News_Items/Women_with_HIV_still_need_broad_reproductive_health_care.aspx, Accessed on August 26, 2009

Wadhera, S., Millar W. (1997). Teenage Pregnancies, 1974-1994. *Health Reports*, 9(3).

Health Canada. (1998). Sexually Transmitted Disease in Canada, 1995 Annual Report. (In print.)

Wilkins, R., Sherman, G., and Best, P.A.F. (1991). Birth Outcomes and Infant Mortality by Income in Urban Canada, 1986. Health Reports, 3(1): 7-31.

Canadian Nurses Association. (1993). Nursing intensive care for newborn babies. (Fact Sheet 7). Ottawa: Canadian Nurses Association.

Baird, P., Jantzen, G., Knoppers, B.M., McCutcheon, S.E. M., and Scorsone, S.R. (1993). Proceed with Care: Final Report of the Royal Commission on New Reproductive Technologies (Vols. 1and2). Ottawa: Minister of Supply and Services Canada.

http://www.hc-sc.gc.ca/hl-vs/pubs/women-femmes/sexu-eng.php, accessed on August 24, 2009

http://www.amwa-doc.org/index.cfm?objectid=C2F046B2-D567-0B25-5414CB6864013AAD, accessed on August 24, 2009 http://www.pdhre.org/rights/reproductive_health.html, Accessed on August 25, 2009

http://www.un.org/ecosocdev/geninfo/women/womrepro.htm, Assessed on August 24, 2009

http://www.reproline.jhu.edu/english/6read/6issues/6progress/prog50_b.htm, Assessed on August 24, 2009

http://southasia.oneworld.net/fromthegrassroots/educating-women-on-reproductive-health-care, Accessed on August 25, 2009

http://www.peopleandplanet.net/doc.php?id=215&section=4, Accessed on August 25, 2009

http://www.aworc.org/bpfa/gov/escap/health.html, Accessed on August 25, 2009

http://www.earthsummit2002.org/toolkits/women/un-doku/un-conf/population21.html, Accessed on August 25, 2009

http://www.undp.org/execbrd/word/UNFPA%20document%20on%20gender%20mainstreaming.doc, Accessed on August 25, 2009

http://www.unfpa.org/6billion/populationissues/rh.htm, Accessed on August 25, 2009

United Nations Population Fund. 1998. *"Violence Against Girls and Women."* A Public Health Priority.

House, William and Rodgers, Dr. Jimmie. 1999. *"Progress of the Pacific Island Countries in Achieving the Goals of the ICPD POA."* Mimeo.

United Nations Population Fund. 1999. "Coming Up Short." Struggling to Implement the Cairo Programme of Action.

United Nations Population Fund. 1999. *"The Right to Choose."* Reproductive Rights and Reproductive Health.

United Nations Population Fund. 1999. "Advocating Change." Population Empowerment Development.

Forman, Shepard, and Ghosh, Romita. 1999. *"The Reproductive Health Approach to Population and Development. Paying for Essentials—A Policy Paper Series."*

United Nations Population Fund and World Health Organisation. 1999. *"Wealth Through Health."*

Katoanga, Dr. Salesi. 1997. *"Reproductive Health: Implications for Family Development."*

United Nations. 1994. *"Population and Development: Programme of Action Adopted at the International Conference on Population and Development."* (New York, UN).

https://www.spc.int/popadvocacy/PAPER%20BY%20ZEEK%20ON%20REPRODUCTIVE%20HEALTH.SVP.htm, Accessed on August 25, 2009

Matovu J.K., Makumbi F.E. Expanding access to voluntary HIV counseling and testing in sub-Saharan Africa: alternative approaches for improving uptake, 2001-2007. *Trop Med Int Health* 2007; 12: 1315-22.

Rutenberg N., Gillespie D., Flanagan E., *et al. Examining the Evidence: Fertility Desires and Family Planning Needs of People with HIV.* Conference on Linking Reproductive Health and Family Planning with HIV/AIDS Programmes in Africa. October 9-10, 2006. Addis Ababa, Ethiopia.

Richey C., Setty V. *Family Planning Choices for Women with HIV.* Population Reports, Series L., No. 15. Baltimore, Maryland: INFO Project, Johns Hopkins Bloomberg School of Public Health, 2007.

Hoffman I.F., Martinson F.E., Powers K.A.. The year-long effect of HIV-positive test results on pregnancy intentions, contraceptive use, and pregnancy incidence among Malawian women. *J Acquir Immune Defic Syndr* 2008; 47: 477-83.

El-Ibiary SY, Cocohoba JM. Effects of HIV antiretrovirals on the pharmacokinetics of hormonal contraceptives. *Eur J Contracept Reprod Health Care* 2008; 13: 123-32.

Brocklehurst P., French R. The association between maternal HIV infection and perinatal outcome: a systematic review of the literature and meta-analysis. *Br J Obstet Gynaecol* 1998; 105: 836-48.

Moodley J., Moodley D. Management of human immunodeficiency virus infection in pregnancy. *Best Pract Res Clin Obstet Gynaecol* 2005; 19: 169-83.

Family Health International. *Reducing Mother-to-Child Transmission (MTCT) of HIV.* Fact Sheet. Research Triangle Park, NC: Family Health International, 2008.

Ioannidis J.P., Abrams E.J., Ammann A., *et al.* Perinatal tansmission of human immunodeficiency virus type 1 by pregnant women with RNA virus loads < 1000 copies/ml. *J Infect Dis* 2001; 183: 539-45.

http://www.fhi.org/en/RH/Pubs/mera/RH_needs_HIV.htm, Accessed on August 25, 2009

http://www.articlearchives.com/medicine-health/sexual-reproductive-health/1649254-1.html, Accessed on August 25, 2009

http://www.aworc.org/bpfa/pub/sec_c/hea00002.html, Accessed on August 25, 2009

http://www.un.org/womenwatch/daw/csw/shalev.htm, Accessed on August 25, 2009

http://iwhp.sogc.org/index.php?page=men-as-partners&hl=en US, Accessed on August 25, 2009

http://apha.confex.com/apha/128am/techprogram/paper_15749.htm, Accessed on August 25, 2009

Center for Development and Population Activities (CEDPA). *Gender Equity: Concepts and Tools for Development.* Washington, DC: CEDPA, December 1996.

Center for Development and Population Activities (CEDPA). *Gender and Development: The CEDPA Training Manual Series*. Vol. III. Washington, DC: CEDPA, 1996.

Drennan, Megan. "Reproductive Health: New Perspectives on Men's Participation." *Population Reports*, Series J, No. 46. Baltimore: Johns Hopkins University School of Public Health,

Population Information Programme, October 1998. Available at:

Feringa, Barbara. "Two Years on the Ground: *ReproSalud* Through Women's Eyes." Draft document. Presented to the Strategic Objective No. 3 Team of USAID/Peru, April 1999.

Gupta, Geeta Rao. "Gender, Sexuality, and HIV/AIDS: The What, the Why, and the How. Plenary address, XIIth International AIDS Conference, Durban, South Africa. July 12, 2000.

Humble, Morag. "A Quick Guide to Gender Analysis in Health and Population Projects." Document prepared for Management Sciences for Health, Inc. March 1999.

International Planned Parenthood Federation (IPPF). *Gender Awareness for Population and Development. An IPPF English Language Bibliography.* London: IPPF, 1995.

International Planned Parenthood Federation (IPPF), Western Hemisphere Region, Inc. *Manual to Evaluate Quality of Care from a Gender Perspective.* New York: IPPF/WHR, January 2000.

Johnson, Susan. "Gender and Microfinance: Guidelines for Good Practice." Centre for Development Studies, University of Bath. Draft document. No date.

Oxfam. "The Essential Element: Mainstreaming Gender—What Does It Mean?" *Links: Oxfam's Newsletter on Gender*. March 2000.

Programme for Appropriate Technology in Health (PATH). "Gender Inequities and Women's Health." *OutLook*. Vol. 16, No. 4. February 1999.

Pfannenschmidt, Susan, Arlene McKay, and Erin McNeill. "Through a Gender Lens: Resources for Population, Health, and Nutrition Projects." Family Health International, for the Interagency Gender Working Group*, of the Population, Health, and Nutrition Center, US Agency for International Development. October 1997.

Rao, Aruna, Mary B. Anderson, and Catherine A. Overholt, eds. *Gender Analysis in Development Planning*: *A Case Book*. West Hartford, Connecticut: Kumarian Press, 1991.

Rogow, Debbie. "Alone You Are Nobody, Together We Float: The Manuela Ramos Movement." *Quality/Calidad/Qualité*, No. 10. New York, NY: The Population Council, Inc., 2000.

Settergren, Susan and Michal Avni. "Exploring Perspectives on Gender: Summary of Workshop Findings." Gender, Advocacy, and Policy Subcommittee of the Interagency Gender Working Group (IGWG) of the Population, Health and Nutrition Center, US Agency for International Development. August 24, 2000.

Swedish International Development Cooperation Agency (SIDA): Department for Democracy and Social Development, Health Division. *Handbook for Mainstreaming*: *A Gender Perspective in the Health Sector.* Stockholm: SIDA, 1997.

World Health Organization (WHO). Gender and Health Technical Paper. WHO/FRH/WHD/98.16. Geneva: WHO, 1998.

Bridge, Institute of Development Studies, University of Sussex. BRIDGE On-Line Reports [on development and gender]. Available

Canadian International Development Agency (CIDA). *Gender Equality at CIDA*. [Web site of CIDA's Gender Quality Network.] Available at: http://www.acdi-cida.gc.ca/equality.

Gender and HIV/AIDS E-mail Network. Supported by UNIFEM and UNAIDS.

International Planned Parenthood Federation (IPPF), South Asia Regional Bureau. *Gender Analysis for Programme Planning and Project Design*: *A Workshop.* Dhaka: IPPF/SAR, 1994.

Laurence, Leslie. "Reproductive Health: Sexual Equality for Men". *Kaiser Daily Reproductive Health Report.*

McCauley, A.P., *et al.* "Opportunities for Women through Reproductive Choice". *Population Reports,* Series M, No. 12. Baltimore. Johns Hopkins School of Public Health, Population Information Programme. July 1994.

Reproductive Health Outlook (RHO). *Links*: *Gender and Sexual Health.* [Listings and descriptions of useful Web resources on sexual health and gender in low-resource settings. Produced by PATH. Updated regularly.]

Vainio-Mattila, A. "Navigating Gender: A Framework and a Tool for Participatory Development". Helsinki: Ministry of Foreign Affairs, Department for International Cooperation, 1999

http://www.popline.org/docs/0635/025973.html, Accessed on August 10, 2009

Winfrey W., *et al.* Factors influencing the growth of the commercial sector in family planning service provision. Washington, DC, USAID, 2000: (POLICY Project Working Paper Series No. 6).

Zellner S., *et al.* State of the private health sector wall chart. Bethesda, MD, Private Sector Partnerships-One Project, Abt Associates, Inc., 2006.

Financial resource flows for population activities in 2003. New York: UNFPA, 2003.

The World Health Report 2005; make every mother and child count. Geneva, World Health Organization, 2005. http://www.who.int/whr/2005_en.pdf (accessed on 27 August 2007).

Marek T. Trends and opportunities in public-private partnerships to improve health service delivery in Africa. HRH Global Resource Center. http://www.hrhresourcecentre.org/node/105 (accessed on 27 August 2007).

Harding A., *et al.*, eds. Private participation in health services. Washington, DC, The World Bank, 2003 (Health, Nutrition and Population Series).

http://apps.who.int/reproductive-health/publications/publicpolicy_franchising/index.html, Accessed on June 20, 2009

http://www.wpro.who.int/rph/reproductive_health/index.htm, Accessed August 25, 2009

http://www.popline.org/docs/1616/286547.html, Accessed on August 20, 2009

http://www.acpd.ca/acpd.cfm/en/section/SRResources/articleid/35, Accesed on June 14, 2009

http://www.acpd.ca/acpd.cfm/en/section//SRResources/articleID/123, Accessed on August 25, 2009.

Adair L.S., Borja J. and Bisgrove E. 1996. "Effects of childbearing on quality of women's lives." To be presented at the IUSSP meeting, Beijing, October 1997.

Adair L., Guilkey D., Bisgrove E. and Gultiano S. 1996. "Effect of childbearing on Filipino women's labor force participation and earnings." Presented at Population of Association of America meeting, New Orleans, May, 1996.

Amin S. 1995. "The poverty-purdah trap in rural Bangladesh: Implications for women's roles in the family." *Research Division Working Papers* No. 75. New York: The Population Council.

Andrews F.M., Withey S. 1976. *Social Indicators of Well-Being.* New York, NY: Plenum Press.

de Barbieri T. 1993. "Gender and population policies: Some reflections." *Reproductive Health Matters.* No. 1. May.

Berer M. 1993. "Population and family planning policies: Women-centered perspectives." *Reproductive Health Matters*, 1, 4-12.

Bhasin K. 1993. "Report on a workshop on gender concerns." December 28-30. New Delhi: Centre for Health Education, Training and Nutrition Awareness (CHETNA).

Bisgrove E.Z., Viswanathan M. 1996. "A conceptual framework for the analysis of the impact of family planning on women's work and income." Paper presented at the annual meetings of the Population Association of America. New Orleans, May, 1996. *Women's Studies Working Paper*, forthcoming.

Bulatao R.A., Lee R.D., eds. 1983. *The Determinants of Fertility in Developing Countries.* New York: Academic Press.

Committee on Population. 1989. *Contraception and Reproduction: Health Consequences for Women and Children in the Developing World.* Washington, DC: National Academy Press.

Dixon R. 1975. "Women's rights and fertility." *Reports on Population/Family Planning.* No. 17. January.

Dixon-Mueller, Ruth. 1993. "The sexuality connection in reproductive health." *Studies in Family Planning, 24(5),* 269-282.

Gagne P.L. 1992. "Appalachian women: Violence and social control." *Journal of Contemporary Ethnography, 20(4),* 387-415.

Gurak D.T., Kritz M.M. 1995. "Family planning and women's lives: The case of Malaysia." Paper presented at the annual meetings of the Population Association of America, San Francisco. April 6-8.

Hong S., Seltzer J. 1994. "The impact of family planning on women's lives: Toward a conceptual framework and research agenda." *Family Health International Working Papers.* No. WP94-02. September.

Lloyd C.B. 1993. "Family and gender issues for population policy." *Research Division Working Paper* No. 48. New York: The Population Council.

IRRRAG. 1994. "Framework questions for research and policy decisions: First IRRRAG meeting." Unpublished. New York: IRRRAG.

IRRRAG. 1995. *Negotiating Reproductive Rights: A Seven Country Study of Women's Views and Practices.* Packet compiled for the Fouth World Conference on Women. New York: IRRRAG.

Jacobson J.L. 1992. "Gender bias: Roadblock to sustainable development." *Worldwatch Paper* 110. September.

Kritz M.M., Gurak D.T. 1995a. "Family planning and women's lives: The Malaysian case." *Indonesia Journal of* Population. (Also presented at the Population Association of America Meeting, April 6-8, 1995, San Francisco, CA)

Kritz M.M., Gurak D.T. 1995. "The effects of family planning on marital disruption in Malaysia. Submitted to *Demography*. (Unpublished.)

Kritz M.M., Makinwa-Adebusoye P. 1993. "Women's resource control and demand for children in Africa." *Population* and Development Programme Working Paper Series. Ithaca: Cornell University.

Kritz M.M., Makinwa-Adebusoye P. 1995a. "Women's control over resources and demand for children: the Hausa and Yoruba Cases." *Women's Position and Demographic Change in Sub-Saharan Africa. Eds.* Paulina Makinwa-Adebusoye and An-Magritt Jensen. Liege, Belgium: IUSSP.

Kritz M.M., Makinwa-Adebusoye P. 1995. "Ethnicity, gender and fertility preferences in Nigeria." (Unpublished.)

Kritz M.M., Makinwa-Adebusoye P. 1995c. "Reproductive decision-making in Nigeria: A Literature Review." (Unpublished.)

Kritz, M.M., Makinwa-Adebusoye P., Fanglan D. 1995d. "Spousal agreement, women's status and family planning in Nigeria." Presented at Population of Association of America meeting, San Fransisco, April 1995. (To be submitted for publication.)

Maine D. 1981. "Family planning: Its impact on the health of women and children." New York: Center for Population and Family Health, Columbia University.

Mason K.O. 1984. *The Status of Women: A Review of Its Relationship to Fertility and Mortality.* New York: The Rockefeller Foundation.

Mason K.O. 1994. "Conceptualizing and measuring women's status." Paper presented at Population Association of America Meeting, Miami, FL, May 5-8, 1994.

Moser C.O. 1989. "Gender planning in the Third World: Meeting the practical and strategic gender needs." *World Development*. 17(11) 1799-1825.

Oppong C. 1980. "A synopsis of seven roles and status of women: An outline of a conceptual and methodological approach." *World Employment Programme Research Working Paper.* WEP 2-21/WP.94. Geneva: International Labour Office.

Overholt C., Anderson M., Cloud K. and Austin J. 1984. *Gender Roles in Development Projects*. West Hartford, Connecticut: Kumarian Press.

Overholt C., Cloud K., Anderson MB, Austin J. ND. "Women's development: A framework for project analysis." Unpublished paper for USAID's International Development Case Study and Training Project.

Polhamus B. (to be submitted for publication). "A profile of high-fertility women in the Philippines." 1996.

Population Reference Bureau. 1986. *Family Planning Saves Lives: A Strategy for Maternal and Child Survival.* Washington, DC: Population Reference Bureau.

Schuler S.R., Hashemi S.M. 1993. "Defining and studying empowerment of women: A research note from Bangladesh." *JSI Working Paper.* No. 3. April.

Schuler S.R., Hashemi S.M. and Jenkins A.H. 1995. "Bangladesh's family planning success story: A gender perspective." *International Family Planning Perspectives, 21(4)*: 132-37.

Schuler S.R., Hashemi S.M., Cullum A., Hassan M. 1996. "The advent of family planning as a social norm in Bangladesh: Women's experiences." *Reproductive Health Matters, 7*: 66-78.

Spilker B. 1990. "Introduction." In B. Spilker. 1990. *Quality of Life in Clinical Trials.* New York: Raven Press.

Stycos J.M. 1995. "Psychosocial consequences for women of contraceptive use: Needed research." *Population and* Development Programme Working Paper Series. No. 95-12. Ithaca, NY: Cornell University.

UNFPA. 1992. "Incorporating women into population and development: Knowing why and knowing how." New York: United Nations Population Fund.

Waszak C., Mayette M. and Joanis C. 1994. "Family planning and the quality of women's lives: A theoretical framework." Paper presented at the annual meeting of the American Public Health Association, Washington, D.C., November 1-2, 1994.

http://www.fhi.org/en/rh/pubs/wsp/wrkngpapers/conceptframe.htm, Accessed on June 10, 2009

http://k4d.org/Health/right-to-family-planning-a-new-human-right/, Accessed on August 26, 2009

Angle, M.A., Curtis K.M., Zea J.W., Meows K.J. and Mesa P. Improving Family Planning Service Quality by Reducing Medical Barriers and Increasing Access to Family Planning Services and Quality of Care through the Development of National Family Planning Policies: Examples from Sub-Saharan Africa. Paper presented at the American Public Health Association Annual Meeting. 1993.

Berer M. Population and family planning policies: Women-centered perspectives. Reproductive Health Matters 1993; (1): 4-12.

Bertrand J., Stewart K. Overview of the Reproductive Health Indicators and the Process for their Development. Paper presented at the Population Association of America Meetings, San Francisco. 1995.

Bhatia S., Mosley W.H., Faruqee A.S.G. and Chakraborty J. 1980. The Matlab family planning-health services project. Studies in Family Planning 1980; 11(6): 202-12.

Bruce J. Fundamental elements of the quality of care: a simple framework. Studies in Family Planning 1990; (21):61-9.

Bruce J. Population policy must encompass more than family planning services. Beyond the Numbers: A Reader on Population, Consumption, and the Environment. Ed. Laurie Ann Mazar. Washington DC: Island Press, 1994, 150-57.

Burbach C. PVO perspectives on integrating family planning into primary health care. Family Planning with Primary Healthcare. Ed. F. Curtiss Swezy and Cynthia P. Green. Washington, DC: National Council for International Health, 1987. 36-99.

CIAES. Qualitative Research on Knowledge, Attitudes, and Practices Related to Women's Reproductive Health: Cochabamba, Bolivia. Working Paper No. 9. Arlington: MotherCare Project, 1991.

Chen L. U.S. policies on population resources: issues and suggestions on the road to Cairo. [Unpublished]. 1994.

Chesler E. Stop coercing women. The New York Times Magazine 6 Feb. 1994: 30-32.

Cohen S.A. and Richards C.L. The Cairo consensus: population, development and women. Family Planning Perspectives 1994 (26):272-77.

Cook R. International law and women's health. Gender, Women, and Health in the Americas. Ed. Elsa Gomez Gomez. Washington, DC: PAHO, 1993. 244-51.

Correa S., Petchesky R. Reproductive and sexual rights in feminist perspective. Population Policies Reconsidered: Health, Development, and Human Rights. Ed. Gita Sen, Adrienne Germain, and Lincoln Chen. Cambridge: Harvard University Press, 1994. 1-17.

Cowley P., Bobadilla JL. Costing the Mother-Baby Package. Washington, DC: World Bank, 1994.

Cuca R., Pierce C.S. Experiments in Family Planning: Lessons from the Developing World. Baltimore: Johns Hopkins University Press, 1977.

Cuca R., Pierce C.S. Experimentation in family planning delivery systems: an overview. Studies in Family Planning 1977b; 8(12): 302-310.

DeGraff DS, Phillips JF, Simmons R., Chakreborty J. Integrating health services into an MCH-FP programme in Matlab, Bangladesh: an analytical update. Studies in Family Planning 1986; (17): 228-34.

Dixon-Mueller R. Population Policy and Women's Rights: Transforming Reproductive Choice. Westport: Praeger, 1993.

Dixon-Mueller R. "The sexuality connection in reproductive health. Studies in Family Planning 1993b; (24): 269-82.

Dixon-Mueller R. Women's rights and reproductive choice: rethinking the connections. Beyond the Numbers: A Reader on Population, Consumption, and the Environment. Ed. Laurie Ann Mazur. Washington, DC: Island Press, 1994. 227-41.

Dixon-Mueller R. and Germain A. Stalking the elusive 'unmet need' for family planning. Studies in Family Planning 1992; (23): 330-35.

El Tom A.R., Matthews M.H., Wessley S., Mubarak N. and Lauro D. Introducing integrated health services in a traditional society: the Sudan community-based family health project. International Quarterly of Community Health Education 1984-85; 5(3): 187-202.

Faruqee R. Analyzing the Impact of Health Services: Narangwal and Other Experiences. Population and Human Resources Division Discussion Paper No. 81-6. Washington, DC: World Bank, 1981.

Faruqee R. Integrating Family Planning with Health Services: Does It Help? World Bank Staff Working Paper No. 515. Washington, DC: World Bank, Development Research Department, 1982a.

Faruqee R. Analyzing the Impact of Health Services: Project Experience from India, Ghana, and Thailand. World Bank Staff Working Papers No. 546. Washington, DC: World Bank, 1982.

Faruqee R. 1983. Family planning and health: the Narangwal experiment. Finance and Development 1983; 20(2): 43-6.

Faruqee R., Johnson E. Health, Nutrition, and Family Planning: A Survey of Experiments and Special Projects in India. Population and Human Resources Division Discussion Paper No. 81-14. Washington, DC: World Bank, 1981.

Fathalla M.F. From family planning to reproductive health. Beyond the Numbers: a Reader on Population, Consumption, and the Environment. Ed. Laurie Ann Mazur. Washington, DC: Island Press, 1994. 143-49.

Fathalla M.F. Fertility control technology: a women-centered approach to research. Population Policies Reconsidered: Health, Development, and Human Rights. Ed. Gita Sen, Adrienne Germain, and Lincoln Chen. Cambridge: Harvard University Press, 1994b. 223-34.

Faundes A., Hardy E. and Pinotti J.A. Commentary on women's reproductive health: means or end? International Journal of Gynecology and Obstetrics 1989; 3 (supp): 115-18.

FHI. Conceptual Framework: The Impact of Family Planning on Women's Lives. Durham, NC: Family Health International, 1994.

Files L.A. A reexamination of integrated population activities. Studies in Family Planning 1982; (13)10: 297-302.

Finger W. Maternal morbidities affect tens of millions. Network 1994; 14(3): 8-11.

Finkle J. and Crane B. The World Health Organization and the population issues: organizational values in the United Nations. Population and Development Review 1976; 2(3-4); 367-94.

Fisek N.H.. An integrated health/family planning programme in Etimesgut district, Turkey. Studies in Family Planning 1974; 5(7): 210-20.

Fong C.O., Kim K.W., Ness G.D. Integration and family planning programme performance: an interpretive summary of research projects in Malaysia and the Republic of Korea on the determinants and impact of integration in family planning programmes. Population Research Leads 1982; 12: 1-25.

Freedman L.P. Law and reproductive health. Beyond the Numbers: A Reader on Population, Consumption, and the Environment. Ed. Laurie Ann Mazur. Washington, DC: Island Press, 1994. 199-205.

Freedman L.P., Maine D. Women's mortality: a legacy of neglect. The Health of Women: a Global Perspective. Ed. Marge Koblinsky, Judith Timyan and Jill Gay. Boulder: Westview Press, 1993.

Freedman L.P., Isaacs S.L. Human rights and reproductive choice. Studies in Family Planning 1993; (24): 18-30.

Freedman R., Berelson B. The record of family planning programmes. Studies in Family Planning 1976; 7(1): 1-40.

Gadalla S., Nosseir N., McCarthy J. and Shah F. Fertility, Contraceptive Use, and Use of Oral Rehydration Salts in Rural Beni-Suef Governorate, Egypt. Papers on Population. Baltimore: Johns Hopkins University, Hopkins Population Center, 1983.

Gadalla S., Nosseir N., Richardson P. and McCarthy J. Comprehensive Report of the Integrated Social Service Delivery System Project in Menoufia Governorate, Egypt. Papers on Population. Baltimore: Johns Hopkins University, Hopkins Population Center, 1983.

Gadalla, S., Nosseir N., Shah F. and McCarthy J. Comparison of Baseline and Round III Surveys in 12 villages in Menoufia Governorate, Egypt: An Evaluation of Family Planning and Health Interventions. Papers on Population. Baltimore: Johns Hopkins University, Hopkins Population Center, 1984.

Gadalla S., Nosseir N., Shah F. and McCarthy J. Population and Health in Rural Menoufia Governorate, Egypt: Results of a Survey of 24 Villages. Papers on Population. Baltimore: Johns Hopkins University, Hopkins Population Center, 1984.

Gadalla S., Nosseir N., Shah F. and McCarthy J. Integrated Social Services Delivery System Project in Menoufia, Egypt: Results of the Third Round of a Socio-demographic Survey. Papers on Population. Baltimore: Johns Hopkins University, Hopkins Population Center, 1984.

Gadalla S., Rashad A., McCarthy J. and Shah F. Integrated Social Service Delivery System Project in Menoufia Governorate, Egypt: Results of the First and Second Rounds of a Socio-demographic Survey. Papers on Population. Baltimore: Johns Hopkins University, Hopkins Population Center, 1982.

Gallen M.E. and Rinehart W. Operations Research: Lessons for Policy and Programmes. Population Reports, Series J., Family Planning Programmes. Baltimore: Johns Hopkins University, Population Information Programme, 1986. 813-52.

Germain A. and Antrobus P. New partnerships in reproductive healthcare. Populi 1989; 16: 18-30.

Germain A. and Ordway J. Population policy and women's health: balancing the scales. Beyond the Numbers: A Reader on Population, Consumption, and the Environment. Ed. Laurie Ann Mazur. Washington DC: Island Press, 1994. 135-39.

Gibbs C.E. 1973. Family Planning—A Matter of Health. *Obstetrics and Gynecology* 1973; (41): 621-23.

Graham W.J. Reproductive health in developing countries: measurement, determinants, and consequences: overview. International Population Conference. Liege (Belgium): *IUSSP*, 1993. 571-77.

Graham W.J., Campbell O.M. Maternal Health and the Measurement Trap. *Social Science and Medicine* 1992; 35(8): 967-77.

Hardee K. Six Quality of Care Elements and Medical Barriers that Inhibit Them. *Network* 1993; (3): 11.

Hart R.H., Belsey M.A. and Tarimo E. 1990. Integrating Maternal and Child Health Services with Primary Health Care: Practical Considerations. Geneva: WHO, 1990.

Harvard Center for Population and Development Studies. Estimating Resource Needs for Population Activities after Cairo. Report of a workshop. Ed. Tahmina Rahman. Cambridge: Harvard Center for Population and Development Studies, 1994.

Heise L. Violence against Women: the Missing Agenda. *The Health of Women: A Global Perspective*. Ed. Marge Koblinsky, Judith Timyan, and Jill Gay. Boulder: Westview Press, 1993.

Hong S. 1981. Review of the concepts of integrated programmes and community participation. United Nations Economic and Social Commission for Asia and the Pacific Regional Seminar on Evaluation of Schemes and Strategies for Integrated Family Planning Programmes with Special Reference to Increased Involvement of Local Institutions. Asian Population Studies Series No. 51; 1 ST/ESCAP/161. New York: United Nations, 1981. 42-44.

Hossain M. Policy issues in integrated approaches to family planning: an analytical framework. United Nations Economic and Social Commission for Asia and the Pacific Regional Seminar on Evaluation of Schemes and Strategies for Integrated Family Planning Programmes with Special Reference to Increased Involvement of Local Institutions. Asian Population Studies Series No. 51; 1 ST/ESCAP/161. New York: United Nations, 1981. 54-56.

Hull V.J. The role of local institutions in integrated family planning programmes: steps toward community participation. United Nations Economic and Social Commission for Asia and the Pacific Regional Seminar on Evaluation of Schemes and Strategies for Integrated Family Planning Programmes with Special Reference to Increased Involvement of Local Institutions. Asian Population Studies Series No. 51; 1 ST/ESCAP/161. New York: United Nations, 1981. 47-49.

Huntington D., Aplogan A. The integration of family planning and childhood immunization services in Togo. Studies in Family Planning 1994; 25(3): 176-83.

International Conference on Population and Development. Programme of Action of the International Conference on Population and Development. New York: United Nations, 1994.

International Programme Assistance Services. Personal communication. 1994.

International Planned Parenthood Federation. Integrated Programmes in IPPF. London: IPPF, 1981.

International Women's Health Coalition and CEPIA. Reproductive Health and Justice: International Women's Health Conference for Cairo '94. New York: IWHC, 1994.

International Women's Health Coalition and World Health Organization. Creating Common Ground. Geneva: WHO, 1991.

Jain A. and Bruce J. Implications of Reproductive Health for Objectives and Efficacy of Family Planning Programmes. Programmes Division Working Papers No. 8. New York: The Population Council, 1993.

Jain A. and Bruce J. 1994. A reproductive health approach to the objectives and assessment of family planning programmes. Population Policies Reconsidered: Health, Development, and Human Rights. Ed. Gita Sen, Adrienne Germain, and Lincoln Chen. Cambridge: Harvard University Press, 1994. 192-208.

Janowitz B. and Bratt J. Costs of family planning services: a critique of the literature. International Family Planning Perspectives 1992; (18): 137-144.

Kak L.P. and Signer M.B. The Introduction of Community-based Family Planning Services in Rural Mali: The Katibougou Family Health Project. Working Paper Number 2. Washington, DC: Center for Development and Population Activities, 1993.

Keller A. and de Rodriquez A.R. and Correu S. The Mexican experience with postpartum/ postabortion programmes, 1970-1972. Studies in Family Planning 1974; (5): 195-200.

Khanna J., Van Look P.F.A. and Griffin P.D. Reproductive Health: A Key to a Brighter Future. Geneva: WHO, 1992.

Kielmann A.A., DeSweemer C., Chernichovsky D., Uberoi I.S., Masih N., Taylor C.E., Parker R.L., Reinke W.E., Kakar D.M. and Sarma R.S. 1983. Child and Maternal Health Services in Rural India: The Narangwal Experiment. Volume 1. Integrated Nutrition and Health Care. Baltimore: Johns Hopkins University Press, 1983.

Kiereini E.M. the role of nurses in reproductive health. Reproductive health In Africa. Baltimore: Johns Hopkins Programme for International Education in Reproductive Health, 1984.

Koblinsky M.A., Campbell O., Harlow S. Mother and more: a broader perspective on women's health. The Health of Women: A Global Perspective. Ed. Marge Koblinsky, Judith Timyan, and Jill Gay. Boulder: Westview Press, 1993. 33-62.

Koblinsky M.A., Timyan J., Gay J., eds. The Health of Women: A Global Perspective. Boulder: Westview Press, 1993.

Koblinsky M.A., Tinker A. and Daly P. Programming for safe motherhood: a guide to action. Health Policy and Planning 1994; 9(3): 252-66.

Korten D.C. Integrated Approaches to Family Planning Services Delivery. Cambridge: Harvard Institute for International Development, 1975.

Kunii C. How integration of family planning and maternal and child health should be initiated and developed. JOICFP Review 1984; (7): 15-19.

Ladipo O.A. and Delano G.E. Team approach to reproductive health. Reproductive Health in Africa. Ed. JKG Mati, OA Ladipo, Ronald T. Burkman, Ronald H. Magarick and Douglas Huber. Baltimore: Johns Hopkins Programme for International Education in Gynecology and Obstetrics, 1984. 32-42.

Laing J. 1981. Methods for evaluation of integrated programmes. United Nations Economic and Social Commission for Asia and the Pacific Regional Seminar on Evaluation of Schemes and Strategies for Integrated Family Planning Programmes with Special Reference to Increased Involvement of Local Institutions. Asian Population Studies Series No. 51; l ST/ESCAP/161. New York: United Nations, 1981. 52-54.

Lande R.E. and Geller J.S. Paying for Family Planning. Population Reports, Series J., No. 39. Baltimore: Johns Hopkins University, Population Information Programme, 1991.

Lewis M.A. Do contraceptive prices affect demand? Studies in Family Planning 1986; (17): 126-35.

Maguire E. Changing Paradigms and Lessons for the Public Sector in Population and Reproductive Health. Paper presented at the 21st Annual NCIH International Health Conference. Arlington, VA. 26-29 June, 1994.

Mahmoed A. Self-help through an integrated project: the Majene case. JOICFP Review 1988; (15): 18-23.

Maine D. Safe Motherhood Programmes: Options and Issues. New York: Columbia University, Center for Population and Family Health, n.d.

Mauldin W.P. Family planning programmes and fertility declines in developing countries. Family Planning Perspectives 1975; 7(1): 32-38.

Mitchell M., *et al.*, Ed. Managing integrated services. The Family Planning Manager 1994; (3): 1-22.

Mora G., Betts C., Gay J., Hardee K., Chambers V. and Fox L. Quality of Care in Women's Reproductive Health: A Framework for Latin America and the Caribbean. Washington, DC: Pan American Health Organization, 1993.

Morris R., Lescohier I.H. Service integration: real versus illusory solutions to welfare dilemmas. The Management of Human Services. Ed. RC Sarri and Y Hasenfeld. New York: Columbia University Press, 1978.

Murray C.J.L. and Chen L.C. 1992. Understanding morbidity change. *Population and Development Review 1992*; (18): 481-503.

Nasah B.T. General principles in delegation of maternity functions to community based health workers. International Journal of Gynecology and Obstetrics 1992; 38(supp): S23-S27.

National Council for International Health. Approaches to Integrated Programmes: Health, Family Planning, and Development. Washington, DC: NCIH, 1982.

Ness G.D. Organizational Aspects of Integrating Family Planning with Development Programmes in the ESCAP Region. Asian Population Studies Series No. 36. Bangkok: ESCAP, 1977.

Ness G.D. Existing patterns of integrated programmes their strengths and weaknesses. United Nations Economic and Social Commission for Asia and the Pacific Regional Seminar on Evaluation of Schemes and Strategies for Integrated Family Planning Programmes with Special Reference to Increased Involvement of Local Institutions. Asian Population Studies Series No. 51; ST/ESCAP/161. New York, United Nations, 1981.

Nigam A. and Parker D. Resources for human development. How much is needed? How much is available? Florence: UNICEF, 1994.

Office of Population. Mission Statement: Family Planning, Reproductive Health, and Other Related Activities. Washington, DC: U.S. Agency for International Development, 1994.

Older Women's League. Campaign for Women's Health: A Model Benefits Package for Women in Health Care Reform. Washington, DC: OWL, 1994.

Pai Panandiker V.A. Strategies for increased involvement of non-governmental organizations, local governments and institutions for promoting greater community participation. United Nations Economic and Social Commission for Asia and the Pacific Regional Seminar on Evaluation of Schemes and Strategies for Integrated Family Planning Programmes with Special Reference to Increased Involvement of Local Institutions. Asian Population Studies Series No. 51; 1 ST/ESCAP/161. New York: United Nations, 1981. 49-51.

Pan American Health Organization and Family Health International. Quality of Care in Reproductive Health: Developing an Integrated Framework. Final Report of a Workshop. Durham, NC: FHI, 1994.

Parker R.L. and Sarma R.S. Efficiency and equity of project services. Child and Maternal Health Services in Rural India: the Narangwal Experiment. Volume 2. Integrated Family Planning and Health Care. Ed. CE Taylor, RL Parker, RS Sarma, WA Reinke, R Faruqee. Baltimore: Johns Hopkins University Press, 1983. 191-213.

Phillips J.F., Simmons R., Chakraborty J. and Chowdhury A.I. Integrating health services into an MCH-FP programme: lessons from Matlab, Bangladesh. Studies in Family Planning 1984; (15):153-61.

Phillips J.F., Simmons R., Chakraborty J. and Chowdhury A.I. Integrating Health Service Components into a Comprehensive Family Planning and Basic MCH Programme: Lessons from the Matlab Family Planning Health Services Project. Paper presented at the NCIH 11th Annual International Health Conference, Arlington, VA. 11-13 June 1984.

Phillips J.F., Simmons R., Simmons G.B. and Yunus M. Transferring health and family planning service innovations to the public sector: an experiment in organization development in Bangladesh. Studies in Family Planning 1984c; 15(2): 62-73.

Population Action International. Personal communication. 1994.

Population Council. Lessons learned: September 15, 1984-September 14, 1990. INOPAL I. Final technical report: operations research to improve family planning and maternal-child health service delivery systems in Latin America and the Caribbean. Operations Research Findings, Impacts, and Lessons Learned in Project Development. Vol. 1. New York: The Population Council, 1991.

Population Reference Bureau. Women's Concerns about Global Population Issues. Washington, DC: Population Reference Bureau, 1993.

Pratt R., Acharya S., Lubis F., Pillsbury B., Rana M., Shipp P., Pandey M.R. Evaluation of the USAID/NEPAL Integrated Rural Health/Family Planning Services Project. No. 367-0135. Population Technical Assistance Project. Report No. 88-004-075. Arlington, VA: Dual and Associates, 1989.

Queen H.F., Ward H., Smith C., Woodroffe C. Women's health: potential for better coordination of services. Genitourinary Medicine 1991; (67): 215-19.

Randall C. The obstetrician-gynecologist and reproductive health. American Journal of Obstetrics and Gynecology 1977; (129): 715-22.

Rockefeller Foundation. Improving the Quality and Reach of Reproductive Health Service Delivery: A Strategy Paper. New York: Rockefeller Foundation, 1994.

Rosen J.E., Foreit J.R., Salvador L., De Vargas T., Sevilla F. Integration and Home Visiting: Necessary Ingredients for Acceptance of Family Planning Services in Indigenous Communities? Results from an Experiment in Ecuador. Paper presented at the 117th Annual Meeting of the American Public Health Association, Chicago, 1989.

Rosenfield A. Integrated maternal-child health and family planning services. Gynecology and Obstetrics. Ed. John W. Sciarra. Philadelphia: Harper and Row, 1982. 1-7.

Rosenfield A. The Integration of Health, Nutrition, and Family Planning Services. New York: Center for Population and Family Health, 1984.

Rosenfield A., McNamara R. Community-oriented Health, Nutrition and Family Planning Services: Overview and Lessons from Operations Research. CPFH Working Paper No. 21. New York: Columbia University, Center for Population and Family Health, 1985.

Ross J.A. Family Planning Pilot Projects in Africa: Review and Synthesis. CPFH Working Paper No. 24. New York: Columbia University, Center for Population and Family Health, 1986.

Ross J.A., Isaacs S.L. Costs, payments, and incentives in family planning programmes: a review for developing countries. Studies in Family Planning 1986; 19(5): 270-83.

Rukanuddin A.R., Hardee-Cleaveland K. Can family planning succeed in Pakistan? International Family Planning Perspectives 1992; (18): 109-21.

Sai F.T., Nassim J. The Need for a Reproductive Health Framework. Paper presented at the Christopher Tietze International Symposium on Women's Health in the Third World. Rio de Janeiro. 29-30 Oct. 1988.

Sai F.T., Nassim J. The need for a reproductive health approach. International Journal of Gynecology and Obstetrics 1989 (Suppl 3): 103-13.

Sarma R.S., Faruqee R. 1980. Achievements in family planning use. Integration of Family Planning and Health Services: The Narangwal Experience. Ed. C.E. Taylor, R.S. Sarma, R.L. Parker, W.A. Reinke, R. Faruqee. Washington, DC: World Bank, 1980.

Sarma R.S., Faruqee R. The use of family planning. Child and Maternal Health Services in Rural India: the Narangwal Experiment. Volume 2. Integrated Family Planning and Health Care. Ed. C.E. Taylor, R.L. Parker, R.S. Sarma, W.A. Reinke, R. Faruqee. Baltimore: Johns Hopkins University Press, 1983, 59-84.

Satia J.K. Issues in integrated approaches to family planning programmes. United Nations Economic and Social Commission for Asia and the Pacific Regional Seminar on Evaluation of Schemes and Strategies for Integrated Family Planning Programmes with Special Reference to Increased Involvement of Local Institutions. Asian Population Studies Series No. 51; 1 ST/ESCAP/161. New York: United Nations, 1981. 45-47.

Sciarra J.J. 1993. Transactions of the sixteenth annual meeting of the Central Association of Obstetrics and Gynecology. American Journal of Obstetrics and Gynecology 1993; (168): 1649-53.

Seward S.B., Fong CO. Integrated Family Planning Programmes: Rationale, Concepts and Methodology for Evaluation. Paper presented at Research on the Regulation of Human Fertility: An International Symposium Organized by the Karolinska Institute and the University of Uppsala, Stockholm. 7-9 Feb. 1983.

Shelton J., Angle M., Jacobson F. Medical barriers to access to family planning. The Lancet 1992. 340: 1339-1335.

de Sherbinin A., Ashford L., Gelbard A. What I Hear When You Say "Population": Interpretation of Key Population Terms. Paper Presented at the Annual Meeting of the National Council for International Health. 29 June 1994.

Simmons G.B., Balk D., Faiz K.K. Cost-effectiveness analysis of family planning programmes in rural Bangladesh: evidence from Matlab. *Studies in Family Planning* 1991; 22: 83-101.

Simmons R., Koenig M.A., Huque A.A. 1990. Maternal-child health and family planning: user perspectives and service constraints in rural Bangladesh. *Studies in Family Planning* 1990; 21(4): 187-96.

Simmons R.S., Ashraf A. 1978. Implementing family planning in a ministry of health: organizational barriers at the state and district levels. *Studies in Family Planning* 1978; (9)2-3: 22-34.

Simmons R., Phillips J.E. The integration of family planning with health and development. Organizing for Effective Family Planning Programmes. Ed. R.J. Lapham, G.B. Simmons. Washington, DC: National Academy Press, 1987. 185-211.

Simmons R., Phillips J.F., Rahman M. Strengthening government health and family planning programmes: findings from an action research project in rural Bangladesh. *Studies in Family Planning* 1984; 15: 212-21.

Simmons R., Fajans P., Lubis F. Contraceptive introduction and the management of choice: the role of Cyclofem in Indonesia. Contraception 1994; 49: 509-25.

Sinding S.W., Ross J.R. Seeking common ground: unmet need and demographic goals. *International Family Planning Perspectives* 1994; 20: 23-32.

Sivin I. 1971. Fertility decline and contraceptive use in the international postpartum family planning programme. *Studies in Family Planning* 1971; 2(12): 248-56.

Taylor C.E., Newman J.S., Kelly N.U. 1976. Interactions between health and population. Studies in Family Planning 1976; 7(4): 94-100.

Taylor C.E., Parker R.L., Sarma R.S., Reinke W.S. Faruqee R. eds. Child and Maternal Health Services in Rural India: The Narangwal Experiment. Volume 2. *Integrated Family Planning and Health Care.* Baltimore: Johns Hopkins University Press, 1983.

Taylor C.E., Reinke W.A., Faruqee R., Parker R.L., Sarma R.S. Main research findings on policy issues. Child and Maternal Health Services in Rural India: The Narangwal Experiment. Volume 2. *Integrated Family Planning and Health Care*. Ed. CE Taylor, RL Parker, RS Sarma, WA Reinke, R. Faruqee. Baltimore: Johns Hopkins University Press, 1983.

Taylor C., Sarma R.S., Parker R., Reinke W., Faruqee R. Benefits of Integrating Family Planning with Health Services: the Narangwal Experiment. Population and Human Resources Division Discussion Paper No. 81-62. Washington, DC: World Bank, 1981.

Taylor C.E., Sarma R.S., Parker R.L., Reinke W.A., Faruqee R. Integration of Family Planning and Health Services: The Narangwal Experience. Washington, DC: World Bank, 1980.

Taylor H.C., Berelson B. 1971. Comprehensive family planning based on maternal/child health services: a feasibility study for a world programme. *Studies in Family Planning* 1971; 2: 22-54.

Taylor HC Jr., Lapham R.J. A programme for family planning based on maternal/child health services. Studies in Family Planning 1974; 5: 71-82.

Technical Guidelines Working Group. Recommendations for Updating Selected Service Practices in Contraceptive Use: Results of a Technical Meeting. Volume I: Combined

Oral Contraceptives, Progestin-Only Injectables, NORPLANT Implants, Copper-bearing Intrauterine Devices. Chapel Hill: INTRAH, 1994.

Thaddeus S., Maine D. Too Far to Walk: Maternal Mortality in Context. New York: Columbia University, Prevention of Maternal Mortality Programme, Center for Population and Family Health, 1990.

Thaddeus S., Maine D. Too far to walk: maternal mortality in context. Social Science and Medicine 1994; 38(8): 1091-1110.

Tinker A., Daly P., Green C., Saxenian H., Lakshminarayanan R., Gill K. 1994. Women's Health and Nutrition: Making a Difference. Discussion Paper Number 256. Washington, DC: World Bank, 1994.

Tinker A., Koblinsky M.A. Making Motherhood Safe. World Bank Discussion Papers No. 202. Washington, DC: World Bank, 1993.

Tsui A.O. A Conceptual Framework for the Evaluation of Reproductive Health. Chapel Hill: The Carolina Population Center, 1994.

Tuladhar J.M., Stoeckel J. The relative impacts of vertical and integrated FP/MCH programmes in rural Nepal. Studies in Family Planning 1982; 13(10): 275-86.

United Nations Fund for Population Activities. General Lessons Learned from Evaluations of MCH/FP Projects in Botswana, Malawi, Swaziland and Zambia. New York: UNFPA, 1984.

United Nations Fund for Population Activities. Botswana: Programme Review and Strategy Development Report. New York: UNFPA, 1991.

United Nations Fund for Population Activities. Background Note on the Resource Requirements for Population Programmes in the Years 2000-2015. New York: UNFPA, Technical and Evaluation Division, 1994.

Vernon R., Lopez-Canales J.R., Carcamo J.A., Balindo J. The impact of a perinatal reproductive health programme in Honduras. *International Family Planning Perspectives* 1993; 19: 103-09.

Vernon R., Ojeda G., Murad R. Incorporating AIDS prevention activities into a family planning organization in Colombia. *Studies in Family Planning* 1990; 21(6): 335-43.

Walley J.D., McDonald M. Integration of mother and child health services in Ethiopia. Tropical Doctor 1991; 21: 32-35.

Warwick, D.P. The Indonesian family planning programme: government influence and client choice. *Population and Development Review* 1986; 12(3): 453-90.

Wasserheit J.N. 1989. The significance and scope of reproductive tract infections among Third World women. *International Journal of Gynecology and Obstetrics* 1989; (Supp) 3: 145-68.

Weiss E.M. The Calabar. Rural Maternal and Child Health/Family Planning Project: Evaluation and Research Component. International Programmes Working Paper No. 16. New York, Population Council, 1982.

Williamson N.E. The Bohol project and its impact. *Studies in Family Planning* 1979; 10(6-7): 195-210.

Winikoff B. Women's health: an alternative perspective for choosing interventions. *Studies in Family Planning* 1988; 19: 197-214.

World Bank. World Development Report 1993. New York: Oxford University Press, 1993.

World Health Organization, Global Programme on AIDS and Programme of Maternal and Child Health Including Family Planning. AIDS Prevention: Guidelines for

MCH/FP Programme Managers, Vol. I: AIDS and Family Planning. Geneva: WHO, 1990b.

World Health Organization, Global Programme on AIDS and Programme of Maternal and Child Health including Family Planning. AIDS Prevention: Guidelines for MCH/FP Programme Managers, Vol. II: AIDS and Maternal and Child Health. Geneva: WHO, 1990.

World Health Organization. Women's Health Across Age and Frontier. Geneva: WHO, 1992.

World Health Organization. Creating Common Ground in Asia. Geneva: WHO, 1994.

World Health Organization. Care of Mother and Baby at the Health Center: A Practical Guide. Geneva: WHO, 1994.

Wulf D., Wolff J., Miller J. Cairo and beyond: addressing the critical management challenges. *The Family Planning Manager* 1994; 3(4): 1-26.

Zurayk H., Younis N., Khattab H. Rethinking Family Planning Policy in Light of Reproductive Health Research. Paper prepared for the Population Council Symposium on Family, Gender, and Population Policy: International Debates and Middle Eastern Realities. 1994.

http://www.fhi.org/cn/RH/Pubs/wsp/wrkngpapers/rhetreal.htm, Accessed on August 12, 2009

http://www.health.state.ny.us/community/pregnancy/family_planning/index.htm, Accessed on August 26, 2009.

Almaz, Terefe and Charles P. Larson. (1993). "Modern Contraception Use in Ethiopia: Does Involving Husbands Make a Difference?" American Journal of Public Health 83(11):1567-1576.

Bashin, Michelle E. and Hubert A. Allen, Jr. (1989). Family Planning Comes of Age in Niger. A Post-Project Survey of Family Planning Knowledge, Attitudes, and Practice in Niamey, Maradi, and Zinder October 1989. Ministry of Health and Social Affairs Directorate of Family Planning, Niger, and the Johns Hopkins University Population Communication Services.

Chirambo, Kondwani. (1992). "Men Targeted for Family Planning in Zambia." Network. 13(1):16-17. *Family Health International.*

Danforth, Nick. (1994) Involving Men in Family Planning: Kenya and Baltimore. Paper presented at the Lessons Without Borders Conference in Baltimore, M.D., October 4, 1994.

Ellerston, Charlotte. (1992). African Men and Family Planning, Paper Prepared for the U.S. Agency for International Development, September, 1992.

Ezeh Alex C., Seroussi Michka, Raggers Hendrik, Male Fertility, Contraceptive Use and Reproductive References, Demographic Health Surveys Comparative Studies No. 17, March 1996, Macro International Inc.

Finger, William R. (1992). "Pilot Programmes Increase Men's Involvement." Network. 13(1):8-9. *Family Health International.*

Green, Cynthia P., Sylvie I. Cohen, and Dr. Hedia Belhadj-El Ghoayel. "Male Involvement in Reproductive Health, Including Family Planning and Sexual Health." Technical Report 28, UNFPA.

Hawkins, Kirstan. (1992). Male Participation in Family Planning; A Review of Programme Approaches in the Africa Region. Paper presented at a Workshop on Male Participation, Banjul, The Gambia, 25-28 November 1991. London.

International Planned Parenthood Federation. (1984). Male Involvement in Family Planning. 73-76, 79-80.

Johns Hopkins Population Communication Services/Population Information Programme, Male Involvement in Reproductive Health, Summary of Activities, For distribution at AVSC Meeting, November 30, 1994.

Kim, Y.M., C. Marangwanda, and A. Kols. (1996). Involving Men in Family Planning: The Zimbabwe Male Motivation and Family Planning Method Expansion Project, 1993-1994. Baltimore: Johns Hopkins School of Public Health, Center for Communication Programmes.

Kim, Young Mi, Opia M. Kumah, Phyllis Tilson Piotrow, *et al.* (1992). Family Planning IEC Project in Ghana: Impact on Ghanaian Males. Paper presented at the 120th APHA Annual Meeting, Washington, D.C., November 1992.

Kumah, Opia Mensah, Philippe F. Langlois, Cheryl L. Lettenmaeir, Sharon K. Rudy, Florence Chikara, and Mary A. Kotei. Changing the Attitudes and Behaviour of African Men Towards Contraception: Myths, Facts, Obstacles and Opportunities.

Lewis, Gary L. A Review of Recent Findings on Family Planning Service Delivery Quality and the Roles of Men in Family Planning in Zimbabwe, 1990-1992. Baltimore: Johns Hopkins University Center for Communication Services.

Mason, Kate. (1992). "Not for Women Only: Child Spacing Clubs for Malawian Men." AVSC News.

Mbuya, Isabel. (1986). The Forgotten Men of Kenya. People. 13(1). Olukoya, Adepeju A. (1985). "The Changing Attitude and Practice of Men Regarding Family Planning in Lagos, Nigeria." Public Health. 99:349-355.

Piotrow, Phyllis T., D. Lawrence Kincaid, Michelle J. Hindin, *et al.* (1992) "Changing Men's Attitudes and Behaviour: The Zimbabwe Male Motivation Project." Studies in Family Planning, 23(6):365-373.

Population Council and the Family Planning Association of Kenya. (1995). Increasing Male Involvement in the Family Planning Association of Kenya (FPAK) Family Planning Programme.

Population Council and the Ministry of Public Health, Cameroon. (1993). Promotion and Delivery of Family Planning Services in the Donga Mantung: an Operations Research Study on the Role of Male Opinion Leaders in Rural Cameroon.

Rogow, Debbie. (1990). "Man/Hombre/Homme: Meeting Male reproductive Health Care Needs in Latin America." Quality/Calidad/Qualité, No. 2. The Population Council.

Swalehe, R.M.A. and M. Mwaipopo. (1994). Knowledge of, Attitude Towards and Practices of Family Planning, Family Welfare Issues Among Male Wage Workers in Tanzania. A Preliminary Baseline Survey Report for the Male Motivation and Education Project. Ministry of Community Development, Women Affairs and Children.

Tapsoba, Placide, Robert Miller, and Lilia Rajoelison Ralalahavirenty. (1993). Involving Husbands to Increase the Acceptability of NORPLANT in Antanarivo, Madagascar. Paper presented at the annual meeting of the American Public Health Association, San Francisco, CA, October 1993

Tipping, Sharon. (1991). Male Approval and Acceptance of Condoms in Diverse Cultural Settings: The SOMARC Social Marketing Experience. SOMARC/The Futures Group. Paper presented at the APHA Annual Conference, Population and Family Planning Section. Session entitled: Contraceptive Social Marketing. November 12, 1991.

Wambui, Catherine. (1995). Parents, Kenya: Male Only Centers: A New Concept in Family Planning, published in Conveying Concerns: Women Write on Male

Participation in the Family. Publications of the Women's Edition Project, Population Reference Bureau, Inc.

Wambui, Catherine. (1994). Male Only Centers: A New Concept in Family Planning. Published in Conveying Concerns: Women Write on Male Participation in the Family, Population Reference Bureau, Inc.:18-19.

Yanyi, Djamba. (1990). "Rôle différentiel des époux dans la planification familiale en Afrique: Recherche méthodologique." Cahiers Economiques et Sociaux, XXIV:(1-2). Revue trimestrielle publiée par l'Institut de Recherches Economiques et Sociales, Université de Kinshasa, Zaire.

"Encouraging Men's Cooperation." *Population Reports* XXII(1):25-29, July 1994.

"How Can Family Planning Programmes Benefit Women?" Population Reports, XXII (1):15-25, July 1994.

"Who Makes Reproductive Decisions?" *Population Reports*, XXII (1):18-19, July 1994.

"Media Images Can Inspire New Behaviour." Population Reports, XXII (12):21, July 1994.

"Men—New Focus for Family Planning Programmes." *Population Reports*, XIV (33):911-913. November-December 1986.

http://sara.aed.org/publications/reproductive_health/family_planning/html/male.htm, Accessed on June 11, 2009.

http://www.amchp.org/MCH-Topics/A-G/FamilyPlanning/Pages/default.aspx, Accessed on August 26, 2009

http://www.un.org/popin/unfpa/taskforce/guide/iatfreph.gdl.html, Accessed on August 12, 2009

http://www.eldis.org/go/topics/resource-guides/health/key-issues/sexual-and-reproductive-health-and-rights/what-does-it-mean, Accessed on August 26, 2009

http://lao.unfpa.org/defcon.htm#indicators, Accessed on May 13, 2009.

http://www.supportwomenshealth.org/resourcecenter/informationclearninghouse/whatisrh.aspx, Accessed on August 26, 2009

Senderowitz, J. 1995. Adolescent Health: Reassessing the Passage to Adulthood. *World Bank Discussion Papers* No. 272.

AIDSCAP. 1996. *Descriptive Analysis of AIDSCAP/Haiti BCC Projects: Some Lessons from the Field. Family Health International.*

Brabin, L. 1995. "Preventive and Curative Care for Adolescents: The Role of the Health Sector." (Prepared for WHO/UNFPA/UNICEF Study Group on Programming for Adolescent Health.)

Fee, N. and M. Youssef. 1993. "Young People, AIDS and STD Prevention: Experience of Peer Approaches in Developing Countries." Global Programme on AIDS, WHO.

International Planned Parenthood Federation (IPPF). 1995. "Working with Youth." (A Report of IPPF's Youth Task Force and Youth Consultation Meeting).

Merritt, A.P. and M. Raffaeli. 1993. "Creating a Model HIV Prevention Programme for Youth." *The Child, Youth and Family Services Quarterly* 16(2). American Psychological Association.

Barker, G., J. Hirsh, and S. Neidell. 1991. *Serving the Future: An Update on Adolescent Pregnancy Prevention Programmes in Developing Countries.* Washington, DC: International Center on Adolescent Fertility, Center for Population Options.

Moore, K. and D. Rogow, eds. 1994. "Family Planning, Gender and Adolescence." (Family Planning and Reproductive Health Briefing Sheets for a Gender Analysis). New York: Population Council.

International Planned Parenthood Federation (IPPF). 1994. "Understanding Adolescents." (IPPF Report on Young People's Sexual and Reproductive Health Needs).

Marie Stopes International. 1995. "A Cross Cultural Study of Adolescents to Family Planning and Reproductive Health Services." (Final Report to the World Bank).

Kauffman, C., J. Brower, L. Hue and S. Randolph. 1996. *AIDSCAP Subproject Final Narrative Report: Together We Can, HIV/STD Peer Education Project*. American Red Cross and Jamaica Red Cross.

Weiss, E., D. Whelan and G.R. Gupta. 1996. *Vulnerability and Opportunity: Adolescents and HIV/AIDS in the Developing World.* Washington, DC: International Center for Research on Women.

Barker, G., and S. Rich. 1992. Influences on Adolescent Sexuality in Nigeria and Kenya: Findings from Recent Focus-Group Discussions. *Studies in Family Planning* 23(3).

Townsend, J. *et al.* 1987. Sex Education and Family Planning Services for Young Adults: Urban Strategies in Mexico. *Studies in Family Planning* 18(2): 103-108.

Hawkins, K., D. Ojakaa, and B. Moshesha. 1992. *Review of the Youth Programme of the Family Guidance Association of Ethiopia*. London: IPPF.

McCauley, A. and C. Salter. 1995. Meeting the Needs of Young Adults. *Population Reports* Series J (41).

Perry, C. and R. Sieving. 1991. "Peer Involvement in Global AIDS Prevention Among Adolescents." (Unpublished review commissioned by the WHO Global Programme on AIDS).

UNICEF. 1996. *Youth Health—For a Change: A UNICEF Notebook on Programming for Young People's Health and Development*. (Working Draft I.)

WHO/UNFPA/UNICEF. 1995. "Programming for Adolescent Health." (Discussion paper prepared for the WHO/UNFPA/UNICEF Study Group on Programming for Adolescent Health.)

Panos Institute. 1996. AIDS and Young People. *Panos AIDS Briefing* No. 4.

http://www.pathfind.org/pf/pubs/focus/IN%20FOCUS/if%20outre%20form.html, Accessed on July 18, 2009.

Johns Hopkins School of Public Health, Center for Communication Programmes 1995. Population Reports: Meeting the Needs of Young Adults Series J (41).

Piotrow P.T. D.L. Kincaid, J.G. Rimon 2nd and W. Rinehart. 1997. *Health Communication: Lessons from Family Planning and Reproductive Health.* Westport, CT: Praeger.

John Hopkins School of Public Health, Center for Communication Programmes (1995). "Reaching Young People Worldwide: Lessons Learned from Communication Projects, 1986-1995." *Working Paper* No. 2.

John Hopkins School of Public Health, Center for Communication Programmes.

Smith W.A., M.J. Helquist, A.B. Jimerson, K. Carovano and S.E. Middlestadt. 1993. *A World Against AIDS: Communication for Behaviour Change*. Washington, DC: Academy for Educational Development.

McCombie S., R. Hornik and J.K. Anarfi. 1992. *Evaluation of a Mass Media Campaign to Prevent AIDS among Young People in Ghana, 1991-1992*. AIDS Technical Support. Washington, DC: United States Agency for International Development.

http://www.pathfind.org/pf/pubs/focus/IN%20FOCUS/massmedia.htm, Accessed on July 22, 2009

Kitt, M.M., Khalid G., Rahimi S. and McCarthy B.J. An occupational health services initiative at a women's hospital in Kabul, Afghanistan *Public Health Reports* 2006; 121(6):650-657.

Dott M.M., Orakail N., Ebadi H., Hernandez F., MacFarlane K., Riley P.L., Prepas R., McCarthy B.J. Implementing a facility-based maternal and perinatal health care surveillance system in Afghanistan, *Journal of Midwifery and Women's Health* 2005; 50(4):296-300.

Williams J.L., McCarthy B. Observations from a maternal and infant hospital in Kabul Afghanistan-2003, *Journal of Midwifery and Women's Health* 2005; 50(4): e31-e35.

http://www.cdc.gov/reproductivehealth/Global/HCapacity.htm, Accessed on August 26, 2009

http://www.usaid.gov/our_work/global_health/pop/techareas/capacity, Accessed on August 26, 2009

http://www.acdi-cida.gc.ca/CIDAWEB/acdicida.nsf/En/EMA-21813178-PGC, Accessed on August 26, 2009

Ezeh A.C., Seroussi M., Raggers H. Men's Fertility, Contraceptive Use, and Reproductive Preferences—DHS, Comparative Studies No. 18. Calverton, MD: Macro International, Inc., 1996.

Kak L.P., Signer M.B. The Introduction of Community-based Family Planning Services in Rural Mali: The Katibougou Family Health Project. CEDPA Working Paper No. 2. Washington: Centre for Development and Population Activities, 1993.

Valente T.W., Saba W.P., Merritt A.P., *et al.* Reproductive Health Is in Your Hands: Impact of the Bolivia National Reproductive Health Programme Campaign. IEC Field Report No. 4. Baltimore: The Johns Hopkins Center for Communication Programmes, 1996.

Ringheim K. Whither methods for men? Emerging gender issues in contraception. Reprod Health Matters, 1996 No. 7:79-89.

AVSC International, Busoga Diocese's Family Life Education Programme. Reaching Men in Uganda: A Case Study of the Busoga Diocese's Family Life Education Programme. (New York: AVSC International, 1997) 10.

http://www.fhi.org/en/RH/Pubs/Network/v18_3/NW183ch1.htm, Accessed on August 26, 2009

http://www.infoforhealth.org/pr/J45/j45print.shtml, Accessed on August 26, 2009

http://www.familycareintl.org/en/issues/24, Accessed on August 25, 2009, Accessed on August 26, 2009

http://www.cdc.gov/reproductivehealth/index.htm, Accessed on August 26, 2009

Report of the International Conference on Population and Development, Cairo, 5-13 September 1994, Sales No. E. 95.XIII. 18, New York: United Nations, 1995; Adrienne Germain and Rachel Kyte, The Cairo Consensus: The Right Agenda for the Right Time (New York: International Women's Health Coalition, 1995).

United Nations Development Programme, *Human Development Report* 2003, Millennium Development Goals: A Compact among Nations to End Human Poverty (New York: Oxford University Press, 2003).

United Nations General Assembly, Report of the Ad Hoc Committee of the Whole of the Twenty-first Special Session of the General Assembly, Addendum, Key Actions for the Further Implementation of the Programme of Action of the International Conference on Population and Development, A/S-21/5Add. 1 (1 July 1999): paragraphs 64, 70.

Reproductive Health Indicators for Global Monitoring: Report of the Second Interagency meeting, WHO, Geneva, 18-19 July 2000, WJP/RHR/01.19 (Geneva: World Health Organization, 2001).

Carla AbouZahr and Tessa Wardlaw, "Maternal Mortality in 2000: Estimates Developed by WHO, UNICEF and UNFPA" (2004).

Kristin Luker, Taking Chances: Abortion and the Decision Not to Contracept (Berkeley, CA: University of California Press, 1975); Robey, Ross and Bhushan, Meeting Unmet Need, 12.

United Nations Millennium Project Task Force on Child Health and Maternal Health, "Who's Got the Power?"

Akinrinola Bankole, Susheela Singh, and Taylor Haas, "Reasons Why Women Have Induced Abortions: Evidence from 27 Countries," *International Family Planning Perspectives* 24, No. 3 (1998): 121.

Sarah S. Brown and Leon Eisenberg, eds., The Best Intentions: Unintended Pregnancy and the Well-being of Children and Families (Washington, DC: National Academy Press, 1995); John Santelli, *et al.*, "The Measurement and Meaning of Unintended Pregnancy," Perspectives on Sexual and Reproductive Health 55, no. 2 (2003): 94-101; Cicely Marston and John Cleland, The Effects of Contraception on Obstetric Outcomes (Geneva: WHO, 2005): 18-33.

Brown and Eisenberg, The Best Intentions, 31-33, 106-176; Akinrinola Bankole, Susheela Singh, and Taylor Haas, "Characteristics of Women Who Obtain Induced Abortion: A Worldwide Review," *International Family Planning Perspectives* 25, no. 2 (1999): 68-77.

World Health Organization, Safe Abortion: Technical and Policy Guidance for Health Systems (Geneva: World Health Organization, 2003): 69-73; World Health Organization, Unsafe Abortion: Global and Regional Estimates of the Incidence of Unsafe Abortion and Associated Mortality in 2000, 4th ed. (Geneva: WHO, 2004): 7.

Huntington, Mensch, and Miller, "Survey Questions," 156; Etienne van de Walle and Elisha P. Renne, eds., Regulating Menstruation: Beliefs, Practices, Interpretations (Chicago: University of Chicago Press, 2001).

http://www.users.interport.net/i/w/iwhc/cgsel.html, Accessed on August 17, 2009

United Nations Population Fund. Programme of Action adopted at the International Conference on Population and Development, Cairo, 5-13 September 1994.

http://www.paris21.org/betterworld/repro.htm, Accessed on August 27, 2009

http://www.spc.int/statsen/English/News_and_Events/RMHPS2005/Meeting_Docs/Information/1_Information.doc, Accessed on August 27, 2009

Cates, W. (1997). "A risk-assessment tool for ntegrated reproductive health services", International Family Planning Perspectives, 23.

China (1995). Family Planning In China (Beijing, the State Council of the People's Republic of China).

Chowdury, S.N.M, J.V. Gomes and S.Md. Hossain (1997). Strengthening STD Services for Men in an Urban Clinic Based Programme (Dhaka, Population Council).

Cook, R.J and M.F. Fathalla (1996). "Advancing Beijing", *International Family Planning Perspectives*, 22.

Department of Public Health (1998). National Standards and Minimum Medical Standards for Family Planning Services (Male, Department of Public Health, Ministry of Health).

Deodata, G. (1996). "Efforts undertaken by WPR to integrate STD/HIV prevention activities into other reproductive health services", paper prepared for a thematic workshop held in WHO, Geneva, 21-25 October.

EPS (1997). Essential Package of Services. First Stage Prioratization (Dhaka, EPS Task Force).

Epstein, E.E. (1990). Enterprise in the Philippines: a Strategic Approach to Private Sector in Family Planning (Arlington VA., John Snow Inc.).

Family Health Bureau (1996). Annual Report on Family Health, Sri Lanka 1994 (Colombo, Evaluation Unit, Family Health Bureau, Ministry of Health).

____ (1997). Handbook on Contraceptive Technology (Colombo, Family Health Bureau, Ministry of Health).

Fort C.J., and C. Hart (1989). Market-based Family Planning: the Enterprise Programme Experience (Arlington V.A., John Snow Inc.).

Germain A., K.K. Holmes, P. Piot and J.N. Wasserheit (1992). Reproductive Tract Infections. Global Impact and Priorities for Women's Reproductive Health (New York Plenum Press).

Government of Bangladesh (1997). Health and Population Strategy (Dhaka, Ministry of Health and Family Welfare).

Hannenberg, R.S., W. Rojanapithayakom and P. Kunasol (1994). "Impact of Thailand's HIV control programme as indicated by the decline in sexually transmitted disease", Lancet, 344.

Harvey, P.D. (1996). "Let's not get carried away with reproductive health", *Studies in Family Planning*, 27.

ICDDRB (1996). Health and Population Extension Division, MCH-FP Extension Project-Intervention Updates (Dhaka, International Centre for Diarrhoeal Disease Control, Bangladesh).

Jain, A. (1995). "Implementing the ICPD's Message", Studies in Family Planning, 26.

Jajoo, U.N. (1992). "Risk-sharing in rural health care", World Health Forum, 13.

Janowitz, B. and B.J. Gould (1995). Options for Financing Family Planning: Increasing Private Sector Participation and User Fees, Technical report No.26, Report on Family Planning Programme Sustainability (New York, United Nations Population Fund).

Janowitz, B., D. Hubacher, K. Jamil and K. Rahman (1996). Productivity and Costs for Family Planning Service Delivery in Bangladesh: the Government of Bangladesh Programme (Research Triangle Park NC, *Family Health International*).

Janowitz. B., M. Holtman, D. Hubacher and K. Jamil K. (1997). "Can the Bangladeshi family planning programme meet rising needs without raising costs?", International Family Planning Perspectives, 23.

Katoanga, S. (1996). "Progress of integrating sexually transmitted disease (STD), HIV and AIDS programmes and services into reproductive health services among the Pacific island countries since the ICPD, Cairo, 1994", paper prepared for a thematic workshop held in WHO, Geneva, 21-25 October.

Kay B., A. Germain and M. Bangser (1991). The Bangladesh Women's Health Coalition, Quality/Qalidad/Qualite 3 1991 (New York, Population Council).

Myanmar (1993). National Health Plan, 1993-1996 (Yangon, Ministry of Health).

____ (1994). National Report on Population (Yangon, National Population Committee).

NIPHP (1997). National Integrated Population and Health Programme, Results Package, July 1997-June 2004 (Dhaka, National Institute for Population Research and Training).

Nowak, R. (1995). "New push to reduce maternal mortality in poor countries", Science, 269.

UNFPA (1996). Expert Consultation on Operationalizing Reproductive Health Programmes, Technical Report No. 37 (New York).

____ (1997). Country Programme for Bangladesh, 1998-2002 (Dhaka).

____ (1997). Strengthening the Logistics System of the Health and Family Welfare Programme (New Delhi).

____ (1997). Report of the UNFPA Programme Support to Thailand (Bangkok).

United Nations (1998). World Urbanization Prospects: the 1996 Revision (New York).

Usmani, F. (1997). A Concept Paper: Prevention and Treatment of Infertility (New Delhi, UNFPA).

Walley, J. (1997). "The implementation of integrated mother and child health and family planning services", Tropical Doctor, 27.

WHO (1994). Maternal Health and Safe Motherhood Programme. Research Progress Report 1987-1992 (WHO/FHE/MSM/94.18. Geneva).

____ (1996). Investing in Health Research and Development. Report of the Ad Hoc Committee on Health Research Relating to Future Intervention Options (Geneva).

____ (1996). Regional Reproductive Health Strategy for South-East Asia (New Delhi, WHO Regional Office for South-East Asia).

____ (1997). Annual Technical Report 1996, UNDP/UNFPA/WHO/World Bank Special Programme of Research, Development and Research Training in Human Reproduction (Geneva).

World Bank (1993). World Development Report. Investing in Health (New York, Oxford University Press).

____ (1995). India's Family Welfare Programme—Towards a Reproductive and Child Health Approach (New Delhi).

____ (1996). Improving Women's Health in India, Development in Practice Series (Washington, DC).

http://www.unescap.org/esid/psis/population/icpd/sec4.asp, Accessed on August 18, 2009.

http://www.reproline.jhu.edu/english/6read/6issues/6progress/prog54_a.htm, Accessed on August 27, 2009

Considerations for formulating reproductive health laws. A discussion paper. Geneva, World Health Organization, 1998 (Document WHO/FRH/WOM/98.1).

Cook R.J. Women's health and human rights. Geneva, World Health Organization, 1994.

http://www.prb.org/Reports/1999/ReproductiveHealthinPolicyPractice BrazilIndiaMoroccoandUganda.aspx, Accessed on August 27, 2009

World Bank, 1999, *Intensifying Action Against HIV/AIDS in Africa*: *Responding to a Development Crisis,* Washington, D.C.

World Bank, 1999, *Population and the World Bank*: *Adapting to Change,* Washington, D.C.

World Bank, 1999, *Safe Motherhood and the World Bank*: *Lessons from 10 Years of Experience,* Washington, D.C.

World Bank, 2000, *Improving Women's Health*: *Issues and Interventions,* Washington, D.C.

World Bank, 2000, *Contracting-out for Reproductive Health: A Guide,* Washington, D.C. (Also available in French and Spanish)

World Bank, 2001, *Condom Procurement Guide,* Washington, D.C.

Bulletin of the World Health Organization, Volume 79 No. 3 2001, Estimates of maternal mortality for 1995. Kenneth Hill, Carla AbouZahr, & Tessa Wardlaw.

http://web.worldbank.org/WBSITE/EXTERNAL/TOPICS/EXTHEALTHNUTRITIONANDPOPULATION/EXTPHAAG/0, contentMDK:20722992~menuPK:64229770~pageP K:64229817~piPK:64229743~theSite PK:672263,00.html, Accessed on August 18, 2009

http://www.savethechildren.org/programs/health/reproductive-health/reproductive-health.html, Accessed on August 18, 2009

http://www.usaid.gov/our_work/global_health/pop/, Accessed on August 18, 2009

http://www.guttmacher.org/pubs/journals/25s5099.html, accessed on August 18, 2009

"Developing Health Promotion and Education Initiatives in Reproductive Health: A Framework for Action Planning", WHO, RHR, Geneva, 1998.

"Facts for Life", UNESCO/UNICEF/WHO. "Guide to Planning Health Promotion for AIDS Prevention and Control", WHO AIDS Series 5, Geneva, WHO, 1989.

"Refugee Reproductive Health Needs Assessment Field Tools", RHR Consortium, 1997.

"Tools for Project Evaluation: A Guide for Evaluating AIDS Prevention Interventions", *Family Health International*, AIDSTECH/*Family Health International*, Durham, NC, 1992.

http://www.unfpa.org/emergencies/manual/a1.htm, Accessed on August 24, 2009

http://www.un.org/popin/books/popinsoj.htm, Accessed on August 24, 2009.

UNFPA "Review and Analysis of Premarital/Newlywed Education Activities in Mexico, Indonesia and the Philippines", Technical and Evaluation Division, November 1990.

3/Varusay, Fauziah "Investing in Youth" in Challenges, Vol. 1, No. 2, Oct. IPPF-ESEAOR, Kuala Lumpur, 1994.

http://www.mpsacsb.org/iec.html, Accessed on August 24, 2009

http://www.un.org/popin/regional/asiapac/fiji/disc/disc7.htm, Accessed on August 24, 2009

Bolider, C., Diana Santana, Diana Santillan, Karen Hardee, Margaret E. Greene, and Sidney Schiller. *The So What Report: A Look at whether Integrating a Gender Focus into Programmes Makes a Difference to Outcomes*. An Interagency Gender Working Group Task Force report, March 2004.

Kane, S. *Working with Victims of Organized Violence from Different Cultures*: A Red Cross and Red Crescent Guide. Geneva: IFRCRC. 1995

Marie Stopes International and Women's Commission for Refugee Women and Children. Displaced and Desperate: Assessment of Reproductive Health for Colombia's Internally Displaced. February 2003.

Saving Women's Lives: *Responding to Emergency Situations.* UNFPA Fact Sheet, 2001.

Women's Commission for Refugee Women and Children. *Refugee Women and Reproductive Healthcare*: *Reassessing Priorities.* New York, Women's Commission, 1994.

"Reproductive Health in Refugee Situations: An Interagency Field Manual". United Nations High Commissioner for Refugees (UNHCR), 1999.

UNIFEM. *Women, War, Peace*: *The Independent Experts'Assessment,* Chapter 3, "Progress of the World's Women, Volume 1," 2002.

McGrew, Laura, Kate Frieson, and Sambath Chan. *Good Governance From The Ground Up*: *Women's Roles in Post-Conflict Cambodia,* Women Waging Peace Policy Commission, Washington DC, 2004.

UNIFEM. *Women, War, Peace*: *The Independent Experts' Assessment,* Chapter 3, "Progress of the World's Women, Volume 1," 2002.

Vann, B., Meriwether Beatty, and Lisa Ehrlich. "Supporting displaced communities to address gender-based violence." In *Forced Migration Review* 19.

Alonso, C., Laura Miranda, Sally Hughes, and Lucy Faveau. "Reducing maternal mortality among repatriated populations along the Guatemala-Mexico border." In *Forced Migration Review* 19.

Botha, Mbuyiselo. South Africa: "Using men to address gender discrimination." In Gender and Peacebuilding Programme's *Newsletter Engendering Peace.* Volume 1, Issue 4. Spring 2004. *International Alert*

http://www.huntalternatives.org/download/47_sexual_reproductive.pdf, Accessed on September 10, 2009

http://www.id21.org/health/clusters/conflictrh.html, Accessed on September 10, 2009

http://www.id21.org/health/h6ja3g1.html, Accessed on September 10, 2009

http://www.who.int/reproductivehealth/topics/emergencies/en/index.html, Accessed on September 10, 2009

http://www.womensrefugeecommission.org/programs/rh/56-rh/67-reproductive-health, Accessed on September 11, 2009

http://womenwarpeace.org/node/14, Accessed on September 11, 2009

http://www.id21.org/health/h6br2g1.html, Accessed on September 11, 2009